EAST ANGLIAN ARCHAEOLOGY

Aspects of Anglo-Saxon Inhumation Burial: Morning Thorpe, Spong Hill, Bergh Apton and Westgarth Gardens

by Kenneth Penn and
Birte Brugmann

with Karen Høilund Nielsen

illustrations by
Steven Ashley, Birte Brugmann, David Dobson,
and Karen Høilund Nielsen

East Anglian Archaeology
Report No.119, 2007
Historic Environment
Norfolk Museums and Archaeology Service

EAST ANGLIAN ARCHAEOLOGY
REPORT NO.119

Published by
Historic Environment
Norfolk Museums and Archaeology Service
Union House
Gressenhall
Dereham
Norfolk NR20 4DR

in conjunction with
ALGAO East
www.algao.org.uk

Editor: Brian Ayers
Managing Editor: Jenny Glazebrook

Editorial Committee:
Brian Ayers, County Archaeologist, Norfolk Museums and Archaeology Service
Owen Bedwin, Head of Historic Environment, Essex County Council
Adrian Tindall, County Archaeologist, Cambridgeshire County Council
Keith Wade, Archaeological Service Manager, Suffolk County Council
Peter Wade-Martins, Director, Norfolk Archaeological Trust

Set in Times Roman by Jenny Glazebrook using Corel Ventura ™
Printed by Geerings of Ashford Ltd., Kent

©HISTORIC ENVIRONMENT,
NORFOLK MUSEUMS AND ARCHAEOLOGY SERVICE

ISBN 978 0 905594 45 3

This volume was published with the aid of a grant from English Heritage

East Anglian Archaeology was established in 1975 by the Scole Committee for Archaeology
in East Anglia. The scope of the series expanded to include all six eastern counties and
responsibility for publication was transferred in 2002 to the Association of Local Government
Archaeological Officers, East of England (ALGAO East).

For details of reports in *East Anglian Archaeology*, see last page

Cover photograph
Glass beads of group A1 from Grave 16 at Morning Thorpe

Contents

List of Plates vi
List of Figures vi
List of Tables vii
Contributors viii
Acknowledgements viii
Abbreviations ix
Summary/Résumé/Zusammenfassung ix

1. Introduction: circumstances and origins of the project
1.1 Background 1
1.2 Aims 3
1.3 The report 3

2. East Anglian cemeteries
2.1 Background 4
2.2 The distribution of Early Anglo-Saxon cremation and inhumation cemeteries in East Anglia 5
2.2.1 Geology 5
2.2.2 Parish boundaries 6
2.3 East Anglia as a geopolitical concept 6
2.4 The local context of the four cemeteries 8
2.4.1 Spong Hill 8
2.4.2 Bergh Apton 9
2.4.3 Morning Thorpe 9
2.4.4 Westgarth Gardens 11
2.5 Conclusions 11

3. Social and chronological analysis: theory and method
3.1 Background 12
3.2 Previous research on the four cemeteries 12
3.2.1 Social structure 12
3.2.2 Chronology 15
3.2.3 Conclusions 16
3.3 Methods 16

4. Grave-good analysis
4.1 Background 17
4.2 Weapons and associated objects, based on a report by K.Høilund Nielsen 17
4.2.1 Spearheads 17
4.2.2 Shield bosses 22
4.2.3 Seaxes, swords and axe 23
4.3 Dress accessories and associated objects of females 24
4.3.1 Brooches 24
4.3.2 Pendants 26
4.3.3 Glass beads 26
4.3.4 Wrist-clasps 28
4.3.5 Finger-rings 29
4.3.6 Slip-knot rings 29
4.3.7 Girdle-hangers and keys 30
4.3.8 Weaving batten 30
4.4 Objects in the graves of males and females 30
4.4.1 Pins 30
4.4.2 Necklet 31
4.4.3 Buckles 31
4.4.4 Strap-ends 32
4.4.5 Lace-tags 32
4.4.6 Knives 34
4.4.7 Firesteels/pursemounts 34
4.4.8 Tweezers and possible ear-scoop 36
4.4.9 Lyres 36
4.4.10 Glass vessels 36
4.4.11 Copper-alloy and wooden vessels 36
4.4.12 Pottery 38

5. A chronological framework
5.1 Background 42
5.2 Weapons and associated objects, based on an archive report by K.Høilund Nielsen 42
5.2.1 Relative chronology 42
5.2.2 Absolute chronology 45
5.3 Female dress accessories and associated objects 48
5.3.1 Relative chronology 48
5.3.2 Absolute chronology 58
5.4 A correlation of the chronological frameworks for males and females 58
5.4.1 Grave-goods 58
5.4.2 Vertical stratigraphy 59
5.4.3 Horizontal stratigraphy 68
5.4.4 Relative and absolute chronology 71

6. Burial practice
6.1 Backgound 76
6.2 Grave lengths and depths 76
6.3 Double graves 77
6.4 Grave features 82
6.5 Grave orientation and body position 84
6.6 Cemetery layout 86
6.7 Conclusions 87

7. Social structure
7.1 Background 88
7.2 Age 88
7.3 Sex and gender 88
7.4 Grave-goods 89
7.4.1 Background 89
7.4.2 Materials 90
7.4.3 Association scores 92
7.4.4 Quantity and quality 92
7.4.5 Graves without gender-indicating grave-goods 94
7.5 5th- and 6th-century Anglo-Saxon social structure 94
7.6 Inhumation and cremation burial practice 96
7.7 Summary 97

8. Conclusions 98

Gazetteer of East Anglian cemeteries 101
Bibliography 113
Index, by Sue Vaughan 119

List of Plates

Plate 1   Glass beads of bead Group A1: 'Traffic Light' (1) and 'Blue' beads (2) from Grave 16 at Morning Thorpe. Scale 2:1   27

Plate 2   Glass beads of bead Group A2: 'Segmented Constricted' (1), 'Constricted Cylindrical' (2), 'Miniature Dark' (3) and 'Norfolk Melon' (4) from Grave 38 at Spong Hill. Scale 2:1   27

Plate 3   Glass beads of bead Group A2: 'Norfolk Short' from Grave 407 at Morning Thorpe. Scale 2:1   27

Plate 4   Glass beads of bead Group A2: 'Norfolk YellowRed' from Grave 65 at Bergh Apton. Scale 2:1   27

Plate 5   Glass beads of bead Group A2: 'Norfolk Crossing Trails' from Grave 65 at Bergh Apton. Scale 2:1   28

Plate 6   Glass beads of bead Group A2: 'Norfolk Melon' with amber and other glass beads from Grave 303 at Morning Thorpe. Scale 2:1   28

Plate 7   Glass beads of bead Group A2: 'YellowGreen' from Grave 209 at Morning Thorpe. Scale 2:1   28

Plate 8   Glass beads of bead Group A2b: 'Melon', of Group B: 'Cylindrical Round', 'Cylindrical Pentagonal', and a biconical bead from Grave 18 at Bergh Apton. Scale 2:1   29

Plate 9   Glass beads of bead Group B: 'Cylindrical Round' (1), 'Koch 20' (2), 'Koch 34' (3), 'Dot34' (4) from Grave 371 at Morning Thorpe. Scale 2:1   29

List of Figures

Fig. 1.1   The location of the four Anglo-Saxon inhumation cemeteries discussed in this volume   xii

Fig. 2.1   Spong Hill, the local context   7

Fig. 2.2   Bergh Apton, the local context   8

Fig. 2.3   Morning Thorpe, the local context   9

Fig. 2.4   Westgarth Gardens, the local context   10

Fig. 4.1   Measurements and angles recorded from spearheads. Not to scale   17

Fig. 4.2   Blade lengths of the spearheads from the four cemeteries. Arrows mark the steps in length which have been used to define ranges   18

Fig. 4.3   Speahead types. a lanceolate, b concave, c angular, d parallel, e rhomboid, f mid-ribbed, g corrugated. Not to scale   18

Fig. 4.4   Apex shapes. V V-shaped outline, T T-shaped outline, VT half-way between V-shaped and T-shaped outline, n stopper-shaped, o knob. Not to scale   22

Fig. 4.5   Morning Thorpe. The distribution of buckles with and without plates, and of Type *Buckle1*   33

Fig. 4.6   Morning Thorpe. The distribution of knives in general and of blades 10cm or more in length   35

Fig. 4.7   Morning Thorpe. The distribution of pottery in general and of pottery with stamp decoration   37

Fig. 4.8   Morning Thorpe. The distribution of pottery with stamps that were used for more than one pot from the site   39

Fig. 5.1a   The four cemeteries. Correspondence analysis 1, weapon types   46

Fig. 5.1b   The four cemeteries. Correspondence analysis 1, graves   46

Fig. 5.1c   The four cemeteries. Correspondence analysis 1, sorted matrix   46

Fig. 5.2a   The four cemeteries. Correspondence analysis 2, weapon types   47

Fig. 5.2b   The four cemeteries. Correspondence analysis 2, graves   47

Fig. 5.2c   The four cemeteries. Correspondence analysis 2, sorted matrix   47

Fig. 5.3a   Morning Thorpe. Correspondence analysis 3, bead types   48

Fig. 5.3b   Morning Thorpe. Correspondence analysis 3, graves   48

Fig. 5.3c   Morning Thorpe. Correspondence analysis 3, bead types, sorted matrix   49

Fig. 5.4a   The four cemeteries. Correspondence analysis 4, bead types   50

Fig. 5.4b   The four cemeteries. Correspondence analysis 4, graves   50

Fig. 5.4c   The four cemeteries. Correspondence analysis 4, sorted matrix   51

Fig. 5.5a   The four cemeteries. Correspondence analysis 5, types of female dress accessories   52

Fig. 5.5b   The four cemeteries. Correspondence analysis 5, graves   52

Fig. 5.5c   The four cemeteries. Correspondence analysis 5, sorted matrix. Associations with certain functional types of objects not included in the analysis are also shown   52

Fig. 5.6a   The four cemeteries. Correspondence analysis 6, types of female dress accessories   55

Fig. 5.6b   The four cemeteries. Correspondence analysis 6, graves   55

Fig. 5.6c   The four cemeteries. Correspondence analysis 6. Associations with certain

Fig. 5.7	functional types of objects not included in the analysis are also shown	54
Fig. 5.7	Morning Thorpe. Correspondence analysis 7, sorted matrix	56
Fig. 5.8	Spong Hill and Bergh Apton. Correspondence analysis 10, sorted matrix	57
Fig. 5.9	The four cemeteries. The date range of some female dress accessories. Dark grey indicates the main occurrence of a type of object in Phases FA1, FA2a, FA2b or FB; light grey indicates that a type of object is not common but occurs in that phase	58
Fig. 5.10	Morning Thorpe. The distribution of graves dated to Phases FA1 and MA1	60
Fig. 5.11	Morning Thorpe. The distribution of graves dated to Phases FA2 and MA1–2	61
Fig. 5.12	Morning Thorpe. The distribution of graves dated to Phases FB and MB	62
Fig. 5.13	Morning Thorpe. The distribution of 'unfurnished' graves (undisturbed or slightly disturbed), pottery, and buckles not associated with gender-specific grave-goods. The extent of the distributions of graves dated to Phases FA1/MA1a or FB/MB is encircled	63
Fig. 5.14	Spong Hill. The distribution of graves dated to Phases FA1 or MA1	64
Fig. 5.15	Spong Hill. The distribution of graves dated to Phases FA2 or MA1–2	65
Fig. 5.16	Bergh Apton. The distribution of graves dated to Phases FA2 or MA1–2	66
Fig. 5.17	Bergh Apton. The distribution of graves dated to Phases FB or MB	67
Fig. 5.18	Westgarth Gardens. The distribution of graves dated to Phases FA1 or FB and to MA1 or MB	68
Fig. 5.19	Westgarth Gardens. The distribution of graves dated to Phases FA2 and MA1–2	69
Fig. 5.20	The four cemeteries. The correlation of phases for males and females, number of graves represented by these phases and the date spans of the cemeteries	69
Fig. 5.21	The four cemeteries. Types of objects defining Phase FA1. Not to scale	70
Fig. 5.22	The four cemeteries. Types of objects defining Phase FA2a. Not to scale	72
Fig. 5.23	The four cemeteries. Types of objects defining Phase FA2a–b. Not to scale	73
Fig. 5.24	The four cemeteries. Types of objects defining Phase FA2b. Not to scale	72
Fig. 5.25	The four cemeteries. Types of objects defining Phase FB. Not to scale	73
Fig. 5.26	The four cemeteries: types of weapons defining Phase MA1. Not to scale	74
Fig. 5.27	The four cemeteries: types of weapons defining Phase MA2. Not to scale	75
Fig. 5.28	The four cemeteries: types of weapons defining Phase MB. Not to scale	75
Fig. 6.1	Spong Hill. Schematic site plan showing grave lengths and ring-ditches	78
Fig. 6.2	Spong Hill. Schematic site plan showing grave depths and ring-ditches	79
Fig. 6.3	Morning Thorpe. Schematic site plan showing grave lengths and the distribution area of graves dated to Phases FA1/MA1a and to FB/MB	80
Fig. 6.4	Morning Thorpe. Schematic site plan showing grave depths	81
Fig. 6.5	Bergh Apton. Schematic site plan showing grave lengths	84
Fig. 6.6	Westgarth Gardens. Schematic site plan showing grave lengths	85
Fig. 6.7	Westgarth Gardens. Distribution of age and sex	86
Fig. 7.1	The four cemeteries. The ratio of undated and dated graves with one to ten types of objects as listed in Table 7.2. Only undisturbed graves are included; only graves dated to one of the phases for males and females are 'dated'	91
Fig. 7.2a	The four cemeteries. Graves dated to Phases FA1, FA2 or FB sorted according to the number of types of grave-goods found in them	91
Fig. 7.2b	The four cemeteries. Graves dated to Phases MA1, MA2 or MB sorted according to the number of types of grave-goods found in them	91
Fig. 9.1	East Anglia showing location of Anglo-Saxon cemeteries listed in the Gazetteer	111

List of Tables

Table 4.1	The four cemeteries. Spearhead measurements	19
Table 4.2	The four cemeteries. Shield boss measurements	19
Table 5.1	The four cemeteries. Graves and types used for the definition of Phases FA1, FA2 and FB	43–45
Table 6.1	The four cemeteries. Grave lengths sorted after sites, gender and chronological phases	77
Table 7.1	The four cemeteries. Number of individuals identified as male or female on the basis of human bone (sex) and/or grave-goods (gender)	89
Table 7.2	The four cemeteries. Association scores for the main types of objects from the graves, sorted into three groups	90

Contributors

Birte Brugmann, Dr phil, FSA
Heritage Consultant

Karen Høilund Nielsen, DPhil
Senior Research Associate

Kenneth Penn, BEd, FSA, MIFA
Senior Project Officer, NAU Archaeology

Acknowledgments

Thanks are due first to the excavators of the four East Anglian cemeteries which are the subject of this work, who made these sites available for study by their swift publication. Peter Wade-Martins, Bob Carr and then Catherine Hills excavated the large cremation and inhumation cemetery at Spong Hill, a project initiated by Barbara Green, who was also the co-author of the reports on Bergh Apton and Morning Thorpe, excavated by Christopher Green and Andrew Rogerson. Stanley West investigated the cemetery at Westgarth Gardens, Bury St Edmunds.

It is also a pleasure to acknowledge the encouragement of English Heritage, who funded work on these four sites and their eventual publication, and was keen to see a work of synthesis undertaken. Philip Walker is owed special thanks for his continuing interest and help over several years, and more recently, Brian Kerr, Kath Buxton, Kim Stabler and Christopher Scull, who were the source of many pertinent comments and helpful advice.

Kenneth Penn is grateful to a number of people who gave information about other cemeteries, often before their full publication, and their help is gratefully acknowledged; John Newman and Colin Pendleton (Suffolk), Alison Taylor, Nesta Rooke and Tim Malim (Cambs), Andrew Rogerson (Norfolk) and David Buckley (Essex), gave information from their respective County Sites and Monuments Records. Christopher Scull kindly made available a draft of his own list of Anglo-Saxon finds from East Anglia and Stanley West made a copy of his Suffolk Corpus (West 1998) available in advance of publication, and discussed this work. Reference to Penn forthcoming *Excavations along the Bacton to King's Lynn Gas Pipeline, Volume II: Anglo-Saxon Cemetery at Tittleshall, Norfolk* (working title) was possible due to the kind permission of Transco through Network Archaeology Ltd.

Tim Pestell discussed with Kenneth Penn current work on the cemetery at Snape, and allowed access to a draft catalogue, as did Dominic Powlesland for West Heslerton (Yorks). Cathy Haith at the British Museum sent records of the cemetery at Sleaford (Lincs), and discussed the new finds from Buckland, Dover. At University College, London, Clive Orton was helpful in arranging a preliminary computer analysis of the Morning Thorpe record, carried out by his student Tim Carew, and offered support to Jane Brenan for her subsequent analysis of the material which has aided thinking on this subject (Brenan 1997). John Hines and Karen Høilund Nielsen worked together on the correspondence analysis (Hines and Høilund Nielsen 1997) and also gave advice on more general matters. Karen Høilund Nielsen made a further study of grave goods from the male graves (Høilund Nielsen 2003).

Kenneth Penn's thanks are due to Charlotte Roberts for access to unpublished articles, and to John Blair for information regarding burials in Oxfordshire. Professor Brian Funnell of the University of East Anglia provided information on geology, for which the writer is very grateful. Chris Mycock arranged access to Moyses Hall Museum, Bury St Edmunds to study material from Westgarth Gardens in the possession of the museum, and colleagues at the Castle Museum and Art Gallery, Norwich, arranged access to material from the other cemeteries. Nick Stoodley sent information from his current work.

The writers are grateful to Seamus Ross for his permission to refer to his unpublished PhD thesis (Ross 1991). Kenneth Penn is also grateful for advice and information on various aspects of their work from David Gurney, Jude Plouviez and John Hines; Karen Brush, Dido Clark and Janet Parker allowed access to their own research. The illustrations are in part taken from the original catalogues, with additions by Birte Brugmann; tables and diagrams are also largely the work of Birte Brugmann, with maps by Kenneth Penn. David Dobson prepared the illustrations for publication. Birte Brugmann wishes to thank Jayne Bown for her steady support as project manager (2003/4) and Karen Høilund Nielsen, Chris Scull, John Hines and Jan Bemmann for their specialist comments on a wide range of subjects. Professor Irwin Scollar's helpful comments on the computer programme *Socistat* and Jacqueline McKinley's on cremation burial practice are also gratefully acknowledged.

Various drafts or sections of this report have been read by Liz Shepherd, Andrew Rogerson, Catherine Hills, Stanley West, Helen Geake, Jez Reeve and Chris Scull, whose comments and advice have been gratefully received. John Hines' comments on the entire volume greatly improved the final version of the text.

Abbreviations

BA   Bergh Apton
MT   Morning Thorpe

SH   Spong Hill
WG   Westgarth Gardens

Summary

Excavations at the four cemeteries of Morning Thorpe, Bergh Apton, Spong Hill and Westgarth Gardens were carried out in the 1970s and published as catalogues in *East Anglian Archaeology*, but full discussions of the results were withheld, with the intention that catalogue publication would be followed by a single discussion of the four cemeteries. This publication policy has turned East Anglia into a particularly well represented region in national samples of Anglo-Saxon cemeteries. The c.500 inhumations from the four cemeteries form 15–20% of the total number of inhumation graves recorded in East Anglia since the 19th century and had produced the largest body of early Anglo-Saxon material from formal excavations of inhumation cemeteries until, in 1997, a large part of an inhumation cemetery at Lakenheath, Suffolk was excavated.

The aim of the report is an analysis of the material culture and inhumation burial practice at the four cemeteries as a source of information on Anglo-Saxon social structure. For this purpose, a chronological framework has been created which allows for distinctions between developments over time and contemporary diversity in the material culture and burial practice at the four cemeteries. This required a selective grave-good analysis focussed on a typology of objects suitable for correspondence analysis, on external dating evidence for types of grave-goods, and on the use of material culture in Anglo-Saxon burial practice. The relative chronological framework for the four cemeteries is based on correspondence analyses of grave-good associations and on the vertical and horizontal stratigraphy (in particular at Morning Thorpe). This relative chronological framework is supported by results from research on a national sample of weapon graves carried out as part of the project *Anglo-Saxon England c. 570–720: the chronological basis* funded by English Heritage, and by a chronological framework for glass beads from Anglo-Saxon graves. Absolute date ranges for the relative chronological phases defined on the basis of the results from correspondence analyses are based on types of objects which are dated by regional frameworks for Early Medieval cemeteries on the Continent, in particular for the Lower Rhine valley and the South of Germany.

The four cemeteries were largely but not entirely contemporary. Inhumation burial at Spong Hill began c. AD 450 at the earliest and ended AD 550 at the latest. Burial at Morning Thorpe and Westgarth Gardens started at about the same time but was finally given up in the second half of the 7th century. Bergh Apton was mainly in use from the late 5th to the late 6th centuries. Inhumation burial at each of the four cemeteries seems to have started as dispersed graves, the area becoming fully occupied by graves in the following phases. Towards AD 500, the burial ground at Morning Thorpe was expanded on a scale that suggests it was more than the expansion of existing plots. In the second half of the 6th century, a substantial part of the site seems to have been given up, both at Morning Thorpe and Bergh Apton. This development may be part of socio-economic changes that eventually led to the founding of so-called 'Final Phase' cemeteries.

The evidence from the four cemeteries supports the interpretation of Anglo-Saxon inhumation cemeteries as the burial grounds of communities which may reflect status differences within rather than between families and/or households. A detailed analysis of the grave-good associations from the four cemeteries confirms certain aspects of interpretations of Anglo-Saxon weapon burial practice and of recent research on gender. At the four cemeteries, as at other Anglo-Saxon sites, burial with female dress accessories or weapons became more common towards the end of the 5th century, and included individuals of younger age groups; these tended to be buried with simpler 'kits' than adults, drawing out the scale of 'wealth' and 'status' indicated by grave-good associations. The evidence from the four cemeteries suggests that this development led to an 'inflation' of burials with female dress accessories or spears in the early 6th century and that this was related to a decline in the average manufacturing quality of copper-alloy dress accessories and in the length of spearheads. Around the mid 6th century wrist-clasps and girdle-hangers were either not worn or no longer buried, and annular brooches became less common grave-goods. By then, new types of great square-headed brooches had become the privilege of a relatively few females, who were buried with a brooch that required considerably more copper-alloy than annular brooches and wrist-clasps put together and on which gilding and silver-plating was regularly used. It seems likely that these square-headed brooches fulfilled their display function for only a generation or so and marked the changes which led to the formation of a new elite in the 7th century, a development also indicated by the evidence of weapon graves. Weapon burial at this time used particularly long spearheads and became mostly the privilege of adults. The concentration of wealth in the graves of particular males and females forms a stark contrast to the previously wide use of female dress accessories and spearheads. The analysis demonstrates that changes in burial practice over time require a differentiated approach to the data if it is to be used as a source of information on Anglo-Saxon social structure.

Résumé

Au cours des années 70, des fouilles furent entreprises dans les quatre cimetières de Morning Thorpe, Bergh Apton, Spong Hill et Westgarth Gardens. Les résultats furent publiés sous forme de catalogues dans l'*East Anglian Archaeology*, sans être toutefois accompagnés de commentaires exhaustifs. Il fut en effet décidé que la publication des catalogues serait suivie d'un seul commentaire portant sur les quatre cimetières. Cette politique de publication a fait de l'East Anglia une région très bien représentée au niveau national sur le plan des cimetières anglo-saxons. Les inhumations datant environ de l'an 500 contenues dans les quatre cimetières représentent de 15 à 20 % du nombre total des tombes d'inhumation dénombrées dans l'East Anglia depuis le dix-neufième siècle. Jusqu'à la découverte en 1997 d'une grande partie d'un cimetière d'inhumations à Lakenheath dans le Suffolk, elles constituaient la part la plus importante des matériaux de la première période anglo-saxonne provenant des fouilles menées en bonne et due forme dans des cimetières d'inhumation.

Le rapport a pour objectif d'analyser les pratiques funéraires d'inhumation et la culture matérielle des quatre cimetières comme source d'informations sur les structures sociales anglo-saxonnes. C'est dans ce but qu'a été créé un cadre chronologique qui permet de distinguer entre les développements établis dans la durée et la diversité contemporaine sur le plan de la culture matérielle et des pratiques funéraires mises en oeuvre dans les quatre cimetières. Cette approche a nécessité une analyse sélective des objets funéraires s'appuyant sur une typologie des objets adaptée à une analyse par correspondance, sur des preuves de datation externes pour les types d'objets funéraires, et sur l'utilisation d'une culture matérielle pour les pratiques funéraires anglo-saxonnes. Le cadre chronologique relatif des quatre cimetières est fondé sur les analyses par correspondance des associations d'objets funéraires et sur la stratigraphie verticale et horizontale (en particulier à Morning Thorpe). Ce cadre est conforté par les résultats de recherches menées sur un échantillon national de tombes contenant des armes. Ces recherches, financées par l'English Heritage, font partie d'un projet intitulé *Anglo-Saxon England c.570–720: the chronological basis*. On peut également remarquer qu'un cadre chronologique appliqué aux perles de verre provenant des tombes anglo-saxonnes vient confirmer le cadre chronologique relatif des quatre cimetières. Les fourchettes de dates absolues concernant les phases chronologiques relatives définies sur la base des résultats provenant des analyses par correspondance reposent sur les types d'objets qui sont datés selon les cadres régionaux pour les cimetières du début du Moyen Âge sur le continent, en particulier dans la vallée inférieure du Rhin et dans le sud de l'Allemagne.

Les quatre cimetières étaient en grande partie contemporains sans l'être toutefois complètement. Les inhumations à Spong Hill ont commencé au plus tôt vers 450 de notre ère et se sont terminées au plus tard vers 550. Les inhumations à Morning Thorpe et à Westgarth Gardens commencèrent à peu près à la même époque et furent définitivement abandonnées pendant la seconde moitié du septième siècle. Bergh Apton fut utilisé principalement entre la fin du cinquième siècle et la fin du sixième siècle. Il semble que les inhumations dans les quatre cimetières aient d'abord pris la forme de tombes dispersées, l'espace devenant par la suite entièrement occupé par les sépultures. Vers 500 de notre ère, l'expansion du cimetière de Morning Thorpe fut telle qu'on peut légitimement penser qu'elle dépassait la zone existante. Dans la seconde moitié du sixième siècle, il semble qu'une part importante du site ait été abandonnée aussi bien à Morning Thorpe qu'à Bergh Apton. Cette évolution est peut-être due aux changements socio-économiques qui ont finalement conduit à la création des cimetières de la «phase finale».

Les fouilles entreprises confortent l'idée que ces quatre cimetières anglo-saxons servaient de lieux d'inhumation à des communautés et reflétaient des différences de statut entre les membres des familles ou des foyers plutôt qu'entre des familles ou des foyers. Une analyse détaillée des associations entre les objets funéraires provenant des quatre cimetières confirment, dans une certaine mesure, les interprétations sur les pratiques funéraires anglo-saxonnes impliquant des armes et sur les recherches récentes en fonction du sexe. Dans les quatre cimetières comme dans d'autres sites anglo-saxons, les inhumations contenant des accessoires vestimentaires féminins ou des armes devinrent plus fréquentes vers la fin du cinquième siècle; elles concernaient des individus de classes d'âge plus jeunes qui étaient souvent enterrés avec des «ensembles» plus simples que les adultes, ce qui eut pour effet d'éliminer l'échelle de la «richesse» et du «statut» indiquée par les associations entre les objets funéraires. Les objets provenant des quatre cimetières suggèrent l'idée que ce développement conduisit à une «inflation» d'inhumations comportant des accessoires vestimentaires féminins ou des lances au début du sixième siècle. Ce phénomène s'accompagna d'un raccourcissement des pointes de lance et du déclin de la qualité moyenne de fabrication des accessoires vestimentaires en alliage de cuivre. Vers le milieu du sixième siècle, les anneaux portés au poignet et les bijoux suspendus à la ceinture ne furent plus portés ou enterrés et les broches de forme circulaire devinrent moins fréquentes parmi les objets funéraires. A cette époque, de nouveaux types de broches aux extrémités carrées devinrent le privilège d'un nombre relativement restreint de femmes qui étaient enterrées avec des broches plus riches en alliage de cuivre que les broches de forme circulaire et les anneaux au poignet réunis. En outre, ces broches présentaient régulièrement des dorures et des argentures. Il est vraisemblable que ces broches aux extrémités carrées remplirent leur fonction d'apparat pendant seulement une génération environ et furent la marque des changements qui conduisirent à la formation d'une nouvelle élite au septième siècle, ce phénomène se manifestant également par les traces découvertes dans les sépultures contenant des armes. Pendant cette période, les inhumations présentent des armes dotées de pointes de lance particulièrement longues étaient surtout le privilège des adultes. La concentration de richesses dans les tombes de certains individus, hommes ou femmes, constitue un contraste marqué avec l'usage autrefois largement répandu de pointes de lance et d'accessoires vestimentaires féminins. L'analyse démontre que les changements survenus dans les pratiques funéraires envisagées dans la durée nécessitent une approche différenciée des données si l'on compte les utiliser comme source d'informations sur les structures sociales anglo-saxonnes.

(Traduction: Didier Don)

Zusammenfassung

Auf den vier Gräberfeldern von Morning Thorpe, Bergh Apton, Spong Hill und Westgarth Gardens fanden in den 1970er Jahren Ausgrabungen statt, die in der Reihe *East Anglian Archaeology* in Katalogform veröffentlicht wurden. Die Ergebnisse wurden nicht vollständig diskutiert, da geplant war, der Katalogveröffentlichung eine Gesamterörterung zu allen vier Gräberfeldern folgen zu lassen. Diese Veröffentlichungsstrategie hat dafür gesorgt, dass East Anglia unter den britischen Beispielen angelsächsischer Gräberfelder besonders gut vertreten ist. Die etwa 500 Erdbestattungen auf den vier Gräberfeldern machen 15% bis 20% aller in East Anglia seit dem 19. Jh. dokumentierten Körpergräber aus. Bis 1997, als ein Großteil des Körpergräberfelds bei Lakenheath in Suffolk ausgegraben wurde, lieferten diese vier Stätten den umfangsreichsten frühangelsächsischen Materialkomplex aus offiziellen Ausgrabungen.

Der Bericht unternimmt eine Analyse der materiellen Kultur und der Praxis der Körperbestattung auf den vier Gräberfeldern, die als Informationsquelle über die angelsächsische Sozialstruktur angesehen werden kann. Zu diesem Zweck wurde ein chronologischer Rahmen entwickelt, der es möglich macht, zeitlich bedingte Entwicklungen genauso festzuhalten wie zeitgleich auftretende Unterschiede in der materiellen Kultur und bei den Bestattungssitten auf den vier Gräberfeldern. Dazu war eine selektive Analyse der Grabbeigaben erforderlich, die sich auf Objekttypen konzentrierte, die sich für eine Korrespondenzanalyse eignen, sowie auf externe Datierungsmerkmale bei verschiedenen Arten von Grabbeigaben und die Nutzung materieller Güter bei angelsächsischen Bestattungen. Der relative chronologische Rahmen für die vier Gräberfelder beruht auf Korrespondenzanalysen vergesellschafteter Grabbeigaben sowie auf vertikalen und horizontalen Stratigraphien (vor allem beim Gräberfeld von Morning Thorpe). Dieser relative chronologische Rahmen wird durch Ergebnisse aus der Untersuchung einer landesweiten Stichprobe an Waffengräbern unterstützt, die im Rahmen des von English Heritage geförderten Projekts *Anglo-Saxon England c. 570–720: the chronological basis* durchgeführt wurde, wie auch durch einen chronologischen Rahmen für Glasperlen aus angelsächsischen Gräbern. Die absoluten Datenbereiche für die relativen chronologischen Phasen, die auf der Grundlage der Ergebnisse der Korrespondenzanalysen definiert wurden, stützen sich auf Objekttypen, die durch regionale Rahmen für frühmittelalterliche Gräberfelder in Kontinentaleuropa, vor allem im unteren Rheintal und in Süddeutschland, datiert wurden.

Die Nutzung der vier Gräberfelder erfolgte zum großen Teil, wenn auch nicht durchweg, zur selben Zeit. Bei Spong Hill begannen die ersten Körperbestattungen frühestens um 450 n. Chr., spätestens im Jahr 550 n. Chr. wurden sie beendet. Die Bestattungen bei Morning Thorpe und Westgarth Gardens begannen etwa zur selben Zeit, wurden jedoch in der zweiten Hälfte des 7. Jh. beendet. Bergh Apton wurde hauptsächlich vom späten 5. Jh. bis zum späten 6. Jh. genutzt. Wie es scheint, waren die Körpergräber auf jedem der vier Gräberfelder zunächst weiträumig verteilt; die Fläche wurde erst in den darauf folgenden Phasen voll genutzt. Gegen 500 n. Chr. wurde das Gräberfeld von Morning Thorpe in einem Maß erweitert, das darauf schließen lässt, dass es um mehr ging als um eine reine Erweiterung des bestehenden Geländes. In der zweiten Hälfte des 6. Jh. wurde ein Großteil des Geländes offenbar aufgegeben, sowohl bei Morning Thorpe als auch bei Bergh Apton. Diese Entwicklung könnte im Rahmen der sozioökonomischen Veränderungen erfolgt sein, die schließlich zur Einrichtung sogenannter Gräberfelder der »Endphase« führten.

Die Befunde aus den vier Gräberfeldern stützen die Deutung, dass angelsächsische Körpergräberfelder als Begräbnisstätte ganzer Gemeinschaften dienten, die womöglich eher Statusunterschiede innerhalb und weniger zwischen Familien bzw. Haushalten verdeutlichen. Eine detaillierte Analyse von Grabbeigaben aus den vier Gräberfeldern bestätigt gewisse Interpretationsaspekte, die im Zusammenhang mit angelsächsischen Waffengräbern und kürzlichen Studien zur Geschlechterforschung aufgetaucht sind. Auf allen vier Gräberfeldern zeigte sich, ebenso wie an anderen angelsächsischen Orten, dass gegen Ende des 5. Jh. vermehrt Begräbnisse mit weiblichem Kleidungsschmuck oder Waffen als Beigaben stattfanden Dies betraf oft auch jüngere Menschen, deren »Ausstattung« jedoch meist einfacher war als die der Erwachsenen, wodurch sich das »Wohlstands-« und »Statusspektrum« erweiterte, das die vergesellschafteten Grabbeigaben anzeigten. Die Befunde aus den vier Gräberfeldern deuten an, dass es zu Beginn des 6. Jh. zu einer »Inflation« von Bestattungen mit weiblichem Kleidungsschmuck bzw. Speeren kam und dass dies mit dem Niedergang der durchschnittlichen Produktionsqualität bei kupferlegiertem Kleiderschmuck und der Länge der Speerspitzen einherging. Um die Mitte des 6. Jh. wurden als Ärmelverschluss dienende Hakenspangen und Gürtelgehänge entweder nicht mehr getragen oder nicht mehr mit bestattet, ebenso kamen immer weniger Ringfibeln als Grabbeigaben zum Einsatz. Zu jener Zeit erwiesen sich neue Formen großer Kreuzkopffibeln als Privileg einiger weniger Frauen, denen eine Fibel beigegeben wurde, die deutlich mehr Kupferlegierung erforderte als Ringfibeln und Hakenspangen zusammen genommen und für die regelmäßig Gold- und Silberauflagen verwendet wurden. Es erscheint wahrscheinlich, dass diese Kreuzkopffibeln ihre Renommierfunktion nur etwa eine Generation lang erfüllten und die Veränderungen anzeigten, die zur Formierung einer neuen Elite im 7. Jh. führten — eine Entwicklung, die auch in den Funden der Waffengräber sichtbar wird. Zur damaligen Zeit wurden Waffengräber, in denen fast nur noch Erwachsene beerdigt wurden, mit besonders langen Speerspitzen versehen. Die Anhäufung reicher Gaben in den Gräbern bestimmter Männer und Frauen stehen in deutlichem Kontrast zu der zuvor beobachteten weiten Verbreitung von Kleidungsschmuck und Speerspitzen. Die Analyse zeigt, dass zeitlich bedingte Veränderungen bei den Bestattungssitten eine andere Interpretation der Daten nötig machen, falls diese als Informationsquelle zur Sozialstruktur der Angelsachsen dienen sollen.

(Übersetzung: Gerlinde Krug)

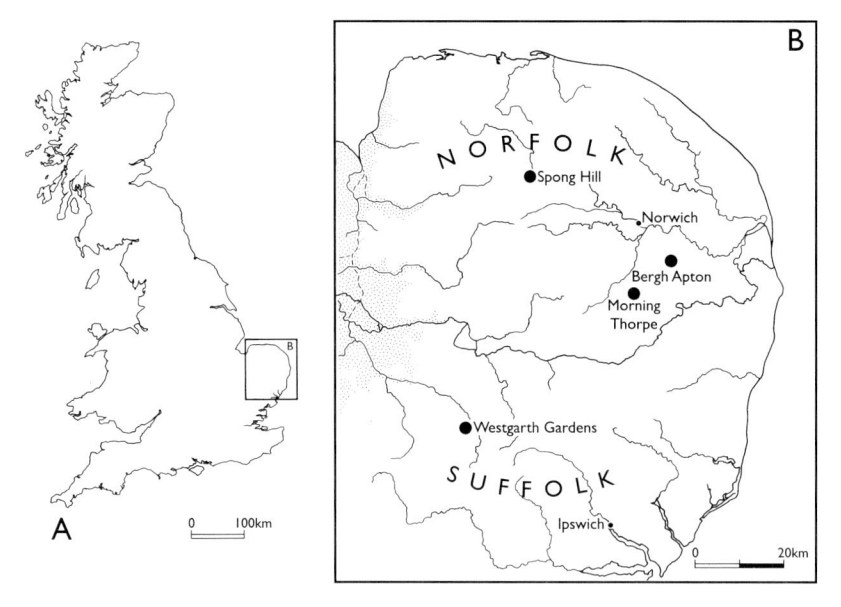

Figure 1.1 Location of the four Anglo-Saxon inhumation cemeteries discussed in this volume

1. Introduction: circumstances and origins of the project

1.1 Background

This work is concerned with an analysis of four inhumation cemeteries excavated in East Anglia (Fig. 1.1) and now published as catalogues of the grave-groups: Bergh Apton (Green and Rogerson 1978), Westgarth Gardens (West 1988), Morning Thorpe (Green *et al.* 1987) and Spong Hill (Hills 1977b; Hills *et al.* 1984). The *c.* 500 inhumations from these sites have produced the largest body of early Anglo-Saxon material from formal excavations of inhumation cemeteries in East Anglia until 1997 when excavations on a large part of an inhumation cemetery at Lakenheath, Eriswell (Gaz. no. S95) began.

Until the increase due to metal-detector searches, nearly all known East Anglian sites were found by chance during development involving earthmoving, and it could be presumed that a similar density of development across the whole of East Anglia would result in a proportional number of new finds. Deliberate searching for metal objects by metal-detector is the main reason for the dramatic increase in new finds over the last twenty years, although the significance of surface finds, that is, whether cemetery or settlement, is often uncertain at first. Discovery is frequently made after disturbance of buried remains (by ploughing mostly), and the greater the surface evidence the more severe is below-ground disturbance. Thus a metal-detector survey of a possible barrow in west Norfolk at Oxborough (Gaz. no. N72) recovered several dozen fragments of metal objects, whilst subsequent excavation revealed ten surviving burials, nearly all plough-damaged (Penn 1999). The finding of a few fragments of brooch or wrist-clasp on the surface could indicate a better-preserved site than extensive scatters of objects, and reports of small numbers of artefacts may prove to be the first signs of a cemetery lying undisturbed whilst the larger collections may represent a site surviving only as disassociated finds in the ploughsoil.

The history of Anglo-Saxon cemetery excavations in East Anglia is largely the same as in other regions — sites were often found by chance during some other earthmoving operation, including the excavation of prehistoric barrows by antiquaries, and most have been found during periods of change and development. Before the early 19th century there were only very occasional finds in East Anglia, although these include Spong Hill (found 1711 in agricultural work; Gaz. no. N66), Burgh Castle (*c.* 1756; Gaz. no. N14), Chatteris (*c.* 1757; Gaz. no. C19, a barrow with skeletons), and Bloodmoor Hill, Pakefield (1758; Gaz. no. S35), found by antiquaries investigating an upstanding barrow (Newman 1996b). At Great Walsingham (Gaz. no. N38), many urns were found *c.* 1658, but their precise location is uncertain, a problem with several early discoveries.

The pace of discovery and destruction of funerary monuments quickened in the early 19th century with expansion of agriculture, enclosure of commons, and the clearance of mounds and barrows, activities which brought to light the burials at Moneypot Hill, Redgrave (late 18th century; Gaz. no. S69), Sporle (*c.* 1820; Gaz. no. N84) and Warren Hill, Mildenhall (1820; Gaz. no. S61), where horse-burials were also found. The levelling of barrows for agricultural improvement continued, with occasional finds being recorded, with discoveries at Little Wilbraham (*c.* 1847; Gaz. no. C43), Linton Heath (1853; Gaz. no. C41), Earsham (1850; Gaz. no. N29), Thetford (*c.* 1868; N86), Allington Hill, Bottisham (1876; C6), and other places including, as late as 1936, Langham, at Blakeney in north Norfolk (Gaz. no. N8).

Agricultural activity has ensured that barrows survive best on the unimproved heaths and commons, for example at Snape and Sutton Hoo (Gaz. nos S75, 77), whilst early accounts of finds sometimes hint at the former existence of barrows.

Growing antiquarian interest in the 19th century was directed deliberately at visible mounds and monuments, sometimes with unfortunate results, as at Snape in 1827 when barrows were opened and objects carted away by 'gentlemen from London' with no record of the campaign nor even of the identity of its directors (Filmer-Sankey 1992; Filmer-Sankey and Pestell 2001). Subsequent careful excavation by the landowner, Septimus Davidson in 1862–3 revealed a ship burial, whose significance was enhanced by the discoveries at the Sutton Hoo barrows in 1938–9, and by recent excavations at both places in the late 1980s. Frequently, the first discoveries were followed by further excavations or investigations of varying value, sometimes leading to some confusion over what was found and its associations, so that a coherent picture of a complete site was lost. Canon Greenwell was amongst the early excavators in East Anglia, with investigations on Risby Heath (Gaz. no. S73), where he excavated a barrow with secondary Anglo-Saxon cremations, about 1869.

Standards of recording improved, and some pioneers conducted thorough investigations of their sites and left a published record which included details of finds and individual burials. In Cambridgeshire the Hon. R.C. Neville followed early finds at Streetway Hill, Little Wilbraham (Gaz. no. C43) with a campaign of excavation in 1851, recovering 188 inhumations, 121 cremations and a horse-burial. All this he catalogued and illustrated in his *Saxon Obsequies* of 1852, although neither a full cemetery plan nor plans of individual graves were included. He also excavated at Linton Heath (Gaz. no. C41) in 1853 and discovered over one hundred inhumations in a prehistoric barrow, which he published soon afterwards in the *Archaeological Journal* for 1854. The first finds at Holywell Row (Gaz. no. S62) were made about this time, but the site was not excavated until 1931 (and then partially), by T.C. Lethbridge, after further finds.

The period 1840–1870 saw an increase in the discovery of cemeteries and burials, many connected with railway construction (*e.g.* Finningham in the 1840s, Gaz. no. S32) and suburban development, but frequently these circumstances permitted either very little record, or the immensity of the task seems to have prevented a proper record of discoveries. Thus, over the years, cemeteries and occasional burials have been found around most large towns in East Anglia (and also Ely, Swaffham and Bungay), but any record was the result of chance and the presence of some formal agency. Cemeteries around Cambridge, Caistor St Edmund and Burgh Castle may relate to some reuse of the Roman walls in the Early Saxon period, but the contemporary context for early cemeteries near towns is best understood as the 'river corridors' in which they lie.

Whilst building work has, at all times, revealed burials across the region, and often allowed time for some salvage and record to be made, one of the most destructive agencies has been large-scale quarrying, because the evidence of any cemetery and its setting may be entirely removed, perhaps unwittingly, although this is naturally not possible to prove. Discoveries have been made during quarrying since the early 19th century, mostly with scant record, but modern machine-sorting has further reduced the chance of odd finds being noticed. Amongst early gravel-pit discoveries, diggings at Eye, Suffolk (Gaz. no. S30) in 1818 revealed a large cremation cemetery, but little was kept or recorded, although some 150 urns were discovered.

Quarrying at West Stow (Gaz. no. S83) in 1849 also brought to light burials (West 1985), and in 1852 another 100 burials were found (published by C. Roach Smith in *Collecteana Antiqua*), long before the nearby and possibly contemporary settlement became known; gravel-extraction also revealed cemeteries at Brettenham, Kenninghall and Rockland in Norfolk (Gaz. nos N9, 49, 76) amongst others, whilst in Cambridgeshire, coprolite-digging at Barrington (1840), Haslingfield (1865) and Hauxton (1879) led to the discovery of other important cemeteries (Gaz. nos C3, 35, 36) although the circumstances and casualness of the early finds had raised problems on matters of exact location of some of the reported sites. At Barrington in 1879, coprolite diggers found and destroyed several graves, before some 114 graves were excavated the following year.

Even large numbers of burials might easily escape proper publication. At St John's College, Cambridge (Gaz. no. C14), many hundreds of burials were said to have been destroyed before 1888, before further investigations recovered another 200 burials (both cremation and inhumation), which have not been properly published either. Whether sites were recorded depended on some individual to undertake the work and see the results through to publication. At Sleaford in Lincolnshire, an important cemetery was discovered during railway construction in the early 1880s and then excavated in difficult circumstances by G.W. Thomas. This was undertaken to a high standard, given the conditions, and Thomas took some pains to catalogue and publish his findings, with his observations on the positions of the grave-goods and an estimate of the ages of the individuals buried (Thomas 1887).

Thomas's effort affords an interesting contrast with some rather less useful work in west Norfolk, on the parish boundary between West Acre and Castle Acre (Gaz. no. N22), where a cremation cemetery was explored in 1891 by Housman and others for the local society: 'At first it was proposed to mark on the plan the exact position of each urn as it was discovered, but owing to the frequency of their occurrence this became impracticable, and, in fact, would serve no useful end' (Housman 1895, 100). Of the urns from West Acre, about a dozen found their way into the collections of the Norfolk Museums and Archaeology Service. The dispersal and disappearance of finds from large, virtually unrecorded, cemeteries such as West Acre renders these sites of little value in any inter-site comparisons.

Cataloguing of finds in their associated grave-groups had become more usual by this time, and Layard's excavation at Hadleigh Road, Ipswich (Gaz. no. S42), supported by Ipswich Museum, revealed 159 graves, part of a larger cemetery of quite distinctive character (Layard 1907). This report is still very useful, even if, as elsewhere, a plan of the cemetery and individual graves was not attempted, mostly for lack of time and resources. Layard's catalogue is descriptive, but has no illustrated grave-groups, although there are drawings and photographs of the outstanding objects, and figures of all the spears, pots, and shield bosses together as unnumbered groups. Recent research into notes and correspondence has made it possible to reconstruct some of the grave-groups (Plunkett 1994, 1).

The work of T.C. Lethbridge for the Cambridge Antiquarian Society at Burwell, Holywell Row and Shudy Camps (Gaz. nos C7, S62, C50) suffers from selectivity as it was practiced at the time, and illustration of just the more interesting burial groups, although his work remains very informative. In cataloguing Shudy Camps, Lethbridge stated that 'It is not thought necessary to describe here burials which were not accompanied by grave-goods' (Lethbridge 1936, 2), although it was, amongst other things, the high number of these unaccompanied burials (71 of the 148) which helped him deduce a 7th-century date for this, and for the Burwell cemetery (Lethbridge 1931, 48). Lethbridge continued his work after the war with the excavation of the large cremation cemetery at Lackford in 1947, when around 500 urns were found — doubtless part of a much larger group — but poorly recorded, with the urns unnumbered on his plan and grave-groups not systematically presented (Lethbridge 1951).

Investigations by Commander-Surgeon F.R. Mann at Caistor St Edmund (Gaz. no. N18) in 1932–7 resulted in the finding of over 500 urns, and later work by G.P. Larwood at nearby Markshall (Site 16) in 1948–9 recovered over 100 urns, both discoveries coming from larger cemeteries. These sites were published in 1973 by J.N.L. Myres and B. Green, who added a gazetteer to their report, with a map of cemeteries in East Anglia. This gazetteer has been updated at the end of this report.

The quality of the discoveries at Sutton Hoo in 1938 and 1939 (Gaz. no. S77; Bruce-Mitford 1975; 1978; 1983) has put the evidence from all other known Anglo-Saxon burial sites in the shade. The outbreak of war stopped further work at Sutton Hoo, but also brought new finds to light in the course of airfield construction in East Anglia, at Lakenheath and Mildenhall in Suffolk. Excavations at Sutton Hoo were continued in the 1960s, 1980s and early 1990s (Carver 2005), and more recently a substantial

Anglo-Saxon burial site was excavated at Lakenheath (Gaz. no. S95) and over 200 burials recorded.

Research on Anglo-Saxon social structure has often focused on social developments leading to the formation of kingdoms (see Scull 1993). The contrast between the evidence from Sutton Hoo and the majority of known Anglo-Saxon burial sites labelled 'folk' cemeteries by Carver (1992, 363) invites such a discussion in particular in regard to the East Anglian evidence. Most of the graves from Spong Hill, Morning Thorpe, Bergh Apton and Westgarth Gardens, however, pre-date the mounds at Sutton Hoo, and need to be judged by the standards of their time.

The four inhumation cemeteries owe their joint discussion in this volume to the fact that the grave catalogues were published in anticipation of a detailed analysis to follow. This publication policy, begun in the 1970s, has made East Anglia a particularly well-represented region in national samples of 6th-century grave-good associations. No single synthesis of the four cemeteries has been attempted; their joint discussion provides the opportunity to deal with the individual sites in a regional context that goes beyond the scope of a cemetery report focused on the publication of a single site. The archive for the four cemeteries project is held by Norfolk Museums and Archaeology Service.

1.2 Aims

The aim of this report is to demonstrate the importance of changes over time in East Anglian material culture and inhumation burial practice for an analysis of Anglo-Saxon social structure. The analysis is based on the inhumation cemeteries at Spong Hill, Morning Thorpe, Bergh Apton and Westgarth Gardens and required:

- a selective grave-good analysis focused on dating evidence and on the social context of the material culture,
- the creation of a chronological framework,
- an analysis of the burial practice at the four cemeteries,
- an analysis of grave-good associations as indicators of social status.

The changes in material culture and burial practice identified at the four cemeteries suggest changes in the social structure of the communities burying at Spong Hill, Morning Thorpe, Bergh Apton and Westgarth Gardens related to economic and socio-political changes.

1.3 The report

With two exceptions, the report is based on the data from the four cemeteries as they were published in the grave catalogues. The report does not reproduce information given in these catalogues but should be used in conjunction with them. The two exceptions are formed by the glass bead typology, which is based on first-hand examination by Birte Brugmann (see Brugmann 2004), and some first-hand measurements of shield bosses and spearheads from Westgarth Gardens which were kindly provided by Heinrich Härke.

To avoid repetition in the text, the grave-goods are discussed in Chapter 4 by type and not by site. Chapter 5 on chronology takes advantage of the broad basis formed by the four cemeteries as a regional sample. Chapter 6 on burial practice gains from a joint discussion of the evidence in which local variations can be set against common features. The gazetteer of East Anglian burial sites provides useful information on the regional context of the four cemeteries.

The report was completed in 2004 and was not updated during the editorial stages in 2006–7.

2. East Anglian cemeteries

2.1 Background

Well over 200 Anglo-Saxon cemeteries and burial places are now known in East Anglia, a figure which includes single burials, burials in barrows, and cemeteries containing hundreds of burials, inhumations and cremations. For most of these sites, no figure can be put on the original number of graves each represents, but the known numbers produce a total of at least 3,000 inhumations and some 4,000 cremation burials and probably more, since most are represented by odd finds or surface scatters. Most of these cemeteries are poorly understood, often discovered in the course of building, quarrying or agricultural operations, whilst many of the more recent discoveries of Anglo-Saxon material have been made by the use of metal-detectors, and are therefore surface scatters of metal objects with no grave associations; these scatters of finds are mostly of dress fittings and thus are assumed to represent cemeteries. The *c.* 500 inhumations from Spong Hill, Morning Thorpe, Bergh Apton and Westgarth Gardens had produced the largest body of early Anglo-Saxon material from formal excavations of inhumation cemeteries in East Anglia until excavations began in 1997 on a large part of an inhumation cemetery at Lakenheath, Eriswell (Gaz. no. S95).

Although the number of known Anglo-Saxon burials is much higher than that of known Roman period burials, because the burial practice is more visible in the archaeological record, it has been argued that even larger numbers of graves should have been found if Anglo-Saxon cemeteries represent a burial practice for the entire population (Hills 1993). Hodges (1989) and Higham (1992) argued that the known figures for the early Anglo-Saxon period may be consistent with relatively small numbers of élite settlers, with the remainder of the population (surviving Romano-Britons or other Anglo-Saxons) using a different burial practice not yet recognised. Scull's arguments against such an interpretation, however, suggest a more complex answer to the problem (Scull 1995, 78).

The term 'Early Anglo-Saxon' will be used in this volume in a strictly chronological sense for the period covered by the four cemeteries (mid 5th to 7th centuries), if not clearly indicated otherwise. The term 'Anglo-Saxons' will be used, for want of a better term, for the population of East Anglia in this period regardless of their provenance, ethnic identity or fate in the time span under discussion. This solution is far from elegant but will have to suffice until a more differentiated but clear terminology has been developed that reflects the current unease with a terminology that is oversimplifying at best and misleading at worst.

The four cemeteries owe their joint discussion in this volume to the fact that the grave catalogues were published in anticipation of a detailed analysis to follow. East Anglia is thus a particularly well-represented region in national samples of 6th-century grave-good associations (see, *e.g.,* Härke 1992; Stoodly 1999; Brugmann 2004). As a sample, however, on which to base a detailed chronological and social analysis, the four cemeteries are arbitrary in a number of ways.

The analysis will be based on inhumation graves only and thus exclude a large number of Early Anglo-Saxon burials excavated in East Anglia: excavations at Spong Hill produced almost 2500 cremations, the more limited excavations at Morning Thorpe a minimum of six cremations and Westgarth Gardens four cremations. With the exception of Westgarth Gardens, the archaeological record of these individuals is largely restricted to grave features and associated grave-goods because of the prevailing soil conditions. The general acidity of East Anglian soils on sands and gravels has often reduced the skeletal evidence to a few scraps of bone or stains at best. Information on age and sex at Westgarth Gardens is taken from the published identifications, except for Grave 50, where a more recent identification is preferred (see Crawford 1991).

The quality of the four cemeteries as local samples varies. Only Spong Hill had been known prior to excavation, and the site owes its extensive excavation primarily to academic interest and not to rescue excavation. Though not even Spong Hill could be fully excavated to more modern standards due to prior disturbances, it was possible to excavate the entire area. At Morning Thorpe, Bergh Apton and Westgarth Gardens it was not possible to assess the entire areas, and the obviously incomplete samples from these sites may not be representative of the full range of burial activity originally defining the cemeteries.

Excavations at Lakenheath, at Beckford in Worcestershire (Evison and Hill 1996) and Buckland, Kent (Parfitt and Anderson forthcoming), for example, have shown that identifying the limit of a cluster of Anglo-Saxon graves is no guarantee that there were no others adjacent. Burials found in the vicinity of the graves at Westgarth Gardens and metal-detector-finds not far from the excavated area at Bergh Apton might prove the point. In most cases there is no evidence for natural boundaries limiting the extent of Anglo-Saxon burial plots, and the reasons for some plots being crowded with graves and others being scattered are not clear. The modern concept of a cemetery as a demarcated piece of ground attached to a central place (a church) has influenced the interpretation of Anglo-Saxon cemeteries but may be misleading.

Most of the inhumation graves at the four cemeteries preceded the 7th century, but the sites do not cover exactly the same date-span. Burial at Spong Hill, Morning Thorpe and Westgarth Garden began in the second half of the 5th century, at Bergh Apton towards the end of the 5th century. Burial ceased at Spong Hill in the mid 6th century, at Bergh Apton possibly before the end of the 6th century, and Morning Thorpe and Westgarth Gardens have produced some evidence which suggests they were still used in the second half of the 7th century.

Comparison with the richly furnished boat graves at Sutton Hoo and Snape (Gaz. no. S75 and S77) shows that the four cemeteries do not cover the entire range of contemporary burial practice known from East Anglia. This may not only be due to the difference between 'folk' cemeteries (see Carver 1992, 363) and the burial grounds of elites but may well also have a geographical background. Boat burial is a practice naturally connected with a coastal setting (see Müller-Wille 1995), a fact that points to the geographical limitations of the four cemeteries as a regional sample. Of all four cemeteries, Bergh Apton, positioned c. 20km from the coast, provided the best access to the sea through the valley of the River Chet. Morning Thorpe, Spong Hill and Westgarth Gardens in particular were further inland. As an East Anglian sample, the four cemeteries have a strong bias towards south-east Norfolk and are not fully representative.

The caveats presented here are not meant to demonstrate that the four cemeteries are worthless for chronological and/or social studies of Early Anglo-Saxon East Anglia. Quite the contrary, 500 systematically and individually recorded inhumation graves in the heartland of an emerging Anglo-Saxon kingdom provide a set of data that can be called rich in terms of Early Anglo-Saxon archaeology. The point made here is that the data are heterogeneous in some ways and limited in others and therefore require careful interpretation. The four cemeteries are typical of much but not all of what is known about Early Anglo-Saxon burials in East Anglia.

2.2 The distribution of Early Anglo-Saxon cremation and inhumation cemeteries in East Anglia

2.2.1 Geology

The general distribution of Early Anglo-Saxon cemeteries in England coincides with certain geological and soil regions, especially where the succession of geological zones is quite marked. This may also be true of East Anglia, a region of subdued geography, but with distinct soil zones dominated by a central tract of Boulder Clay bearing most of the woodland recorded at Domesday (Darby 1971, figs 29, 45 and 61) and largely devoid of prehistoric and Early Saxon settlement. It seems that over much of Norfolk, Suffolk and west Cambridgeshire, the heavy clays and dry sands inhibited Early Saxon occupation, and the few Anglo-Saxon cemeteries or other finds recorded in these areas were mostly in the river valleys, on gravel soils. It will take systematic surveys to establish a pattern of settlement evidence that can be compared to what is suggested by cemetery evidence. This is particularly important in view of theories on cremation cemeteries serving larger areas of settlement than inhumation cemeteries (see Williamson 1993, 64 ff., West 1998 and Wade 2000, 23 for a more detailed discussion).

The tract of East Anglian Boulder Clay is not continuous, but dissected by many small streams and rivers, along which are patches of lighter sands and gravels. Areas of brickearths, sands and loams cover parts of north-east Norfolk, apparently sparsely settled until later times, with broad river valleys and estuaries reaching the sea at Great Yarmouth. South-east of the tract of Boulder Clay in Suffolk is a belt of sands, the 'Sandlings', until recently an area of extensive heathland. West of the Boulder Clay, in Norfolk and Suffolk, lay another area of poor sands, over chalk, the Breckland or Fielding, mostly acid and dry soils, although easily worked. In west Norfolk, skirting the fens, lies a broad belt of chalk, sandstone and greensand, with patches of Boulder Clay. Early Anglo-Saxon cemeteries lay in stream valleys (often where crossed by routeways), and elsewhere in the valleys of the Rivers Little Ouse, Thet, Nar, Wissey and the Stiffkey, and the valleys of the Rivers Wensum, Tas and Chet and their tributaries in the Boulder Clay regions of central Norfolk, including Spong Hill (Gaz. no. N66), Morning Thorpe (Gaz. no. N58) and Bergh Apton (Gaz. no. N6). In parts of East Anglia, such as the fen edge, the dominant topography is very subdued, with few marked slopes or prominent locations, but even here a fen-edge and possibly 'liminal' situation seems to have been preferred.

In Suffolk, Early Anglo-Saxon cemeteries lie in the south-east along the River Gipping, and in the 'Sandlings' along the Rivers Deben, Stour, Orwell, Alde and Butley River. The Boulder Clay 'Woodlands' separated the south-eastern cemeteries and settlement to the north and north-west in the sandy Breckland, where cemetery locations mostly follow the Rivers Lark and Linnet, and Black Bourn (West 1985, 170; 1998). The River Lark runs north past Bury St Edmunds and on across Breckland to the Fens and thence to the sea. The group of cemeteries along the upper reaches of the River Lark, including Westgarth Gardens (Gaz. nos S17–20, and further upstream no. S74) lie within but close to the edge of the tract of Boulder Clay and may represent the local limit of 6th-century occupation. The cemetery and its contributory population stood on the edge of that area of north-west Suffolk which looked towards the north-west and the Cambridge area, in contrast to the cemeteries of south-east Suffolk and the valley of the River Gipping. Newman's fieldwork in south-east Suffolk suggests heavy clays inhibited 5th- and 6th-century settlement there (Newman 1992). West's maps of Early Anglo-Saxon sites and finds in Suffolk show the absence of settlement on the central claylands, except where they are dissected by river systems (West 1998, figs 143a-b).

The Icknield Way ran along the chalk corridor into Cambridgeshire, an area divided by a series of linear earthworks, with fen to the north and the wooded clays of north-west Essex to the south; some of the earthworks are certainly of Early Saxon date. In Cambridgeshire, cemetery distribution is associated with the Roman walled town of Cambridge, the fen edge, and the valleys of the Rivers Cam, Granta and Rhee (Bourn Brook), which dissect the dry open chalk upland, devoid of cemeteries. West of Cambridge, in the tract of heavy clay, the two known cemeteries (Gaz. nos C24 and 48) lay in river valleys. Several cemeteries lie on the low 'islands' within the fen, usually near the fen edge, and indicate Early Saxon settlement (Gaz. nos C19, 23, 25–6, 34, 46, 51–2 and 61); the 'wood' names on the clays of west and east Cambridgeshire probably testify to the wooded nature of these areas. The cemetery next to the Roman walled town at Great Chesterford, and finds at Wendens Ambo, in the extreme north-west corner of Essex, are included in the map and gazetteer of East Anglia because of clear material links to the Anglian cemeteries around Cambridge (Evison 1969; Fox 1923, 291), and their separation from the other Anglo-Saxon cemeteries in south-east Essex by a tract of Boulder Clay.

Where topography allowed, preferred cemetery locations appear to be on valley crests, with a few exceptions, for example around the Roman walled enclosures of Cambridge and Caistor St Edmund, and by Roman roads. Valley bottom sites were not usually selected for cemeteries, and early reports of urns associated with small barrows at Earsham (Gaz no. 29) seem uncertain for this reason. It has been noted, however, that the cemetery at Westgarth Gardens was positioned unusually close to the bottom of the river valley (see below) and the pattern may not be as clear-cut as archaeological activity seems to suggest.

The distribution of barrows and ring-ditches in East Anglia and beyond, along river valleys and in areas of light soils and along the chalk ridge into Cambridgeshire, resembles that of Anglo-Saxon cemeteries. In Suffolk, barrows have a concentration along the lower reaches of the river valleys, and on the light soils of the Sandlings along the east coast. They appear to be absent on the Boulder Clays of central Norfolk and Suffolk. The association of Anglo-Saxon burial sites with prehistoric barrows may have been a deliberate choice or the result of coincidence to do with settlement geography as well as a need for prominent siting (Lawson *et al.* 1981, 56).

The distribution of Anglo-Saxon cemeteries seems to indicate a 'retreat' from the pattern of settlement in the Roman period, which extended across the whole county, with extensive settlement on the central clays. Anglo-Saxon cemeteries are found in areas of former dense Roman settlement in Suffolk, but mainly on the lighter soils. A similar pattern is seen in Norfolk, especially in the west, where several cemeteries lie along and west of the Boulder Clay plateau, also heavily settled in Roman times, and in minor river valleys in north Norfolk. Using place-name evidence and locational analysis, Oosthuizen (1998, 93–99) has argued for some Roman to Early Anglo-Saxon continuity of settlement location and possibly population in Cambridgeshire, except in areas of heavy clay, which seems to be the pattern in Suffolk, too.

2.2.2 Parish boundaries

Cemetery locations are often close to parish boundaries, suggesting their deliberate placement 'remote' from settlement and on marginal land, and even the pre-existence of the boundaries (*cf.* Bonney 1966; 1972; 1979; Goodier 1984), although Middle Saxon 'estates' and *parochiae* were very much larger than the high-medieval parish. However, Goodier has pointed out that on a random basis one would expect to find cemeteries near parish boundaries quite frequently (Goodier 1984) since more of any parish lies towards the boundary than the centre.

Of the burial sites in East Anglia, about 40% lie somewhere near a parish boundary, arguably lending support to the idea that these boundaries were already in existence. Cemeteries are almost never on parish boundaries, however, unless that boundary also happens to follow an existing feature, usually a stream, sometimes a Roman road or a linear feature such as an earthwork. A few cemeteries are also more central within a parish, and several were clearly sited in relation to a Roman walled enclosure. Of some 250 cemetery sites, only about fifteen or sixteen were close to parish boundaries that did not coincide with such features (Gaz. nos C6; N8, 21, 35, 59, 60, 62, 74, 90, 98; S6, 13, 27, 28, 46, 85). Even in these cases, some other locational determinant is more likely. In Cambridgeshire, Gazetteer no. 6 lies on a parish boundary. There a single burial of 7th-century or later date in a barrow on Allington Hill lay within sight of the Icknield Way, possibly the locational determinant (*cf.* Sporle, Gaz. no. N84).

In Norfolk, Gazetteer nos N21, N35 and N62 lay on small promontories overlooking small streams, whilst Gazetteer no. N8 is a barrow burial, possibly re-used as a boundary landmark. Gazetteer nos N59 and N60 lie on the coast, where the original topography is lost. Gazetteer no. 90 at Thornham is a 7th-century cemetery in a Roman enclosure, doubtless the determinant for both this and the line of the later parish boundary. Gazetteer nos N74 and N98 are the only good parish boundary locations, and even these may be burials associated with barrows which provided a landmark for later boundary surveyors.

For Suffolk, West counted about 24% (15/63) of Anglo-Saxon cemeteries that 'could be said to have a close relationship' to parish boundaries. He went on to note at least five or six with barrows or those situated near rivers, leaving about 14% within 400m of a parish boundary rather than a river, and without known monuments (West 1998, 274–5). Gazetteer nos S46 and S85 lay in elevated positions, overlooking rivers (at a little distance). Gazetteer no. S13 was a barrow burial, and no. S6 lay on a promontory, leaving nos S27 and S28, both at Eriswell, as the sole examples of 'parish boundary only' locations.

Cemeteries have been found on boundaries between parishes once united, *i.e.* West Acre/Castle Acre (Gaz. no. N22) and Little/Great Thurlow (Gaz. no. S37). It seems possible that some feature of the cemetery, possibly a barrow, was chosen to mark the later division of a single land unit. If the stretches of parish boundary which follow some other feature are omitted, then in East Anglia, cemetery locations and parish boundaries are almost mutually exclusive; those cases of coincidence cannot be used to argue for the antiquity of the parish boundary.

2.3 East Anglia as a geopolitical concept

The four cemeteries date mainly in the late 5th and 6th centuries and therefore in a phase in which Anglo-Saxon material culture had developed overall characteristics closely related to but in detail different from Scandinavian and continental contemporary evidence. Attempts at defining 'Anglian' and 'Saxon' female dress produced regional patterns but also mixed groups instead of sharp geographical boundaries (see Vierck 1978b). K. Høilund Nielsen's trend surface map of brooch types shows Norfolk in a zone together with the North, and Suffolk and Cambridgeshire in a more southerly zone (Høilund Nielsen 1997, fig. 2.3). This suggests that the material culture from each of the four cemeteries needs to be analysed in its regional context rather than unquestioningly being treated as an East Anglian melting pot (see also Filmer-Sankey and Pestell 2001, 265 on the Sandlings).

Carver's statement 'If equations can really be made between brooch types and place of origin, East Anglia can have recognized itself as a separate territory, if not a

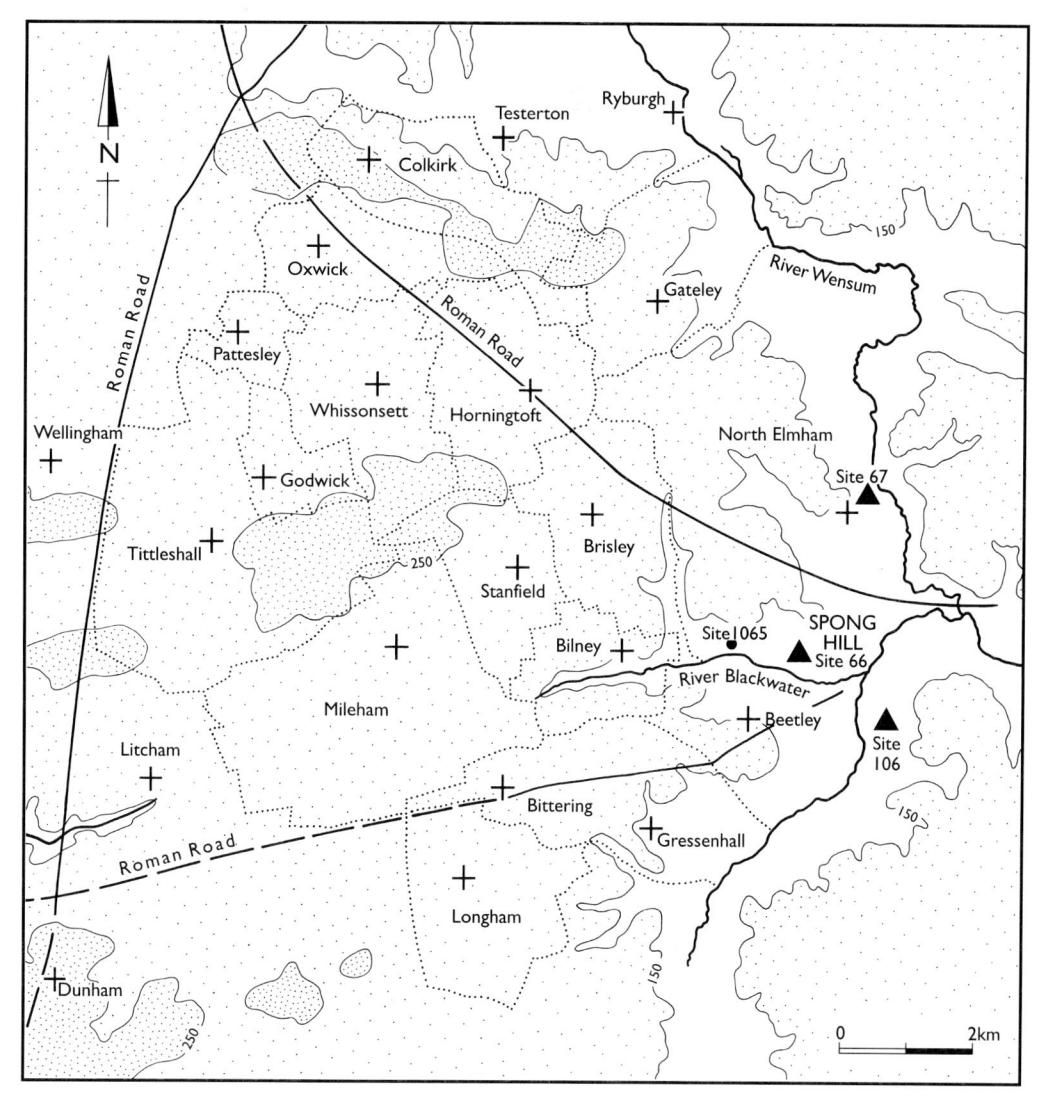

Figure 2.1 Spong Hill, the local context. Crosses represent churches

kingdom, as early as the early fifth century' (Carver 1989, 148) does not hold up to the archaeological evidence (Hills 1993). This does not mean, however, that differences, in turn, give archaeological evidence for the existence of ethnic or political groups, as the relationship between political boundaries, ethnic groups and regional characteristics of material culture is far from clear.

At the four cemeteries, individuals were buried who witnessed or were involved in an emerging Anglo-Saxon kingdom. The Tribal Hidage as the earliest written source, probably compiled in the second half of the 7th century (Davies and Vierck 1974, 227; but see Brooks 1989), does not list territories but groups of people, among them the 'east engle' (Davies and Vierck 1974, 234 fig. 3). By the time Bede finished his Ecclesiastical History in AD 731, the East Anglians had a king with a claim to royal ancestors, who was probably buried at Sutton Hoo (for surveys on East Anglia as an Early Anglo-Saxon kingdom see Carver 1989 and Scull 1992; 1993; 1995). The extent of the East Anglian kingdom or hegemony in the 6th and 7th centuries is difficult to define, not only due to the scant written evidence but probably also to a concept of overlordship over people rather than territory (Scull 1992; 1993). In a largely agricultural society, however, land was an important resource and source of power, and would therefore need definition and protecting. To what extent Roman structures may have survived into the Anglo-Saxon period is not clear (Scull 1992, 14). The possible early existence of small 'tribes' or groups within the larger kingdom may be significant in interpreting local variations in burial practice.

The spatial distribution of settlement cells on which Vierck based his 'tribal areas' in East Anglia (Davies and Vierck 1974) has not held up to the increase of finds since the 1970s (pers. comm. C. Scull) but distribution maps still show concentrations of finds linked to river systems (Scull 1992, 15). On a regional level, Spong Hill may have been part of a different infrastructure than Morning Thorpe and Bergh Apton in the south-east and Westgarth Gardens in the south-west. Scull (1992, 17), however, points out that 'The territorial identification of any fifth- or sixth-century polities, British or Anglo-Saxon, within the region must remain speculative'.

The difficulties attached to precisely matching archaeological and historical records are demonstrated in the archaeological marker that has been used to define the region covered by the Gazetter of East Anglian Cemeteries — the distribution of wrist-clasps. Wrist-

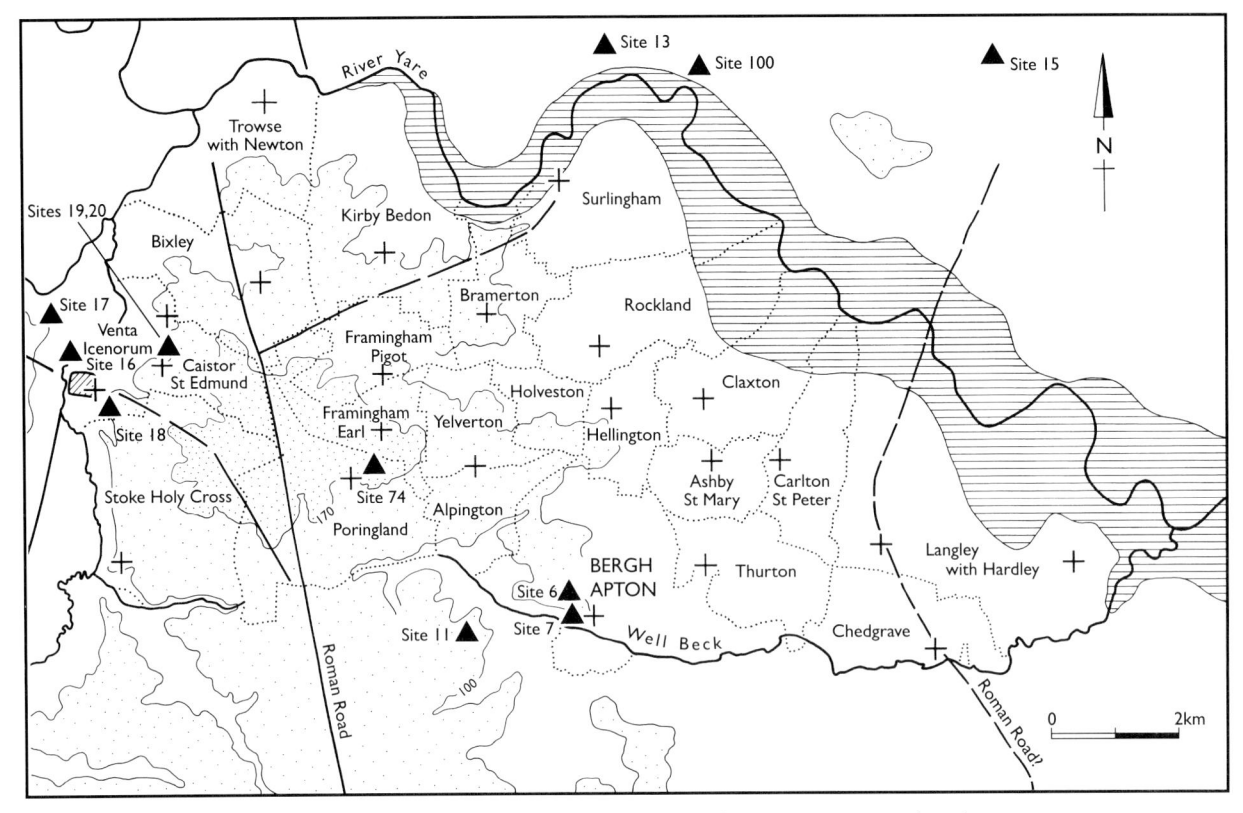

Figure 2.2 Bergh Apton, the local context. Crosses represent churches

clasps are considered a female dress accessory related to 'Anglian', but not specifically East Anglian material culture (Hines 1984). Their distribution includes the south part of Cambridgeshire and the extreme north-west corner of Essex (*i.e.* including Great Chesterford) and possibly extends the boundaries of East Anglia as an early Anglo-Saxon geo-political concept. Cemeteries here are separated by a tract of wooded clayland from south-east Essex, where wrist-clasps are absent from Early Saxon female burials.

The only indisputable boundary of East Anglia as the home of the East Angles was the coastline to east and north. The River Wissey and its estuary, beginning at Wisbech, may have helped mark the western limits of the East Anglian kingdom, with the fen 'island' of March on the boundary. Bede (HE IV, 19) mentions Ely and its district as a part of East Anglia, although perhaps with its own ruling family, whilst the later diocese of Norwich comprised Norfolk and Suffolk, whose boundary with the diocese of Ely (a late creation including an area from south Cambridgeshire to Wisbech in the north) was the earthwork known as Devil's Dyke. It is possible that the River Granta (Cam) was an older frontier which was re-used soon after AD 410, becoming the East Anglian frontier with Mercia (Oosthuizen 1998, 89).

The Cambridgeshire Dykes appear to mark the south-west boundary of East Anglia. Recent work points to the initial construction of Fleam Dyke in the Early Saxon period or perhaps as early as the early 5th century, with its second phase (and the first phase of Devil's Dyke) a little later but still within the Early Saxon period (Malim *et al.* 1997). These earthworks may indicate the existence of some powerful authority able to command the resources for such a venture. By around AD 600 the shared boundary between the East Anglian and the East Saxon kingdom to the south ran along the River Stour for much of its length. The four cemeteries lie well to the north.

2.4 The local context of the four cemeteries

2.4.1 Spong Hill

The graves at Spong Hill are positioned on the southern part of a low ridge that forms the side of a small valley, the Blackwater draining into the Wensum (Hills 1977b, 2, fig. 2). Finds from an Anglo-Saxon cemetery were recorded as early as 1711, and in 1968 systematic excavation began an assessment of the site in view of ongoing damage by erosion and ploughing and in advance of possible destruction by road works and gravel-extraction. The site owes its excavation until 1981 to a research project aiming to be the first ever total excavation of an East Anglian Anglo-Saxon cemetery (Hills 1977, 6). Adjacent to an area with *c.* 2500 cremations a small cemetery of fifty-five inhumation graves was found. While the south-western and north-eastern extent of the scatter of inhumation graves was clearly reached, it seems possible that further inhumation graves lie beyond the excavated area in the north and west.

The graves were placed within the enclosures of a Roman farmstead and accompanied by an adjacent scatter of Anglo-Saxon buildings (see Rickett 1995). The cemetery was probably situated *c.* 2 miles from the junction of two roads crossing the Wensum at a Roman settlement (Hills 1977b, fig. 1). There is some further evidence of Early Saxon activity in North Elmham parish: an occupation site to the west (County Sites 1065 and 1100) and another 6th-century cemetery to the north (Gaz. no. N67) closer to North Elmham village. Except for this cemetery, evidenced by surface finds, and that at Spong

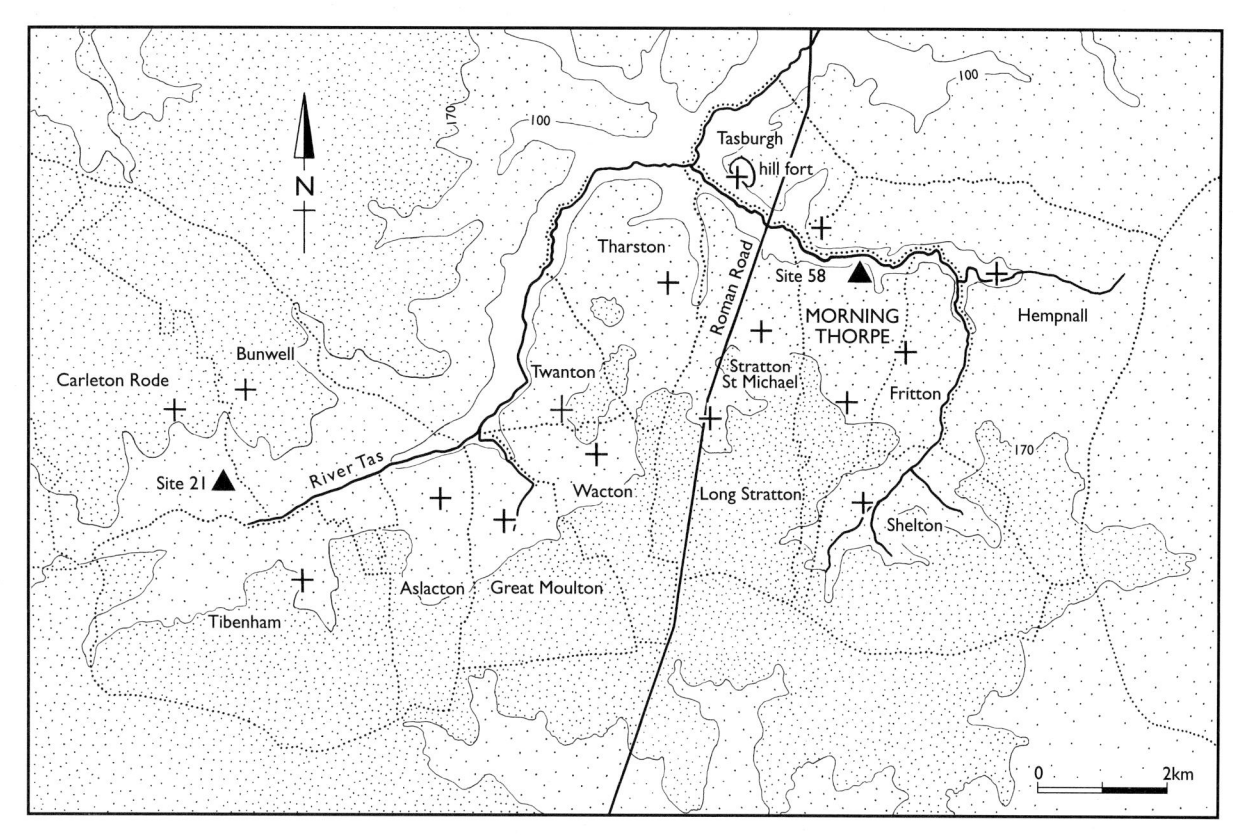

Figure 2.3 Morning Thorpe, the local context. Crosses represent churches

Hill, no other Early Saxon cemeteries are known in the Wensum valley system until Gaz. no. N50: Kettlestone, about 10km to the north, and Gaz. no. N109: Morton on the Hill, about 13km to the east and downstream (Fig. 2.1).

Excavations at North Elmham have revealed three phases of Middle Saxon occupation, possibly beginning as early as the late 7th century, with the earliest datable finds being two early 8th-century coins (Wade-Martins 1980, 628). North Elmham may have been the site of a bishop's see from AD 673, when the East Anglian see was divided in two, and a new centre established at Elmham (Bede HE IV, 5; Rigold 1980; Fernie 1993, 8–10).

2.4.2 Bergh Apton

The inhumation cemetery at Bergh Apton lies on the top of a small hill on the north side of the Well Beck, one of the main tributaries to the River Chet (Green and Rogerson 1978, 2), c. 40km south-east of Spong Hill. The site was discovered in the course of gravel-extraction in 1973, and sixty-five graves were excavated under time pressure ahead of further destruction. The edge of the quarry clearly cuts across the cemetery in the west and south and further graves may be positioned in the unexcavated area to the east.

Evidence for prehistoric, probably Bronze Age, activity on the site has probably been lost in quarrying for gravel; a large pit or pits (77) at the north end of the site, perhaps on the edge of the Anglo-Saxon cemetery, contained a piece of prehistoric flint-gritted pottery. Other evidence of prehistoric activity came from the south-eastern part of the site (perhaps the eastern edge of the cemetery), where nine features were found, two of which contained probable Bronze Age flint-gritted pottery (Green and Rogerson 1978, fig. 4). An undated north-to-south ditch (23) seemed to underlie some of the graves, although this relationship is not certain (Green and Rogerson 1978, figs 4 and 5). Not enough of the cemetery could be excavated to know whether a prehistoric monument existed and was visible in the Early Saxon period, but this is likely.

The Well Beck, which formed much of the southern parish boundary for Bergh Apton, helps to define a long east-to-west strip bounded by the Rivers Yare and the Tas to the north and to the west. The south boundary was defined by a small tributary to the Tas, a short overland stretch following a narrow lane (Dove Lane), and then the Well Beck flowing eastwards into the River Chet, and then to its confluence with the River Yare (Fig. 2.2). Within this large area several early cemeteries are known, including three around Caistor St Edmund (Gaz. nos N18, 19 and 20), one of which runs into the 7th century, an early record of burials at Poringland (Gaz. no. N74), and ?two cemeteries at Bergh Apton (Gaz. nos N6 and N7). The cremation cemeteries at Caistor St Edmund (Gaz. nos N16 and 18) are mostly earlier than the Bergh Apton cemetery and may relate to a 'central function' within the walls and a wide catchment area.

2.4.3 Morning Thorpe

Morning Thorpe, as Bergh Apton, owes its discovery to gravel extraction in 1974. The cemetery was located on a gentle slope to the south of a valley containing a tributary of the River Tas (Green et al. 1987, 1, fig. 2), c. 10km south-east of Bergh Apton and 35km south-east of Spong Hill. Rescue excavations in the same and the following year recorded 320 inhumations and nine cremations. The southern and western limit of the plot could be determined

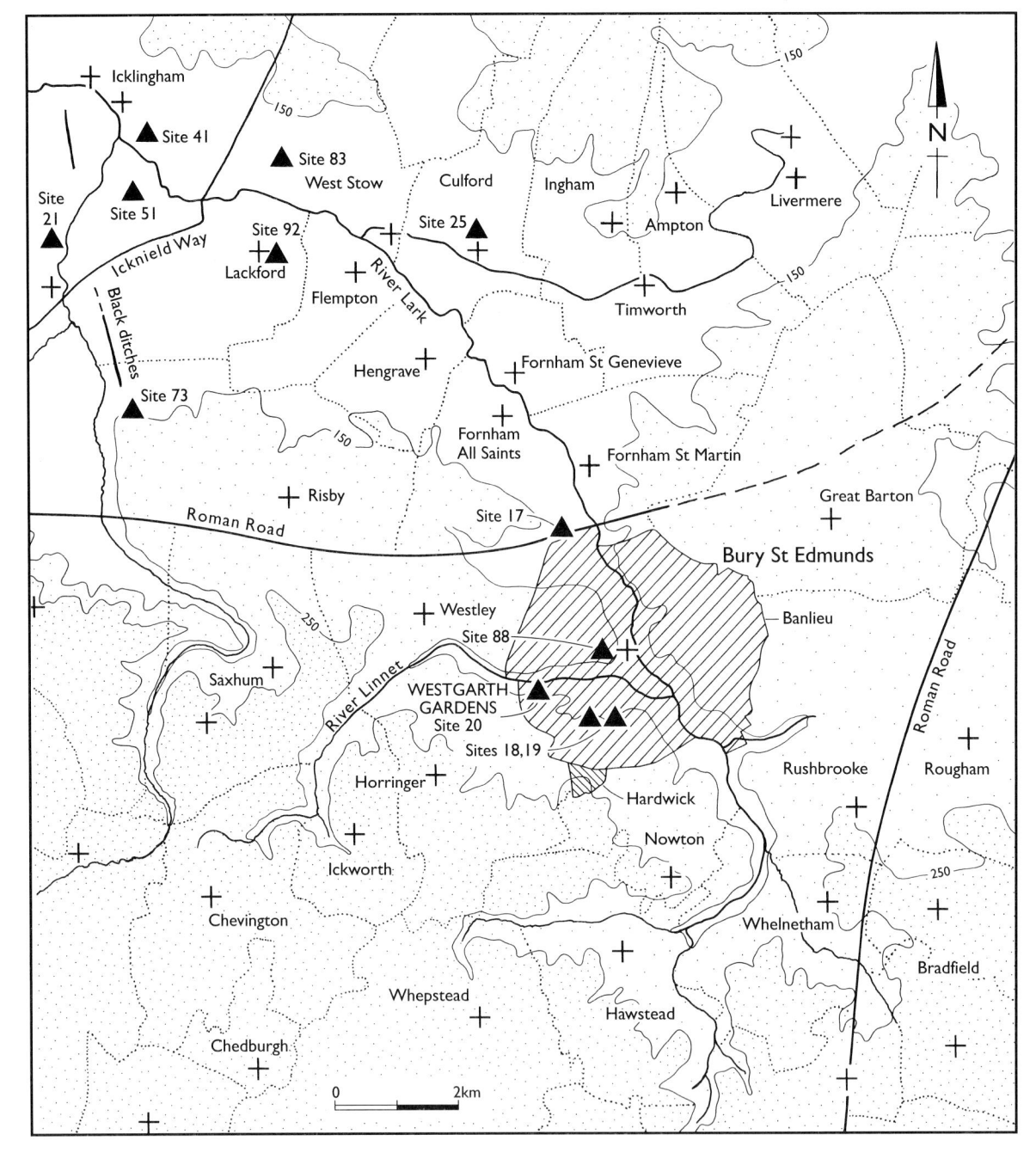

Figure 2.4 Westgarth Gardens, the local context. Crosses represent churches

but a northern part had been cut away by the quarry and the eastern limit of the cemetery lay outside the examined area.

An air photograph taken before the expansion of the quarry at Morning Thorpe shows a ring-ditch (County Site 10179) just to the north of the cemetery, on the slope above the River Tas (Green *et al.* 1987, pl I, fig. 4). This was probably the ditch of a Bronze Age barrow, now destroyed in quarrying, and possibly the deliberate focus for the later Anglo-Saxon cemetery since it lies 100m north of the excavated area (and less to the original north edge of the cemetery). Other evidence for prehistoric burial here was found during excavation, in the quarry face (a Bronze Age cremation urn: Context 431).

The cemetery lies on the northern edge of the parish of Morning Thorpe in a tract of heavy Boulder Clay upland on which lie remnant woods and many small greens and commons. This was a region of wood-pasture with medieval settlement mainly on gravel soils in stream valleys, with evidence of a pre-Roman landscape to the west of Morning Thorpe, which survived into the Anglo-Saxon period. The modern A140 is a Roman road in origin, and at Long Stratton the adjacent field systems may be of the same period (Williamson 1987). Further to the west, in Moulton and Aslacton, another large field system may also be of early date; their south boundary is an ancient lane, the boundary between the Hundreds of Depwade, and Diss and Earsham (Fig. 2.3). Within this large area there is some evidence of other early cemeteries; such as the site on the boundary of Bunwell and Carleton Rode (Gaz. no. N21).

2.4.4 Westgarth Gardens

The cemetery at Westgarth Gardens was positioned at the foot of a hill that forms the south bank of the Linnet, a tributary of the River Lark. It is the most southerly of the four cemeteries and lies *c.* 60km south(-west) of Spong Hill and *c.* 50km south-west of Morning Thorpe. In contrast to the high setting of Spong Hill, Westgarth Gardens is remarkable for being positioned close to the valley bottom rather than higher on the slope (West 1988, 2).

Grave-goods were discovered in a gas main trench in 1972, and it was subsequently possible to excavate seventy graves on the site of two houses ahead of further building works (West 1988, 1). Empty spaces in the south and north-east of the excavated area suggest that some limits of the cemetery were reached but the building works had clearly cut though the north-western and probably also south-eastern part of the plot. Two finds, A and B, came from 20m and 40m east of the excavated area (West 1988, fig. 2) with 'Grave' 67 about 50m to the east, towards burials found between 1955 and 1970 (see below). Except for a shallow ditch in the south-east corner of the excavated area, no other features were found, and no evidence of earlier activity. This could be due to the nature of the site and the circumstances of its recovery.

There is no evidence of prehistoric activity or monument on the site which could have determined the later location of an Anglo-Saxon cemetery here. The site, Gaz. no. S20 lay close to the boundary of the later *banlieu* of the Late Saxon and medieval abbey and town, however, and it is possible that some feature within the cemetery, possibly a barrow, provided a landmark when the boundary was laid out.

As noted, in this area of Boulder Clay, medieval settlement location was strongly determined by rivers and streams. Several other Early Anglo-Saxon burials are known in the immediate area, two small cemeteries to the east (Fig. 2.4, Gaz. nos S18 and 19), and a probable barrow to the north (Gaz. no. S17) which produced several burials. There is also a cemetery near the river at Fornham (St Martin or St Genevieve) to the north. Gazetteer no. S18 at Hardwick Lane produced three burials, no. S19 at Baron's Road, 340m to the east, another two or three, and at no. S17, Northumberland Avenue to the north, the remains of a larger cemetery (thirty burials) have been found; this appears to have run into the 7th century, like Westgarth Gardens.

If these burials were not part of much larger cemeteries, they may have belonged to farmsteads, with both settlements and cemeteries lying along the rivers at intervals. The four cemeteries at Gaz. nos S17–20 in effect occupy a small river basin in the Boulder Clays, close to east-to-west and south-to-north Roman roads. The mid 7th-century (AD 630s) monastic site of *Bedericsworth* was probably founded close by.

2.5 Conclusions

Due to the history of archaeological activity in Norfolk and Suffolk, the four cemeteries are the only substantial East Anglian inhumation cemeteries with date-ranges between the mid 5th and 7th centuries which have been formally excavated and published so far. The *c.* 500 graves excavated at these sites form 15–20% of the total number of inhumation graves recorded in East Anglia since the 19th century and have produced the main evidence for detailed information such as grave-good associations, the position of the objects in the graves and cemetery layout.

The locations of the four cemeteries follow an established pattern. They were situated on the slopes of river valleys (Spong Hill rather high on a slope and Westgarth Gardens rather low), all were dug in areas settled in Roman times and certainly or possibly focused on Bronze Age barrows. Only at Spong Hill could an area be fully excavated, and comparison of the four cemeteries in terms of size, duration, or their individual character as 'mixed' cemeteries with evidence for both inhumation and cremation is therefore limited. It seems possible that Morning Thorpe, Bergh Apton and Westgarth Gardens with their partially excavated plots were parts of burial grounds similar to Spong Hill in their entirety, rather than substantially different in character. The potential for demographic research based on these sites therefore is limited. The poor bone preservation at Spong Hill, Morning Thorpe and Bergh Apton puts further limits on the subject.

The majority of inhumation graves of the four cemeteries date to the 6th century and thus to a phase in which Anglo-Saxon material culture had developed overall characteristics closely related to, but in detail different from, Scandinavian and continental evidence. All four sites include objects generally characterised as 'East Anglian' but there is also evidence for local variation. A sample of the size of the four cemeteries can make it difficult to differentiate between local and regional variations in the evidence, and it seems likely that an analysis of Westgarth Gardens in this respect will be greatly enhanced by the publication of the recently excavated graves at Lakenheath, Eriswell.

3. Social and chronological analysis: theory and method

3.1 Background

The nature of Early Anglo-Saxon inhumation cemetery evidence — human remains of individuals each set in their own context of features and artefacts — appeals to a strong sense of individual identity in modern western society and prompts research focussing on the expression of social, and in particular personal identity in past societies. Such efforts can build on thirty years of research on the theory and method of analysing and interpreting social structures and identity expressed in burial practice. They are usually based on the quantity, quality and diversity of grave-goods and their associations with human remains, on labour investment in the burials and on spatial patterns (for the history of research on cemeteries in general see, *e.g,* Parker Pearson 1999; McHugh 1999; for Anglo-Saxon evidence in particular Scull 1993; Härke 1997; 2000; Lucy and Reynolds 2002b).

Variation in the burial data, if possible a combination of physical anthropological data (age, sex, pathology) and archaeological data (the grave-finds, the treatment of the body and the use of material, space and labour for the burial) are used to define individuals as a component of a pattern expressing social structure. Of these criteria, only the osteological ones are unmitigated evidence of the individual in life. The others create an 'archaeological image' of the individual based on burial practice and the preservation of the evidence in the ground. As meaning is derived from patterns in the record, interpretations of burial evidence are highly dependent on burial practices being consistent in the way they create these patterns. The difference between cremation and inhumation practice and between 'furnished' and 'unfurnished' burial practice often attributed to pagan and Christian influence, are the most obvious examples for variations in burial practices that need to be taken into account when working with the archaeological image of individuals. Changes over time both in burial practice and the material culture used in this practice call for chronological frameworks that differentiate between social variation and changes over time. As it is the interpretation of patterns in the archaeological evidence, not their very existence that is usually being questioned, some quantitative methods are now firmly established in cemetery studies, in particular cluster, factor and correspondence analysis (see Jensen and Høilund Nielsen 1997; McHugh 1999; Ravn 2003).

Detailed investigations of single sites or relatively small regional samples can show a high degree of variation in the data difficult to interpret with confidence. Sam Lucy's research on East Yorkshire sites (Lucy 1998) has led her to promote a 'bottom-up' approach to burial data which questions the validity of general conclusions drawn on the basis of large-scale investigations, arguing that a supra-regional identity exceeded Anglo-Saxon self-awareness, which was shaped by 'local' identities (Lucy 2002, 77). A 'bottom-up' approach has its merits but incorporates the danger of not seeing the wood for the trees. Work on Kentish and Cambridgeshire sites, for example, has demonstrated that the complexity of the material culture raises questions that can be answered only in a regional or supra-regional context (Parfitt and Brugmann 1997; Malim and Hines 1998). Härke's analysis of Anglo-Saxon weapon graves and Stoodley's analysis of gender have shown that far-reaching conclusions on social structure can be promoted on the basis of large samples combining archaeological, osteological and historical data (Härke 1992; Stoodley 1999). It is this supra-regional level on which questions about broad-ranging social issues such as ethnic identity and the formation of kingdoms can be addressed.

3.2 Previous research on the four cemeteries

3.2.1 Social structure

Pader's study *Symbolism, Social Relations and the Interpretation of Mortuary Remains* is notable for including Westgarth Gardens and to a lesser extent Bergh Apton in the analysis besides a particularly systematic approach to the subject. She produced the most explicit theoretical and methodical framework yet published as the basis for an Anglo-Saxon cemetery analysis, a 'framework largely derived from structuralism and Marxism, by which to interpret empirical data concerning mortuary practices' (Pader 1982, 198). Her explicitness does not cover the chronological framework used for the dating of graves, a shortcoming that does not discredit other aspects of her work. The patterns defined by Pader's 'multidimensional' approach are not based on the quantity and diversity in grave-good assemblages alone but allow for local and regional variations in the use of material culture in general and of burial practice in particular. These patterns, however, are too small-scale to be interpreted with confidence:

> Some readers might find it unsatisfactory that after eight chapters of theory and analysis I have not actually attempted to present a reconstruction of the social organisation which underlies the patterning found in the early Anglo-Saxon cemeteries at Holywell Row and Westgarth Gardens, nor tried to interpret the meaning of, for example, the different degrees to which age and sex categories are demarcated between the cemeteries. However, I feel that at this point in our knowledge of the very complex relationship between material culture remains, social relations and ideology, any such attempt would be premature (Pader 1982, 201).

A social status analysis of the four cemeteries was carried out by Jane Brenan in 1997 (Brenan 1997). It was based on an analysis of the combinations of grave-finds, using the *Socistat* computer programme developed at the Institute for Archaeology, University College, London. A variation of the programme is part of the *Bonn Seriation and Archaeological Statistics Package* distributed by the *Unkelbach Valley Software Works*. *Socistat* was first used to analyse social status for Hallstatt graves (Hodson 1977), and has been applied by Brenan (1984–5; 1991) to various Anglo-Saxon cemeteries.

> The programme works basically on two related assumptions, that the 'rich' graves will tend to contain a higher number of objects, or, more specifically, of functional types, and that poorer types such as knives and belt buckles will also be represented in the grave assemblage along with types of higher status. This last assumption can be justified by simply looking at the grave assemblages, for example, the 'rich' female graves contain not only pendants, girdle-hangers and wrist-clasps, but also knives and buckles. Using this assumption, the status of each functional type can be estimated by calculating the average number of types any specific type is associated with. This can then be used as a status score for each type (Brenan 1984–5, 127).

This is an approach based on the model of a social group with a simple vertical structure expressed through grave-finds in a largely cumulative manner. For the programme to produce the desired result, the bulk of 'high' status males, for example, have to share some of their status symbols with males of 'lower status'. Males of 'higher' and 'lower status' will — to use a commonplace example — be buried with a spear, but only the 'higher status' males will have an additional sword. In a gender group with a stronger vertical structure, in which a 'high status' male will be buried with a sword but not with a spear signalling a 'lower status', 'high status' objects will not score appropriately in *Socistat*. Such a model would, however, be compatible with the symbolic use of weapons in Anglo-Saxon burial practice (*cf.* Härke 1992) which does not require a weapon set to be functional. The fact that Anglo-Saxon grave-good associations suggest some degree of accumulation within gender groups might indicate a relatively low degree of social differentiation within these groups.

An interesting aspect of the programme is the 'status index' given to types as the mean number of different types in graves containing the type. Such a 'status index' merits a methodical approach to an aspect of burial practice that is often approached intuitively.

As with any programme, the usefulness of results obtained from *Socistat* depends on the data input. For the purpose of Brenan's analysis,

> All the objects in the cemetery were coded into functional types. A data set was then constructed consisting of a listing of all the graves with grave-goods in the cemetery. Each grave number was followed by a list of functional types occurring in that grave. Functional types are preferable in this sort of analysis since they are likely to remain stable over a long period of time. The results are therefore less likely to be influenced by changes in design and style. Assumptions about the material can also be kept to a minimum... In this way the total number of types occurring in the cemetery can be kept to a minimum. This is useful in comparatively small cemeteries, since the results will be more reliable if the types occur frequently. Conversely the status of a type which only occurs one or two times throughout the cemetery will not be very reliable. Multiple occurrences of types within a grave, such as knives, were also not recorded. It was felt such instances occurred too infrequently to justify an additional type (Brenan 1997).

Brenan's choice of 'functional' types was largely based on the attribute 'practical function'. This included indiscriminate groups such as 'other weapons', 'miscellaneous tools', 'pin', 'copper fragments' and 'pendant/charm/amulet/keepsake'. Rather than keeping assumptions to a minimum, the choice of types was based on generalisations which would need to be tested. This also applies to the assumption that functional types are likely to remain stable over a long period. In Chapter 7 it will be demonstrated that the 5th to 7th centuries saw some changes in Anglo-Saxon burial practice that require a more differentiated approach to the material.

In Brenan's analysis, the ranking of the graves from Morning Thorpe defined girdle-hangers as the highest status object in female graves, followed by keys, wrist-clasps, suspension rings, brooch pairs, single brooches, necklaces, and pendants/trinkets. Swords were defined as the type of weapon with the highest social status attached to it, followed by shields and spears. Buckles being rarer than shields in male graves led Brenan to speculate about a possible function of buckles as scabbard fittings. In Anglo-Saxon graves in general, however, buckles are also found to be combined with no more than a knife or a pot, for example, so that their overall 'status index' is fairly low. An analysis based on a slightly different choice of types has produced a 'status index' for buckles slightly lower than that for shield bosses (Ch. 7) and gives an example of the importance of the choice of data for such an analysis.

Comparative analysis of the type combinations at Spong Hill, Bergh Apton and Westgarth Gardens with *Socistat* produced variations which Brenan attributed mainly to low grave numbers producing statistically unreliable results. Further analysis of the four cemeteries will show, however, that girdle-hangers and wrist-clasps were in use for a shorter period than brooches, for example, thus affecting the 'status index' of objects in use for a longer or different period. It will also be possible to demonstrate that Spong Hill appears to be the richest of the four sites mainly because of its predominantly early date range. These results demonstrate the importance of chronological studies as a basis for an analysis of social aspects of Anglo-Saxon cemeteries and call for a differentiated use of programmes such as *Socistat*.

An analysis of artefact associations from the graves at the four cemeteries has been undertaken by Kenneth Penn (archive report), adapting the model used by Guy Halsall (1995) to analyse Merovingian cemeteries in the region of Metz. In his interpretation of the osteological and archaeological evidence, Halsall was able to draw on written sources and produced an interesting picture of social structure around Merovingian Metz. Unfortunately an analysis of the four cemeteries cannot draw on contextual information in the same way.

The most obvious pattern the artefact association analysis of the four cemeteries produced was similar to the pattern also picked up by Lucy in her analysis of East Yorkshire cemeteries, and it is in fact a regular feature of

Anglo-Saxon burial grounds. Lucy (1998, 41) defined four groups of grave-good assemblages, based on a breakdown of two East Yorkshire cemeteries by grave and assemblage constituents:

- those containing jewellery or ornamentation of some sort…
- those containing weapons…
- those containing goods which do not fall into these previous two categories (including individual beads, knives, buckles or belt-fittings, vessels and animal bones…
- and those containing no surviving artefacts at all

The first two groups are defined by the presence of objects that have been recognised as strongly gender related. Such objects are absent in the archaeological record of the other two groups, a characteristic that needs to be carefully assessed. The idea that 'all the mourners of those burials with other goods assemblages, or with no surviving goods, seem to have felt no compunction to signal anything at all about their gender whatsoever' (Lucy 1998, 49) takes the archaeological record at face-value. It is an obvious but important point that organic components of the burial assemblage usually do not survive. In particular clothing or hair styles were probably distinctive in precisely these terms. In terms of gender, Lucy's groups fall into three categories: graves with types of objects associated with male gender, those associated with female gender and those without gender-related attributes in the archaeological record. Correlations of the four groups with features such as age, position of the body, size or orientation of graves are not strong enough to produce patterns that invite a detailed interpretation of Anglo-Saxon social structure. What they do demonstrate is considerable variation in Anglo-Saxon burial practices at a micro-level (see above) also evident at the four cemeteries. This situation creates a challenge for quantitative approaches to the study of Anglo-Saxon cemeteries (see McHugh 1999).

In his study *The Significance of Form and Decoration of Anglo-Saxon Cremation Urns*, which included the cremations at Spong Hill, Richards (1987, 42) concentrated on Anglo-Saxon cremation vessels as 'a potential set of communicating symbols' related to the 'social identity of the occupant'. The results of this study, which demonstrated links between osteological and archaeological data, have been reviewed by Ravn (2003) in his work on *Death Ritual and Germanic Social Structure (c. AD 200–600),* which includes an analysis of both the inhumation and cremation graves at Spong Hill. Ravn points out that the potential of the quantitative methods available to Richards (1987, 45) at the time (chi-square and Kolmogorov-Smirnov test) was limited in comparison to correspondence analysis used by Ravn (2003, 18ff.; 99) for his own social analysis of the Spong Hill graves. Additionally, Ravn was able to incorporate data on the cremations dug after 1977, an analysis of the human remains from Spong Hill (McKinley 1994) and a chronological analysis of the Spong Hill pots by Karen Høilund Nielsen (Ravn 2003, 99 figs 8.2,3). The most important difference between Richards' and Ravn's analysis of the material in terms of social meaning is, however, Ravn's contextual approach to the data used not only to identify symbols related to social identity but also to suggest their 'secondary meanings' on the basis of later written sources.

Ravn's analysis of the inhumation graves at Spong Hill produces a result for the female graves that leads him to describe them as 'quite homogeneous' (Ravn 2003, 104.). For the male graves he defines two groups. Group A is characterised by weapons, buckles and animal bones, which he describes as 'high[ly] prestigious'. Group B comprises the remaining male graves, associated with certain types of pot decoration and most of the silver. On the basis of stratigraphic and spatial evidence, Ravn proposes an interpretation of individual graves in terms of generations of family relations and household members: a male 'leading person', wives, daughters, spouses, 'servants', 'retainers' and individuals in terms of 'prestige' and 'importance' and concludes:

> I suggest from the chorological distribution as well as the discussion of stratigraphy that the inhumations at Spong Hill can be divided into at least two sections… The eastern section belonged to the most important farm, judging from the quality, quantity as well as combinations of finds in the CA analysis. I suggest that the family of the male spouse in grave 40 was the leader of the area. His son(s) or successor in grave(s) 31 and 32 took over that role after his death. Further analysis awaits a chronological assessment, which will be able to suggest whether the eastern and western groups were contemporaneous (Ravn 2003, 106).

Ravn's search for family members and household plots and in particular for a 'founder grave' follows a line of research better known in Scandinavia and Germany than in Britain (see Härke 2000, 374) and is based on a model of 'Germanic' social structure largely developed from early medieval written sources (see Härke 1997, 141.).

Ravn's analysis of the Spong Hill cremations is particularly interesting in view of the question which part of Anglo-Saxon society may be represented by inhumation cemeteries (see Ch. 2.1). The distribution of sex and age in combination with chronological factors led him to conclude that the cremation cemetery is also comprised of household plots, 'a family based cemetery with internal social division within a farmstead according to age' estimated at '5–6 contemporary nuclear settlements using Spong Hill as a burial ground' with 'a catchment area of a ca 16km elliptical area around Spong Hill' (Ravn 2003, 123). The Spong Hill inhumations are interpreted as a burial practice that forms a demonstrative act of distinction from the cremation cemetery, an emerging elite 'seizing power and ideology, expressing it through their mode of interring their household, poor as well as rich' (Ravn 2003, 129). This is an interesting model in view of the interpretation of small 'elite' cemeteries adjacent to continental row-grave cemeteries (see Härke 2000, 374). A similar interpretation which takes the historical context of the period into account, has been suggested by Böhme (1986, 542). He considered the possibility that representatives of the Late Roman military administration were inhumed at Spong Hill. Whether in the area on duty, or taking charge after the dissolution of the Roman administration, these individuals would have represented an elite.

Ravn (2003, 122) defines three groups of males among the Spong Hill cremations. A 'significant relationship between adult men, horses and play pieces' in the group considered to have the highest status points to 'a relationship between high status, mobility and warfare', possibly indicating that 'older prestigious men were war leaders who led the battle from horseback.' According to Ravn (2003, 122), 'the meaning of play pieces could be that games had intellectual status as chess in the high medieval age, symbolising intelligence, flair for strategic thinking and the ability to lead a battle', the notion that 'horse must have been meaningful in burial ritual and not just reflecting economic aspects, is substantiated by the fact that the presence of horse and dog is much higher at Spong Hill than on for instance settlement sites such as West Stow' (Ravn 2003, 127).

Group II is distinguished by the combination of weapons, copper-alloy tweezers, hone stones and glass vessels among other variables (Ravn 2003, 114). Ravn (2003, 133) associates the tweezers with hair as a symbol of power as is suggested in literary sources, and glass vessels with drinking rituals. He argues that weapons may be a late phenomenon in cremation burial practice and contemporary with the inhumation graves from the same site (Ravn 2003, 123). The adoption of the inhumation burial practice would thus coincide with changes in the use of material culture for burial, such as the increased use of weapons for the expression of an 'ideology of war' (Ravn 2003, 128).

> It may have been the retainers or warriors which distinguished themselves towards the end of the lifetime of the cremation cemetery, possibly developing into the ones of the inhumations. They had a number of stamps on their pots suggesting that they were in a negotiating position between the rich and the poorer, trying to legitimate their power, not only with their weapons but also with a religious relation to the warrior god Thor (Ravn 2003, 127).

The third group of male graves, group I, is the 'least significant of the three groups... buried with iron miniature artefacts' but presumably of higher status than the possibly 'least prestigious social group' of 'the 1151 badly or unfurnished graves' covering between 40% and 46% of the individuals cremated at Spong Hill (Ravn 2003, 127).

The pattern produced by the cremation of females is more homogeneous than that of the males: 'the pattern points to *no clear internal division* among females, as is the case with males. Maybe this lack of internal social division and competition explains the absence of stamps and ornamentation among women...' (Ravn 2003, 118). Ravn (2003, 127) follows Brush (1994) in the interpretation of women 'playing the role as 'ethnic markers' between various regions, as also indicated from brooch types in general and from inhumation graves' and suggests they were '*markers of wealth*, as it is mainly among them that we find precious metals' (Ravn 2003, 135), a role for which Arnold (1980, 132) argued in more detail.

One does not need to wholeheartedly embrace Ravn's interpretations of symbols or suggestions about social structure at Spong Hill to appreciate the effort he has made not just to present a largely descriptive account of the results of his analysis of patterns in the burial data but also to make suggestions about their meaning in a 5th- and 6th-century context. The social structure outlined by Ravn is not far from that developed by Steuer (1982a) for continental row-grave cemeteries (see Härke 2000, 372) and compatible with the model of 'ranked lineages' as an early stage of social relationships proposed by Christopher Scull (1993, 73) for Early Anglo-Saxon East Anglia,

> a model of broadly-equal, internally ranked patrilineal, patrilocal descent groups farming or exploiting their own territories... The cemetery evidence suggests unequal social relations within lineages, and might be taken to imply the existence of central figures, in whose favour the balance of social obligation and responsibility might be tipped, and who may also have had some redistributive power. Such communities might also very well have included a sizable servile or semi-servile element. Although it is more difficult to discern ranking amongst cremations, the size of urnfields such as Spong Hill would not be inconsistent with this model if they were indeed central burial places for a population scattered among a number of small settlements.

For an analysis of the four cemeteries, Ravn's work is particularly interesting because it embraces both the cremation and inhumation graves at Spong Hill. The relative chronological framework developed for the four cemeteries (Ch. 5) meets Ravn's demand for a more detailed chronological framework for the inhumation graves at Spong Hill and corrects some of his suggestions.

The most detailed published studies on aspects of Early Anglo-Saxon social structure based on regional and national cemetery samples, Heinrich Härke's analysis of weapon graves and Nick Stoodley's *Critical Enquiry into the Construction and Meaning of Gender in the Early Anglo-Saxon Burial Rite* (Härke 1992; Stoodley 1999) include Spong Hill, Bergh Apton and Westgarth Gardens, but not Morning Thorpe. Sites included in their regional East Anglian samples are Holywell Row (Suffolk), Little Eriswell (Suffolk), and Swaffham (Norfolk). This puts the weight of Härke's and Stoodley's East Anglian samples on Suffolk, while the weight of the four cemeteries as a sample lies on Norfolk. Høilund Nielsen's study on 'Saxon' and 'Anglian' material culture puts both Suffolk and Norfolk in the area of predominantly Anglian material culture, but the 'gradual change between Anglian and Saxon with a rather mixed group in between' raises the question to what extent this shift may vary results obtained from the different samples. Høilund Nielsen's trend surface map shows Norfolk and Suffolk in different zones (Høilund Nielsen 1997, 85, fig. 23), a result that could be tested and probably improved by including Bergh Apton, Morning Thorpe and the recently excavated site at Eriswell, Lakenheath in Suffolk. It therefore seems possible that not only the overbearing presence of Morning Thorpe can lead to results different from Härke's and Stoodley's, but also the northern bias in the four cemeteries as an East Anglian sample.

3.2.2 Chronology
A chronological framework is here understood as a model. The aim of such a model is not to date every individual grave as closely as possible but to identify general changes over time as accurately as possible. Such a model is likely to be too abstract to do justice to each individual grave in the analysis, but provides a framework that can serve studies with broader aims.

The state of research on Anglo-Saxon chronology has been discussed in detail by Høilund Nielsen (1997) and Hines (1999a). Their criticism of Palm's and Pind's approach to the chronology of *Anglian English Women's Graves in the Fifth to Seventh Centuries AD* (Palm and Pind 1992; Hines 1992) highlights the need for regional chronological frameworks for Anglo-Saxon female dress accessories. Unfortunately, this need for regional approaches makes it impossible to work with large amounts of data such as is available from continental row-grave cemeteries. Research on glass beads from Anglo-Saxon cemeteries, however, suggests that the *c.* 500 graves from the four cemeteries form a regional sample with a good potential for relative chronological studies based on correspondence analysis (see Brugmann 2004). For want of other applicable methods, absolute dates rely on comparative material dated in continental contexts.

A case study of graves from Buttermarket, Ipswich, has demonstrated the use of high precision radiocarbon dating for graves of the 7th and 8th centuries (Scull and Bayliss 1999). The ongoing project *Anglo-Saxon England c. 570–720: the chronological basis* funded by English Heritage makes use of this method for a national sample of Anglo-Saxon graves and has produced promising preliminary results. Weapons are less subject to regional variation than brooches and it is therefore easier to support East Anglian data with a national sample (Ch. 5.2). A detailed chronological framework for East Anglian cremation cemeteries would need to be largely based on the cremation urns. A correspondence analysis of pot attributes by Høilund Nielsen shows promising results but unfortunately is not published in detail (see Ravn 2003).

3.2.3 Conclusion

The history of research on social structure and identity expressed in East Anglian burial practices, and in Early Anglo-Saxon burial practices in general, shows that further research needs to tackle two problems in particular: a chronological framework that reduces the 'background noise' of variations in the data based not on social differentiation but change over time, and a lively discussion of models of Early Anglo-Saxon social structure based on osteological and archaeological evidence, historical sources and ethnographic evidence. The analysis of the four cemeteries will contribute by concentrating on the archaeological evidence.

3.3 Methods

The poor preservation of bones at Morning Thorpe, Bergh Apton and Spong Hill make the four cemeteries a sample largely unsuitable for comprehensive research on individual identity. Over 80% of the burials, however, produced finds, and the strength of the four cemeteries lies in the size of the regional sample and the potential of the material for chronological studies. The four cemeteries are thus suited for an analysis of changes in East Anglian material culture and burial practice over time.

Though there is quite some evidence for intercutting graves at the four cemeteries, few are useful for chronological studies, either because the relationship between the two graves is not clear or because none or only one of them produced objects useful for dating purposes. The position of grave-finds and the outlines of some graves in particular at Morning Thorpe suggest they represent the remains of more than one grave, thus questioning the context of apparent grave-good assemblages. Such cases have been meticulously noted in the grave catalogue and warn against the possibility of further cases which may not have been spotted for a lack of distinctive grave-finds arousing suspicion.

The main method used for the development of a relative chronological framework is correspondence analyses of artefact associations using the programme KVARK developed by Torsten Madsen. For the use of this method for chronological studies see Høilund Nielsen (1995; 1997). The objects are subjected to a grave-good analysis that takes into account not only the practical function of objects but as far as possible also their style, provenance, quality, and quantity. With few exceptions the analysis of the metalwork is based on the published information only (see Ch. 1.3).

The available information is used to develop a typology based on attributes judged to be of chronological significance (see Jensen and Høilund Nielsen 1997). The strong gender relation in grave-good associations requires largely separate correspondence analyses for male and female graves. The four cemeteries are analysed both separately and jointly, taking local variations in the data into account. The results are tested against the stratigraphical relationship of intercutting graves, tested for spatial patterns indicating a horizontal stratigraphy of the individual sites and tested against external dates for objects derived from dated contexts outside the four cemeteries. For practical purposes, gradual changes in the material culture are defined and further treated as a sequence of phases. Absolute dates for the relative chronological framework are derived from frameworks of other regions as far as that is possible.

For the analysis of aspects of social structure, two different scoring methods based on the same typology, a count of the total number of certain types in a grave and their 'status index' as defined by *Socistat* (though not the programme itself), will be used to demonstrate the effect the changes over time in the material culture and burial practice identified at the four cemeteries have on such scores and their interpretation. It will be shown that the detailed analysis of the four cemeteries largely supports and refines Härke's and Stoodley's conclusions on East Anglian Anglo-Saxon burial practice and social structure (Härke 1992; Stoodley 1999). The chronological framework developed for the sites will be used to highlight some changes in burial practice and the material culture used in it that indicate changes in the social structure of the communities using the four cemeteries for burial.

4. Grave-good analysis

4.1 Background

An analysis of grave-goods relevant for a chronological framework for the weapon graves at the four cemeteries was carried out by Karen Høilund Nielsen (2003). Her archive report supersedes analysis carried out by her and John Hines in 1997 and builds on work on a national sample of weapon graves which forms part of the project *Anglo-Saxon England c. 570–720 AD: the chronological basis*, by the same authors in co-operation with the Radiocarbon Dating Laboratory at Queen's University, Belfast, and English Heritage.

In the grave-good analysis, Høilund Nielsen made use of existing typologies where possible and created new typologies of objects if they were required for the chronological framework developed in Chapter 5. She also reviewed published data on external datings for objects which can help to support, correct or refine this framework. The same method has been applied to the grave-good analysis of objects from the graves of females. It is based on the definition of typology not as the identification of an inbuilt order in the material but as a purpose-led analysis of attributes that aims at definitions of objects according to clearly defined criteria in a particular context.

The regional focus of the analysis and the use of correspondence analysis required purpose-designed typologies in particular for the main functional types of weapons and dress accessories, that is spearheads and shield bosses, cruciform, small-long and annular brooches, some types of beads and wrist-clasps, and girdle-hangers. The type definitions and names used for spearheads and shield bosses may not be retained in the forthcoming publication on the project *Anglo-Saxon England c. 570–720 AD: the chronological basis*. The chronological phases for the four cemeteries referred to below, MA1, MA2 and MB for males and FA1, FA2 and FB for females, are defined in Chapter 5. For references to gender see Chapter 7.3.

4.2 Weapons and associated objects
based on a report by Karen Høilund Nielsen (2003)

4.2.1 Spearheads
The typology developed by Karen Høilund Nielsen for the spearheads from the four cemeteries is based on a combination of measurements and not on an intuitive definition of their outline. In this, the approach differs from Swanton's typology of Anglo-Saxon spearheads (Swanton 1973).

The four cemeteries produced 103 spearheads which could be fully or partly measured. All measurements were based on the drawings in the cemetery catalogues. The Westgarth Gardens report does not give information on the scale of the drawings, but first-hand measurements kindly made available by Heinrich Härke made it possible to reconstruct their scale. The drawings of spearheads in the catalogues for Bergh Apton, Morning Thorpe and Spong Hill were published at a scale of 1:2. Therefore all calculations are based on measurements at half size. In Tables 4.1 and 4.2, these numbers have been changed to calculated full size. The use of drawings instead of first-hand examination produced some problems, one of them the identification of the transition from the socket or shank to the blade of a spearhead, which had to be defined as the narrowest point in the drawing.

The following measurements were recorded and the following values calculated on the basis of these measurements (Fig. 4.1). Measurements are given in centimetres, angles in degrees:

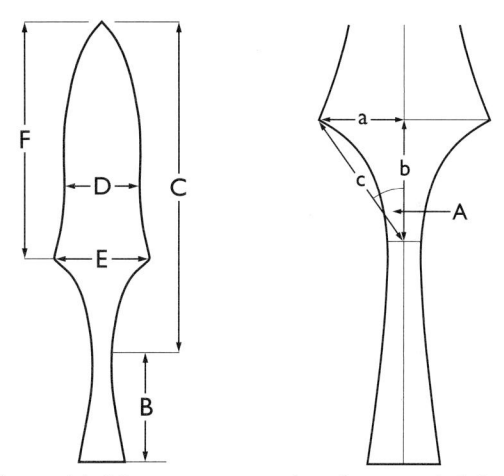

Figure 4.1 Measurements and angles recorded from spearheads. Not to scale

A	The angle between the socket/shank and the maximum width of the spearhead. Degrees = $\text{Acos}((b^2+c^2-a^2)/2bc)$
a	Half of the maximum width of a blade
b	The distance from the point of the maximum width of a blade to the socket/shank along the centre line
c	The distance from the edge of the maximum width of a blade to the socket/shank along the centre line
B	The length of a socket/shank
C	The length of a blade
D	The width of a blade three quarters from its point to its maximum width
E	The maximum width of a blade = $2*a$
F	The distance from the point of a blade to its maximum width = $C-b$
G	The length of a socket/shank (B) as a percentage of the total length of the spearhead = $(B/(C+B))*100$
H	The distance from the point of a blade to its maximum width as a percentage of the total length of the blade = $(C-b/C)*100$
I	E as the percentage of the length of a blade = $(E/C)*100$
K	The relative difference in the width of a blade = $((E-D)/E)*100$

Size groups

Five groups based on blade length (C) can be defined on the basis of small steps that occur in the range of blade lengths (Fig. 4.2):

small: up to a blade-length of 10cm
medium 1: above 10cm and up to a blade-length of 14cm
medium 2: above 14cm and up to a blade-length of 21cm

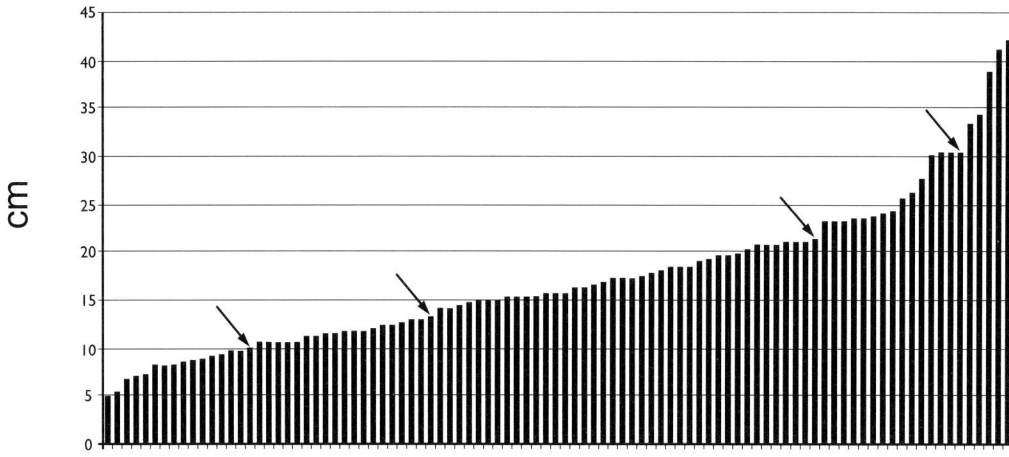

Figure 4.2 Blade lengths of the spearheads from the four cemeteries. Arrows mark the steps in length which have been used to define ranges

long 1: above 21cm and up to a blade-length of 32cm
long 2: above 32cm and up to a blade-length of 42cm

Of these size groups *medium2* forms the largest group, whereas *long2* is the smallest. For all groups the socket is never more than 55% of the total length of the spearhead, except in one case where it is 70% (Grave 41 at Bergh Apton). This one has been kept apart in the general analysis. The same applies to the spearhead from Grave 218 at Morning Thorpe, which has a long socket (50%).

Definitions of outline
Combinations of spearhead proportions were used to define types. The analysis was done for each length group separately, but in most cases a general definition can be applied to each outline type. Four main outline types and four additional but rare types have been defined. The four main types are *angular, concave, lanceolate* and *parallel*. Additional types are *rhomboid* (or *broad angular*), *midribbed, long shank/socket* (not illustrated) and *corrugated* (Fig. 4.3). Further details of the measurements for the various types are given in Table 4.1.

The primary measurements for the definitions are the relative distance from the point to the maximum width (H) and the relative difference in width (K). In general *lanceolate* spearheads have a value for H below 62% and a value for K below 10%. The *angular* and the *concave* spearheads have a value for H between 62% and 89%. For the *angular* spears the value of K is below or equal to 21% and for the *concave* spears it is above 21%. *Parallel* spears have a value for H above 85% and a value for K below or equal to 17%.

The outline groups *rhomboid* (or *broad angular*) and *ribbed* fall outside this general definition and will be dealt with below.

Lanceolate spearheads
Lanceolate spearheads are rare. They are found in the size groups *small, medium1* and *long1*. None of these is associated with ferrules. The blade of a *lanceolate* spearhead has no side points, its maximum width (E) is fairly close to the middle of the blade and the edges are fairly evenly curved from socket/shank to point.

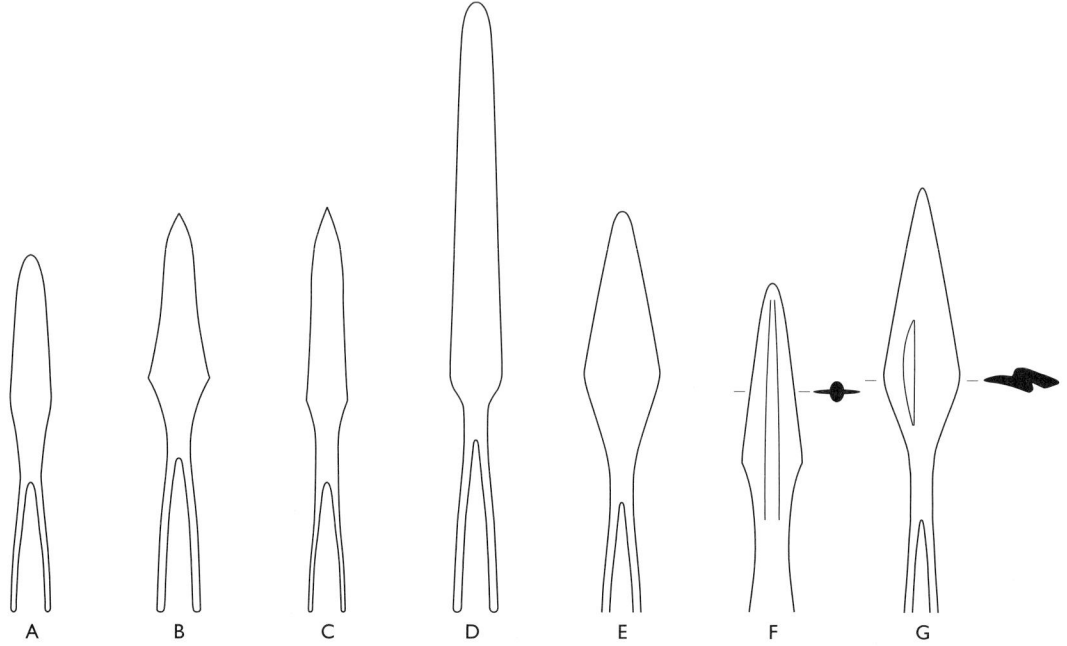

Figure 4.3 Spearhead types a) *lanceolate* b) *concave* c) *angular* d) *parallel* e) *rhomboid* f) *mid-ribbed* g) *corrugated*. Not to scale

	No. of spears measured	Max width (E) cm	Angle (A)°	Total length (B+C) cm	Blade length (C) cm	Socket/shank length (B) cm	Socket length (G) %	Measurement (H) %	Width (I) %	Width (D) cm	Measurement (K) %
Angular Small	7+1	1.8–2.2	25–34	11–18	4.8–9.8	5.6–9.2	37–55	62–79	19–25(38)	1.5–2.0	(6)10–20
Angular Small Long So/Sh BA41	1	2.2	43	17.5	5.4	12.2	70	77	42	2.0	10
Concave Small	6	2.0–2.7	17–31	15–18	7.0–10.2	6.6–9.6	43–52	62–75	23–33	1.1–2.1	23–29
Lanceolate Small	2	2.0–2.8	17–19	13–17	6.6–8.9	6.8–7.8	47–51	51–56	30–31	1.9–2.6	5–8
Rhomboid Small	1	3.0	30	16	8.0	7.6	49	68	38	2.5	20
Angular Medium 1	9	2.0–3.0	19–38	17–23	10.6–13.0	6.8–11.2*	39–45(51)*	65–88	17–26	1.9–2.6	4–20
Concave Medium 1	9	2.2–3.8	19–28	16–23	10.6–13.2	(5.0)8.4–10.2*	(32)41–46*	70–76(81)	19–30	1.8–3.1	22–44
Lanceolate Medium 1	1+2	2.3	13	20	11.8	8.4	42	57	19	2.1	10
Angular Medium 2	16+2	2.0–3.1(3.7)	13–40	22–41	14.2–20.2	6.4–21.2	27–52	68–92	13–18(21)	1.9–3.2	4–20
Concave Medium 2	14	2.8–4.1	14–31	22–33	14.4–21.0	7.0–12.8*	30–44*	65–82	15–24	2.2–3.0	23–46
Concave Med2 Long So/Sh MT218	1	3.5	27	31	15.6	15.4	50	78	22	2.7	30
Rhomboid Medium 2	1	4.0	15	- - - -	15.4	8.4*	- - - -	53	26	2.9	38
Midribbed Medium 2	1	3.4	- - - -	- - - -	14.0	>10	c. 40	c. 60	24	2.4	42
ZConcave Medium 2	6	3.6–4.9	21–40	23–33	15.0–21.0	6.2–16.2	27–49	62–83	17–33	2.0–3.3	27–80
Concave Long 1	10+1	2.7–6.6	10–37	35–56	23.0–30.2(42.0)	11.6–18.4*	24–39*	69–86	8–25	2.2–4.2	21–57
Lanceolate Long 1	2	2.4	5–7	35	31.4–23.0	12.0*	34*	48–55	10–11	2.2–2.3	4–9
Parallel Long 1	5	2.7–3.7	25–39	35–43	21.0–27.6	12.0–15.8*	34–40*	86–92	10–16	2.4–2.7(3.4)	8–17
Parallel Broad Long1 MT409	1	5.2	23	46.5	30.2	16.4	35	79	17	4.9	6
Parallel Long 2	4	2.5–3.2	35–49	46–50	33.4–41.0	11.0–13.6*	22–28*	95–96	7–8	2.4–3.0	4–8

*Means that some spears are damaged and cannot give a precise measurement

Table 4.1 The four cemeteries, spearhead measurements. For key see p. 17

	number	Cone shape	Apex type	Outline of transistion from cone to wall	Wall shape	Rivet types	Flange width (cm)	Diameter of rivets (cm)	Boss height (cm)	Measurement (M) in %	Measurement (N) in %	Measurement (O) in %	Measurement (P) in %
SOC1	6	straight	V	overh car	concave	disc	2.0–3.2	1.6–2.0	7.8–9.6	34–64	61–75	34–39	57–67
SOC2	4	straight-slight convex	VT	overh car	concave	disc	2.2–3.0	1.5–2.6	7.2–8.0	33–50	66–75	26–33	57–63
SOC3	5	straight-slight convex	n	overh car	concave	disc	1.9–2.8	1.4–2.3	8.0–9.1	24–37	73–81	33–40	65–70
COV	4	convex	T	overh car	vertical	disc	1.7–2.5	1.6–2.2	7.8–8.3	49–57	64–67	38–43	71–77
COS	18	convex	T	overh car	sloping	disc	1.0–2.5	1.3–2.4	6.0–8.8	30–53	65–77	28–41	60–84
CAV	2	convex	none	angle	vertical		0.6–1.2		7.8–9.0	29	77	67–75	73–83
S	1	straight	o?	none	sloping-vertical	knob	1		11.2		100	81	77
CAS	5	Convex	o	angle	sloping-vertical	knob	0.7–1.6		8.0–8.8	18–42	70–85	44–54	74–87
SOS	2	Straight	T	overh/angle	sloping	knob	0.9–2.0		7.5–8.6	36–55	65–74	45–47	72–80
other	6												

Table 4.2 The four cemeteries, shield boss measurements. For key see p. 22

The relative distance from the point of the spear to maximum width (H) is below 62%. The relative difference in the width of the blade (K) is below 10%. Consequently the angle (A) is small and varies between 5 and 19 degrees — the longer the spear, the smaller the angle.

The type corresponds with Swanton's leaf-shaped spears, type C.

Type C1 equals type *lanceolate small*. Swanton dates it relatively early, that is, it runs out before the end of the 6th century in his terms.

Type C2 may include all of *lanceolate medium1*. Swanton does not date them more closely than the 5th to 7th centuries.

Type C3 has short sockets. It seems that this type more likely is related to type *parallel long2*, which however also includes Swanton type E3. Swanton dates it relatively late.

Type C4 corresponds with type *lanceolate long1*. It is dated relatively late by Swanton.

The correspondence analysis in Chapter 5 includes only *lanceolate medium1* spearheads, which fall in Phase MA2. *Lanceolate long1* and *lanceolate small* spearheads are probably both early types (Phase MA1). On the Continent *lanceolate* spearheads are known from the 5th and first half of 6th centuries (see, *e.g.*, Koch 2001).

Finds list:
Lanceolate Small (LaSma)   MT022 and 274
Lanceolate Medium1 (LaMed1)   BA12 and MT40 and 388
Lanceolate Long1 (LaLo1)   BA8 and WG30A

Angular spearheads
Angular spearheads together with *concave* spearheads are the most common spearhead types. They are found in the size groups *small, medium1*, and *medium2*. Ferrules occur with about a quarter of the angular spearheads; a preference for certain types is not discernible. The blade of an *angular* spearhead has its maximum width (E) or its side points (angles) located fairly close to the transition from blade to shank/socket, and there is no concavity above the angles.

The relative distance from the point of the spear to maximum width (H) is 62–89%. For size group *medium2* it is, however, defined as being 62–92%. The relative difference in the width of the blade is equal to or below 21%. Angle (A) is generally larger than that of the *lanceolate* spears. It varies between 13 and 40 degrees, with most below 30 degrees.

Type *angular medium2* was sub-divided on the basis of the relative difference in width (K). At sub-type *a* K is below 6%, at sub-type *b* 8–18% and at sub-type *c* equal to 20% or above, which means the blade tapers more and more.

This type only includes type E of Swanton's angular spears.

Type E1 equals type *angular small*. Swanton dates it relatively early. There may be an overlap with *angular medium1*.

Type E2 corresponds with *angular medium2* and partly *medium1*, although some of the spears of E2 have a more concave outline. Swanton dates his type to the 6th and 7th centuries.

Types E3–E4 have a short socket and is related to Swanton's type C3. There seem to be no parallels to Swanton's type among the angular spears, but *parallel long1–2* seem to come closest. Swanton dated them to the 6th and 7th centuries.

Angular together with *concave* spearheads dominate Phase MA. *Angular medium2a* and probably *angular medium2c* spearheads are dated in Phase MA1, *angular small, angular medium1* and *2b* and possibly *angular medium2c* spearheads fall in Phase MA2. Type *angular medium2a* is used to define sub-Phase MA1a on the basis of its distribution at Morning Thorpe (see Ch. 5.2.1). *Angular* spearheads on the Continent were used in a period that includes the first half of the 6th century (see Koch 2001).

Finds list:
Angular Small (AnSma)   BA27, MT67, 269, 275, and 297, SH50, WG50 and 62
Angular Medium1 (AnMed1)   BA50, MT126, 211, 340, SH32, WG5, 41, 51, 63 and 68
Angular Medium2a (AnMed2a)   MT389, SH31, WG04
Angular Medium2b (AnMed2b)   BA2, 66 and ?71, MT35, 61, ?100, 304, 362, 380, 381, 416, SH27
and   WG10
Angular Medium 2c (AnMed2c)   MT370 and SH49

Concave spearheads
The *concave* spearheads are rather common and also represented in all size groups. About a third of the spears had a ferrule. *Concave* spearheads, which form a subgroup of Swanton's *angular* spearheads, are defined by a blade that has its maximum width (E) or its side points positioned between the transition to the socket and the middle of the blade; it has pronounced concavities below and above these points.

The relative distance from the point of the spear to maximum width (H) is 62–89%. The relative difference in the width of the blade is equal to or above 22%. The angle (A) lies between 10 and 37 degrees, but most vary between 18 and 32 degrees.

Type *concave medium1* was subdivided on the basis of measurement (K). Sub-type *a* has values below 30%, sub-type *b* above 30%. This means that the blades of sub-type *b* are more curved than those of sub-type *a*.

Type *concave medium2* was subdivided on the basis of measurement (H). Sub-type *a* has a value of 75% or lower, for sub-type *b* it is above 77%. This means that the widest part of the blade is higher among the spearheads of subtype *a* and lower among the spearheads of subtypes *b*.

The four cemeteries produced only a single concave spearhead of size group *long2*. As it does not form a group by itself, it is included in type *concave long1*.

Type *concave long1* was subdivided on the basis of the relative distance between point and max. width (H) and the relative difference in width (K). Sub-type *a* is defined by an H equal to 80% or lower (*i.e.* the points are placed higher on such a blade) and a K below 45%. Sub-type *b* is defined by an H over 80% (*i.e.* the points are placed lower on such a blade) and a K below 45%. Sub-type *c* is defined by a K equal to or above 45% (*i.e.* this blade has a rather pronounced outline).

This type includes Swanton's type H of the *angular* spears.

Type H1 corresponds with types *concave small* and *concave medium1*.

Type H2 corresponds with type *concave medium2*.

Type H3 corresponds with type *concave long1*.

Swanton dates all spearheads of his type H early.

Concave spearheads form part of Phase MA: *concave medium1b* and *2a* and *concave long1b* fall in Phase MA1, type *CoMed2a* links the sub-Phases MA1a and MA1b;

concave medium1a and *2b, concave small* and *concave long1a* spearheads fall in Phase MA2. Similar types of spearheads found on the Continent are dated in the period AD (500–)555–580 (Koch 2001), and in Scandinavia in the period AD 525–600 (Nørgård Jørgensen 1999).

Finds list:
Concave Small (CoSma)	MT117, 225, 327, 337 and 402
Concave Medium1a (CoMed1a)	BA26, MT62, 142, 238 and WG53
Concave Medium1b (CoMed1b)	MT259, SH41 and 51
Concave Medium2a (CoMed2a)	BA52/53, MT132, 296, 319, 330, 332 and WG25
Concave Medium2b (CoMed2b)	MT69, 339, SH40, 54 and WG5
Concave Long1a (CoLo1a)	BA12, MT85, 341 (long 2) and WG30B
Concave Long1b (CoLo1b)	MT97, 265 and WG 11
Concave Long1c (CoLo1c)	BA20, MT19, 129, 157

Parallel spearheads

The *parallel* spearheads are defined only for size groups *long 1* and *long 2* and are not very common. The appearance of the *parallel* spearhead is a blade with maximum width (E) or the angles very close to the transition to the shank/socket and with sides parallel or almost parallel until shortly before the point. They have rather short sockets/shanks and for most the distance (c) between the angles and the socket is very short. None of the *parallel* spearheads are associated with ferrules.

The relative distance from the point of the spear to maximum width (H) is 86–92% for size group *long 1*, and 95–96% for Long 2. The relative difference in the width of the blade (K) is equal to or below 17%, for *long2* even below 8%. The angle A is 25–39% for type *parallel long1* and 35–49% for type p*arallel long2*, and thus clearly larger than for the *angular, concave* and *lanceolate* types. The p*arallel long1*-like spear of MT409 does not fit into this type, but is broader and heavier. It is, however, closely related to this type.

In Swanton's analyses the parallel spears form a sub-group of the *angular* spears.

Type E3 has a short socket, is closely related to Swanton's type C3, and it has a blade with the same variation in width as found by *parallel long1*. Type E4 has almost parallel sides and resembles more *parallel long2*. Swanton dated them to the 6th and 7th centuries.

Type G1 and G2 have short sockets and almost parallel sided blades. Both types seem to correspond with types *parallel long1–2*, although some of the G1 spears are shorter and thus overlap with *angular medium2* as no parallel types are defined for that size group. Swanton dates them fairly late, that is in the late 6th and 7th centuries.

In the correspondence analysis in Chapter 5 these spearheads fall in Phase MB.

Finds list:
Parallel Long1 (PaLo1)	Ba16, MT42, 333, 367, and 398
Parallel Broad Long1 (PaBrLo1)	MT409
Parallel Long2 (PaLo2)	MT215, 255 and 351

Spearheads with a long socket/shank

Only one spearhead of the type *angular small* and one of the type *concave medium2* have relatively long socket/shanks. This demonstrates that long sockets or shanks are not a typical feature among the spearheads from the four cemeteries. The *angular small* spearhead from Grave 41 at Bergh Apton has a shank/socket of 70% of the total length of the spearhead and probably belongs to Swanton's type D3, which is dated to the 6th century. It was not possible to date this spearhead through correspondence analysis. The *concave medium2* spearhead from Grave 218 at Morning Thorpe has a shank/socket of 50% of the total length of the spearhead (unusual for spearheads type *concave medium2*) and probably belongs to Swanton's type F2 dated to the late 6th and 7th centuries. This spearhead, not itself part of the correspondence analysis, belongs to a grave that is and thus falls in early Phase MB by association.

Finds list:
Angular Small Long Shank/Socket (AnSmLoSh)	BA41
Concave Medium2 Long Shank/Socket (CoMed2LoSh)	MT218

Rhomboid or broad angular spearheads

Rhomboid spearheads are wider than the *angular* spearheads, in absolute as well as in relative terms. They have a value for H close to 50% and a value for K well over 22%. The value of the *broad angular* spearheads for H (62–92%) falls within the *angular* group and its value for K (21%) is close to the upper limit of the *angular* group, but the relative and absolute width of the *broad angular* spearheads is larger. The type is subsumed under the *rhomboid* spearheads.

Two of the spearheads from the four cemeteries are labelled *rhomboid*, a *small* one from Grave 28 at Spong Hill, which is actually a *broad angular* one, and a *medium2* one from Grave 154 at Morning Thorpe, which is a proper *rhomboid* spearhead. In Swanton's typology they would probably just fall within the angular group — E1–2 and F1–2. It was not possible to date these spearheads through correspondence analysis.

Finds list:
Rhomboid Small (RhSm)	SH28
Rhomboid Medium2 (RhMed2)	MT154

Spearhead with a midrib

Only the spearhead from Grave 356 at Morning Thorpe has a midrib along the vertical axis of the blade and would probably fall into type B2 of Swanton's derivative forms, which is not closely dated by Swanton. It was not possible to date this spearhead through correspondence analysis.

Finds list:
Midribbed (MRib)	MT356

Corrugated spearheads

Corrugated spearheads have a fuller or stepped section hammered into one blade half, which makes the spearhead less heavy and strengthens it lengthwise (Swanton 1973, 115 and 121). The outline of the spearheads from the four cemeteries is concave, and they follow the same definitions as for *concave* spearheads in general, although the relative difference in width (K) is often much higher. The type is in some cases associated with a ferrule.

Six *corrugated concave medium2* spearheads have been identified. The variation in shape within this group define Swanton's types I1, J and L. Swanton dated type I1 to the very early settlement phase and type J a little later, contemporary with type H. Type L was also considered relatively early by Swanton.

Correspondence analysis assigns type *ZCoMed2* to Phase MA1.

Finds list:
Corrugated Concave Medium2 (ZCoMed2)	MT1, 68, 148, 170 and SH13 and 36

Undefined
The spearheads from Graves 52, 167, and 361 at Morning Thorpe could not be assigned to any of the types because they were too fragmentary.

4.2.2 Shield bosses
The typology for the fifty-three shield bosses from the four cemeteries is based on measurements and outlines. The following attributes were defined.

Figure 4.4 Apex shapes. Not to scale

Shapes:
A   Apex (Fig. 4.4)
    V   V-shaped outline
    VT   half-way between a V-shaped and a T-shaped outline
    T   T-shaped outline
    n   stopper-shaped
    o   knob
B   Cone shapes: *convex, slightly convex,* or *straight*
C   The outline of the transition between the cone and the wall: *overhanging carination, angle* or *none*
D   Wall shapes: *concave, sloping* or *vertical*
E   Rivet shapes: *disc-headed* or *knob-headed*

Measurements in cm:
F   Height of boss
G   Height of cone
H   Height of wall
I   Width of flange
J   Diameter of rivets if disc-shaped
K   Total diameter of boss
L   Smallest inner width measured between the walls

Calculated proportions:
M   between wall and cone, given in percent = (H/G) x 100
N   Cone height in relation to the sum of wall and cone height, given in percent = (G/(G+H)) x 100
O   Boss height in relation to boss width, given in percent = (F/K) x 100
P   Inner width between the walls in relation to the total diameter, given in percent = (L/K) x 100

The attributes used for the definition of boss types were mainly formal ones (Table 4.2). A reasonably clear division could be identified between bosses with straight cones and concave walls, and bosses with convex cones and sloping or vertical walls. Both groups have disc-headed rivets and relatively broad flanges. A third group has a tall convex cone, a sloping or vertical wall and knob-headed rivets and a fourth group has no division between a sloping wall and cone and also knob-headed rivets. These types of bosses are combined with various apex types. A fifth boss group has a convex cone, a vertical wall and no apex.

Comparison of these boss types with those defined by Dickinson and Härke (1992) shows similarities but a one-to-one correlation of types is not possible because the typologies do not have the same basis.

Bosses with straight cones and concave walls
This group comprises three types which differ mainly in the type of apex used, but also in some proportions. All types have disc-headed rivets 1.4–3.2cm in diameter. The flange is 2–3cm wide and the boss has a maximum height of 9.6cm. The cones of types *SOC1* and *SOC2* take up almost three quarters of the height below the apex, while the cone of type *SOC3* takes up just over four fifths of the height, which means that the wall is quite low. The height/width index (O) shows that the bosses of types *SOC1–3* are all relatively short.

These shield boss types approximately relate to Dickinson and Härke's typology as follows:
SOC1   Group 1   *c.* AD 450–600
SOC2   Group 1.1   *c.* AD 450–600
SOC3   Group 1.2   *c.* AD 450–550/600

This suggests a 5th- to 6th-century date for types *SOC1–3*.

It seems that continental finds of shield bosses — in particular the early Merovingian ones — have not been intensively studied so far. The only explicit typology that deals with both the very early types of shield bosses as they are included in Böhme's analyses of 4th- and 5th-century graves between the Elbe and the Loire (Böhme 1974) and shield bosses of the Merovingian period, can be found in Hinz's publication of the Eick cemetery (Hinz 1969). The definition of type *SOC3* finds its best approximation in Hinz's type A1, dated in the 5th century. Type *SOC3* is also found at the Pleidelsheim cemetery and dated by Koch (2001) to the period AD 430–480. Shield bosses with concave walls and straight cones associated with the swords discussed by Menghin (1983) can be found in his Phases A and B (*c.* AD 450–*c.* AD 525) and in a few cases in his Phase C. Related types are also known from Norway, in particular Bemmann's and Hahne's shield boss type VIII, a south-west Norwegian type (Bemmann and Hahne 1994). This type first appears in the late Øvsthus-group, is most popular in the Snartemo-group, and found only rarely in the Nerhus-group. This suggests the type was created shortly after AD 450 and was in use until the very early 6th century. Stylistically, type *SOC* is developed from the continental type Liebenau.

Finds list:
SOC1   BA8, MT1, 22, 36, 319, and 389, SH31
SOC2   MT97, SH41 and 49, ?WG1 and WG25
SOC3   MT68, 259 and 265, SH36 and 51

In the correspondence analysis this type of shield boss appears early, in Phase MA1, and in the order *SOC1, SOC2* and *SOC3*. The basis for the analysis is too small to prove a chronological development within the type but the horizontal stratigraphy at Morning Thorpe suggests that type *SOC1* was indeed the earliest of the three types. As a correlation of the chronological frameworks for males and females required a subdivision of Phase MA1, this type has been used in the definition of a sub-Phase MA1a (see Ch. 5.2.1).

Low bosses with a convex cone
This group is the most numerous group and includes two types, the difference being the angle of the wall, which is either vertical or sloping. Both types have disc-headed rivets and a flange 1.0–2.5cm wide. The height/width index (O) shows these bosses are relatively low and have a low wall.

These shield boss types approximately relate to Dickinson and Härke's typology as follows:
COV   Group 3   *c.* AD 500–650
COS   Group 3 and possibly 2   *c.* AD 500–650 (group 3) and *c.* AD 500–600 (group 2)

This suggests a date for types COV and COS in the 6th and first half of the 7th century.

Type *COS* is related to the common Merovingian shield bosses of Hinz's type A2 dated to the first half of the

6th century (Hinz 1969). This continental version appears in Menghin's late Phase B and his Phase C, that is *c.* AD 500–575 (Menghin 1983). In Koch's chronological framework for South Germany the continental parallels fall in her Phases 4–6 (*c.* AD 510–580; Koch 2001). In the Lower Rhine region type *COS* corresponds with Nieveler's and Siegmund's type SBu3 with flat rivets, dated to Phase 3–4 (*c.* AD 480–560; Nieveler and Siegmund 1999). The Scandinavian version of this type, Bemmann's and Hahne's type IX, belongs to the Nerhus-group, which is dated to the first half of the 6th century (Bemmann and Hahne 1994).

Finds list:
COV MT45 and 183, WG11 and 51
COS BA?12, 26 and ?66, MT35, 52, 85, 115, 126, 211, 225, 380, and 388, SH27, 40, WG5, 8, ?41, 49, 50, 60, 62, and ?68

The correspondence analysis places both types in Phase MA2.

The shield bosses from Graves 61 and 154 at Morning Thorpe do not correspond with any of the type definitions given above but are broadly related to type *COS*. The boss from Grave 61 is probably related to the bosses in Phase MA1 (or perhaps MA2) and probably falls in Nieveler's and Siegmund's type SBu2 dated in Rheinland Phase 3 (*c.* AD 480–530; Nieveler and Siegmund 1999). The boss from Grave 154 is related to the bosses in Phase MA2 and probably falls in type SBu4 dated in Phases 6–7 (*c.* AD 570–610).

Bosses with 'tall' cones
This group includes two types, *CAS* with a convex cone and a knob-headed apex, and *SOS* with a straight cone and a T-shaped apex. Both types have a narrow flange, less than 2.0cm in width, and the rivets are always knob-headed.

The approximate equivalent of types *CAS* and *SOS* in Dickinson's and Härke's typology is Group 6 dated *c.* 575–650 AD (Dickinson and Härke 1992). Koch's chronological framework for South Germany (Koch 2001) has no corresponding types. Type *CAS,* however, seems to be related to type SBu3 with hemispherical rivets after Nieveler and Siegmund (1999) dated to Rheinland Phases 5–6 (*c.* 550–590 AD) and Phase 5–6 (*c.* AD 565–610/20) after Müssemeyer *et al.* (2003), though the rivets of this continental type probably are slightly larger than those used for the Anglo-Saxon flanges.

Finds list:
CAS MT215, 218, 333, 367 and 374
SOS MT42 and 255

The correspondence analysis places both types in Phase MB.

Bosses with a 'tall' convex cone and without apex
This type is rare and it stands apart from the other types because of the absence of an apex. The flange is very narrow and the rivets are knob-headed. Type *CAV* was found in Grave 19 at Bergh Apton and Grave 67 at Westgarth Gardens. Neither grave is included in the correspondence analysis.

The approximate equivalent of this type in Dickinson and Härke's typology is type 8 dated *c.* AD 575–650 (Dickinson and Härke 1992). The type may also find parallels in shield bosses of the late 6th century in South Germany. It seems that comparable shield bosses in Siegmund's chronology for the Lower Rhineland can be found in his Phase 8 (*c.* AD 610–640; Siegmund 1998). The Anglo-Saxon type may also be related to type SBu5b after Nieveler and Siegmund (1999) dated to Phase 6 (*c.* AD 570–590) and to Phase 5 (*c.* AD 565–580/90) after Müssemeyer *et al.* (2003). This suggests a date for the two shield bosses from Bergh Apton and Westgarth Gardens in Phase MB.

Boss type S: 'Muysen' after Stein (1967)
Stein's 'type Muysen', here listed as type *S*, is defined by an almost entirely straight cone, mostly without a distinct wall, a short flange, knob-headed rivets and a knob-headed apex (Stein 1967). The only boss of this type from the four cemeteries, found in Grave 66 at Westgarth Gardens, is taller than any of the other types discussed above.

The approximate equivalent of 'type Muysen' in Dickinson's and Härke's typology is Group 7 dated *c.* 650–700 AD (Dickinson and Härke 1992). It seems, however, that this Group includes a diverse range of shield bosses and therefore requires a wider date range. Stein dated her 'type Muysen' broadly to the 7th century. It falls in Siegmund's Lower Rheinland Phases 6–7 (*c.* AD 570–610; pers. comm. Frank Siegmund). This suggests the boss from Westgarth Gardens falls in Phase MB.

4.2.3 Seaxes, swords and axe

Two or perhaps three short seaxes were found at the four cemeteries (Graves 265 and perhaps 339 at Morning Thorpe and Grave 1 at Westgarth Gardens). The lengths of their blades vary between 18 and 20cm (only 16cm in Grave 339), and they are less than 3cm wide in the Morning Thorpe graves and a little wider at Westgarth Gardens. On the Continent, seaxes of this very early type are usually dated from *c.* AD 530 onwards (see Siegmund 1998 and Koch 2001) but may have been buried as early as *c.* AD 480/90 (see Nieveler and Siegmund 1999). In the correspondence analysis they link the types of spearheads and shield bosses defining Phases MA1 and MA2.

The four cemeteries produced only five swords, two of them with cocked hat pommels (type *sw1*). The sword from Grave 51 at Westgarth Gardens has a cocked hat pommel with concave sides, a metal mouthpiece to the scabbard and an amber sword bead. This is a type of sword dated in Phase C (*c.* AD 525–575) after Menghin (1983). The type of cocked hat pommel found with the sword in Grave 218 at Morning Thorpe is of a type dated in Phases late B, C and D (*c.* AD 500–625) after Menghin. The date range given for South German material is closer: Phases 5–6 (*c.* AD 530–580; Koch 2001). In the correspondence analysis type *sw1* links Phases MA2 and MB.

The swords from Grave 51 at Westgarth Gardens and from Grave 40 at Spong Hill both have metal mouth pieces and sword beads (*sw2*), which fall in Phase MA2 in the correspondence analysis. The mouthpieces are dated to Phases A, B and early C after Menghin (1983), that is to the mid 6th century at the latest. In Koch's chronological framework for South Germany the type is dated to Phase 4 (*c.* AD 480–510; Koch 2001).

The sword from Grave 66 at Westgarth Gardens has a little flat knob on the terminal of the tang, whereas the sword from Grave 19 at Bergh Apton has a bare tang. These two swords cannot be dated on stylistic grounds. They were associated with shield bosses of types *CAV* and *S* respectively, both types that could not be used in the correspondence analysis but dated to Phase MB on external evidence (see above).

Grave 362 at Morning Thorpe produced an axe, possibly a 'francisca' of a type that is dated roughly to the 6th century on the Continent, an absolute date mainly covered by Phase MA2.

4.3 Dress accessories and associated objects of females

4.3.1 Brooches

Equal-armed brooches
At the four cemeteries, two types of equal-armed brooches were found. The 'chip-carved' and gilt 'Saxon' equal-armed brooch with additional Animal Style decoration on the outer borders from Grave 55 at Westgarth Gardens falls in Böhme's type 'Nesse', found both in Lower Saxony and in England and dated to the second half of the 5th century (Fig. 5.21) (Böhme 1986, 542–51). Grave 55 is dated to Phase FA1 on the basis of the associated bow brooches.

The 'Anglian' equal-armed brooches from Grave 36 at Westgarth Gardens and Grave 46 at Spong Hill are comparatively small and plain (Figs 5: 21–22) (Hines 1984, 253–9; MacGregor and Bolick 1993, 150f.). The type is not common and therefore difficult to date other than on the basis of associated objects. The Spong Hill grave falls in Phase FA1, the Westgarth Gardens grave in Phase FA2a.

Cruciform brooches
An overview of the history of research on the chronology of cruciform brooches from Anglo-Saxon contexts has been given by Høilund Nielsen (1997, 79). In an analysis of cruciform brooches from the Continent, Scandinavia and England published more recently, Bode (1998, 23ff.) has taken account of the heterogeneous designs used for this type of brooch by treating the brooches as composite designs. This enabled her to analyse the design of head-plates, bows and foot-terminals separately and she avoided a situation in which type definitions had to be made on the basis of forced choices. This is an approach that would probably produce interesting results if applied to all of the cruciform brooches found in England, brooches with lappets and florid cruciform brooches included, and would have formed an ideal basis for the classification of the cruciform brooches from the four cemeteries as a regional sample. A classification of these brooches suitable for correspondence analysis had to be based on simpler methods, however, and adapts classifications by Åberg (1926) and Mortimer (1990) in general and the classification of the cruciform brooches from the four cemeteries created by Høilund Nielsen and Hines in the archive report (1997) in particular. The requirement was to define types based on chronologically significant attributes which are found with groups of brooches large enough to make an impact on the sorting of the matrix of a correspondence analysis but small enough not to dominate other components. Accordingly, the brooches were divided into three groups of brooches with combinations of attributes defined as types *X1*, *X2* and *X3*.

Type *X1* (Fig. 5.21) covers all cruciform brooches of the 'classic' design with animal-shaped foot-terminals and without lappets or any other additional designs to the head- or foot-plate. The brooches with head-knobs labelled small-long brooches in the published catalogues on the basis of their spatula-shaped foot-terminals from Grave 370 at Morning Thorpe, Grave 5 at Spong Hill, and Grave 7 at Westgarth Gardens are included in type *X1* because they are too few to be included in correspondence analyses as a type of their own and because their design and size comes closest to type *X1*. The early contexts of the brooches from the graves at Morning Thorpe and Spong Hill suggest that the Westgarth Gardens grave also dates to Phase FA1.

Type *X2* (Fig. 5.22) comprises all cruciform brooches with lappets to the bow combined with some elements of Style I in their design, either fully executed or retaining recognisable elements. These brooches are larger than most of type *X1* and have foot-terminals exaggerating elements of the horse-heads used for type *X1*, mostly spatula-shaped extensions, some of them extended to form a bar. Type *X2* includes all florid cruciform brooches with the exception of the brooch from Grave 18 at Bergh Apton, with a design that shows a close formal relationship with Hines' Group XXI of square-headed brooches (see Hines 1997 and below) and is dated to Phase FB on the basis of associated grave-goods. The burnt fragment of a florid cruciform brooch from Grave 342 at Morning Thorpe may be derived from a cremation.

Type *X3* (Fig. 5.23–24) covers all cruciform brooches with lappets and abstract designs that do not retain recognisable elements of Animal Style.

The list below shows occurrences of types *X1* and *X2* at all four sites, and finds of type *X3* as the smallest group at Morning Thorpe and Spong Hill.

Finds list:
Type *X1* BA5, BA6, BA37, MT30, MT90, MT97, MT153, MT346, MT353, MT362, MT370, MT371, SH5, SH22, SH26, SH46, WG7, WG52, WG55, WG61
Type *X2* BA6, MT16, MT80, MT91, MT96, MT129, MT208, MT342, MT353, MT370, MT393, MT396, SH2, SH22, SH45, SH57, SH58, WG61
Type *X3* MT131, MT133, MT160, MT209, MT253, MT358, MT397, SH39

Cruciform brooches are considered to have been in use from the mid or later 5th to the late 6th century (Høilund Nielsen 1997, fig. 28). The correspondence analysis in Chapter 5 suggests that type *X1* is the earliest type and mainly part of Phase FA1. Type *X2* was in use for a longer period, and type *X3* is part of the definition of Phase FA2.

Small-long brooches
Small-long brooches are a type of brooch considered to have been introduced in the 5th century and to have been given up in the 6th century (Høilund Nielsen 1997, fig. 28). In his study of 5th-century brooch types distributed both in England and on the Continent, Böhme (1986, 557) pointed out that insular types of small-long brooches were developed at an early stage and that the designs form groups rather than types when compared with continental material. A comprehensive survey of the Anglo-Saxon material which would update Leeds' seminal paper published in 1945 is long overdue. The classification of the small-long brooches used for analysis in Chapter 5 follows the same principles as that of the cruciform brooches. Despite a wide variety of designs among these brooches, only four groups are defined, mostly based on the shape of their head-plates.

Type *sm1* (Fig. 5.21) includes all brooches with square head-plates or lappets to the head-plate but no lappets to the bow. This definition includes brooches of Böhme's 5th-century type 'Bordesholm-Haslingfield' (Böhme 1986, 555 f.).

Type *sm2* (Fig. 5.21) covers the brooches with trefoil heads, a definition that covers Böhme's type 'Borgstedt-Rothwell' among other brooches.

Type *sm3* (Fig 5.22) includes all brooches with lappets to the bow and spatula-shaped foot-plates. Brooch b from Grave 346 at Morning Thorpe has an unusual head-plate and does not fall under any of the type definitions. The excavation records suggest that brooches B from Grave 16 and Grave 48 at Westgarth Gardens were interchanged in the excavation report.

Finds list:
Type *sm1*   MT141, MT148, MT153, MT337, MT342, SH2, SH18, WG48
Type *sm2*   BA5, BA6, MT35, MT96, MT148, MT231, MT328, MT346, SH2, SH14, WG16, WG55
Type *sm3*   MT16, MT316, SH42, WG16

Type *sm1* is part of the definition of Phase FA1, type *sm2* is still in use in Phase FA2a, and type *sm3* falls mainly in Phase FA2a.

Annular and penannular brooches
Annular brooches are the most common brooch type found in 'Anglian' graves, but despite their numbers the type is difficult to date closely. Annular brooches seem to have been introduced to Anglian female dress later than cruciform and small-long brooches, though Scandinavian and continental finds can be used to argue for early forerunners (see Ager 1985 and Høilund Nielsen 1997, 80). There is, however, a noticeable absence of annular brooches in East Anglian graves which are considered to be particularly early, and the fact that the cremation graves at Spong Hill produced the fragments of at least thirty-three cruciform brooches but only two probable fragments of annular brooches also suggests a relatively late date for the introduction of annular brooches to East Anglian dress.

An analysis of the decorative designs on the annular brooches from the four cemeteries did not produce results which would have significantly improved a relative chronological framework. Nor did a check on the distribution of these decorative designs at Morning Thorpe produce patterns which might have indicated that these designs were used to indicate group identity. The construction of the ring of an annular brooch in relation to the pin — either a perforation of the annular ring or a constriction — does also not seem to have changed over time in a way that would make these attributes useful chronological markers.

The only attribute that produced useful results was the shape of the perforation for the pin and the shape of copper-alloy pins themselves. The analysis could only include brooches illustrated in the catalogues in sufficient detail and not covered by iron corrosion, Spong Hill is therefore better represented in the finds list than Morning Thorpe. Brooches that show signs of repair suggesting the visible perforation may not have been the primary one, are excluded from the finds list. The brooches that could be included in the analysis indicate that slots or oval perforations, type *ASlot* (Fig. 5.22), are mostly an earlier feature in annular brooches than round holes, type *ARound* (Fig. 5.24; see Table 5.1 for a finds list). This may find an explanation in the technique used for some copper-alloy pins of early quoit and annular brooches, a flat strip bent to form a loop (see, for example, Ager 1985 fig. 18e). The common iron pins of mostly later brooches were probably made from a simple rod and required round perforations.

In correspondence analysis in Chapter 5, annular brooches are used to define the beginning of Phase FA2. The change from a slot to a round hole for the pin attachment serves as one of the criteria for the subdivision of Phases FA2a and FA2b (see p. 50). Six graves with annular brooches are dated to Phase FB on the basis of beads and square-headed brooches: Grave 7 at Bergh Apton (the earliest among them), also Graves 18 and 64 at Bergh Apton, and Graves 359, 384 and 410 at Morning Thorpe.

Repairs are not uncommon with the annular brooches from the four cemeteries, and evident in all three phases. It may be significant that the annular brooches from the Morning Thorpe graves dated in Phase FB are much worn. The individual in Grave 384 was identified as an older infant or younger juvenile and may have been buried with a dress accessory of the previous Phase.

The unusually high number of penannular brooches found at Morning Thorpe (Graves 43, 304, 328, 369, 378, 385, 403, and 407) was discussed by Mackreth (1987) in the site report. He argued for a late Roman date for most of these brooches. Of the eight graves with penannular brooches, five are dated to Phase FA2 and only one to Phase FA1. It seems possible that most of these brooches were used as a substitute when annular brooches were common Anglo-Saxon fashion. Such a re-use of old objects can be observed in relation to some bead types (see Brugmann 2004).

Great square-headed brooches
Of the ten great square-headed brooches from the four cemeteries, eight form a group that can be included in a correspondence analysis. Groups XVI–XVIII after Hines (1997) and the stylistically closely related brooch from Grave 24 at Spong Hill — subsumed in the correspondence analyses in Chapter 5 under type *SqH1* (Fig. 5.25) — were found in Graves 7 and 64 at Bergh Apton, Graves 214, 288, 359, and 371 at Morning Thorpe, Grave 24 at Spong Hill, and Grave 27 at Westgarth Gardens. The four cemeteries lie within the main distribution of all three types which are considered by Hines to be relatively late developments of great square-headed brooches, dated to his Phase 3, that is roughly in the second and third quarters of the 6th century. Brooch Groups XVI–XVIII are the only ones defining Phase FB in Chapter 5. They are linked to the previous Phase FA2b by the brooch from Grave 24 at Spong Hill (Fig. 5.24).

Three of the four type *SqH1* brooches from Morning Thorpe were found in almost adjacent graves close to the southern edge of the cemetery and the fourth brooch c. 20m further to the east. The associations of square-headed brooches and beads at Hadleigh Road, Ipswich, Suffolk, suggests that the brooches were worn for a relatively short period which ended before AD 600.

Hines (1997, 148) saw the square-headed brooch from Grave 38 at Spong Hill as a likely copy of the form of brooches of Hines' Group XIX and assumed a similar date range. In the correspondence analysis, the brooch falls in Phase FA2a on the basis of associated grave-goods (Ch. 5.3.1). The brooch from Grave 18 at Spong Hill forms part of Hines' Group XX also dated by him to his Phase 3. In the correspondence analysis, this brooch is associated with objects dated in Phase FA1 but the undecorated sheet fragment of a wrist-clasp also found in the grave may suggest a slightly later date in Phase FA2a.

Disc brooches
The disc brooches from Graves 44 and 146 at Morning Thorpe are considered a 'Saxon' type on the basis of their main distribution pattern and are generally dated to the second half of the 5th and first half of the 6th centuries (Høilund Nielsen 1997, 78). Two graves with disc brooches dug *c.* 6m apart may be significant but probably do not constitute a Saxon enclave in an Anglian community. The position of the disc brooch in Grave 44 suggests that it was worn as a central brooch together with a pair of annular brooches. The grave is dated in Phase FA2a on the basis of the annular brooches, wrist-clasps and beads.

4.3.2. Pendants

Bucket pendants
Copper-alloy bucket pendants were found in Grave 397 at Morning Thorpe, in Grave 34 at Bergh Apton and in Grave 13 at Westgarth Gardens together with beads. Of the Morning Thorpe pendant only the base and the wall of the miniature 'bucket' are preserved while the nine pendants from Bergh Apton retain remains of the handle ?soldered to the inside of the wall. The published drawing of the Westgarth Gardens pendant is based on a reconstruction in the site notebook.

Objects Gi-ii from Grave 86 at Morning Thorpe are listed as possible bucket pendants in the grave catalogue but are unlikely to be so because the copper-alloy sheets are too large and show perforations, a feature not typical for bucket pendants. Four copper-alloy sheets of the seven illustrated for Grave 92 and described as 'bucket pendants' in the catalogue, are the right size for bucket pendants but have perforations in what would form the wall. For none of the bucket pendants discussed by Meaney (1981, 166ff.), however, are perforated walls mentioned. The absence of any remains of bases or handles in Grave 92 further suggests that these objects do not represent 'classic' bucket pendants. The same applies to the copper-alloy sheet fragments from Grave 415. A set of copper-alloy objects from Holywell Row, Suffolk, with 'two cut-out rectangular suspension loops at the top of the wall' (Dickinson 1993, 6) suggests that small drums made of perforated copper-alloy sheets were a different type of object, which requires further investigation. The only indication for bucket pendants with perforated walls and swinging handles is a personal comment by Chadwick Hawkes on an object from Grave 15 at Eastry, Updown, Kent (Dickinson 1993, 6).

The distribution of 'classic' bucket pendants suggests they were part of 'Anglian' material culture derived from a migration context (see Hines 1984, 13, list 1.2, map 1.3; Dickinson 1993, 6). Meaney's interpretation of these objects as amulets (Meaney 1981, 166) has been widely accepted (Dickinson 1993, 6). Dickinson dates buckets generally to the 6th century, with the exception of the find from Eastry, Kent, dated to the 7th century. This object, however, is not a 'classic' bucket pendant and was found outside the main distribution of such pendants. The three bucket pendants from Morning Thorpe, Bergh Apton and Westgarth Gardens are dated to Phase FA2 by associated objects.

Bracteates
The pair of bracteates from Grave 80 at Morning Thorpe is unusual for being made of copper-alloy instead of gold or silver. They represent examples of Mackeprang's West Scandinavian group C but were probably produced in 'Anglian' England (Hines 1984, 212; Gaimster 1992, 9). The manufacture of the Morning Thorpe bracteates has been dated to the first half of the 6th century (Gaimster 1992, 9; pers. comm. John Hines).

There can be little doubt that bracteates represent Scandinavian influence on Anglo-Saxon material culture. The function and symbolic meaning of these objects are the subject of an ongoing debate based on the use of gold for the display of an iconography that conveys complex cultural concepts. The pair of copper-alloy bracteates from Morning Thorpe is particularly interesting because they defy the definition of a bracteate as an object that combines iconographic meaning with gold as a demonstration of outstanding material wealth. Interestingly, Grave 80 is the only grave of the four cemeteries that produced a copper-alloy instead of a silver scutiform pendant — with the exception of Grave 322 with a gilt copper-alloy scutiform pendant. Associated objects date Grave 80 to Phase FA2b (Ch.5.3.1).

Scutiform pendants
Six of the graves at the four cemeteries produced scutiform pendants: Grave 21 at Bergh Apton and Graves 80, 322, 359, 369, and 375 at Morning Thorpe. With the exception of the pendants from Grave 80, which were made of copper-alloy (gilt in the case of Grave 322), all the pendants were made of silver. The three copper-alloy disc-shaped pendants from Grave 11 at Spong Hill have central bosses which are too small to make definite scutiform pendants and are therefore not included in the correspondence analyses of Chapter 5.

Scutiform pendants are considered to be material culture with a migration background and were in use up to the mid 7th century (Geake 1997, 37f.). At Buckland, Kent, the type was introduced in Phase 2b and mainly in use in Phase 3, that is second half of the 6th and first half of the 7th century (Parfitt and Anderson forthcoming). In the chronological framework for the four cemeteries discussed in Chapter 5.3.1, scutiform pendants link Phases FA2 and FB.

4.3.3 Glass beads
The beads from the four cemeteries form part of the national sample of glass beads on which a chronological framework for beads from Anglo-Saxon graves has been based (Brugmann 2004). Morning Thorpe, Spong Hill and Bergh Apton proved to be of particular relevance to this framework because they produced beads of so-called 'Norfolk' types, the name referring to their main distribution. Since the research on the national sample of glass beads was carried out, work on amber beads has shown that the combination of certain types of amber beads can also be used to date bead assemblages (Brugmann in Parfitt and Anderson forthcoming). An analysis of the amber beads from the four cemeteries would however have required a detailed first-hand

Plate 1 Glass beads of Group A1
'Traffic Light' (1) and 'Blue' beads (2) from Grave 16
at Morning Thorpe. Scale 2:1

examination and the chronological framework is therefore based on glass beads only.

On the basis of the national sample of glass beads it was possible to define three glass bead combination groups found across Anglo-Saxon England (Brugmann 2004). Group A1 includes combinations of various subtypes of 'Traffic Light' beads (Pl. 1). Group A2 includes 'Constricted Cylindrical' and 'Constricted Segmented' ('gold-in-glass') beads (Pl. 2), Group A2b 'Recticalla' and 'Melon' beads, and Group B 'Cylindrical Round' and 'Cylindrical Pentagonal' beads, type 'Koch 34' beads and a variant of these beads, 'Dot 34' (Pl. 9). In Norfolk, Group A2 forms a regional variation defined by additional 'Norfolk' types in the bead type combinations, so-called 'Norfolk BlueWhite' and 'Norfolk YellowRed' beads (Pl. 3, 4). The interpretation of Groups A1, A2, A2b, and B as an overlapping chronological sequence of bead type combinations is supported by continental dating evidence for types with a main distribution pattern on the Continent.

At Westgarth Gardens, none of the 'Norfolk' types was excavated, but in total four beads were found at Eriswell, Lakenheath and Holywell Row (Gaz. nos S27 and S62; Brugmann 2004). The 'Norfolk' types are, however, represented in a cemetery excavated at Tittleshall, Norfolk, which indicates regional differences in the glass bead fashion represented by Group A2 between Norfolk and Suffolk.

Plate 2 Glass beads of Group A2
'Segmented Constricted' (1), 'Constricted Cylindrical' (2), 'Miniature Dark' (3) and 'Norfolk Melon' (4) from Grave 38 at Spong Hill. Scale 2:1

For the purpose of a more detailed chronological analysis of the four cemeteries, further types not included in the national sample were defined and the definition of 'Norfolk BlueWhite' beads revised. Type 'Norfolk BlueWhite' ('NoBlW') covers small, short beads wound of white glass and decorated with irregular light blue trails. The irregular edge to the perforation (Brugmann 2004, fig. 137) seems to be an effect of the same careless manufacture that resulted in the irregular application of the decorative trails. Plate 3 shows these beads together with beads of 'related manufacture' with green trails and in some cases with red dots. These variations together with the 'Norfolk BlueWhite' beads themselves comprise the new type 'Norfolk Short', defined as short white beads with differing colour combinations applied but produced with the same manufacturing technique. Eighteen graves at Morning Thorpe, Bergh Apton and Spong Hill produced beads of this type, but none of the variations of type 'Norfolk BlueWhite' was found at Westgarth Gardens, a further indication of a divide between Norfolk and Suffolk bead fashion during Glass Bead Phase A2 (see Table 5.1 for finds lists).

A further type not found at Westgarth Gardens but found in nine graves of the other three of the four cemeteries is a type of manufacture probably related to 'Norfolk YellowRed'. The type 'Norfolk YellowRed' is defined by an irregular trail applied to a wound cylindrical body with

Plate 3 Glass beads of Group A2
'Norfolk Short' from Grave 407 at Morning Thorpe.
Scale 2:1

Plate 4 Glass beads of Group A2
'Norfolk YellowRed' from Grave 65 at Bergh Apton.
Scale 2:1

Plate 5 Glass beads of Group A2 'Norfolk Crossing Trails' from Grave 65 at Bergh Apton. Scale 2:1

Plate 6 Glass beads of Group A2 'Norfolk Melon' with amber and other glass beads from Grave 303 at Morning Thorpe. Scale 2:1

Plate 7 Glass beads of Group A2 'YellowGreen' from Grave 209 at Morning Thorpe. Scale 2:1

perforated sides not marvered flat. This is a manufacturing detail different from the marvered perforated sides of the 'Cylindrical Pentagonal' and 'Cylindrical Round' beads. The new type definition 'Norfolk CrossingTrails' covers cylindrical beads produced with the same manufacturing technique and of the same relatively small size as type 'Norfolk YellowRed' but with white crossing trails and yellow or green dots (Pl. 5). The bodies of these beads are wound of red or dark glass.

The bright yellow or green opaque glass used for the application of dots to the 'Norfolk CrossingTrail' beads is probably of the same make or stock as the yellow or green glass used for small ribbed beads, type 'Norfolk Melon' (Pl. 6; Brugmann 2004, fig. 13). The ribs were produced by a few indents made with a tool with a straight edge and quite carelessly applied, so that the result is a bead with an irregular cross section and often a tapering longitudinal section. In this, the 'Norfolk Melon' beads are different from larger ribbed beads more carefully made from opaque glass of dull yellow, which are mostly of an earlier date.

A type of bead of a manufacture probably related to that of 'Traffic Light' beads rather than that of 'Norfolk' beads is represented by opaque yellow beads, cylindrical or globular, with irregularly applied translucent green trails ('YellowGreen'; Pl. 7; 'YellowGr' in correspondence analyses). Three of the fourteen graves with such beads were found at Westgarth Gardens.

The chronological framework for female graves in Chapter 5 is heavily dependent on beads. In the correspondence analysis, the national Group A1 is present with groups of five or more *Blue* beads (wound beads made of translucent blue glass, mostly the well-known 'annular' beads) and *Traffic Light* beads. At Morning Thorpe, they were found mostly in the north-west and the mid-east of the excavated area (Brugmann 2004, fig. 22). A quantification of the *Blue* beads was necessary because *Blue* beads as such were in use throughout the Anglo-Saxon period and only larger numbers are typical of early bead associations. The national Group A2 is represented not only by types found across Anglo-Saxon England (*ConSeg,* and in particular *ConCyl*) but at Spong Hill, Morning Thorpe and Bergh Apton also by the regional *Norfolk* types discussed above.

At Morning Thorpe, the distribution of the bead types of Group A2 differs from that of the glass beads of Group B, which are restricted to the south-eastern half of the excavated area (Brugmann 2004, fig. 22). In three of the graves at Morning Thorpe the beads of Group B were associated with silver 'bell' beads made of hollow halves which are bell-shaped (Fig. 5.25). Geake (1997, 43) dated beads of this type in the late 6th and the 7th centuries.

The glass beads from the four cemeteries form the backbone of the relative chronological framework for the graves of females presented in Chapter 5.3. Phase FA1 includes most beads of Group A1, Phase FA2 beads of Group A2 and in the early part of this Phase (FA2a) also beads of Group A1. Phase FB begins with bead Groups A2b and includes mostly beads of Group B.

4.3.4 Wrist-clasps
The wrist-clasps from the four cemeteries were part of a comprehensive study of Anglo-Saxon and Scandinavian finds of wrist-clasps by Hines (1993) and therefore do not need to be discussed here in detail. Wrist-clasps were introduced to 'Anglian' female dress in the 5th century and abandoned in the second half of the 6th century. Later attempts at dating individual types (see Høilund Nielsen 1997, 80) include an analysis of female graves in Cambridgeshire (Hines 1999b).

Among the numerous wrist-clasps from the four cemeteries, three classes proved useful for a relative chronological framework. Class A (Fig. 5.21) after Hines was found in Graves 396 at Morning Thorpe and Grave 5 at Spong Hill. The Morning Thorpe grave was listed by Hines (1993, 10) among the 'earliest-looking' datable contexts for this type in England. Class B12 (type *wcB12*, Fig. 5.21, Table 5.1) was found in Graves 97, 253 and 392 at Morning Thorpe, Graves 29 and 38 at Spong Hill and Graves ?2 and 48 at Westgarth Gardens. The clasp from Grave 16 at Westgarth Gardens was assigned to Class 20 by Hines on the basis of its cast plate/bar (1993, fig. 124, i) but is here reassigned to Class B12 on the basis of the protruding ears flanking a protruding central design, a

Plate 8 Glass beads of Group A2b: 'Melon' and of Group B: 'Cylindrical Round', 'Cylindrical Pentagonal' and a biconical bead from Grave 18 at Bergh Apton. Scale 2:1

composition typical of Class B12 rather than the divers examples of Class 20. Class B7 (clasps with repoussé decoration) was subdivided into clasps with a design that includes or consists of a row of large bosses along the length of a clasp-half (type *wcB7a*, Fig. 5.22, Table 5.1) and clasps with other types of decoration (type *wcB7b*, Fig. 5.24, Table 5.1).

A fourth type used for the relative chronological framework in Chapter 5 comprises clasps falling into several sub-classes of Hines' Class B. The attribute shared by all these relatively narrow clasps is the emphasis of the design on bars in a parallel position when the two halves of the clasp are closed. Clasps with bars cast in one with the rest of the clasp seem to have been contemporary with clasps made of sheet metal with a bar attached. This group of clasps, which is quite varied in the detail of their designs, was found in twenty-five graves (Type *wcBar*; Fig. 5.23, Table 5.1). As it seems possible that plain square clasps originally had either bars or other types of decoration soldered on, such as the repoussé sheets of Class B13c, rather than being plain clasps of Class B7, these clasps were not used for correspondence analysis.

At the four cemeteries, wrist-clasps of Hines' Classes A and B12 fall mainly in Phase FA1, type *wcB7a* in Phase FA2a, type *wcBar* in Phase FA2, and type *wcB7b* in the later Phase FA2 (Ch. 5.3.1). The correspondence analysis in Chapter 5 suggests that wrist-clasps did not survive the change in dress fashion that marks the transition from Phase FA to FB.

4.3.5 Finger-rings
The identification of finger-rings at the four cemeteries can be difficult because of the poor preservation of human remains. There are, however, three silver rings which can be identified as finger-rings, from Graves 384 and 396 at Morning Thorpe and Grave 38 at Spong Hill. The rings from Spong Hill and from Grave 396 are dated in Phase FA2a on the basis of associated grave-goods, and that from Grave 384 in Phase FB. It seems that finger-rings were not a regular part of East Anglian female dress in any of the phases.

4.3.6 Slip-knot rings
All in all seventeen slip-knot rings were found in twelve graves in contexts indicating female gender. The single

Plate 9 Glass beads of Group B: 'Cylindrical Round' (1), 'Koch 20' (2), 'Koch 34' (3) and 'Dot34' (4) from Grave 371 at Morning Thorpe. Scale 2:1

ring from Grave 323 at Morning Thorpe was associated with two beads likely to be from a female context. Only the pair of large copper-alloy rings from Grave 395 at Morning Thorpe was not associated with other objects.

A pair of large copper-alloy slip-knot rings from Grave 379 and a group of three large rings from Grave 64 are dated to Phase FA2 by their grave-good associations. While the rings in these graves were made of solid wire, the pairs of large rings from Graves 70 and 106 (also Phase FA2) were made of rolled sheets of copper-alloy. Smaller rings made of copper-alloy wire were found in Graves 80, 306 and 325 at Morning Thorpe and in Grave 36 at Westgarth Gardens, the dated ones falling in Phases FA2 or FB. Graves 227 and 375 at Morning Thorpe (Phase FB) and Grave 5 at Spong Hill (Phase FA1) produced single silver slip-knot rings. A ring from Grave 13 at Westgarth Gardens is made of iron, an unusual material for a slip-knot wire ring. The variations in size, material and number of the rings from the four cemeteries suggest that they served a range of purposes.

4.3.7 Girdle-hangers and keys

While the term *Gürtelgehänge* is used in German cemetery publications as a collective term for a bunch of objects suspended from the belt of a female, the term 'girdle-hanger' is used for large ornamental 'keys' as a regular but not common accessory associated with 'Anglian' female dress. These keys are usually found in pairs and sometimes linked by a loop. As no practical function can be assigned to girdle-hangers, they are considered to have had a symbolic meaning as pairs of imitation keys (Meaney 1981, 178ff.; Steuer 1982b; Hirst 1985, 87).

The girdle-hangers from the four cemeteries are sorted into three groups for correspondence analysis: type *gh1* (Fig. 5.21) has bird head terminals (Graves 18, 353 and 396 at Morning Thorpe and Grave 9 at Westgarth Gardens). Type *gh2* (Fig. 5.23) has rounded or S-shaped terminals (Graves 108 and 253 at Morning Thorpe and 38 at Spong Hill). Type *gh3* (Fig. 5.24) has angled terminals cut off straight (Graves 29 and 45 at Bergh Apton, 358, 393, and 397 at Morning Thorpe, and Grave 24 at Spong Hill). The probable fragment of a girdle-hanger shaft from Grave 214 at Morning Thorpe cannot be assigned to any of the groups.

Girdle-hangers are best represented in Phase FA2. Type *gh1* is also found in earlier contexts, type *gh2* is associated with objects defining Phase FA2 and type *gh3* helps to define Phase FA2b. Grave 214 dated in Phase FB produced the probable fragment of a girdle-hanger. Incomplete and repaired girdle-hangers are, however, not only a late feature. The girdle-hanger of type *gh1* from Grave 396 at Morning Thorpe was re-used after it was broken and is dated to Phase FA2a.

The stylistic development in the designs of girdle-hangers from types *gh1* to *gh3* seems to follow a general trait also found among cruciform brooches, that is an overall change from zoomorphic to abstract designs.

Iron keys were found almost exclusively in graves dated to Phase FA2 on the basis of associated grave-goods. The only exceptions are Graves 22 at Spong Hill and 370 at Morning Thorpe dated to Phase FA1 and Grave 238 at Morning Thorpe dated to Phase FB. Stoodley (1999, 111) was able to demonstrate that keys were mostly buried with adult women. It seems likely that keys demonstrated control of and access to resources and were therefore 'status goods'. The fact that these keys were buried with their owners suggests that either the containers they locked were buried with them or that it was possible to replace the keys — in which case they may have been more symbolic than functional. The locks to these keys could have been made out of wood and the boxes, if buried with the keys, need not be visible in the archaeological record. The reason boxes are well known from 7th-century contexts is that iron was used for their handles.

4.3.8 Weaving batten

Iron weaving battens are rare objects in Anglo-Saxon graves. The twenty or so known finds suggest that weaving battens were made longer over the course of time (Walton Rogers in Parfitt and Anderson forthcoming, and pers. comm.). This would place the batten from Grave 24 at Spong Hill, only *c*. 56cm long and most likely a recycled sword (Gilmour 1984, 161), among the earliest battens from Anglo-Saxon graves. Most Anglo-Saxon graves with weaving battens are dated after the mid 6th century (Walton Rogers in Parfitt and Anderson forthcoming). On the Continent, iron weaving battens are a largely East Merovingian feature and dated in Phases 5–6 (AD 530–580) of Koch's South German chronology (Koch 2001). In Norway, however, weaving battens were common in the graves of females in both the 5th and 6th centuries (Kristoffersen 2000, 122). The weaving batten from Grave 24 at Spong Hill is dated to Phase FA2b on the basis of associated grave-goods.

4.4 Objects in the graves of males and females

4.4.1 Pins

In the context of Anglo-Saxon grave-goods, the term 'pin' is often used to describe anything from a needle to a substantial rod with a round or square section that may or may not have had a point. It therefore seems possible that the description of object Hii from Grave 316 at Morning Thorpe as 'part of a large iron pin' (Green *et al.* 1987, 122) describes part of a rod or tool. In the following, only complete pins are discussed, and rods which either have a point (in Graves 50 and 407 at Morning Thorpe) or can be argued to have had a point originally.

Most of these pins have been found in the graves of females. The only type of pin that seems to be as common in the graves of males as in the graves of females are iron pins with scrolled heads. They are distributed predominantly in East Anglia and Kent (see Ross 1991 *contra* White 1988). In Graves 398, 409 and 414 at Morning Thorpe such pins were found in what seems to have been the area of the upper body, and were associated with spearheads in Graves 398 and 409. An iron pin found with a spearhead and a shield boss in Grave 259 at Morning Thorpe may originally also have had a scrolled head. Iron pins with scrolled heads from Dover Buckland, Kent, may have been used to fasten cloth wrapped around spearheads (Evison 1987, 82). This, however, does not appear to have been the function of such pins found at the later excavations at Buckland (Parfitt and Anderson forthcoming). In Graves 11 at Bergh Apton and Graves 140 and 249 at Morning Thorpe iron pins with scrolled heads were found with pairs of annular brooches and had probably been used as dress fasteners. These graves are dated in Phase FA2, the pin from Grave 398 associated with a male in Phase MB.

Another type of dress pin combined with pairs of brooches is formed by iron or copper-alloy pins with triangular spangles made of a pair of copper-alloy sheets. In Graves 86 and 378 at Morning Thorpe these pins were complete; in Graves 36 at Westgarth Gardens and Grave 42 at Bergh Apton only parts were found. The possible remains of such spangles (and iron pins) from Graves 44 and 62 at Bergh Apton and Grave 37 at Spong Hill may represent further pins of this type. A single perforated triangular sheet attached to a copper-alloy wire found with beads and brooches in Grave 52 at Westgarth Gardens may, however, represent part of the bead arrangement rather than a pin. The remains of iron pins with perforated heads found with brooches in Graves 108, 148, 387 and 369 at Morning Thorpe may have carried spangles as well. Ross (1991) argued for a late 5th/early 6th-century date for pins with spangles (his Group VII), a type fairly common in 'Anglian' England. The pins with spangles and those which may have had spangles were found in graves of Phase FA2.

Pins with solid heads and rods which are assumed to be pins despite a missing tip, were found in Grave 65 at Bergh Apton, Graves 18, 221, 316/321, 351, and 369 at Morning Thorpe, and Grave 47 at Westgarth Gardens. The pins from Bergh Apton and Westgarth Gardens may originally have had organic heads. The latter pin is relatively short and has a moulding in the middle of the shaft for anchorage. Pins with this technical feature and shorter than 6cm in length fall into Phases 5–7 at Dover Buckland, that is probably not before the mid 7th century (Brugmann in Parfitt and Anderson forthcoming). On the basis of this pin, the grave can be dated in Phase FB. The other pins were found in graves dated to Phase FA2a (FA2 in the case of Grave 221 at Morning Thorpe).

4.4.2 Necklet

The necklet from Grave 50 at Bergh Apton has three holes of uncertain function in the flat copper-alloy strip that forms its main component. The excavators considered decorative studs most likely because of small circular marks around each hole (Green and Rogerson 1978, 45). A more recent find of a copper-alloy necklace flattened out at the front from Grave 100 at West Heslerton, North Yorks, has spangles attached. While the Bergh Apton find was associated with a spearhead, the West Heslerton necklet was found with a *circa* five year-old girl (Haughton and Powlesland 1999, 116). Silver necklets with flattened-out central sections from Anglo-Saxon contexts have been discussed in detail by Adams and Jackson (1988/89, 156). These finds suggest that such necklets were not gender-specific items. Grave 50 at Bergh Apton falls in Phase MA2.

4.4.3 Buckles

Seventeen burials at Bergh Apton, 102 at Morning Thorpe, fourteen at Spong Hill, and twelve graves at Westgarth Gardens produced a total of 178 buckles, seventy-one of them with an attached plate. This count does not include fragments of what most probably were buckle loops. One hundred and twenty-four of these buckles are made of iron, for thirty-eight buckles a combination of iron and copper-alloy was used for loops, plates and rivets, and fourteen buckles are made of copper-alloy only. A buckle from Grave 384 combines iron and silver and another buckle from Grave 157 is made of gilt copper-alloy.

Buckles are the most common type of object in Anglo-Saxon graves after knives and were found in 44% of the male and 34% of the female individuals in Stoodley's national sample (Stoodley 1999, 34). Comparison with the four cemeteries is of limited value because the ratio would depend heavily on the number of individuals identified as male or female on the basis of associated grave-goods such as weapons. Buckles were a fairly regular outfit of males buried with weapons but their association with female dress accessories became more common only in the 6th century. This increase may explain why buckles from undisturbed graves which were not associated with female dress fittings or weapons were mostly found in those parts of the excavated areas at Morning Thorpe and Bergh Apton that produced graves dated in Phases FB and MB (Ch. 5.3).

In a survey on early Anglo-Saxon belt buckles, Marzinzik (2003) included most of the buckles from the four cemeteries in her national sample and subjected them to a detailed typological and chronological analysis. The wide date range of most of the buckle types from the four cemeteries means that most of them have relatively little to add to a chronological framework for the four cemeteries. Though there is a tendency for the use of smaller belt buckles from the 5th to 7th centuries, size alone is not datable (see Geake 1997, 79; Marzinzik 2003, 54), in particular because buckles were used for more than just belts, as is demonstrated by pursemounts, shoe buckles or additional sword belts, for example.

The few closely-datable buckle types in the graves of males have been discussed by Karen Høilund Nielsen in her archive report (2003). Buckle J from Grave 367 at Morning Thorpe (type II.6 after Marzinzik) has a kidney-shaped loop and is associated with a rectangular mount with punched geometrical decoration, almost in Nydam style. It falls into relative chronological phases in continental frameworks which date it AD 440–485 after Siegmund (1998), AD 430–480 after Koch (2001) and AD 440–530 after Nieveler and Siegmund (1999). The early date of this buckle type and the later date for the weapons from the same grave support the suggestion by the excavators that Grave 367 represents a male burial cut into an earlier grave (Green *et al*. 1987, 142) that probably falls in Phase MA1 or FA1.

Buckle Biv in Grave 132 at Morning Thorpe (type I.8 after Marzinzik) has transverse ribs and also represents a particularly early type, which is dated AD 480–510 in Koch's chronological framework for South Germany (Koch 2001). The grave falls in Phase MA1. The third early type (type I.3 after Marzinzik) buried with a male is represented by buckle A from Grave 30 at Westgarth Gardens. The loop and tongue of this buckle are made of copper-alloy and the plate of iron. The tongue is decorated with a rectangular shield and the loop, which is flat for its type, with traverse lines. The type is dated AD 480–530 by Koch (2001), AD 480–530 by Nieveler and Siegmund (1999) and 'around AD 500' by Menghin (1983) in his survey on early medieval swords. The grave falls in Phase MA2.

The copper-alloy buckle and plate from Grave 157 at Morning Thorpe were combined with five belt plates decorated with Style I (type II.14b after Marzinzik). They the second half of the 7th and in the 8th centuries (Geake 1997, 64, map 30). The grave is therefore assigned to Phase MB/FB on the basis of absolute dates.

4.4.6 Knives
Knives are the most common object in Anglo-Saxon graves and at Morning Thorpe they are evenly distributed across the entire site, regardless of the period in which different areas were in use. Relative knife length was mainly related to the age and sex/gender of the individuals buried with them but there was also a tendency for longer knives in later periods (Härke 1989). The latter is clearly reflected in the approximate length of the measurable blades at Spong Hill and Bergh Apton: at Spong Hill blade lengths varied from 5–9cm with an average of *c.* 7cm and at Bergh Apton they varied from *c.* 6–15cm with an average of *c.* 9cm. At Morning Thorpe, the distribution of knives with a blade of *c.* 10cm or more — longer than any of the measurable blades at Spong Hill — covers largely the same area as the graves dated in the latest Phases FB and MB (Fig. 4.6; Ch. 5).

Wear that may have changed the length and shape of the cutting edge and the poor preservation of many knives are not encouraging aspects of a detailed knife typology. It has, however, been possible to single out knives with a fairly straight cutting edge as late types, dated mainly to the 7th century at Dover Buckland (Evison 1987, types 4 and 5). Such knives were found in Grave 19 at Bergh Apton and Graves 167, 211, 311 and 350 at Morning Thorpe (Fig. 4.6). Grave 211 at Morning Thorpe is dated to Phase MA2 and the Bergh Apton grave to Phase MB. This corresponds well with a date for such knives not much before Phase 3 at Dover Buckland. As knives with a straight cutting edge are not ideal as multi-purpose knives, it is not surprising that the few knives from the four cemeteries preserved well enough to be classified as such are relatively large and were found in the graves of males or possible males. It seems likely that these knives had a specific function, possibly as a small weapon. This may explain why the knives in Graves 211 and 311 at Morning Thorpe were associated with a second knife. Stoodley (1999, 30), however, noted that of the twenty-two graves with two knives in his national sample, eleven came from female contexts and four from male contexts, which 'may be symbolic of a perceived female-specific task that required multiple knives or a greater range of female-specific roles needing knives'.

Continental knives with straight cutting edges of the later 7th century suggest similarities in an overall typological development, in the Trier region represented by type C after Böhner (1958) and in the Rhine region by type Ger1.2 after Siegmund (1998) and Nieveler and Siegmund (1999) and type S-Ger1.2 after Müssemeyer *et al.* (2003).

4.4.7 Firesteels/pursemounts
The four cemeteries produced two firesteels and ten objects which (originally) had a buckle and probably served as a combination of a pursemount and a firesteel (Brown 1977). The remains of decorated leather attached to the pursemount from Grave 184 at Morning Thorpe probably represent a particularly well-preserved example of such a purse. As it is likely that the iron used for knives was suitable for the production of sparks (Seeberger 1985), both iron pursemounts (as opposed to organic ones) and plain firesteels were probably luxury items in functional terms used by males and females.

The well-preserved firesteel/pursemounts from the four cemeteries represent types which have defined date-ranges on the Continent. These date-ranges are generally derived from male contexts as relatively few women were buried with firesteels in continental row-grave contexts. The firesteel from Grave 30 at Spong Hill has curved terminals extended from the base of the slightly triangular bar of the pursemount and represents the earliest type, dated to Phases 2–4 (*c.* AD 460–530) of the chronology for South Germany defined by Koch (2001). This suggests a date for the grave in Phase MA1/FA1. The two firesteels from Grave 27 at Spong Hill and Grave 184 at Morning Thorpe also have curved terminals which are, however, attached to the sloping sides of the bar. On the Continent, the type cannot be more closely dated than the late 5th and 6th centuries. Grave 27 at Spong Hill falls in Phase MA2 on the basis of associated grave-goods. Grave 184 at Morning Thorpe is likely to date in the same phase.

The firesteel/pursemounts from Grave 29 at Bergh Apton and Grave 5 at Westgarth Gardens are — if only vaguely — shaped as animal heads. Grave 100 at Morning Thorpe produced a fragment including such an animal head. They represent a type of firesteel/pursemount in use in Phase ABD2 (*c.* AD 475–535) after Périn (1998), Phase 2–3 (*c.* AD 440–510/25) after Siegmund (1998) and in Phases 3–4 (*c.* AD 480–530) after Koch (2001). The firesteel/pursemount from Grave 416 at Morning Thorpe shows the remains of animal heads folded over the central bar. This is a type dated to Phase ABD2 (*c.* AD 475–525) in Périn's chronology for the Ardenne/Meuse region (Périn 1998), Phase 3–4 (*c.* AD 480/90–550/60) after Nieveler and Siegmund (1999) and Phase 3–4 (*c.* AD 460/80–565) after Müssemeyer *et al.* (2003) and to the South German Phases 3–4 (*c.* AD 480–530) after Koch (2001). A late 5th- or early 6th-century date therefore also seems likely for these firesteel/pursemounts. Grave 5 at Westgarth Gardens falls in Phase MA2 on the basis of associated grave-goods and Grave 29 at Bergh Apton in Phase FA2b. The two fragments of a firesteel/pursemount from Grave 36 at Westgarth Gardens have been reconstructed at a slightly exaggerated angle (West 1988, fig. 70, J) and represent a type with curved terminals in use roughly at the same time (see Koch 2001). The grave is dated to Phase FA2a on the basis of associated grave-goods.

The firesteel from Grave 381 at Morning Thorpe is roughly triangular in shape, with a straight base and short upturned terminals. This is a type dated to the late Phase III and early Phase IV after Böhner (1958) by Schulze-Dörrlamm (1990, 289 f.). The typological development of firesteels suggested by Pescheck (1996, fig. 20) makes a date of the Morning Thorpe find in Phases 5 and 6 after Siegmund (1998) likely, that is *c.* AD 555–585. The Morning Thorpe grave falls in Phase MA2 on the basis of associated grave-goods.

The firesteel from Grave 69 at Westgarth Gardens has 'curled terminals', a detail not clearly visible in the drawing (West 1988, 38 fig. 85, B) and represents the latest type in the series, which can be generally dated in the 7th or possibly 8th century (Geake 1997, 79 f.). The firesteel from Grave 19 at Shudy Camps, Cambs, provides a particularly close example associated with 7th-century bulla pendants. A late date for firesteels with curved or

Figure 4.6 Morning Thorpe. The distribution of knives in general and of knives with blades 10cm or more in length. Scale 1:300

curled terminals is suggested by continental contexts (Stein 1967, pl. 11,5). The firesteel in Grave 69 at Westgarth Gardens was associated with a late buckle, which supports a date for the grave in Phase MB/FB.

The firesteel/pursemounts from Graves 12 at Westgarth Gardens and Grave 65 at Morning Thorpe are unfortunately incomplete and may represent types of the second half of the 5th or first half of the 6th century.

4.4.8 Tweezers and possible ear-scoop
Three of the four cemeteries produced seventeen pairs of tweezers and a possible ear-scoop, but none of the graves produced sets of toilet implements as are occasionally found in Anglo-Saxon cremation and inhumation graves. The tweezers are made of strips of copper-alloy (Graves 45, 65, 67, 78, 87, 148, 157, 288, 325, 346, 355, 360, 416 at Morning Thorpe, Grave 27 at Spong Hill, and Grave 41 at Westgarth Gardens) or iron (Graves 27 and 281 at Morning Thorpe), either with parallel sides or slightly expanding towards the tip. These are long-lived types which do not date the graves to any specific phase. Most tweezers from the four cemeteries fall in Phase MA2, but there are also finds from all three phases for female equipment. The scoop falls in Phase FA1.

4.2.9 Lyres
The remains of what seem to have been lyres were found in Grave 22 at Bergh Apton and in Grave 97 at Morning Thorpe. The finds were fully discussed by Lawson (1978; 1987) in the grave catalogues. More recently, Lawson (2001, 223) included these two finds in a discussion of a lyre found with a 'warrior-musician' at Snape, Suffolk. The finds from Bergh Apton and Morning Thorpe form part of a number of instruments identified in the region and come from notably unspectacular contexts, in particular in comparison to Sutton Hoo.

Lyres are usually found with males, and it therefore seems likely that the individuals at the four cemeteries probably buried with lyres were also male. A female context in Grave 97 at Morning Thorpe however cannot be entirely excluded because a male burial disturbed a female one, the graves dated in Phases FA1 and MA1 respectively. Neither can Grave 22 at Bergh Apton be identified beyond doubt as that of a male. Stoodley's statement about the positive association of musical instruments with males excludes the Morning Thorpe evidence and does not seem to take account of the disturbed Bergh Apton grave (Stoodley 1999, 33). The associated buckle in this grave is not closely datable, but the shape of the studs used for the lyre suggests a 6th- or 7th-century date for the lyre rather than a 5th-century one. The probable lyre from Morning Thorpe, however, clearly pre-dates the finds made at Snape and Sutton Hoo.

4.4.10 Glass vessels
The four cemeteries produced only three glass vessels, an exceptional bucket-shaped beaker of Group 19 after Evison (2000) from Grave 62 at Westgarth Gardens, a cone beaker with horizontal trails of Group 20 from Grave 51, and a cone beaker with white arcades of Group 21 from Grave 148 at Morning Thorpe. Evison (2000, 61) considers the bucket-shaped vessel to be a development from a Roman vessel type and dates it to the late 4th/early 5th centuries. Cone beakers of her Groups 20 and 21 are dated by Evison to the 5th and early 6th centuries. The Westgarth Gardens graves are dated in Phase MA2 by associated objects.

Evison (2000, 48) has estimated the number of glass vessels from the cremation graves at Spong Hill to be over a hundred. This suggests that at least one in twenty-five cremations involved a glass vessel. These include Kempston cone beakers dated to the 5th and early 6th centuries and claw beakers of the first half of the 6th century (Evison 2000, 62ff.). A comparable number of vessels in the fifty-five inhumation graves at Spong Hill would be two. Not a single glass vessel was found, however. The ratio at Morning Thorpe, a single vessel in over 300 inhumation graves, is also low compared to the Spong Hill cremations. Only the two vessels from the sixty-nine inhumation graves at Westgarth Gardens compare well with Spong Hill, though three vessels would have come even closer to the ratio estimated for the cremations.

4.4.11 Copper-alloy and wooden vessels
Copper-alloy bowls with beaded rims were found in Grave 24 at Spong Hill and Grave 200 at Morning Thorpe. This is a type that is known from continental contexts of the 5th and first half of the 6th centuries (Koch 1977, 154f.). In Anglo-Saxon England, bowls of this type are considered likely to be imports (Evison 1987, 104 fig. 116). With diameters of *c.* 25 and 26cm respectively, the Spong Hill and Morning Thorpe bowls are relatively small examples. A 'scar' on the bowl from Spong Hill indicates that it originally had a footring such as the one on the Morning Thorpe bowl.

The Morning Thorpe bowl was found in the mouth of the likely remains of a Vestland cauldron, a type of vessel with triangular lugs for suspension and a carinated shoulder. Only the upper part of the vessel is preserved but the sloping profile of the wall makes the carinated shoulder of a Vestland cauldron more likely than the rounded profile of a Gotland cauldron (also with triangular lugs for suspension). The most recent overview on the wide distribution of Vestland cauldrons, which covers England, Scandinavia and the Continent, and on their typology, dating and function has been presented by Hoeper (1999). The outline of the Morning Thorpe cauldron suggests that it is a late typological development of a Vestland cauldron related to type 'Donzdorf' (Hoeper 1999, 237 for a discussion). The proportions and probably also the shape of the handle (the section is not illustrated) of the Morning Thorpe cauldron compare well with the cauldron from the coin-dated 'princely' Grave 1782 at Krefeld Gellep with a *terminus post quem* of AD 491 (Siegmund 1998, 524).

The association of Vestland cauldrons and bowls with beaded rims in Grave 200 at Morning Thorpe and in another grave at Sawston, Cambs (Vierck 1972, 32) is particularly noteworthy because the overall distribution pattern of these two types of vessels is not identical. While the distribution of bowls with beaded rims includes Kent, Vestland cauldrons are almost exclusively distributed north of the Thames (Hoeper 1999, fig. 2). This suggests different sources for the two types of copper-alloy vessels, possibly Scandinavia and the Merovingian Continent.

The bowl with a beaded rim and the Vestland cauldron from Grave 200 at Morning Thorpe were associated with a copper-alloy bound stave-built wooden bucket. Copper-alloy bound buckets are a typical feature of the Anglo-

Figure 4.7 Morning Thorpe. The distribution of pottery in general and of pottery with stamp decoration. Scale 1:300

Saxon 'early' phase of the 5th and 6th centuries, while iron-bound buckets are more common in the later 6th and 7th centuries (Cook 2004). All the buckets in the corpus associated with copper-alloy bowls with beaded rims (nos 45, 65, 84, 207) or Vestland cauldrons (nos 60, 149, 199) were copper-alloy bound vessels.

The bucket in Grave 200 may well have been made in 'Anglian' England (see Cook 2004, no. 148 for a detailed description of the bucket). Bifurcated handle mounts with terminals shaped as animal heads (handle mount type 'a' after Cook 2004) and punch marks for decoration tend to be found more often in 'Anglian' than in 'Saxon' contexts. The bucket from Grave 40 at Spong Hill (Cook 2004, no. 154) shows a slightly different construction. The handle of this bucket is attached to an extended upright, a technical detail more common with buckets from 'Saxon' graves. The semicircular strip riveted to the upright and the top hoop probably imitates a bifurcated handle mount. This is a feature also found on a bucket from Grave 60 at Long Wittenham, Oxon (Cook 2004, no. 195). Two cremations at Spong Hill may also have involved copper-alloy bound buckets (see Cook 2004, nos 152–153).

Grave 40 at Spong Hill is dated to Phase MA2 on the basis of associated weapons. Grave 200 at Morning Thorpe is unusual for an Anglo-Saxon grave because the association includes three vessels generally considered to be luxury items but no weapons or female dress accessories. The grave therefore can be dated only on the basis of the vessels themselves. The Vestland cauldron, bowl with beaded rim and copper-alloy bound bucket suggest a date in Phase MA/FA.

Iron-bound buckets (with handles) and tubs (with suspension rings) are a generally though not exclusively later typological development. The best known examples were found at Sutton Hoo (Cook 2004, nos 232, 233, 235–237). Iron-bound vessels tend to be larger than copper-alloy bound buckets and may have had a different function. Iron-bound buckets were found in Grave 19 at Bergh Apton, Grave 218 at Morning Thorpe and Grave 66 at Westgarth Gardens. Grave 35 at Morning Thorpe produced a tub. A further tub was found in Grave 238 at Morning Thorpe combined with a bucket. An iron fragment from Grave 30 at Westgarth Gardens published as the remains of an iron-bound bucket (West 1988, 28) probably had some other function (Cook 2004, no. 245).

In Anglo-Saxon England, both males and females were buried with buckets, objects which presumably served as 'status goods' (see Cook 2004). While the ratio between males and females buried with copper-alloy bound buckets was probably even, iron-bound buckets were buried more often with males than females. The two copper-alloy bound buckets from the four cemeteries were buried with males, as were most of the iron-bound buckets. The bucket and the tub in Grave 238 at Morning Thorpe, however, may have been buried with the male of Phase MA2 or the female of Phase FB. Both graves are dated within the date-range generally known from contexts with iron-bound buckets. The iron-bound tub in Grave 35 at Morning Thorpe was probably buried with the male dated in Phase MA2. The iron-bound buckets from Grave 19 at Bergh Apton, Grave 218 at Morning Thorpe and Grave 66 at Westgarth Gardens were found with males dated in Phase MB on the basis of associated grave-goods.

Finds from waterlogged sites such as Oberflacht and Wremen in Germany (Paulsen 1992; Schön 1999) support the notion that wooden objects — vessels among them — played a larger part in Early Medieval inhumation burial practice than is usually suggested by the archaeological evidence (Morris 1994). In most cases the only indication for such objects are metal fittings. The copper-alloy rims of wooden bowls were found in sixteen graves at the four cemeteries, mostly those of females (Graves 35 and 65 at Bergh Apton, Graves 25, 108, 133, and 358 at Morning Thorpe, Graves 45 and 58 at Spong Hill, and Grave 36 at Westgarth Gardens). Four males (Graves 126 and 274 at Morning Thorpe, Grave 40 at Spong Hill, and Grave 49 at Westgarth Gardens) and three individuals of unknown sex or gender (Graves 87 and 335 at Morning Thorpe and Grave 34 at Spong Hill) were also buried with vessels indicated by rim clips. If such clips indicated repairs rather than having been decorative, their presence may indicate sixteen graves with second-rate bowls rather than exceptional burials including a vessel. All the vessels associated with datable grave-goods fall in Phases FA2 or MA2.

The only obviously decorative mounts were found in Grave 36 at Westgarth Gardens. A copper-alloy strip decorated with repoussé motifs was attached to the rim of a ?maple vessel with the help of a rim mount and rim clips. The decoration is described in the catalogue as 'twenty-one medallions, with debased heads in eighteen and three with eight-pointed stars in lozenges. Lower border of raised dots…' (West 1988, 29). The rivets appear not to respect the decorative scheme very well, but otherwise there is no evidence that the decorated strip was re-used, especially since the area covered by the rim mount was undecorated. The technique used for the decoration of this turned vessel is the same as that used for most buckets: a top hoop held by rim mounts and rim clips. Repoussé decoration is also very common with top hoops from buckets, as is the use of rows of dots along the lower edge of a top hoop (and both edges on lower hoops). The figural motif and the complex geometric motif would, however, be considered as unusual for a bucket as it is for a wooden vessel. A late Roman origin or the use of a late Roman template for the decorated mount is most likely. The same is suggested for a bucket with Christian motifs from Long Wittenham (Cook 2004, no. 199) and a mount from Strood, Kent of unknown function (Cook 2004, no. 129). Grave 36 is dated in Phase FA2a, suggesting that the bowl was an heirloom at the time of burial.

4.4.12 Pottery

The four cemeteries produced the remains of 173 vessels, most of them grave-goods in inhumation graves, and a few cremation pots. Further fragments were found in some of the grave fills. The grave catalogues provide identifications of fabrics and of motifs used for stamp decorations. Most of the pots are plain, and stamps are the most common type of decoration used for the pots in inhumation graves. Comparison between the decoration of the pots used for the Spong Hill cremations and inhumations suggests that the vessels are part of the same pot making tradition (Hills 1994, 47f.). Graves 3, 8 and 16 contained pots of stamp-linked groups known from cremations (Hills et al. 1984, 15).

There are no recent comprehensive studies exploring the relationship between Anglo-Saxon inhumation and cremation graves (Høilund Nielsen 1997, 72f.) but Hills (1994, 47f.) has outlined the potential of this research for

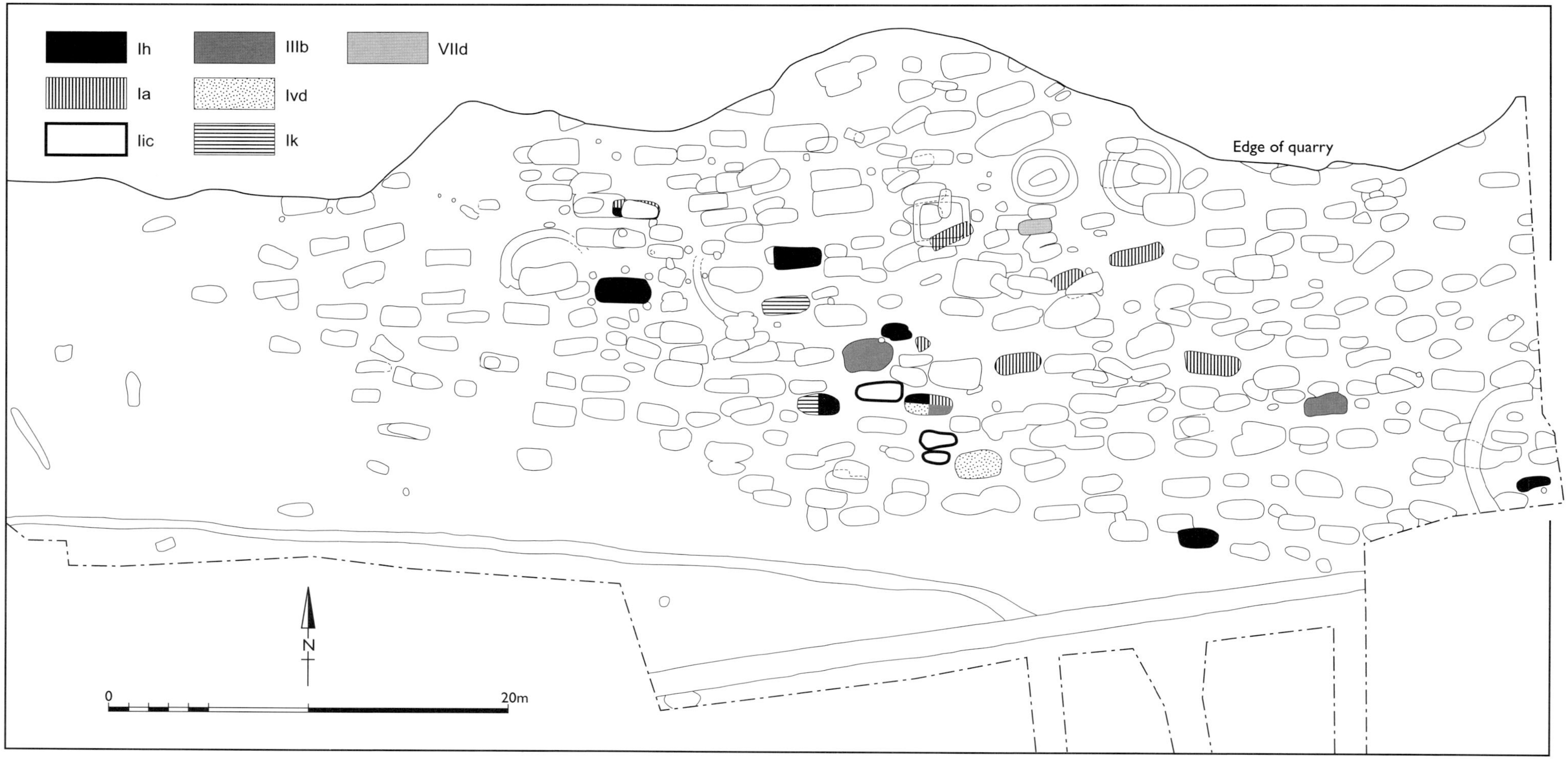

Figure 4.8 Morning Thorpe. The distribution of pottery with stamps that were used for more than one pot from the site. Scale 1:300

the Spong Hill cemetery. Comparison between the pots used for cremations and inhumations at Spong Hill provides some clues for the dating of the pots found with the inhumations. Vessels with plastic and/or line decoration not combined with stamped decoration are considered to be largely earlier than vessels with stamped decoration. According to Hills (1994, 48) 'The stamp-linked pots seem to belong to a phase when local styles had time to develop, after the initial period when pottery had been far closer to its 5th-century (or earlier) continental antecedents. ... Both internal and external arguments therefore coincide in putting all of these burials into the 6th, rather than the 5th century AD'.

Hills' 6th-century date is based on the assumption that the inhumation graves at Spong Hill do not substantially pre-date the 6th century; it would therefore have to shift with a general shift in the dating of the inhumation graves. The pots from the four cemeteries dated by associated grave-goods fall in Phases MA and FA. A few pots in Graves of Phase FB (Grave 27 at Westgarth Gardens and Graves 177 and 227 at Morning Thorpe) demonstrate, however, that graves with pottery cannot be dated early *per se*.

A random use of stamps instead of a carefully executed pattern has been considered a relatively late typological development in the decoration of pots (Hills 1978, 142, 145) but lately doubts about this concept have arisen (Hills 1994, 47). The evidence from the four cemeteries is inconclusive in this respect. One of the two pots with a random pattern of stamps comes from Grave 27 at Westgarth Gardens dated to Phase FB and may support a late date for such pots, but another pot with a random pattern from Grave 387 at Morning Thorpe is dated to Phase FA2a.

The only plain pots with bosses for decoration from the four cemeteries come from Grave 97 at Morning Thorpe dated in Phase FA1 or MA1 and Graves 35 and 47 at Bergh Apton not dated by associated grave-goods. The only pots from the four cemeteries which are decorated with lines not combined with stamped decoration were found in Graves 22 and 56 at Spong Hill and in Grave 40 at Westgarth Gardens. Grave 22 is dated to Phase FA1, Grave 56 to Phase FA2a and Grave 40 to Phase MA2. These datings do not suggest that pots decorated with bosses or lines are generally earlier than pots with a decoration that includes stamps, but the relatively small number of these pots in comparison to the thirty-six pots with stamped decoration from the four cemeteries speaks for themselves.

Hills (1978, 142; 1994, 46) has pointed out that it is difficult to demonstrate that plain pots are about chronology rather than function. There is no significant difference in the range of datings for decorated and undecorated pots in the four cemeteries derived from associated grave-goods but the relatively high number of undecorated pots — *c.* 75% compared to 20% among the cremation pots (Hills 1994, 469) — may imply some chronological factor. A relatively late date for stamped pottery and for an increase in undecorated pots is also suggested by the evidence from cremation graves cutting inhumation graves of Phases MA1–2 and FA1–2 at Spong Hill (see Ch. 5.4.2). Among the urns used for cremations cutting inhumation graves, eight are plain (Cremations 1819, 1879, 1946, 2108, 2131, 2138, 2140 and 2142) and four are decorated (Cremations 1884, 1912, 1941 and 2114), all of the motifs including stamps. The ratio of 1:2 between decorated and undecorated urns is much lower than among the cremations at Spong Hill in general but twice as high as the ratio found among the pottery placed in inhumation graves at Spong Hill.

The evidence from Spong Hill in particular seems to support a relatively late date for stamped pottery and many of the plain pots. It also supports the general notion that cremation burial practice did not cease before the end of the 5th century. It seems possible, however, that the high number of undecorated pots in the inhumation graves at the four cemeteries is based on their function rather than on chronological differences. A detailed comparison of the undecorated pots from inhumation and cremation graves taking account of fabrics, sizes and forms might show basic differences between funeral ware and domestic pottery.

At Spong Hill, Morning Thorpe and Bergh Apton, *circa* three quarters of the pots were undecorated, at Westgarth Gardens slightly less than half the pots. It seems that these undecorated pots were mostly placed in the graves of females, though the number of pots buried with archaeologically invisible gender could even out the numbers at Morning Thorpe and Bergh Apton. The associations of pots with other grave-goods at Morning Thorpe show some further tendencies.

Though decorated and undecorated pots are widely distributed at Morning Thorpe (Fig. 4.7), the pattern is not so regular as that of knives or buckles (Figs 4.5–6). Pottery vessels are relatively common in the north-west of the excavated area and less common in the south-east. This pattern roughly corresponds with the division of the excavated site into an area that was still in use in Phases FB and MB and an area that was apparently not used at this late stage (Ch. 5.4.3). This is a further indication that pottery was more common in the burial practice of Phases FA and MA than in Phases FB and MB.

Stamped pots are found mostly in the southern centre of the excavated area (Fig. 4.7), which was in use in all three phases. Associated grave-goods suggest that most were buried in Phases MA2 and FA2. The distribution of stamp types which were used for more than one pot at Morning Thorpe (Fig. 4.8) shows a tendency for groupings. There is a cluster of such stamps in the lower centre of the excavated area and what looks like a rough north-west/south-east axis across the site. Close datings for the individual types of stamps are sparse and do not indicate a chronological reason for their distribution. This might indicate a 'clan' use of stamps as has been suggested for the cremations at Spong Hill (Hills 1978, 148). Such 'clan' links would then have spanned the cremation and inhumation burial practice and burial communities across the four cemeteries. Unfortunately, the Spong Hill evidence was not available in its entirety when Richards (1987) wrote his thesis on the *Significance of Form and Decoration of Anglo-Saxon Cremation Urns*. Both Hills' and Høilund Nielsen's studies suggest that there is further potential for future studies on this subject (Hills 1994; Ravn 2003, fig. 8,2.3).

The use of ceramic vessels as grave-goods in the graves of females and males raises the question whether these pots can be used to correlate the phases for the two groups. A closer look at the decorative motifs however shows that the designs are too individualistic to form useful groups. Additionally there may have been preferences in the use of composite motifs for pots buried with males and females. Open triangles were mostly used for males (Graves 85, 115, 388 at Morning Thorpe, Grave 36 at Spong Hill, and Graves 11 and 51 at Westgarth Gardens), designs framed by horizontal bands mostly for pots buried with females (Grave 26 at Spong Hill, Graves 140, 208, 387, 396 at Morning Thorpe and Graves 31 and 55 at Westgarth Gardens). A comprehensive analysis of the pottery from the four cemeteries would have to include the cremation graves at Spong Hill and is beyond the scope of the present study.

5. A chronological framework

5.1 Background

The methods used for a chronological analysis of the four cemeteries were set out in Chapter 3.3. The analysis builds on an archive report (Høilund Nielsen and Hines 1997) which identified two specific problems with the correspondence analyses of male and female graves from the four cemeteries. The material basis for the analysis of weapon graves was large enough to produce results, but it was not possible to test their reliability against a national sample. Since then, further research on Anglo-Saxon weapon graves by Høilund Nielsen and Hines has changed the situation (see Ch. 4.1). The situation with regard to a chronological framework for female dress accessories has also changed. Although the East Anglian sample represented by the four cemeteries is relatively large, correspondence analysis showed that the results relied heavily on bead type associations. At the time, research on a national sample of beads was not sufficiently advanced to answer some of the questions raised by the analysis of the four cemeteries. Since then, Norfolk in particular has proved to be a key region for the analysis of 6th-century glass bead chronology (Brugmann 2004).

The difficulties the excavators encountered when trying to define the stratigraphical relationship of some of the intercutting graves at Morning Thorpe make some grave-good assemblages less certain than others. For correspondence analyses, only those grave-good associations considered reasonably certain by the excavators were used. Graves which certainly or possibly represent burials of two individuals of the same gender are either omitted (*e.g.* Grave 30) or listed with the letters representing those objects the excavators considered to form grave-good associations (Table 5.1; Graves 35, 45, 80, 108, 140, 216, 284, 293, 316, 321, 333, 337, 342, 358, 369, and 371). (For a discussion on the stratigraphical relationship between Graves 359 and 360 see Brugmann 2004, 52 note 45).

5.2 Weapons and associated objects
based on an archive report by Karen Høilund Nielsen (2003)

5.2.1 Relative chronology
The typology for spearheads and shield bosses developed for the purpose of a chronological sequence based on correspondence analysis was presented in Chapter 4, as was the grave-good analysis of the seaxes, sword, axe, and the relevant buckle and pin types. Buckles and pins could not be included in the correspondence analysis because they did not occur frequently enough in the relevant grave-good associations. Some spearhead and shield boss types could not be included for the same reason.

Correspondence analysis 1 shown in Figures 5.1a–b presents a result that seems to come reasonably close to a parabola. The matrix of the analysis in Figure 5.1c, however, shows that the smaller and the larger group of graves in Figure 5.1b are linked only by a single type (*sword5*). A separate analysis of the larger group of graves in the matrix (correspondence analysis 2, Figs 5.2a–c) produced a result close to a parabola and retained the order of the graves as it was in the previous analysis. Though a broader basis for the regional sample of graves would be preferable, the result is considered acceptable because the second analysis supports the results of the first, and because both are strenghened by results that have been drawn from the analysis of a national sample of Anglo-Saxon weapon graves (see Ch. 4.1).

The larger group in the analysis is labelled 'MA', the smaller one 'MB'. MA represents types which are generally known to date in the 5th and 6th centuries, and can be subdivided in two sub-groups (Figs 5.1c, 2c), MA1 representing straight-coned shield bosses with concave walls and MA2 concave-coned shield bosses with sloping walls. These groups and sub-groups are considered to represent chronological phases (Phases MA1, MA2 and MB) defined by changes in the design of weapon types.

Phase MA1 is characterised by shield boss types *SOC1–3*. The associated spearheads represent a*ngular, concave* and c*orrugated* types. Spearheads of the *angular* type are relatively long (*medium2a*) and tend to be parallel. Spearheads of the *concave* type appear in three sizes. Those of size *medium1(b)* have a strongly curved outline, those of *medium2(a)* high-positioned points and those of *long1(b)* have low-positioned points. Both the *angular* and *concave* spearheads are often associated with ferrules. The *corrugated* type fall exclusively into Phase MA1. Both *small* and *long1 lanceolate* spearheads can be associated with Phase MA1: spearhead type *LaLo1* from Grave 8 at Bergh Apton and type *LaSma* from Grave 22 at Morning Thorpe were both associated with shield boss type *SOC1*. Phase MA1 includes the earliest short seax.

The correlation of Phases MA1, MA2 and MB with the phases for the graves of females required a tentative subdivision of Phase MA1. Shield bosses of type *SOC1* and spearhead type *AnMed2a* define sub-Phase MA1a, linked with sub-Phase MA1b by spearhead types *CoMed2a* and *ZCoMed2*. Shield bosses of types *SOC2–3* and spearhead types *CoMed1b* and *CoLo1b* define sub-Phase MA1b. This subdivision allows a rough correlation of sub-Phase MA1b with Phase FA2a for females. Eight graves dated to Phase MA1 on the basis of the spearhead types that link sub-Phases MA1a and MA1b (*CoMed2a* and *ZCoMed2*): Grave 52/53 at Bergh Apton, Graves 132, 148, 170 296, 330 and 332 at Morning Thorpe, and Grave 13 at Spong Hill. These graves cannot be assigned to one of the sub-phases.

Phase MA2 is characterised by shield boss types *COS* and *COV*. These are associated with *concave* and *angular* spearheads of almost any length, and *medium1 lanceolate* spears. *Medium2 angular* spearheads are still in use, but are tapering more (*AnMed2b*). *Medium1* and *small angular* spearheads also fall into Phase MA2. The *medium1, medium2,* and *long1 concave* spearheads of Phase MA1 continue in Phase MA2; the *medium1* size with an outline that is less curved than previously (*CoMed1a*), the *medium2* size with low-positioned points (*CoMed2b*), and the *long1* size with high-positioned points (*CoLong1a*).

	5+Blue	ARound	ASlit	bell	buckleI	ConCyl	ConSeg	cuaring	CylPen	CylRound	DarkTL	Dot34	gh1	gh2	gh3	ironring	Koch20	Koch34B	Koch34R	Melon	NoCrTr	NoMelon	NoShort	NoYR	scutiform	sm1	sm2	sm3	SqH1	strapend	TL	wcA	wcB12	wcB7a	wcB7b	wcBar	X1	X2	X3	YellowGr	Phase
MT242	I																																								
MT249																							I								I										FA2
MT251																															I			I							FA2
MT253					I	I			I									I	I												I			I				I	I		FA2
MT256																															I	I									FA2a
MT258							I											I	I																						FB
MT276																		I	I																						FB
MT284AC						I																																			FB
MT288						I		I																					I												FB
MT293GKLNPQR					I																	I	I							I					I						FA2
MT293H					I																																				
MT293M							I	I																																	FB
MT299PQRS								I					I						I																						FB
MT303																		I	I															I	I						FA2
MT304		I			I								I																		I										FA2a
MT306																				I																					FB
MT309			I																																						FB
MT312																																		I							FA2
MT316BFGKHN	I				I													I	I			I																			FA2a
MT321PQST									I									I	I																					I	FA2
MT322					I													I					I																		FB
MT325										I		I					I																								FB
MT328																									I					I											FA1
MT334																															I										FA2a
MT337L					I	I												I	I																					I	FA2
MT337MN																										I															FA1
MT342LMNS						I	I													I																					FB
MT346												I																			I						I				FA1
MT351																																					I				
MT353	I						I																								I						I	I		FA1
MT358ABDJK		I			I													I	I											I							I	I		FA2
MT358LMNPQRSTV						I							I						I																		I		I		FA2b
MT359			I				I	I															I				I														FB
MT360				I	I	I																																			FA2
MT362						I	I											I													I						I	I			FA2a
MT369BCFGHJK																																									FA2b
MT369LMNPTUV					I																																				FA2
MT370						I																															I	I			FA1
MT371CDE																																					I				FA2a
MT371HJ							I	I								I	I	I												I											FB
MT374	I																																								
MT375					I		I	I									I	I	I								I														FB
MT376																I																									FA2/B
MT378			I																				I	I											I						FA2
MT379																						I	I																		FA2
MT384			I	I		I												I	I											I											FB
MT385																							I																		FA2
MT387							I																							I	I				I				I	FA2a
MT393			I	I	I	I			I									I	I											I						I					FA2b
MT396							I	I																					I					I							FA2a
MT397		I				I												I	I															I					I		FA2b
MT400				I			I											I																							FB
MT407						I	I											I	I	I										I											FA2
MT410		I					I										I	I	I	I																					FB
MT415																				I																					FA2
SH02	I									I																	I	I							I					FA2a
SH05	I																									I	I			I										FA1
SH11		I																																							FA2
SH12	I	I				I																																			FA2a
SH14																		I											I												FA2a
SH18																													I		I										FA1/2a
SH19		I																																							FA2
SH22	I																																				I	I			FA1
SH24						I	I							I	I															I	I										FA2b
SH26	I																														I						I				FA1
SH29																I																	I								FA2a
SH37	I	I																													I			I							FA2a
SH38	I	I			I	I			I											I														I							FA2a
SH39		I				I																										I							I	I	FA2a
SH42																				I		I	I				I							I							FA2a
SH44		I			I											I																									FA2

44

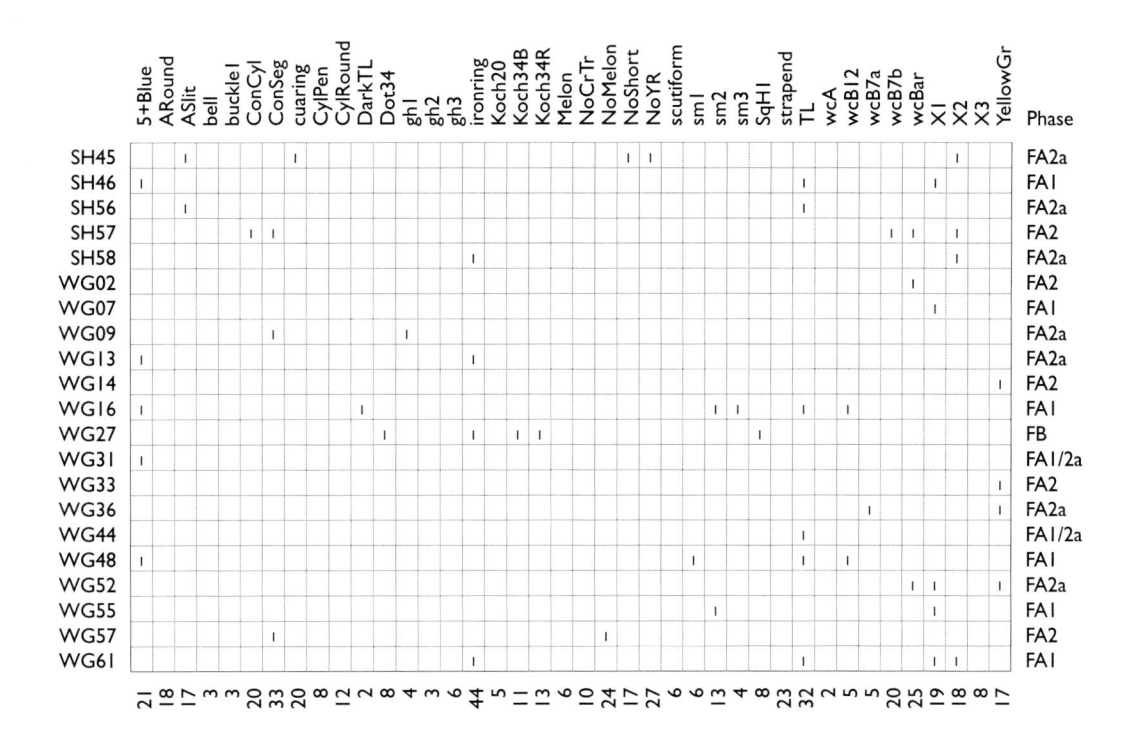

Table 5.1 The four cemeteries. Graves and types used for the definition of Phases FA1, FA2 and FB. Disturbed graves are listed with the letters assigned to objects considered to be from the same grave. The phases to which the graves are assigned are given in the last column. For the abbreviated type names see Ch. 4.3 and 5.3

Small concave spearheads are introduced in Phase MA2, and it seems possible that small spearheads are a feature of Phase MA2 in general. Types *angular* and *concave* can be associated with ferrules. Phase MA2 also includes a continental type of sword and scabbard (*sw1* and *sw2*) and sword beads.

The shield bosses of Phase MB have tall cones with a more or less convex cone, a slightly sloping wall and a narrow flange with knob-headed rivets. The apex is knob- or disc-shaped. The shield bosses are associated with relatively long and almost parallel spearheads, some of them significantly longer than those of the previous phases. It is possible that there is a gap in time between Phases MA2 and MB because they are hardly linked in the correspondence analysis. If such a gap exists, it may indicate a substantial change in the design of weapons from Phase MA2 to Phase MB, or a gap in the evidence from the four cemeteries. For an analysis of the stratigraphical relationships between intercutting dated graves see p.59. Figures 5.26–28 give an overview of the types of weapons defining Phases MA1, MA2 and MB.

5.2.2 Absolute chronology

The absolute chronology of the weapon graves of the four cemeteries relies on absolute chronologies developed for continental and Scandinavian material (see the small-finds analysis in Chapter 3 for details). The spearheads are of little help but some conclusions can be drawn from similarities in the design of shield bosses. A few individual objects such as certain types of buckles are also of some help. Together these can help to date the transition from Phase MA1 to MA2 and from MA2 to MB.

Indications for the absolute dating of Phase MA1 can be derived from shield boss type *COS* with its concave wall and straight cone, attributes dated on the Continent mostly to the 5th century. In Koch's chronology for South Germany they are dated before AD 480 (Koch 2001) but it seems that the type lasted until the very early 6th century. Variations of the type were in use both on the Continent and in South-West Norway. Grave 132 at Morning Thorpe falls into Phase MA1 and includes a buckle with transverse ribs, a type dated on the Continent *c.* AD 480–510. Short seaxes, which are dated to the transition between Phases MA1 and MA2, are a type which can appear as early as AD 480 on the Continent but become more common only around AD 530. The transition between Phases MA1 and MA2 therefore is likely to have occurred soon after AD 500.

Phase MA2 is best dated by shield bosses with a low convex cone and disc-headed rivets and apex (type *COS*). On the Continent, shield bosses with these attributes are given various date ranges that begin between AD 480 and 510 and end between AD 560 and 580, a date span supported by the firesteel in Grave 381 at Morning Thorpe. The two swords in Phase MA2 on the Continent are dated AD 480–510 and AD 525–575 respectively, and a buckle with a square shield-on-tongue to AD 480–530. These dates indicate that Phase MA2 starts between AD 510 and 530 and ends *c.* AD 560/80.

Absolute dates for Phase MB rely mainly on the 'tall' coned shield bosses with knob-headed rivets (type *CAS*). It finds a rough equivalent in Nieveler's and Siegmund's type SBu3b with hemispherical rivets (Nieveler and Siegmund 1999). Such rivets on the Anglo-Saxon bosses seem to be slightly smaller than their continental counterparts. If they were contemporary, they would have been introduced shortly after AD 550/60, which would put the start of Phase MB shortly after AD 560. A sword from this phase is dated to AD 530–580, supporting the start date for Phase MB.

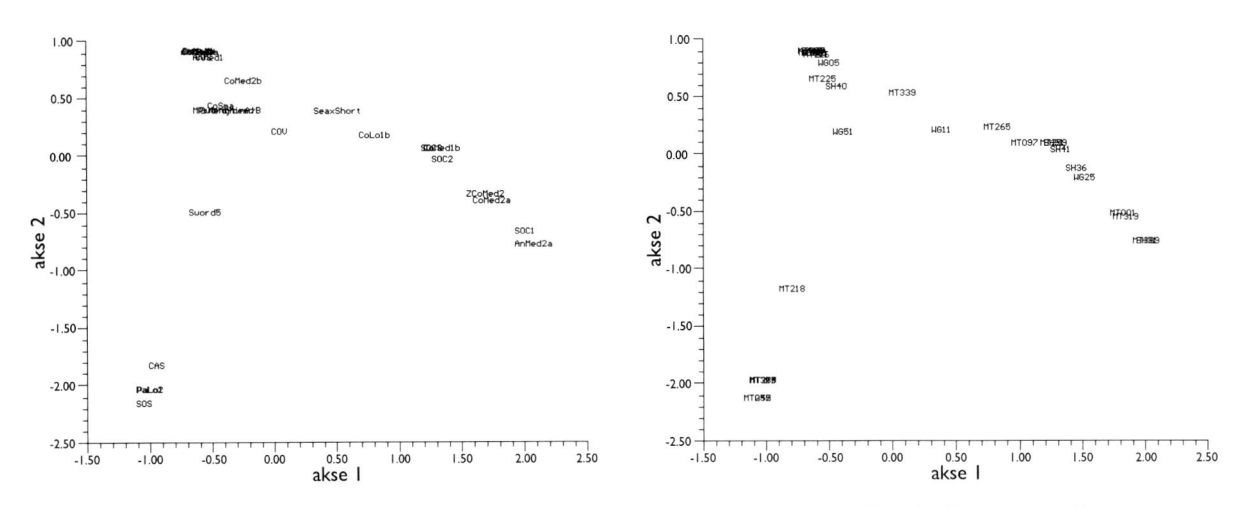

Figure 5.1a The four cemeteries.
Correspondence analysis 1, weapon types

Figure 5.1b The four cemeteries.
Correspondence analysis 1, graves

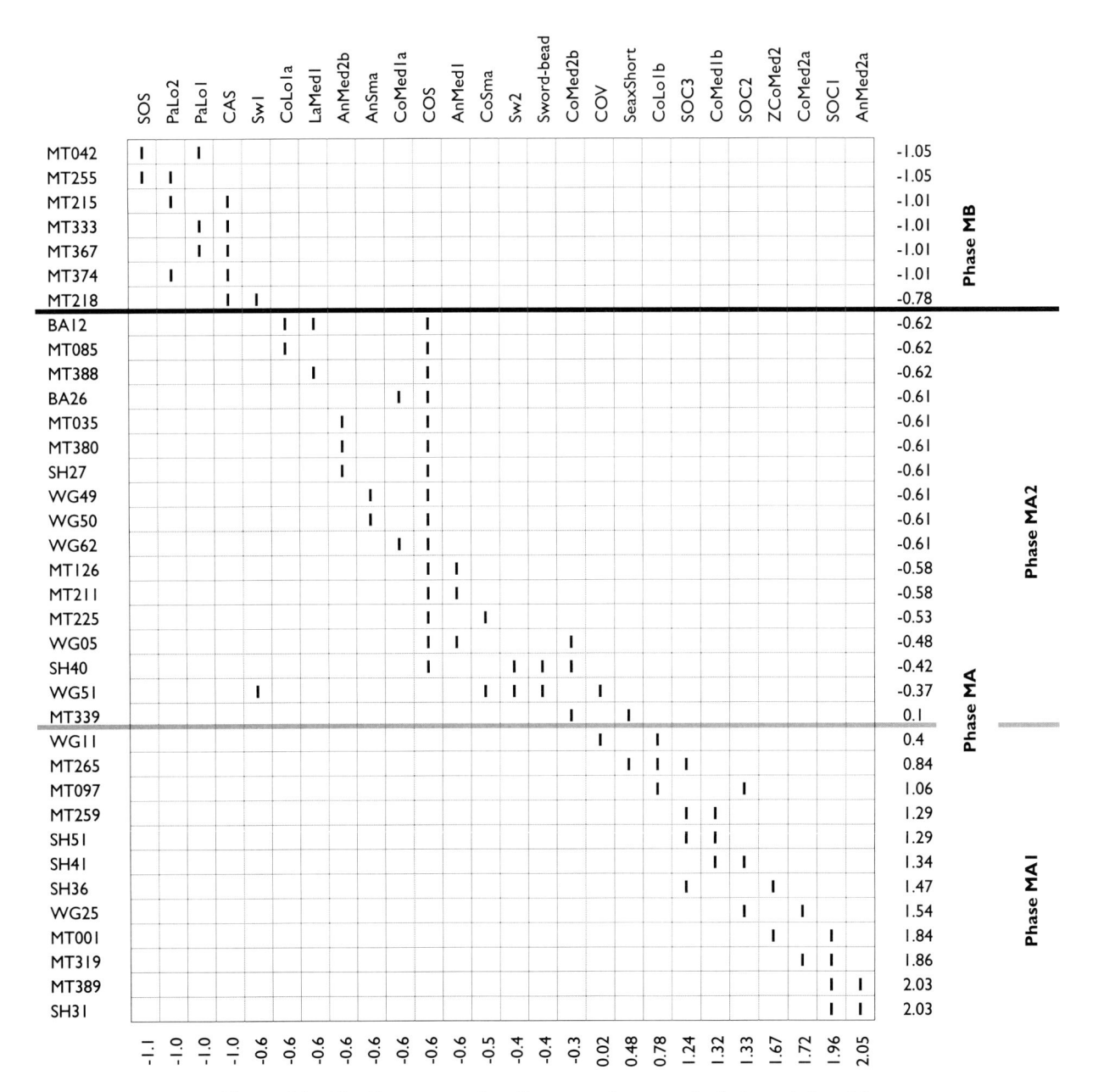

	SOS	PaLo2	PaLo1	CAS	Sw1	CoLo1a	LaMed1	AnMed2b	AnSma	CoMed1a	COS	AnMed1	CoSma	Sw2	Sword-bead	CoMed2b	COV	SeaxShort	CoLo1b	SOC3	CoMed1b	SOC2	ZCoMed2	CoMed2a	SOC1	AnMed2a		
MT042	I		I																								-1.05	
MT255	I	I																									-1.05	
MT215		I		I																							-1.01	Phase MB
MT333		I	I																								-1.01	
MT367		I	I																								-1.01	
MT374	I		I																								-1.01	
MT218					I	I																					-0.78	
BA12						I	I			I																	-0.62	
MT085						I				I																	-0.62	
MT388							I			I																	-0.62	
BA26									I	I																	-0.61	
MT035										I	I																-0.61	
MT380										I	I																-0.61	
SH27										I	I																-0.61	
WG49								I		I																	-0.61	Phase MA2
WG50								I		I																	-0.61	
WG62									I	I																	-0.61	
MT126										I	I																-0.58	
MT211										I	I																-0.58	
MT225										I		I															-0.53	
WG05										I	I				I												-0.48	
SH40										I			I	I	I												-0.42	Phase MA
WG51					I								I	I		I											-0.37	
MT339															I		I										0.1	
WG11																	I	I									0.4	
MT265																		I	I	I							0.84	
MT097																		I			I						1.06	
MT259																			I		I						1.29	
SH51																			I		I						1.29	
SH41																			I			I					1.34	Phase MA1
SH36																			I				I				1.47	
WG25																			I				I				1.54	
MT001																								I	I		1.84	
MT319																								I	I		1.86	
MT389																									I	I	2.03	
SH31																									I	I	2.03	
	-1.1	-1.0	-1.0	-1.0	-0.6	-0.6	-0.6	-0.6	-0.6	-0.6	-0.6	-0.6	-0.5	-0.4	-0.4	-0.3	0.02	0.48	0.78	1.24	1.32	1.33	1.67	1.72	1.96	2.05		

Figure 5.1c The four cemeteries. Correspondence analysis 1, sorted matrix

46

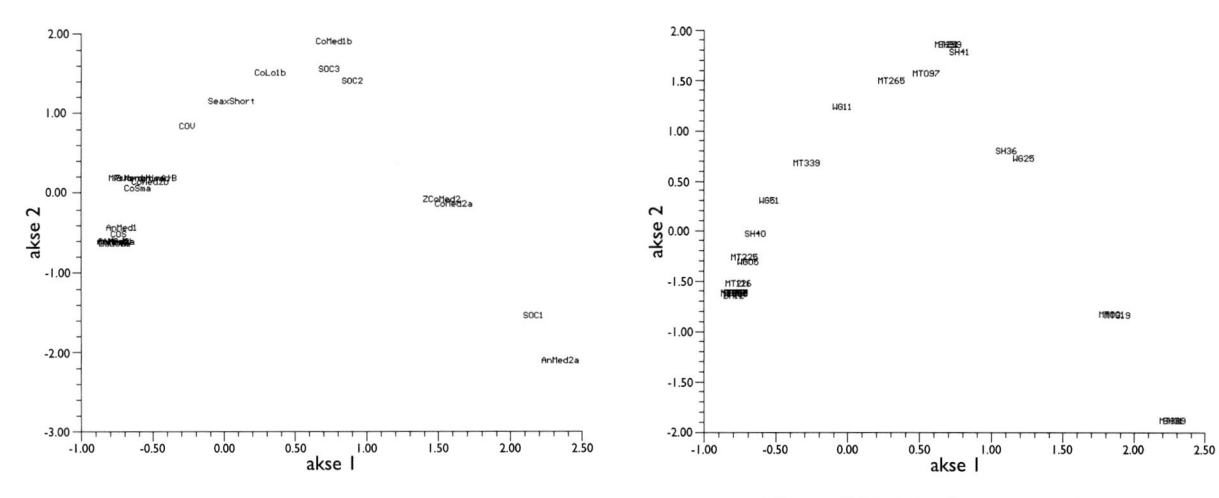

Figure 5.2a The four cemeteries.
Correspondence analysis 2, weapon types

Figure 5.2b The four cemeteries.
Correspondence analysis 2, graves

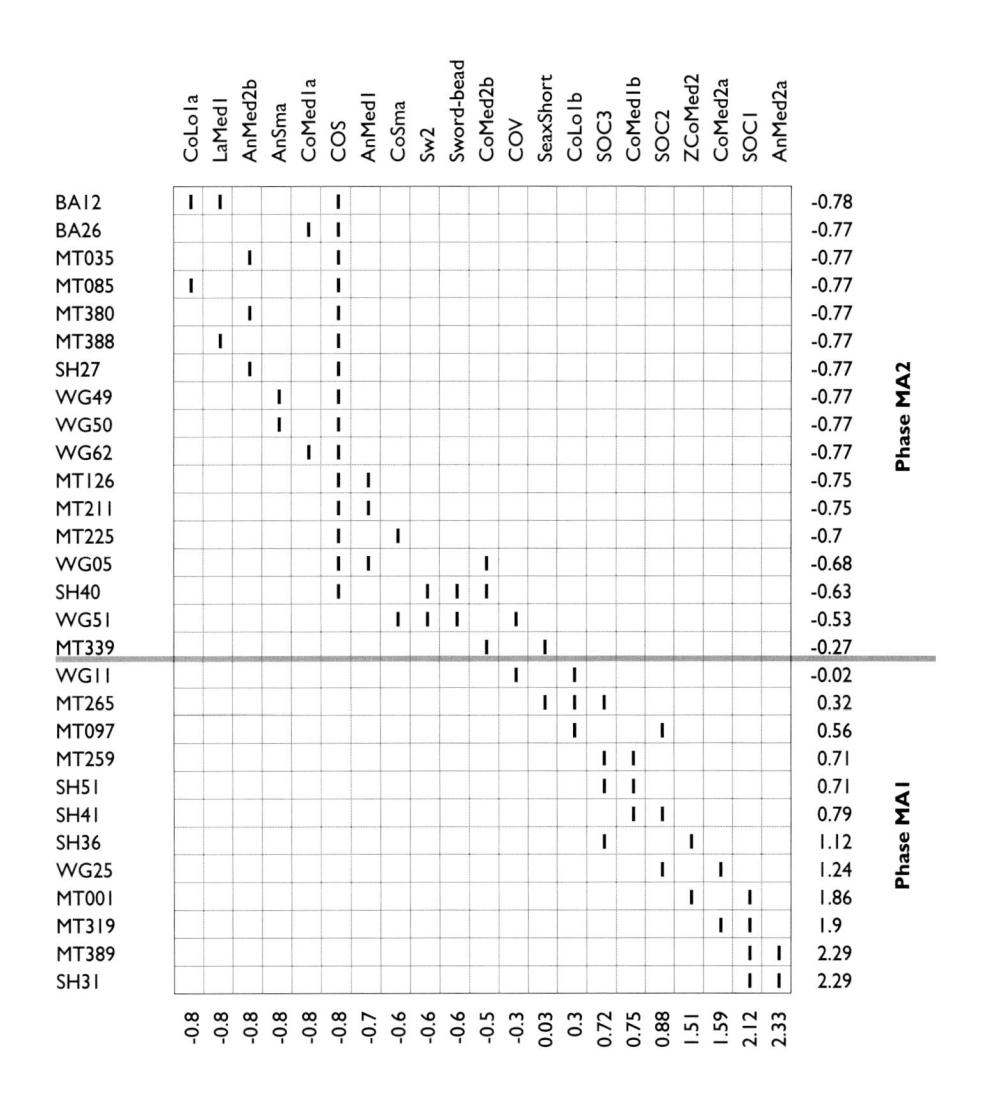

	CoLo1a	LaMed1	AnMed2b	AnSma	CoMed1a	COS	AnMed1	CoSma	Sw2	Sword-bead	CoMed2b	COV	SeaxShort	CoLo1b	SOC3	CoMed1b	SOC2	ZCoMed2	CoMed2a	SOC1	AnMed2a		
BA12	I	I			I																	-0.78	
BA26				I	I																	-0.77	
MT035			I		I																	-0.77	
MT085	I				I																	-0.77	
MT380			I		I																	-0.77	
MT388		I			I																	-0.77	
SH27		I			I																	-0.77	
WG49				I	I																	-0.77	
WG50				I	I																	-0.77	
WG62				I	I																	-0.77	Phase MA2
MT126						I	I															-0.75	
MT211						I	I															-0.75	
MT225						I		I														-0.7	
WG05						I	I			I												-0.68	
SH40						I			I	I	I											-0.63	
WG51									I	I	I	I										-0.53	
MT339											I		I									-0.27	
WG11														I	I							-0.02	
MT265														I	I	I						0.32	
MT097														I			I					0.56	
MT259															I	I						0.71	
SH51															I	I						0.71	
SH41															I	I						0.79	Phase MA1
SH36															I		I					1.12	
WG25															I		I					1.24	
MT001																	I	I				1.86	
MT319																	I	I				1.9	
MT389																			I	I		2.29	
SH31																			I	I		2.29	
	-0.8	-0.8	-0.8	-0.8	-0.8	-0.8	-0.7	-0.6	-0.6	-0.6	-0.5	-0.3	0.03	0.3	0.72	0.75	0.88	1.51	1.59	2.12	2.33		

Figure 5.2c The four cemeteries. Correspondence analysis 2, sorted matrix

5.3 Female dress accessories and associated objects

5.3.1 Relative chronology

In the archaeological record, East Anglian female dress is represented mostly by beads, brooches, wrist-clasps, buckles and relatively few pins and pendants. The function of girdle-hangers is not entirely clear but they can be considered to fall under dress accessories as objects attached to the garments of females. Dress pins form a heterogeneous type of accessory probably serving a variety of functions, and the four cemeteries produced few pins of the same types. Scutiform pendants, in contrast, form a small but homogeneous group and are therefore included. Buckles are a common accessory in female dress, but few types can be shown to have relatively short date ranges and those that have are not common enough for a correspondence analysis with the exception of type *buckle1*.

It has been possible to demonstrate changes in Anglo-Saxon glass bead fashion which help to date a large number of graves across Anglo-Saxon England (Brugmann 2004). The correspondence analysis based on the glass beads from the Norfolk graves in the national sample used for this research can be improved with the help of the additional *Norfolk* types defined in Chapter 4. Only Morning Thorpe produced enough beads to merit a correspondence based on that site alone (correspondence analysis 3, Figs 5.3a-c). This reproduced the bead groups defined in Brugmann (2004). Group A1 is represented by types *Traffic Light* and *5+Blue*, Group A2 by *Constricted Cylinder, Yellow Green* and *Norfolk* types, and beads of Group B are associated with silver *bell* beads. Type *Constricted Segmented* ('gold-in-glass') is included in the analysis to test the association of this common type of bead in Group A2 with the newly defined types *Norfolk Short* and *Norfolk Crossing Trails*. All of these new *Norfolk* types are associated with beads of Group A2 and are therefore in the following considered to be part of this group.

A correspondence analysis that adds the glass beads of the other three cemeteries to the Morning Thorpe beads can include *Melon* from Group A2b and sort these between Groups A2 and B (correspondence analysis 4, Figs 5.4a-c). Relatively few graves from Westgarth Gardens are represented in this analysis because as a Suffolk site, it did not produce any of the *Norfolk* bead types. Group A1 includes two graves from this site, and bead Groups A2 and B are represented by only one grave each from Westgarth Gardens. Bergh Apton is not represented in bead Group A1 and Spong Hill is not represented in Group B. This suggests that Spong Hill has an earlier date range than Bergh Apton but that both sites were in use when bead Group A2 was in fashion (Brugmann 2004).

On the background of the bead chronology it is possible to gain some idea of the overall period of use of pendants, wrist-clasps, girdle-hangers and certain types of brooches. A correspondence analysis of the bead types and of cruciform brooches ('X-form'), florid cruciform brooches ('floridX'), small-long brooches ('smlong'), great square-headed brooches ('sqheaded'), penannular and annular brooches, wrist-clasps ('wrclasp'), pendants, and girdle-hangers ('girdleh') retains the sequence of beads of Groups A1, A2, A2b, and B (Fig. 5.5a–c).

Small-long and cruciform brooches are mostly associated with beads of Group A1 but the association of some of these brooches with square-headed brooches and pendants distorts the parabola because these are the main types that link beads of Group A2 with beads of Group B but in a few cases are also associated with early beads. This suggests that cruciform, small-long and square-headed brooches and pendants as such have long date ranges which only careful stylistic analysis can shorten in relation to individual types. Grave 18 at Spong Hill with a combination of a great square-headed brooch, a small-long brooch and Traffic Light beads is the most obvious example. A long date range is also suggested for florid cruciform brooches. Associations of these brooches with bead types of all three groups suggests that florid cruciform brooches lasted longer than simpler forms of cruciform brooches, but the tendency is not as clear as one might expect. Penannular brooches are associated with beads of Groups A1 and A2, and annular brooches as the most numerous brooch type in the correspondence analysis are mostly associated with beads of Group A2 but also with beads of Groups A1 and B. Wrist-clasps and girdle-hangers are associated with beads of Groups A1 and A2 but not with beads of Group B. The only exception is the fragment of a girdle-hanger in Grave 214 at Morning Thorpe.

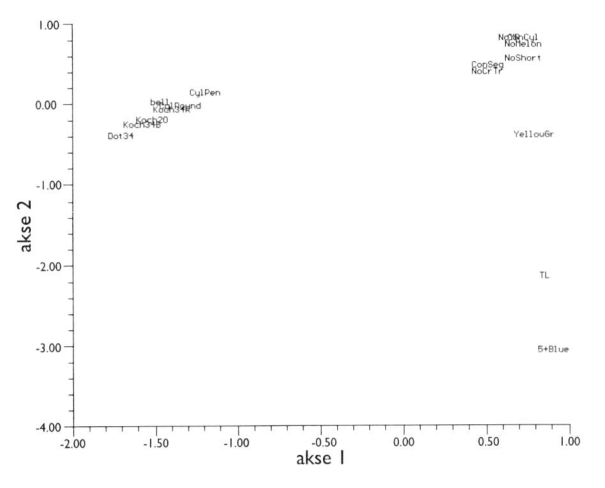

Figure 5.3a Morning Thorpe.
Correspondence analysis 3, bead types

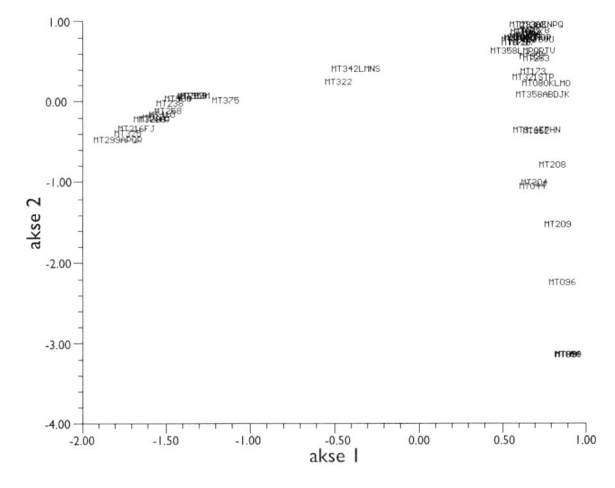

Figure 5.3b Morning Thorpe.
Correspondence analysis 3, graves

Phase	Dot34	Koch34B	Koch20	bell	Koch34R	CylRound	CylPen	ConSeg	NoCrTr	NoYR	NoShort	ConCyl	NoMelon	YellowGr	TL	5+Blue	
								B				**A2**			**A1**		
MT299APQR	I																-1.79
MT325	I	I															-1.73
MT216FJ	I	I	I														-1.68
MT371HJ	I	I	I		I	I											-1.59
MT288	I	I			I	I											-1.58
MT276		I			I												-1.56
MT410		I	I		I	I											-1.53
MT258		I			I	I											-1.49
MT238				I	I	I											-1.48
MT384				I	I		I										-1.43
MT400			I	I			I										-1.43
MT293M					I	I											-1.34
MT359					I	I											-1.34
MT375		I	I		I	I	I										-1.15
MT322			I			I											-0.48
MT342LMNS					I	I		I	I								-0.38
MT379									I	I							0.57
MT358LMPQRTV								I			I						0.62
MT106								I		I							0.62
MT050								I	I			I					0.62
MT207								I				I					0.62
MT360								I			I						0.62
MT092								I		I	I	I					0.65
MT108DJGVU								I	I	I		I					0.65
MT108MNOP								I	I	I		I					0.65
MT407								I	I	I		I					0.65
MT393								I		I	I	I	I				0.66
MT044									I					I			0.68
MT337								I		I	I	I					0.68
IMT303									I			I					0.68
MT397									I			I					0.68
MT173								I			I		I				0.68
MT321STP								I				I	I				0.68
MT304								I						I			0.69
MT253								I		I	I	I	I				0.7
MT362								I				I		I			0.7
MT316EFHN								I		I	I					I	0.7
MT293AENPQ									I		I	I					0.7
MT378									I	I	I						0.7
MT358ABDJK								I		I	I		I				0.74
MT080KLMO												I	I				0.76
MT208									I			I	I				0.8
MT209												I	I				0.83
MT096												I	I	I			0.86
MT016														I	I		0.89
MT090															I	I	0.89
MT091															I	I	0.89
MT353															I	I	0.89
	-1.73	-1.6	-1.54	-1.49	-1.42	-1.37	-1.22	0.49	0.49	0.62	0.7	0.7	0.7	0.77	0.83	0.88	

Figure 5.3c Morning Thorpe. Correspondence analysis 3, bead types, sorted matrix

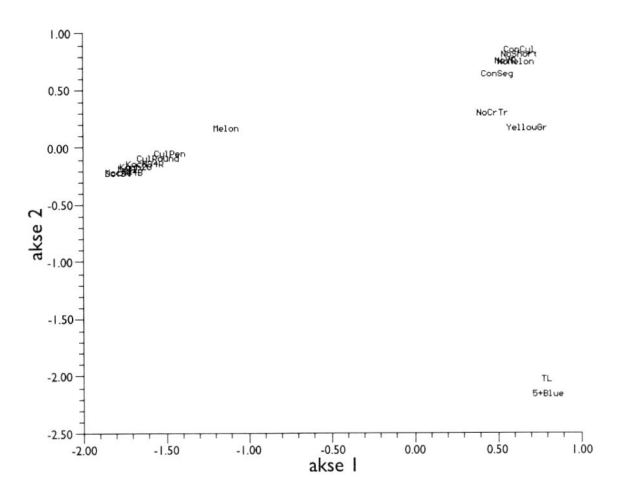

Figure 5.4a The four cemeteries.
Correspondence analysis 4, bead types

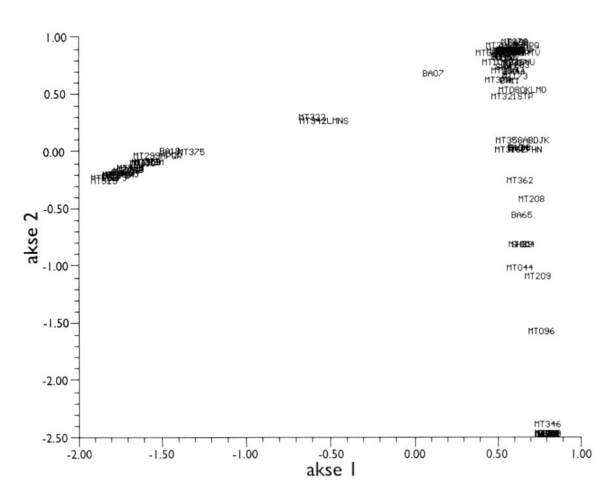

Figure 5.4b The four cemeteries.
Correspondence analysis 4, graves

The associations of the various types of metalwork with dated bead types generally support the results of Høilund Nielsen's analysis of the relative periods in which cruciform, small-long, annular, great square-headed brooches and wrist-clasps were in use (Høilund Nielsen 1997, fig. 28). A correspondence analysis that takes into account the typologies developed in Chapter 4 for stylistic details of the small-long, cruciform, florid cruciform, annular and square-headed brooches, wrist-clasps and girdle-hangers can refine the relative chronological sequence indicated by the glass beads from the four cemeteries.

In correspondence analysis 6 shown in Figures 5.6a–c, the bead types from the previous correspondence analysis are combined with the types of brooches, wrist-clasps and girdle-hangers described in detail in Chapter 4. In this correspondence analysis the sequence of bead Groups A1, A2, A2b and B is retained. The types of small-long and cruciform brooches (*sm1–3* and *X1–3*) are split into overlapping sequences associated with beads of Groups A1 and A2. The positions of the types of wrist-clasps in the sorted matrix suggest an overlapping sequence of *wcB12, wcB7a, wcBar,* and *wcB7*. Type *wcA* could be included in the correspondence analysis with only two examples and are therefore omitted. If included, they would appear in the earliest part of the sequence. The sequences of annular brooches with slots or round holes for the attachment of their pins (*ASlot* and *ARound*) and of girdle-hanger types *gh1–3* are pronounced. Buckles, square-headed brooches and pendants are represented by a single type each, *buckle1* and *SqH1*, and by scutiform pendants. This brooch type and in particular the scutiform pendants link bead Groups A2 and B, now without putting pressure on the sequence.

A definition of phases based on the division of a sequence has to be created with the help of forced choices. The graphs showing the graves and types on the first and second axes of the correspondence analysis (Figs 5.6a–c) give a basis on which these choices can best be made. Both the sorted matrix and the graphs show that there is a marked change in the association of metal dress accessories corresponding with the bead associations labelled Groups F (= female) A and FB. Bead Group A2b shows a closer association to Group FB than to Group FA. These two groups are interpreted as a chronological sequence, Phase FA and Phase FB. Bead Groups A1 and A2 and associated metal dress accessories form Phase FA and bead Groups A2b and B and associated metal dress accessories form Phase FB. The main link between these two phases is formed by scutiform pendants.

A subdivision of the types of objects associated with bead Groups A1 and A2 has to be tentative. The gap between types *sm3* and *wcB7a/ASlot* in Figure 5.6a is relatively wide and can be used to divide types of bead Group A1 and brooch types *sm1–2* and *X1–2,* wrist-clasp *wcB12* and girdle-hanger *gh1* from beads of Group A2, annular brooches (*ASlot* and *ARound*), cruciform brooches of type *X3*, wrist-clasps *wcB7a/b* and *wcBar*, and girdle-hangers *gh2–3*. The type associations including beads of Group A1 are labelled Phase FA1, the associations dominated by beads of Group A2 are labelled Phase FA2.

The sorted matrix of the correspondence analysis shows a gradual change in the type associations in the course of Phase FA2. A tentative sub-division can be made on the basis of this matrix and of the graph showing the first and second axis. Small-long brooch type *sm3*, annular brooches *ASlot*, wrist-clasps *wcB7a* and *wcBar* and beads of type *YellowGreen* are more common in the earlier part of the sequence; annular brooches *ARound*, wrist-clasps *wcB7b* and girdle-hangers *gh3* are more common in the later part (Figs 5.6a–b). On this basis, some graves can be tentatively assigned to sub-Phases FA2a and FA2b.

Of the four cemeteries, only Morning Thorpe is large enough to reproduce substantial parts of the sequence if the graves are analysed by themselves. The sorted matrix of correspondence analysis 7 in Figure 5.7 cannot include the wrist-clasp type *wcB12*, but the remaining matrix reproduced the sequence of the objects defining Phases FA1, FA2 and FB. An analysis of Bergh Apton would be problematic because there would be more types than graves in the analysis, an analysis of Spong Hill could include only ten types and fifteen graves, and an analysis of Westgarth Gardens would be based on even less data, partly due to the lack of *Norfolk* bead types discussed above. A combined analysis of Spong Hill and Bergh Apton (correspondence analysis 8, Fig. 5.8), however, can be based on more substantial data and shows the overall sequence of the types in Phases FA1, FA2a, FA2b and FB.

Spong Hill	Westgarth Gardens	Bergh Apton	Phase	Dot34	Koch34B	bell	Koch20	Koch34R	CylRound	CylPen	Melon	NoCr-Tr	ConSeg	NoYR	NoMelon	ConCyl	NoShort	YellowGr	TL	5+Blue	
				B							A2b	A2							A1		
			MT325	I	I																-1.85
			MT216FJ	I	I		I														-1.82
	WG		WG27	I	I		I														-1.8
			MT276		I		I														-1.77
			MT288	I	I		I	I													-1.76
			MT371HJ	I	I		I	I	I												-1.75
		BA	BA56	I	I			I		I											-1.74
		BA	BA59		I			I													-1.73
			MT238			I		I	I												-1.71
			MT384			I		I		I											-1.69
			MT400			I		I		I											-1.69
			MT258				I	I	I												-1.69
			MT410		I		I	I	I		I										-1.62
			MT293M					I	I												-1.59
			MT359					I	I												-1.59
			MT299APQR	I						I											-1.53
		BA	BA18						I	I	I										-1.46
			MT375		I		I	I	I	I		I									-1.33
			MT322			I						I									-0.61
			MT342LMNS				I	I			I		I								-0.54
		BA	BA07								I		I	I	I						0.11
			MT379								I			I							0.5
		BA	BA45								I	I									0.52
			MT050								I		I	I							0.54
			MT207								I		I								0.55
	WG		WG57								I		I								0.55
SH			SH42								I		I			I					0.55
			MT358LMPQRTV								I					I					0.56
			MT360								I			I							0.56
SH			SH24								I			I							0.56
SH			SH57								I		I								0.56
		BA	BA21								I	I				I					0.56
			MT106								I	I		I							0.56
			MT108DJGVU							I		I		I		I					0.56
		BA	BA11								I	I					I				0.57
			MT092								I	I	I	I							0.57
			MT108MNOP								I	I		I		I					0.57
			MT407								I	I		I		I					0.57
			MT321STP							I		I				I					0.58
			MT303									I		I							0.58
			MT397									I		I							0.58
		BA	BA29								I		I	I							0.58
		BA	BA35								I			I	I						0.58
			MT393								I		I	I	I						0.58
SH			SH45								I			I							0.59
			MT293AENPQ								I	I	I								0.59
			MT173								I		I			I					0.6
		BA	BA44								I		I		I	I					0.6
			MT337								I		I		I	I					0.6
			MT378								I				I	I					0.6
			MT253								I		I	I	I	I					0.61
		BA	BA03										I	I							0.62
		BA	BA34								I	I		I					I		0.62
			MT316EFHN								I	I			I				I		0.62
			MT362								I		I			I					0.63
SH			SH38								I		I	I					I		0.63
			MT044							I								I			0.63
			MT304							I								I			0.64
SH			SH39								I							I			0.64
		BA	BA65							I		I	I					I	I		0.64
			MT080KLMO										I			I					0.65
			MT358ABDJK									I	I	I							0.65
			MT208													I	I	I			0.7
			MT209														I	I			0.74
			MT096													I	I	I			0.76
			MT346															I			0.8
	WG		WG16															I	I		0.8
			MT016															I	I		0.8
			MT090															I	I		0.8
			MT091															I	I		0.8
			MT353															I	I		0.8
SH			SH02															I	I		0.8
SH			SH05															I	I		0.8
SH			SH26															I	I		0.8
SH			SH37															I	I		0.8
SH			SH46															I	I		0.8
	WG		WG48															I	I		0.8
				-1.8	-1.8	-1.8	-1.7	-1.7	-1.6	-1.5	-1.2	0.45	0.48	0.53	0.59	0.61	0.61	0.66	0.77	0.78	

Figure 5.4c The Four Cemeteries. Correspondence analysis 4, bead types, sorted matrix

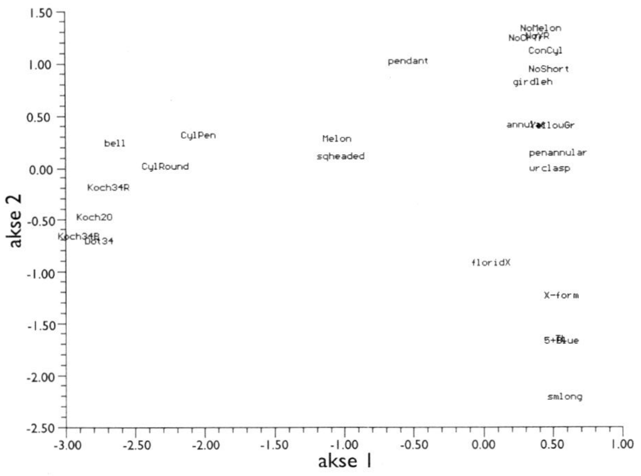

Figure 5.5a The four cemeteries.
Correspondence analysis 5, female dress accessories

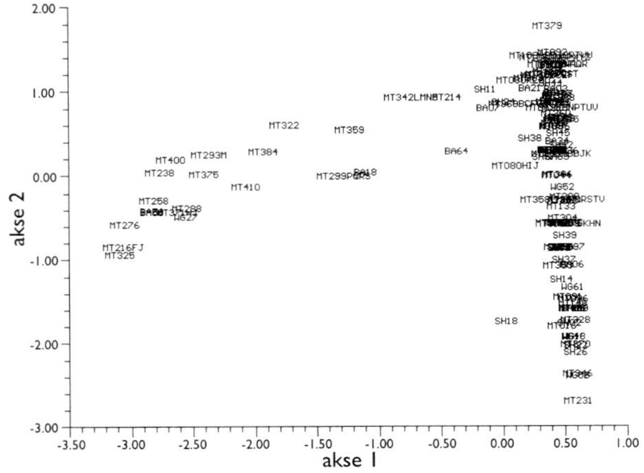

Figure 5.5b The four cemeteries.
Correspondence analysis 5, graves

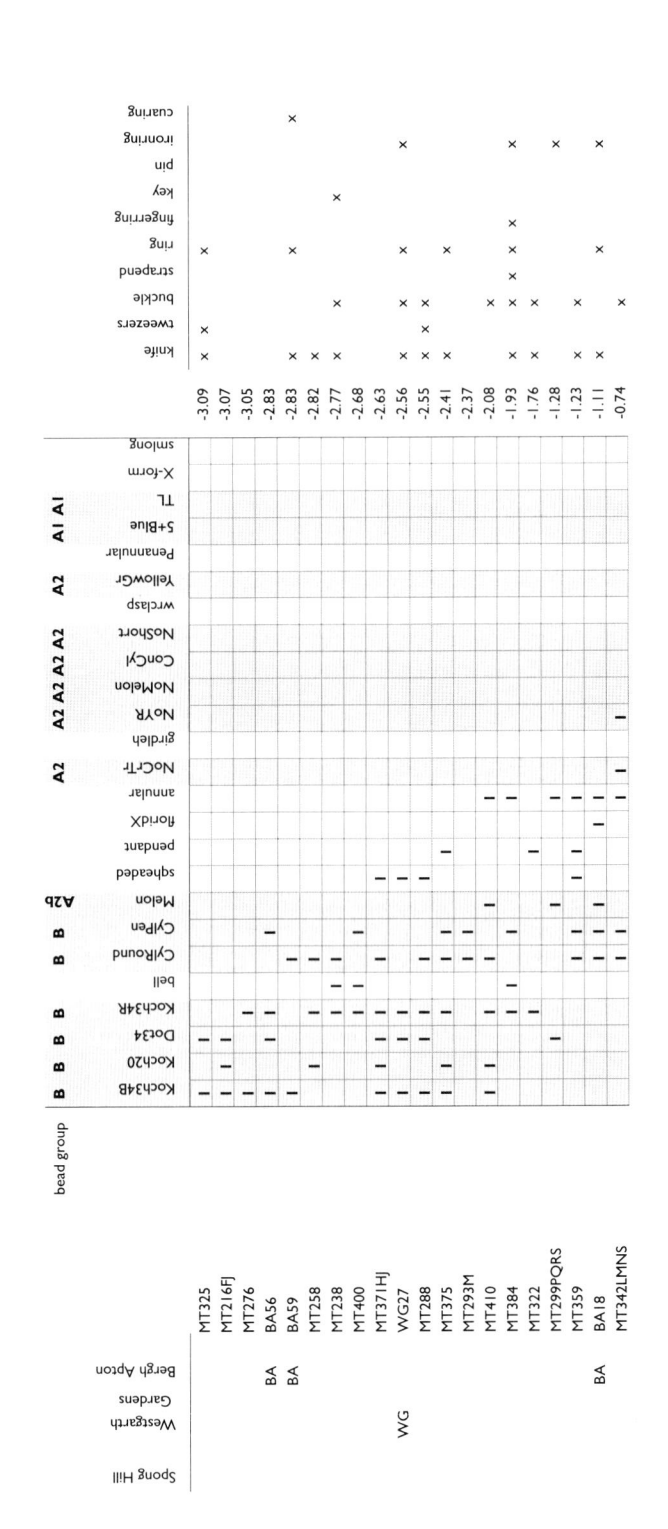

52

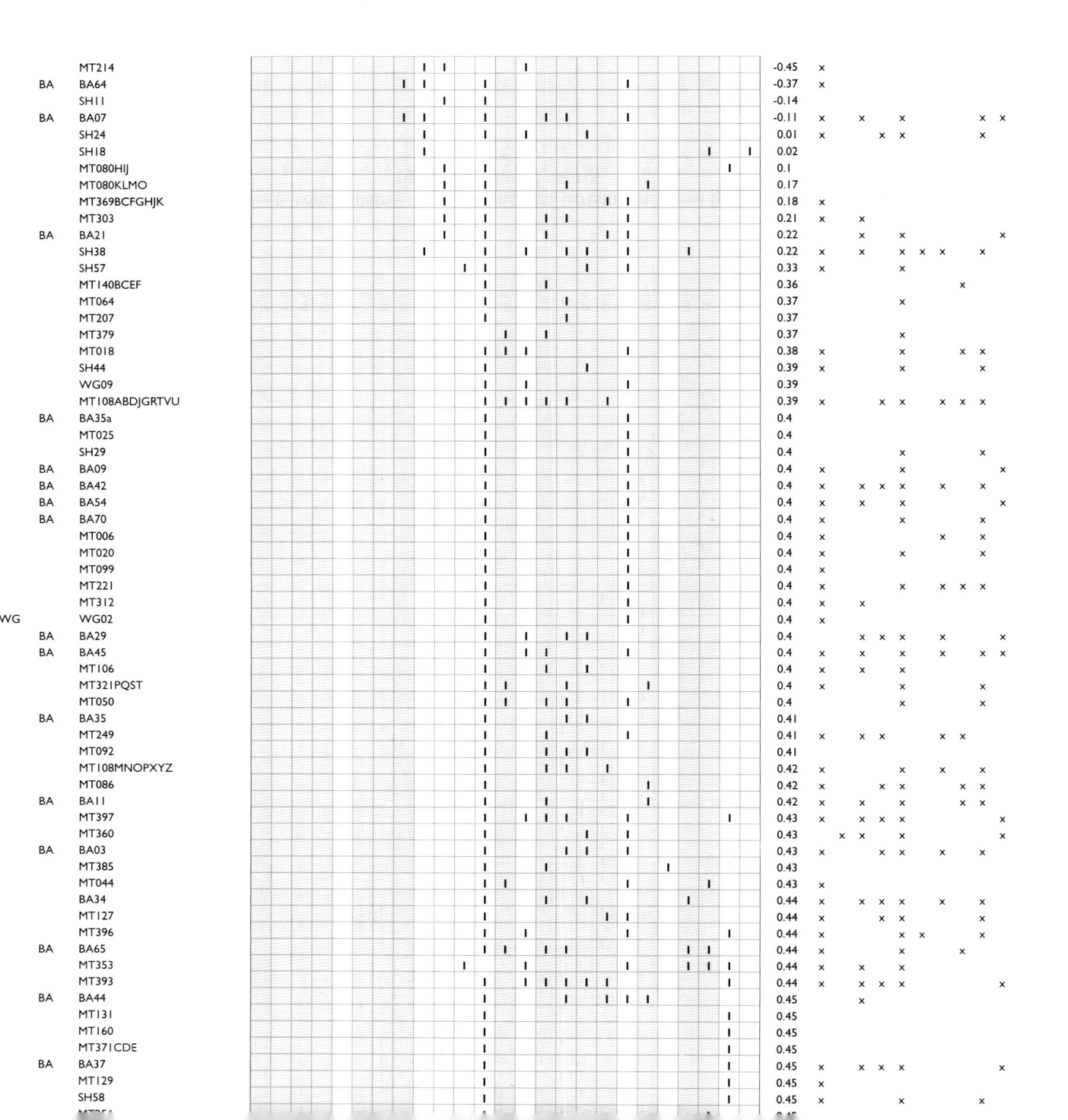

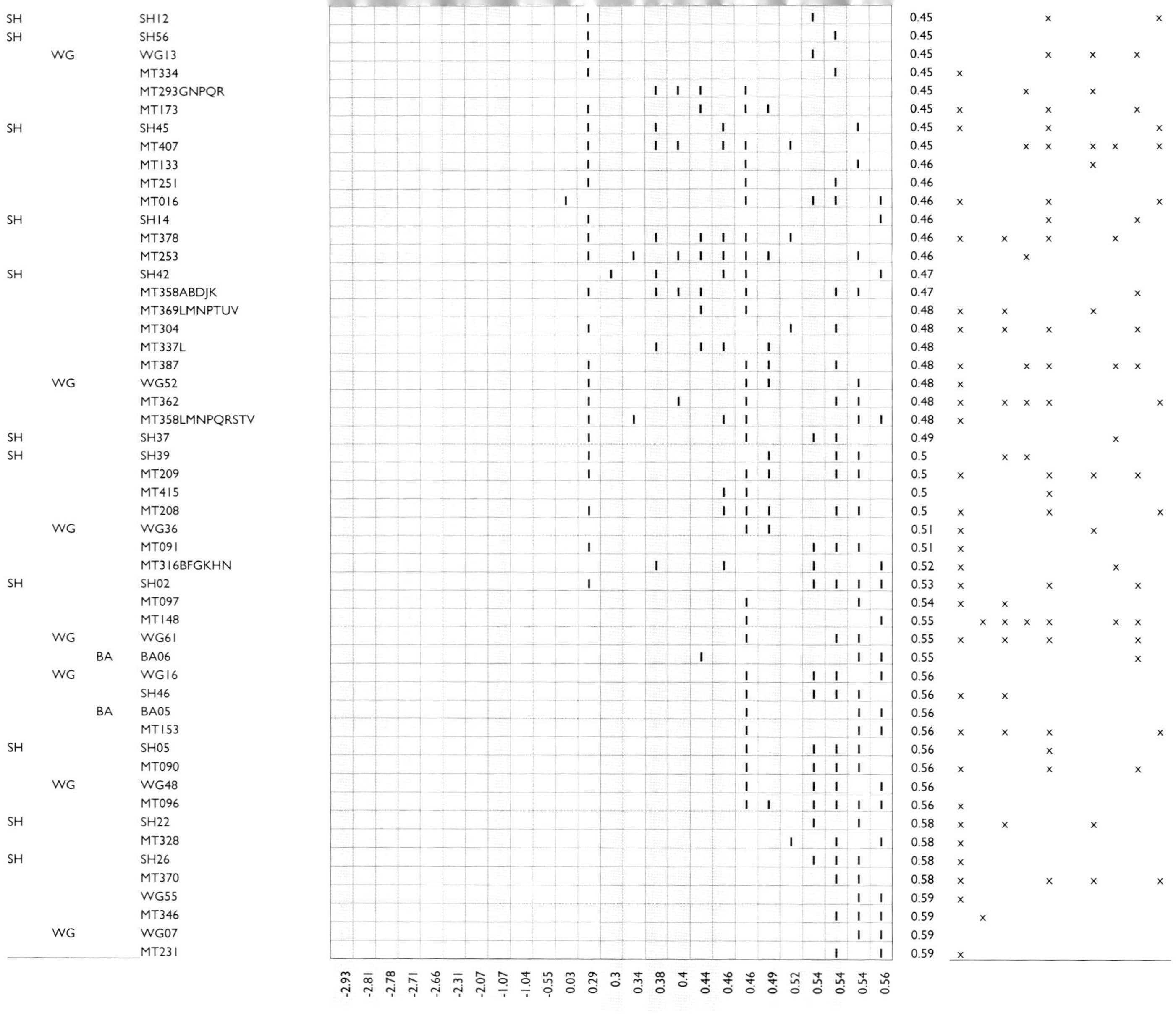

Figure 5.5c The four cemeteries. Correspondence analysis 5, sorted matrix. Associations with certain functional types of objects not included in the analysis are shown to the right of the sorted matrix

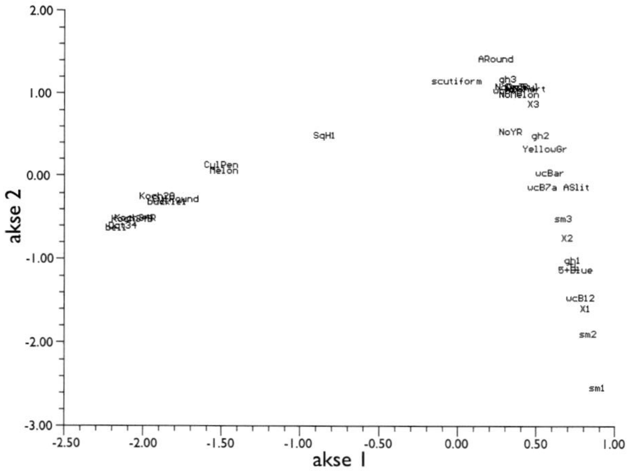

Figure 5.6a The four cemeteries.
Correspondence analysis 6, female dress accessories

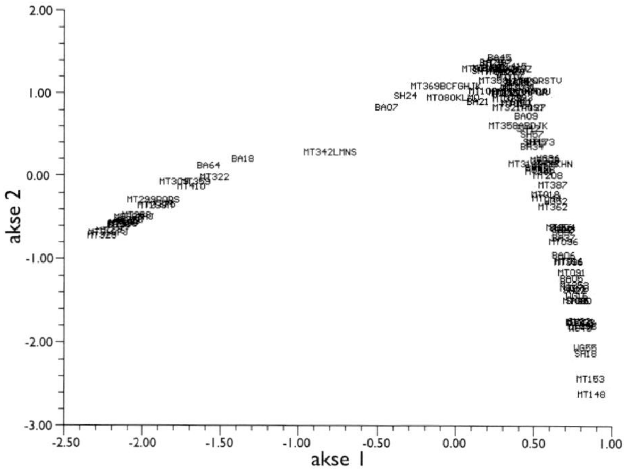

Figure 5.6b The four cemeteries.
Correspondence analysis 6, graves

55

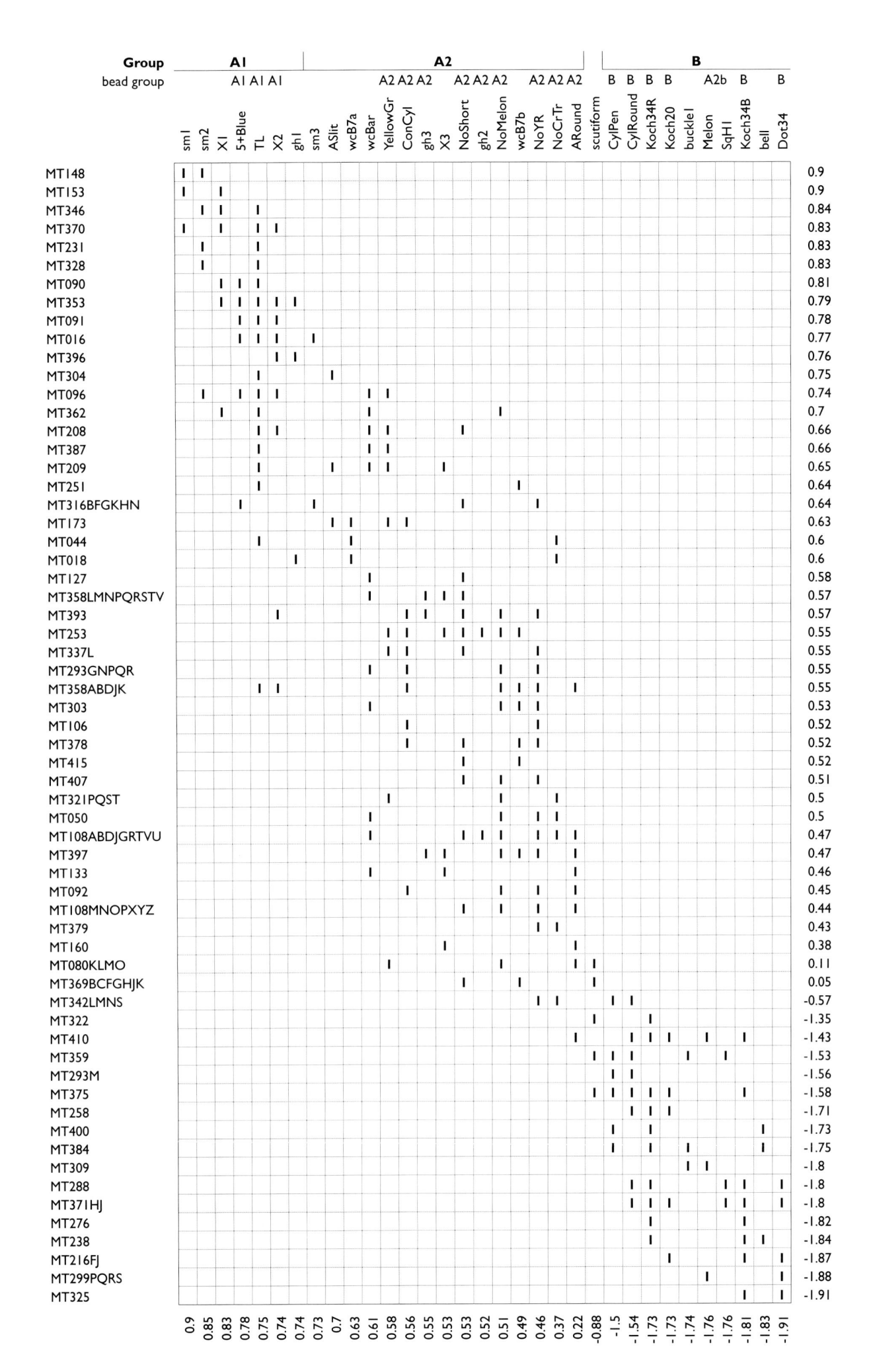

Figure 5.7 Morning Thorpe. Correspondence analysis 7, sorted matrix

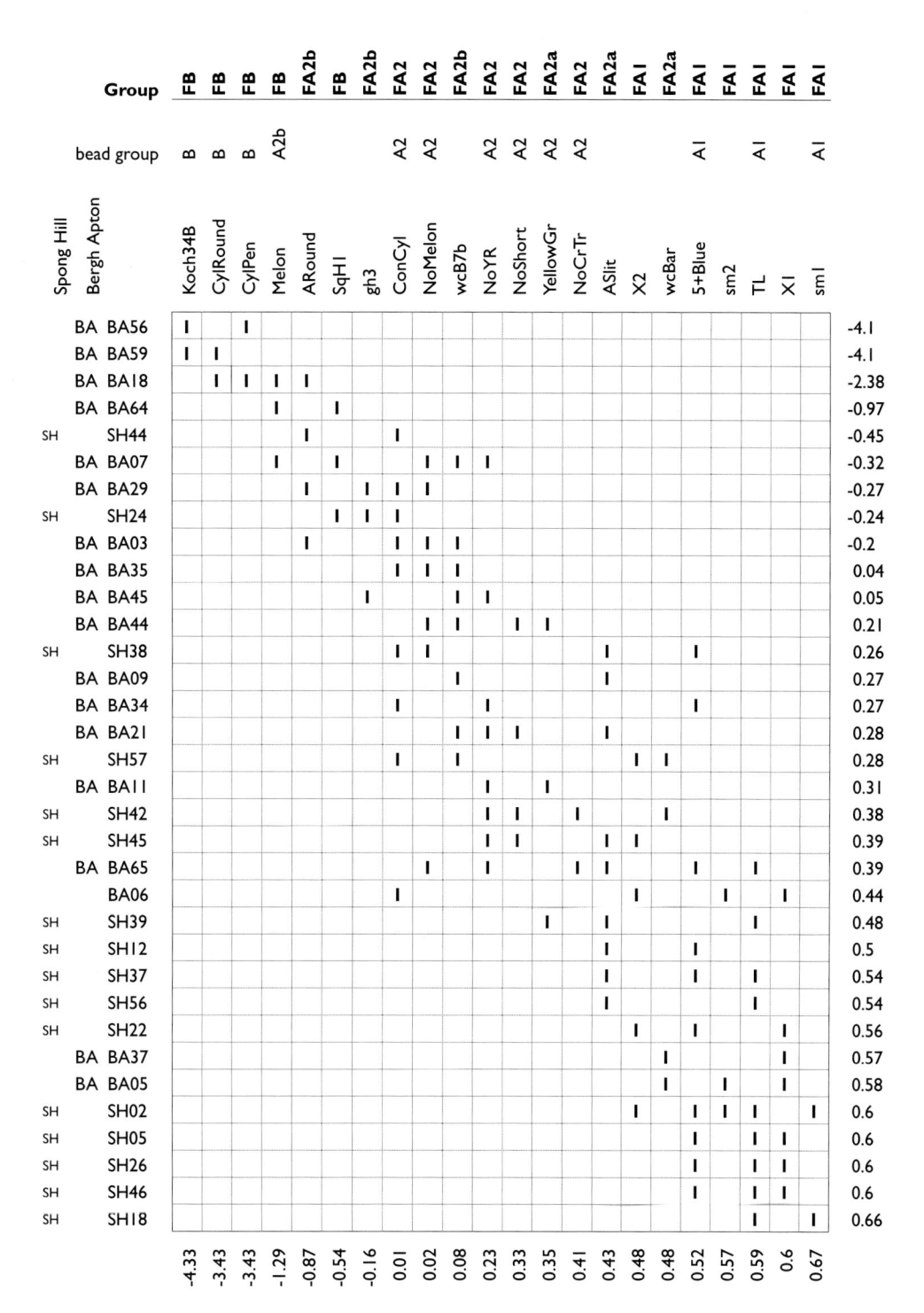

Figure 5.8 Spong Hill and Bergh Apton. Correspondence analysis 10, sorted matrix

The earlier part of the sequence is dominated by Spong Hill, the later part by Bergh Apton.

Figure 5.9 gives an overview of the main periods in which the various types of brooches, wrist-clasps *etc.* were in use. It shows that the bead Groups A1, A2, A2b and B are not exactly equated with Phases FA1, FA2 and FB. The definition of Phase FA2 is based on both annular brooches and beads of Group A2. The end of Phase FA2 is marked by the introduction of beads of Group A2b, which came into fashion before beads of Group B were introduced. Bead groups A2b and B and the square-headed brooches of type *SqH1* define Phase FB. The only brooch of type *SqH1* in a pronounced Phase FA2 context comes from Grave 24 at Spong Hill and represents a forerunner of Hines' Groups XVI–XVIII (see Ch. 4.3.1).

5.3.2 Absolute chronology

There are no coin- or C14-dated graves from the four cemeteries. Therefore absolute dates for Phases FA1, FA2 and FB need to be derived from external sources. The absolute date ranges for the beads given in Brugmann (2004, table 3) give some indication: comparison with continental frameworks suggests that beads of Group A2 were introduced in the late 5th century and that beads of Group A1 went out of fashion in the early 6th century. This suggests a late 5th to early 6th-century date for Phase FA2. Bead Group A2b, the earliest in Phase FB, was introduced on the Continent *c.* AD 530 and bead Group B in the mid 6th century. This suggests a beginning for Phase FB between *c.* AD 530 and 550. The beginning of Phase FA1 and the end of Phase FB are somewhat vague in absolute terms.

The few external datings available for other types of objects support the absolute dates suggested by the beads. The type of firesteel associated with a wrist-clasp of type *wcB7a* of Phase FA2a (and a pair of equal-armed brooches and a pin with spangles) in Grave 36 at Westgarth Gardens is dated to the late 5th and early 6th century on the Continent. The same date range applies to the firesteel in Grave 29 at Bergh Apton dated in Phase FA2b on the basis of annular brooches of type *ARound*, girdle-hangers *gh3* and beads of Group A2. Grave 24 at Spong Hill combined girdle-hangers of type *gh3* and beads of Group A2 with a square-headed brooch of type *SqH1* and thus together with Grave 7 at Bergh Apton marks the transition from Phase FA2 to FB. The Spong Hill grave also included a copper-alloy bowl with a beaded rim and a weaving batten. On the Continent the type of bowl is dated in the late 5th and first half of the 6th century. The batten represents an early type which was probably not buried before *c.* AD 530 but probably before the mid 6th century. This fits well with a presumed beginning of Phase FB between AD 530 and 550.

The only explicitly female dress item dated after the mid 7th century is the dress pin from Grave 47 at Westgarth Gardens. Further objects dated after the mid 7th century by external evidence are the lace-tags from Grave 2 at Morning Thorpe and the iron buckle from Grave 350 at Morning Thorpe. Their presence suggests that Morning Thorpe and Westgarth Gardens were in use after the mid 7th century, though they did not produce the range of grave-goods considered typical of the 'Final' Phase.

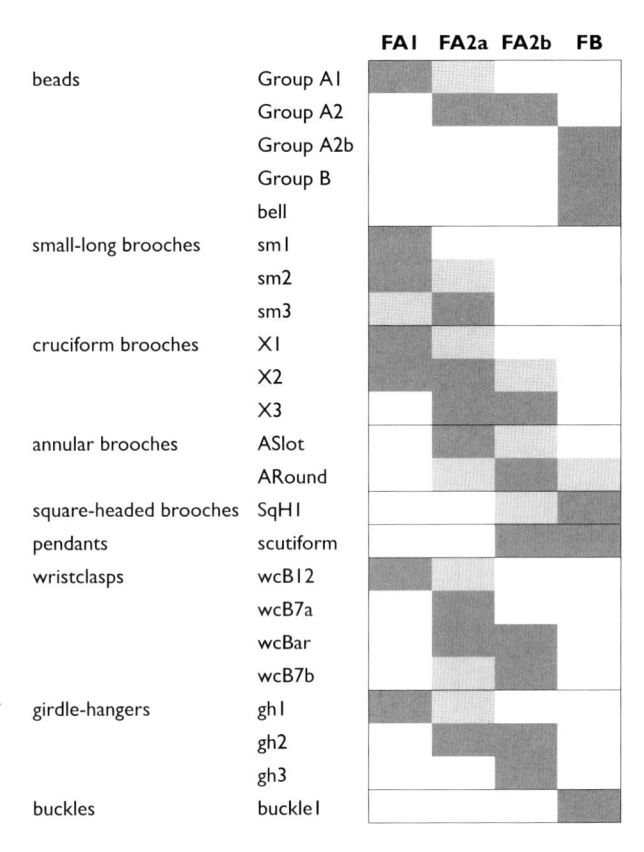

Figure 5.9 The four cemeteries. Date range of some female dress accessories. Dark grey indicates the main occurrence of a type of object in Phases FA1, FA2a, FA2b or FB; light grey indicates that a type of object is not common but occurs in that phase

5.4 A correlation of the chronological frameworks for males and females

5.4.1 Grave-goods

Ideally, it would be possible to correlate Phases MA1, MA2, MB and FA1, FA2 and FB with the help of object types found in the graves of both males and females. Unfortunately, the most common of these objects do not have close date ranges. Among the buckles, only *buckle1* is of some help. Most of the buckles of this type are dated in graves of Phases FB and MB, but there is also a single grave of Phase MA2. This indicates that Phases FB and MB are broadly contemporary, and it might also indicate that Phase MB starts a little later than Phase FB.

Pottery was found in the graves of males and females but it will take further detailed research on Anglo-Saxon pottery from inhumation and cremation graves to make use of the potential of this material. Stamped pottery as far as it is dated by associated grave-goods falls mostly in Phases FA2 and MA2 but Phase FA1, FB and MA1 are also represented with a few graves. The evidence suggests, however vaguely, that Phases FA2 and MA2 are broadly contemporary.

5.4.2 Vertical stratigraphy

Of the large number of intercutting graves, a few involve two dated graves and are therefore useful for the chronological framework. Those stratigraphical relationships that involve two graves dated on the basis of grave-goods support the relative sequence of graves dated in the phases for females and the sequence for the graves of females. They also give some information on the relationship between the two frameworks. The only contradiction between phasing and stratigraphy was found with graves 359 and 360 at Morning Thorpe. This problem has been discussed in detail in Brugmann (2004, 52 note 45) with help from Høilund Nielsen, and an explanation may have been found.

At Morning Thorpe, the following intercutting graves of females are dated:

MT140 dated in Phase FA2 cuts
MT141 dated in Phase FA1.

MT309 dated in Phase FB cuts
MT328 dated in Phase FA1.

MT044 dated in Phase FA2a cuts
MT050 dated in Phase FA2.

MT253 dated in Phase FA2 cuts
MT252 cuts
MT256 dated in Phase FA2a.

In MT358 a burial dated in Phase FA2 cuts a burial dated in Phase FA2b.

In MT369 a burial dated in Phase FA2b cuts a burial dated in Phase FA2.

MT384 dated in Phase FB cuts
MT387 dated in Phase FA2a.

Four of these eight stratigraphical relationships involve graves of the same phase, FA2. This suggests that Phase FA2 was either quite long or that these stratigraphic relationships were not the result of burial ground reclaimed after a lapse of time but part of a deliberate burial practice. The absolute date range for Phase FA2 suggests that the phase lasted fifty to seventy years, short enough to suggest deliberate burial practice.

The following intercutting graves of males are dated:

MT040 dated in Phase MA2 cuts
MT036 dated in Phase MA1a.

MT380 dated in Phase MA2 cuts
MT381 dated in Phase MA2.

The following intercutting graves involve males and females:

In MT097 a burial dated in Phase MA1b cuts a burial dated in Phase FA1.

MT064 dated in Phase FA2 cuts
MT085 dated in Phase MA2.

MT211 dated in Phase MA2 cuts
MT212 cuts
MT251 dated in Phase FA2.

MT177 dated in Phase FB cuts
MT183 dated in Phase MA2.

MT288 dated in Phase FB cuts
MT269 dated in Phase MA2.

In MT351 a burial dated in Phase MB cuts a burial dated in Phase FA2.

MT217/227 dated in Phase FB cuts
MT218 dated in Phase MB.

These stratigraphic relationships suggest that Phases FA2 and MA2 and Phases FB and MB were roughly contemporary because apart from graves of Phase FA2 cutting graves of MB and vice versa, they involve a grave of Phase MA2 cutting a grave of FA2 and vice versa. This supports the notion that the phenomenon of intercutting graves was largely part of a burial practice that involved fairly recent burials.

The stratigraphy at Spong Hill does not involve intercutting inhumations but cremations cutting inhumations and a ring-ditch cutting another ring-ditch. This stratigraphic relationship caused Dickinson and Härke (1992, 12) problems with their dating of shield boss types. The stratigraphic relationship of the two ditches suggests that Grave 31 is later than Grave 40 but the shield typology would make a reverse relationship more consistent with evidence from other sites. Høilund Nielsen encountered the same problem in her analysis of the weapon combinations from the four cemeteries: Grave 31 is dated in Phase MA1 and Grave 40 in Phase MA2.

The ring-ditch around Grave 31, however, also encloses Grave 32 dated to Phase MA2 (Hills *et al.* 1984, fig. 1), and it therefore seems likely that the three graves were dug within a short period. Grave 31 may have been the first grave (possibly re-used soon after for a child rather than robbed, see Ch. 6.3) followed by Graves 40 and 32. The most likely explanation for Graves 31 and 32 in the same ring-ditch seems, however, that they were contemporary and together with Grave 40 mark the transition from Phase MA1 to MA2.

The small Graves 43, 44 and 47 intercutting with the ditch around Grave 40 may have been positioned and orientated with the ring-ditch around Grave 40 in mind, which implies they post-date the ring-ditch (Hills *et al.* 1984, fig. 1). Grave 42 also intercutting with the ring-ditch is larger and orientated roughly east-west as the other graves on the site. It is dated to Phase FA2a and therefore likely to have been dug in the same short period. The dated graves in the south-western part of the inhumation cemetery in fact suggest that most of the burial activity in the area of the ring-ditches was carried out within this period.

Spong Hill inhumation graves cut by cremations include one grave dated in Phase MA1b (Grave 36), two graves dated in Phase FA1 (Graves 22 and 26) and three graves dated in Phase FA2a (Graves 29, 37 and 39). The undated Grave 23 was cut by Cremation 1912 with the fragment of a comb which on the Continent would be dated in the mid third of the 5th century (pers. comm. Jan Bemmann). This suggests an absolute date of the undecorated pot, iron buckle and iron knife from Grave 23 in Phases MA1a or FA1. The evidence from Spong Hill suggests that cremation and inhumation burial practice were contemporary at least until Phase FA2a, but a chronological framework for the Spong Hill cremations that could support the framework for the inhumations is not yet available.

Figure 5.10 Morning Thorpe. The distribution of graves dated to Phases FA1 and MA1. Scale 1:300

Figure 5.11 Morning Thorpe. The distribution of graves dated to Phases FA2 and MA1–2. Scale 1:300

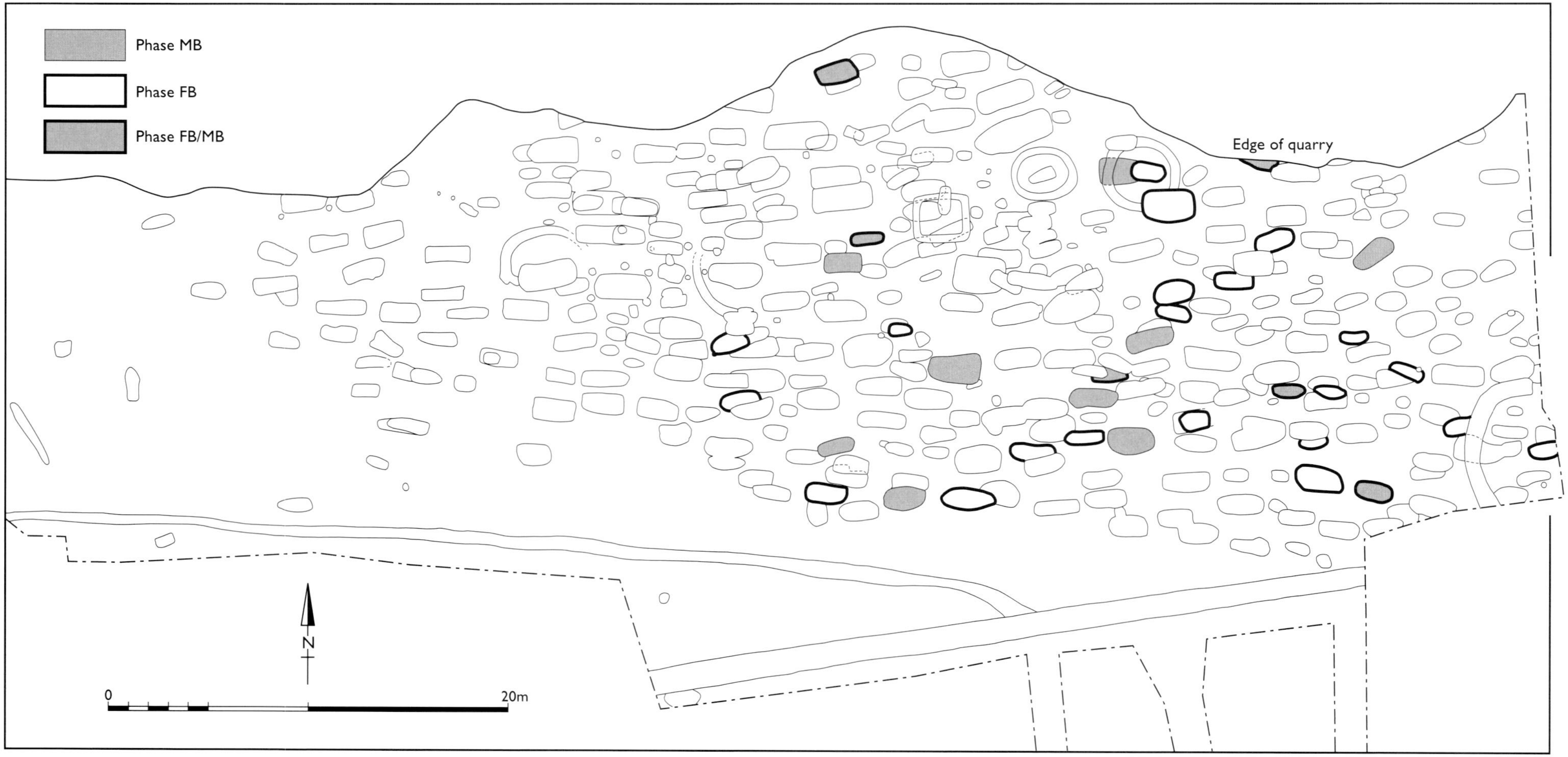

Figure 5.12 Morning Thorpe. The distribution of graves dated to Phases FB and MB. Scale 1:300

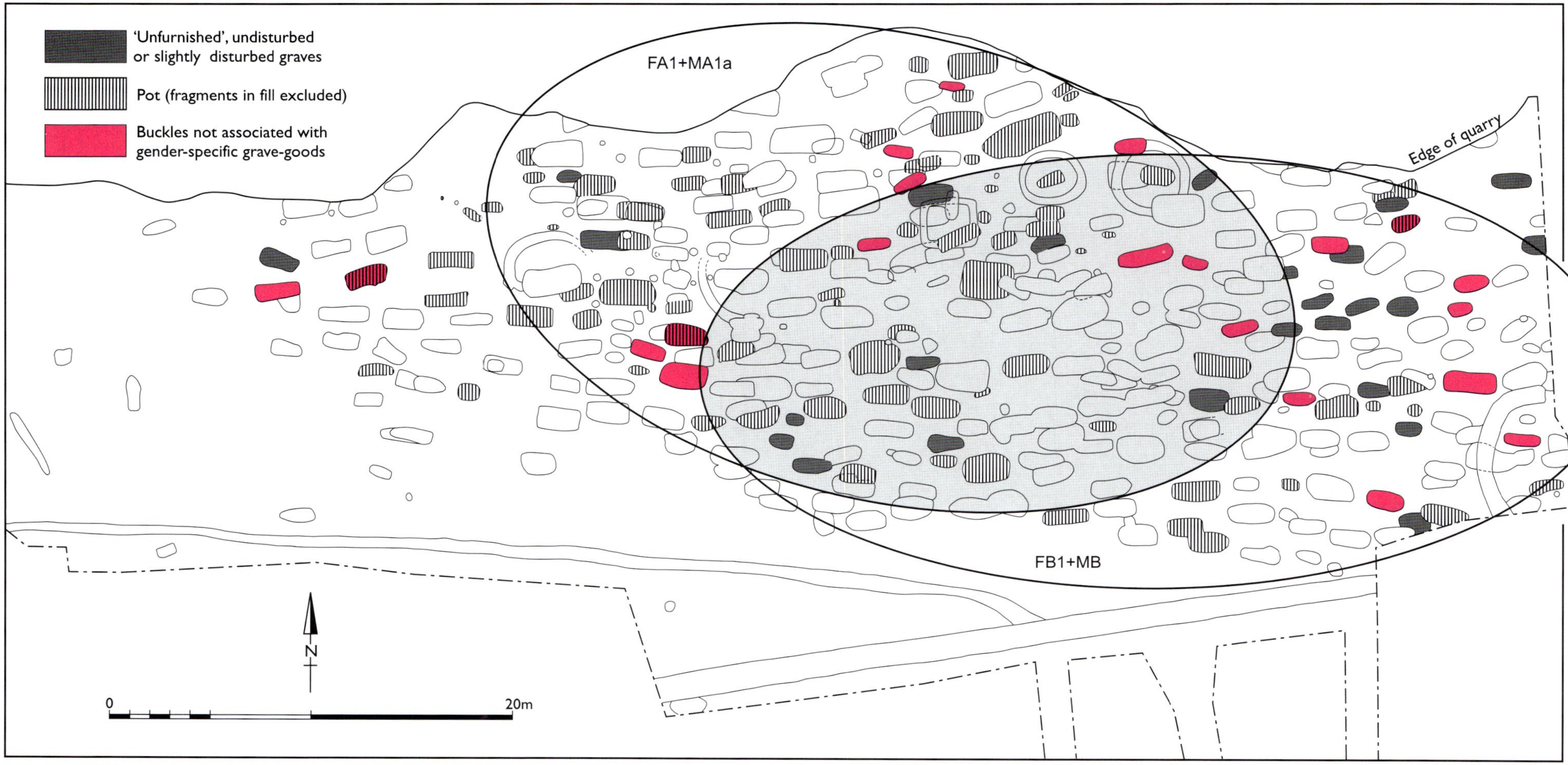

Figure 5.13 Morning Thorpe. The distribution of 'unfurnished' graves (undisturbed or slightly disturbed), pottery, and buckles not associated with gender-specific grave-goods. The extent of the distributions of graves dated to Phases FA1/MA1 and FB/MB is encircled. Scale 1:300

63

Figure 5.14 Spong Hill. The distribution of graves dated to Pases FA1 or MA1. Scale 1:300

Figure 5.15 Spong Hill. The distribution of graves dated to Pases FA2 or MA1–2. Scale 1:300

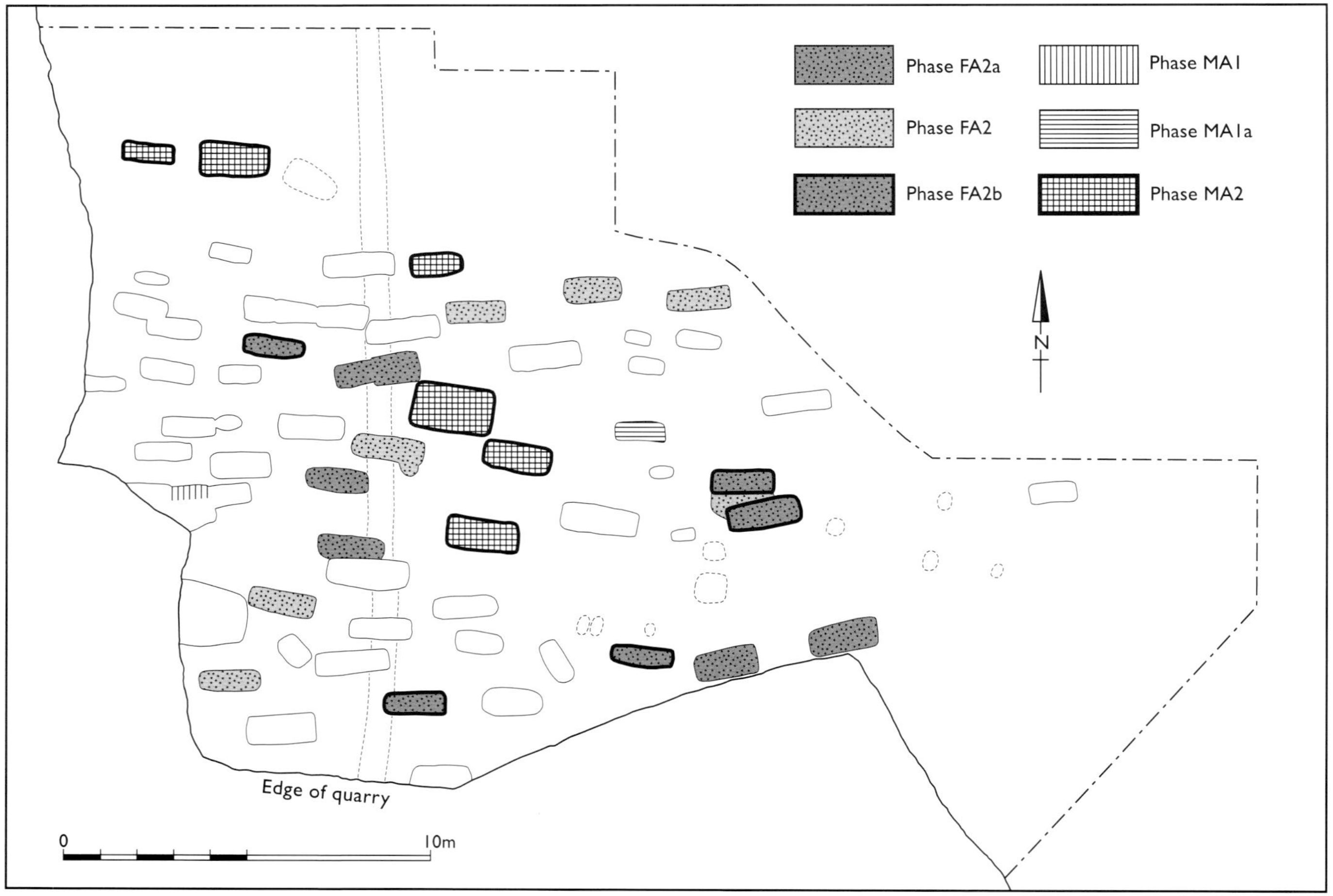

Figure 5.16 Bergh Apton. The distribution of graves dated to Phases FA2 or MA1–2. Scale 1:200

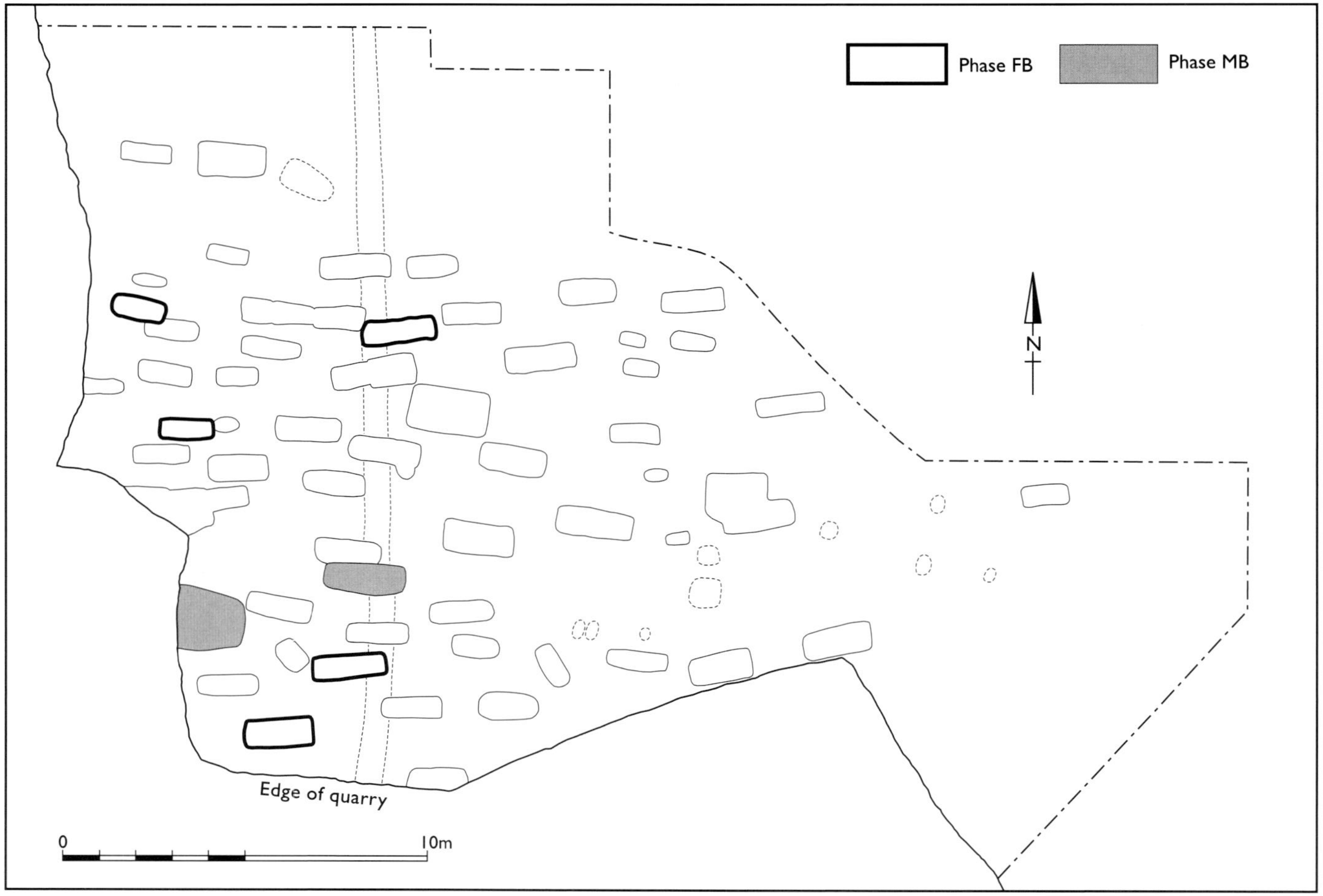

Figure 5.17 Bergh Apton. The distribution of graves dated to Phases FB or MB. Scale 1:200

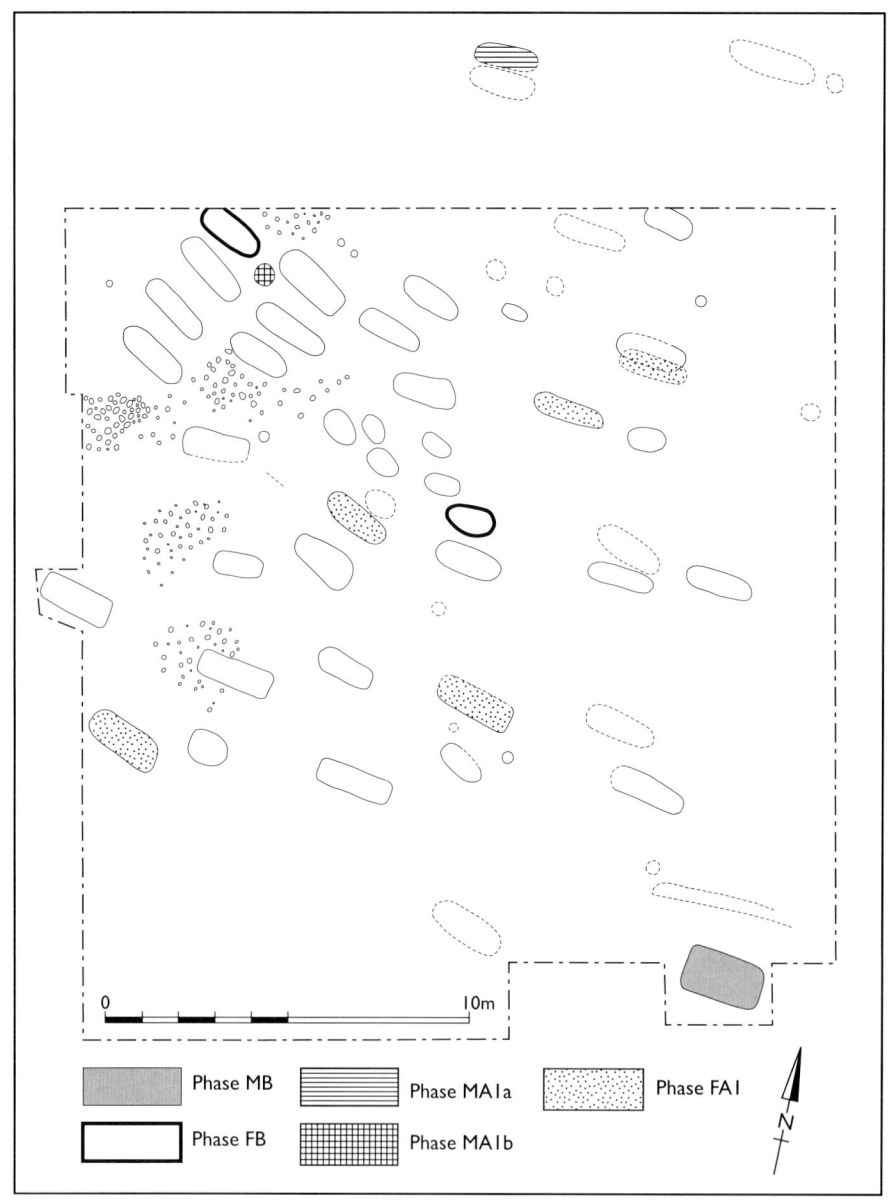

Figure 5.18 Westgarth Gardens. The distribution of graves dated to Phases FA1 or FB and to MA1 or MB. Scale 1:200

5.4.3 Horizontal stratigraphy

Morning Thorpe
The distribution of the dated graves in the four cemeteries gives some indication of how the phases for female and male graves may be correlated though none of the cemeteries has a very clear structure. Morning Thorpe is best suited for such an analysis because it has the largest excavated area, but the site seems to have been polycentric to an extent that makes it impossible to discern cores to individual plots. The graves of Phase FA1 are distributed in the central part of the cemetery, as are the graves of Phase MA1a. The distribution of the graves dated to Phase MA1b extends this area to the west and to the east (Fig. 5.10).

In Phases FA2 and MA2, the graves are scattered across the entire site with the exception of a patch in the north-eastern part of the excavated area (Fig. 5.11). As the differentiation between graves of sub-Phase FA2a and FA2b is only a tentative one and graves assigned to Phase FA2 in general are distributed across the entire site, the distribution of the graves only assigned to sub-Phase FA2b in the south-west may not be significant.

The graves dated to Phases FB and MB were found only in the south-eastern part of the excavated area, the graves of females extending further to the east than the graves of males (Fig. 5.12). The absence of graves dated to Phases FB and MB in the north-west of the excavated area suggests that this part of the site was not in use at the period covered by these phases. Phase FA and FB were probably roughly contemporary, with Phase FB possibly having been longer than Phase MB.

The distribution pattern of the graves dated to Phases FB and MB at Morning Thorpe shows correlations with the distribution of pots, knives and buckles that give some indication of the dating of graves which cannot be dated on the basis of weapon combinations or closely dated female dress accessories. The distribution of pots at Morning Thorpe (Ch. 4.4.12, Fig. 5.13) suggests that fewer pots were placed in graves in Phases FB and MB than in the previous phases. The distribution of large knives (Ch. 4.4.6, Fig. 4.6) and of small graves (Ch. 6.2, Fig. 6.3)

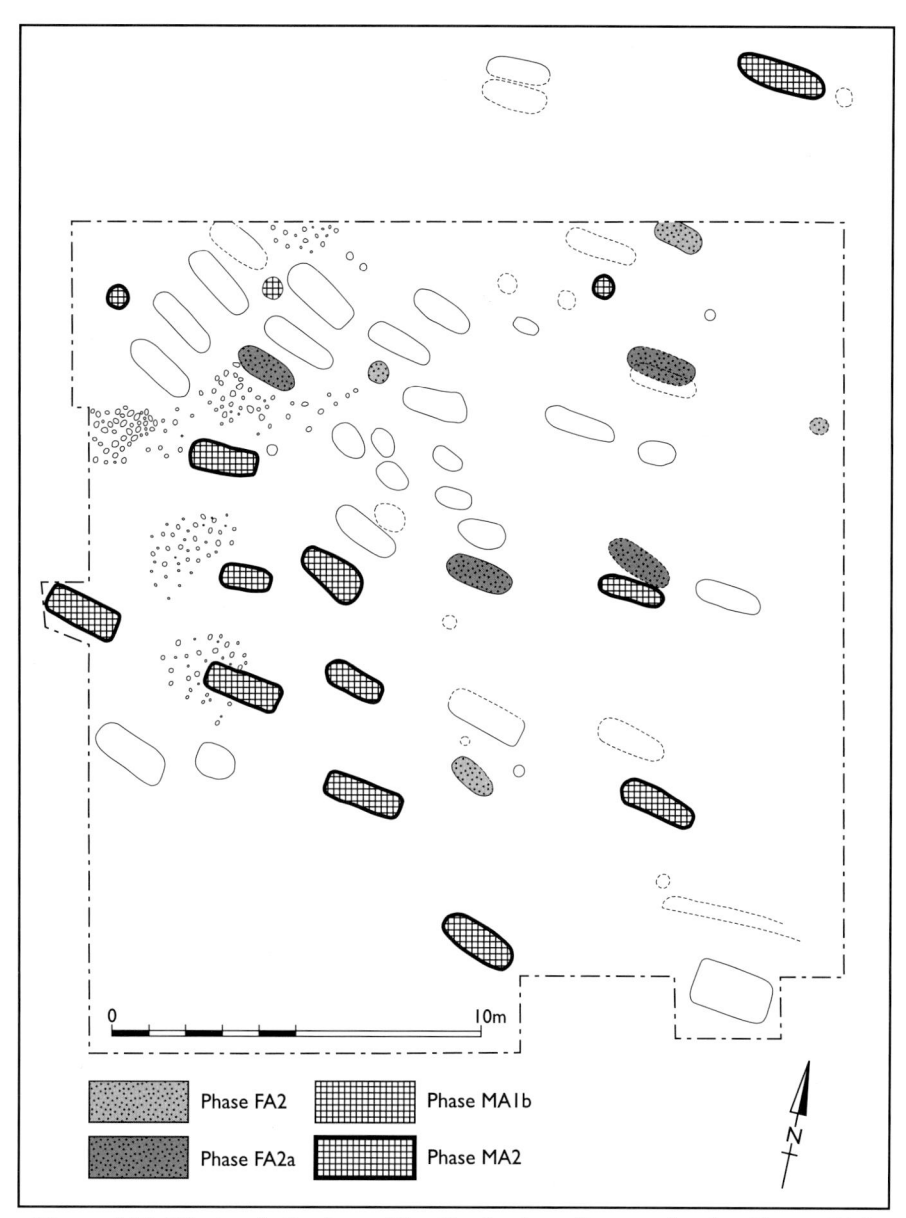

Figure 5.19 Westgarth Gardens. The distribution of graves dated to Phases FA2 and to MA1–2. Scale 1:200

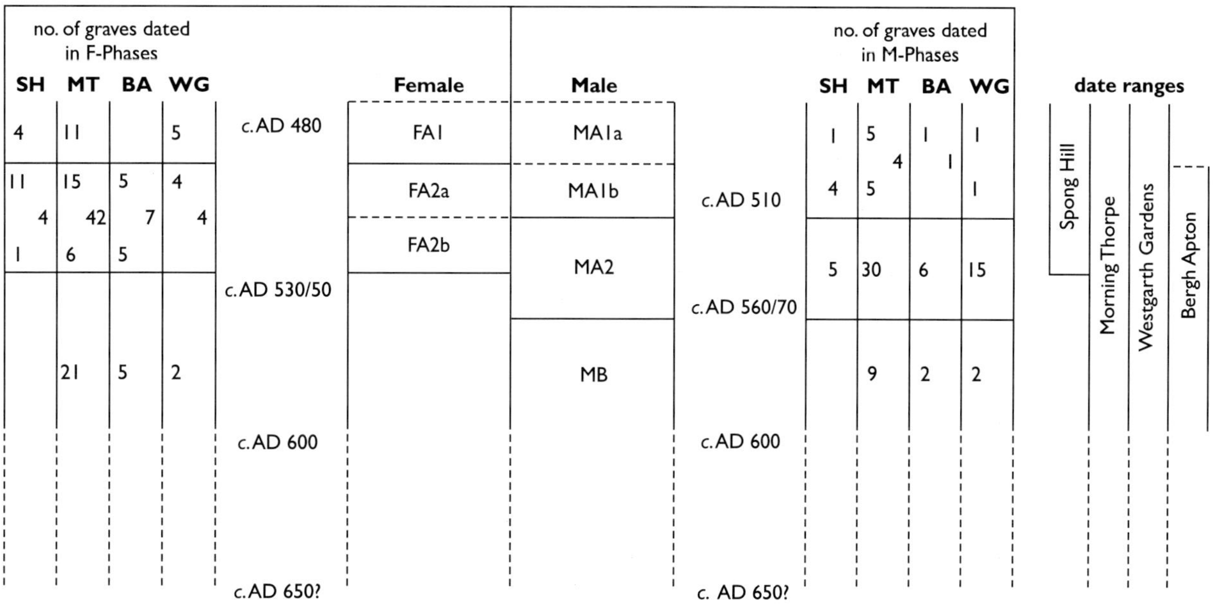

Figure 5.20 The four cemeteries. The correlation of the phases for males and females, the number of graves represented by these phases and the date spans of the four cemeteries.

FA1

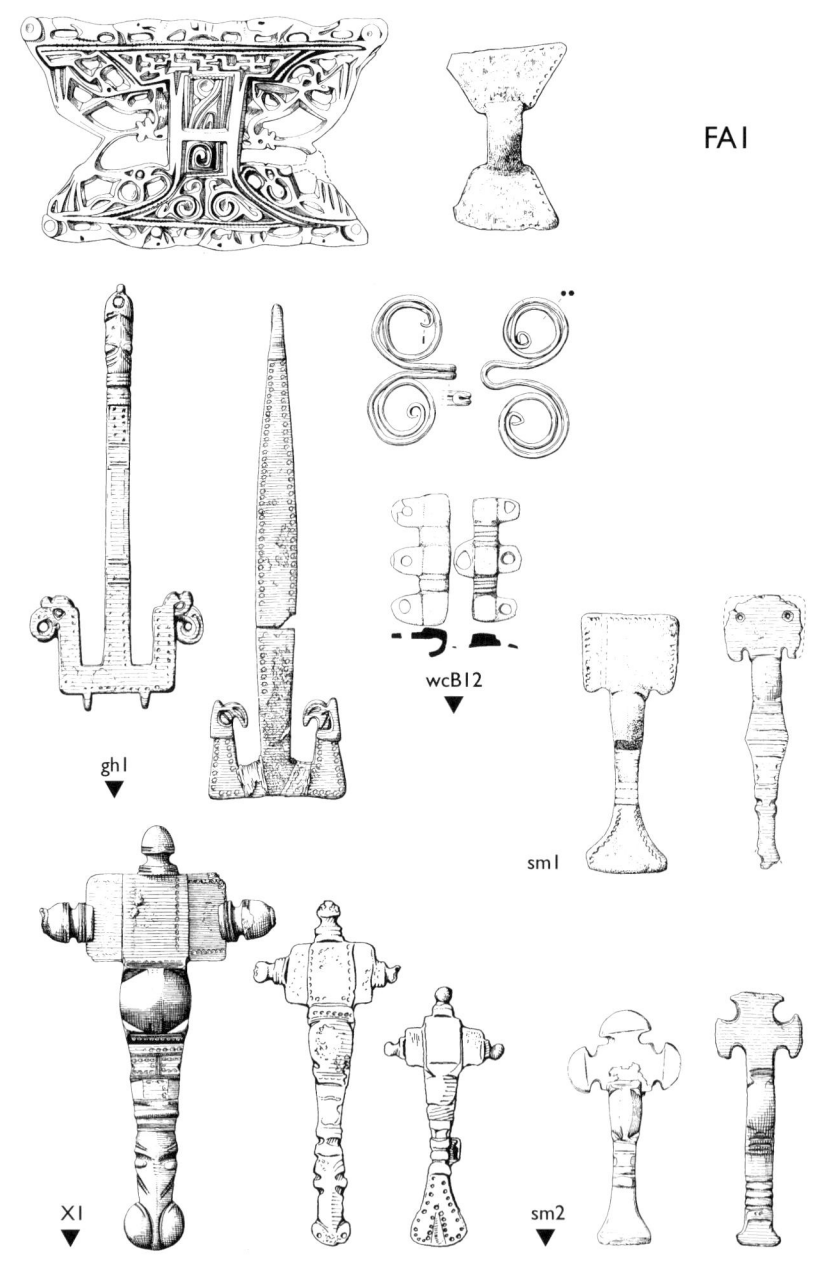

Figure 5.21 The four cemeteries. Types of object defining Phase FA1.
Not to scale

mainly in the area covered by the graves dated in Phases FB and MB agrees with the fact that there was an overall increase in the length of knives over time and that changes in burial practice resulted in fewer archaeologically visible grave-goods such as pots, which were mostly buried with females. Buckles not associated with gender-indicating grave-goods are mostly found in the east of the excavated area (Fig. 5.13) and may indicate the decline of 'furnished' burials towards the end of the 6th century when buckles became the only relatively common dress item.

Though it is impossible to date individual graves on the presence or absence of buckles, knives and pottery alone, the following overall changes over time can be identified: an otherwise undated grave with a pot and a small knife but no buckle in a large pit, such as Grave 55 at Spong Hill or Grave 320 at Morning Thorpe, is likely to be earlier than an otherwise undated burial with a large knife and a buckle but no pot in a small pit, such as Graves 260 and 315 at Morning Thorpe.

Spong Hill
The distribution of graves dated to Phases FA1 and MA1 give the impression of almost separate plots for females and males at the time (Fig. 5.14). Though there is some evidence for clusters of weapon graves in Anglo-Saxon cemeteries (see Ch. 6.6), entirely separate plots are unlikely because the overall distribution of the graves of males and females suggests otherwise (see Hills *et al.* 1984, fig. 4). The graves dated to Phases MA2 and FA2 also show some bias in the distribution of the graves of males and females though the pattern is not as striking (Fig. 5.15). It seems that the entire area covered by the

inhumation graves was in use from the start and that this space was filled in over time.

Unlike Morning Thorpe, the area of inhumation graves at Spong Hill covers too few graves to be of much use for a correlation of the graves of males and females.

Bergh Apton
At Bergh Apton, two graves are dated to Phase MA1, one of them early in this phase, but none to Phase FA1 (Fig. 5.16). This may be result of the clustering of male and female graves in the relatively small excavated area, which may not be representative of the date range of the site. The graves dated to Phases FA2 and MA2 are scattered across most of this area (Fig. 5.16) while the graves dated to Phases FB and MB are found only in the western half of the excavated area (Fig. 5.17). The limited distribution of the graves dated in this latest phase may be significant because it was also found at Morning Thorpe.

Westgarth Gardens
The clustering of male and female graves in the relatively small excavated area does not encourage wide-reaching conclusions on the layout of the site. This area produced graves of all phases but no clear shifts in the use of space (Figs 5.18–19).

Conclusions
The absolute date ranges for the phases for male and female graves suggests that Phases MA1, FA2 and MB were not entirely contemporary with Phases FA1, FA2 and FB. According to these dates, Phase MA1 began later than Phase FA1 and Phase MB began later than Phase FB. The vertical stratigraphy at Morning Thorpe neither contradicts nor supports a 'fine tuning' of the relative phases. The horizontal stratigraphy at Morning Thorpe, however, gives some indication that the absolute dates are correct.

At Morning Thorpe, the graves of sub-Phase MA1b have a distribution that extends that of the graves of Phases MA1a and FA1 both in the west and the east of the excavated area (Fig. 5.10). This suggests that the graves of Phases MA1a and FA1 are roughly contemporary and that the graves of Phase MA1b are contemporary with part of Phase FA2, which has the same wide distribution. Spong Hill is of no help in this matter because the distribution areas of the graves dated in Phases MA1 or FA1 hardly overlap and the excavated areas at Bergh Apton and Westgarth Gardens include too few graves to be of much use. The low numbers of early weapon graves in comparison to well-equipped and therefore datable females of Phase FA1 at Spong Hill, Morning Thorpe and Westgarth Gardens also make comparison difficult. This imbalance in relative numbers makes it the more noteworthy that Bergh Apton has two graves dated to Phase MA1, one of them early within this phase, and no graves dated to Phase FA1, but five graves dated to Phase FA2a. Though it seems quite possible that the excavated area is not representative, it also seems possible that this is further indication of an early start for Phase FA2.

At the four cemeteries, the graves datable to Phases FA2 and MA2 are generally more closely spaced than the graves of Phases MA1 and FA1. It seems that during Phases MA2 and FA2 the burial sites reached their maximum extension. Spong Hill is the only site that has no evidence of the following phases MB and FB. The number of graves dated to Phase FA2b is low compared to the number of graves assigned to Phase FA2a and the number of weapon graves dated to Phase MA2 corresponds in relative terms (Fig. 5.20). It therefore seems likely that Spong Hill was given up during Phase FA2b and before the end of Phase MA2.

The distribution of graves dated to Phases FB and MB at Morning Thorpe and Bergh Apton suggests that parts of the excavated areas were abandoned in these latest phases. It seems possible that the seven graves of females in the east of the excavated area at Morning Thorpe not matched by graves of males dated to Phase MB, pre-date the beginning of Phase MB and the abandonment of this area.

5.4.4 Relative and absolute chronology

According to Høilund Nielsen, the transition from Phase MA1 to MA2 can be dated in the early 6th century and the transition from Phase MA2 to MB *c.* AD 560. The transition from Phase FA1 to FA2 has been dated to the late 5th century and the transition from Phase FA2 to FB to the mid 6th century at latest. The horizontal stratigraphy of Morning Thorpe supports a later beginning of Phase MA2 than of Phase FA2 and also a later beginning of Phase MB than of Phase FB, though the evidence is not that strong. Figure 5.20 shows a correlation of the phases for male and female graves as they are suggested by the absolute dates. Figures 5.21–28 give an overview on the main objects dated to particular phases.

It is easier to put approximate absolute dates to the change from one phase to another than to be precise about when the cemeteries were started and when they were given up. A beginning for Phases FA1 and MA1 soon after AD 450 seems likely considering that Phase FA2 probably began as early as *c.* AD 480 and Phase MA2 around AD 510. The end of Phases FB and MB remains even vaguer. Some evidence suggests that Morning Thorpe and Westgarth Gardens were still in use after AD 650, but none of the types on which the definition of Phases FB and MB is based necessarily dates the graves as late as the mid 6th century.

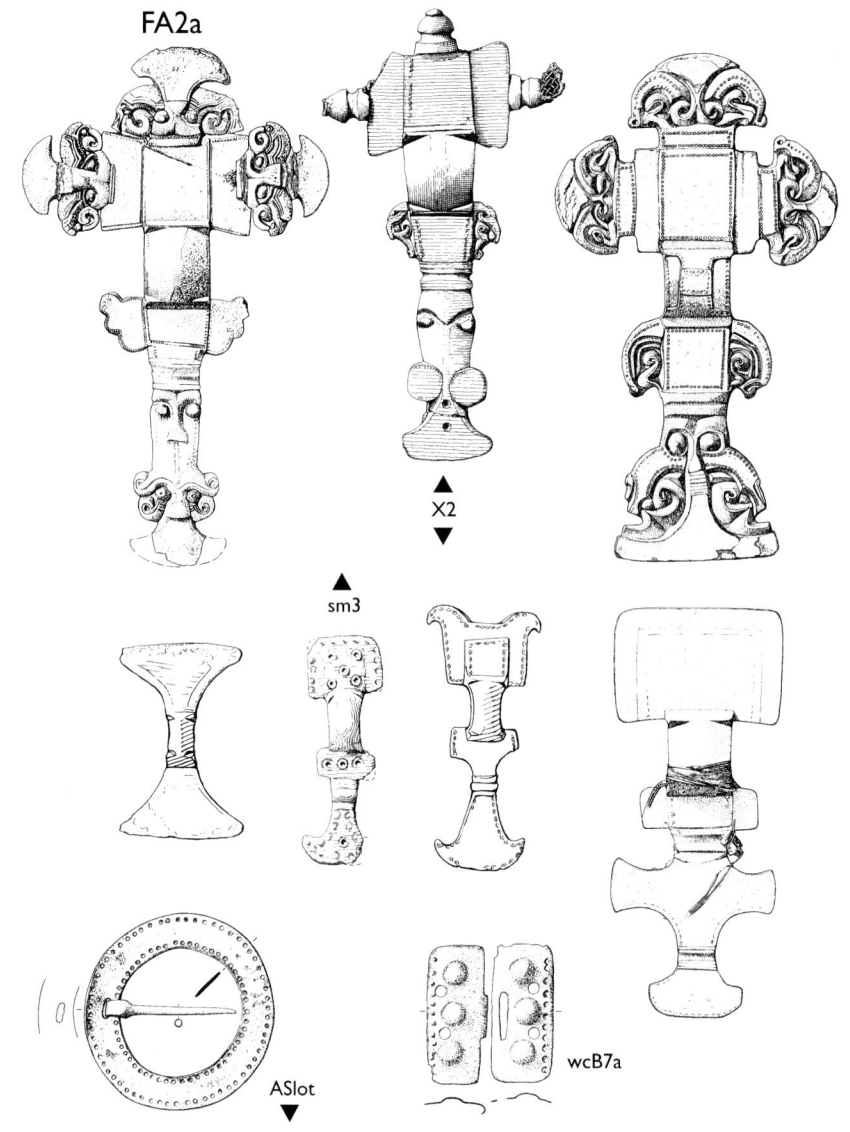

Figure 5.22 The four cemeteries. Types of object defining Phase FA2a. Not to scale

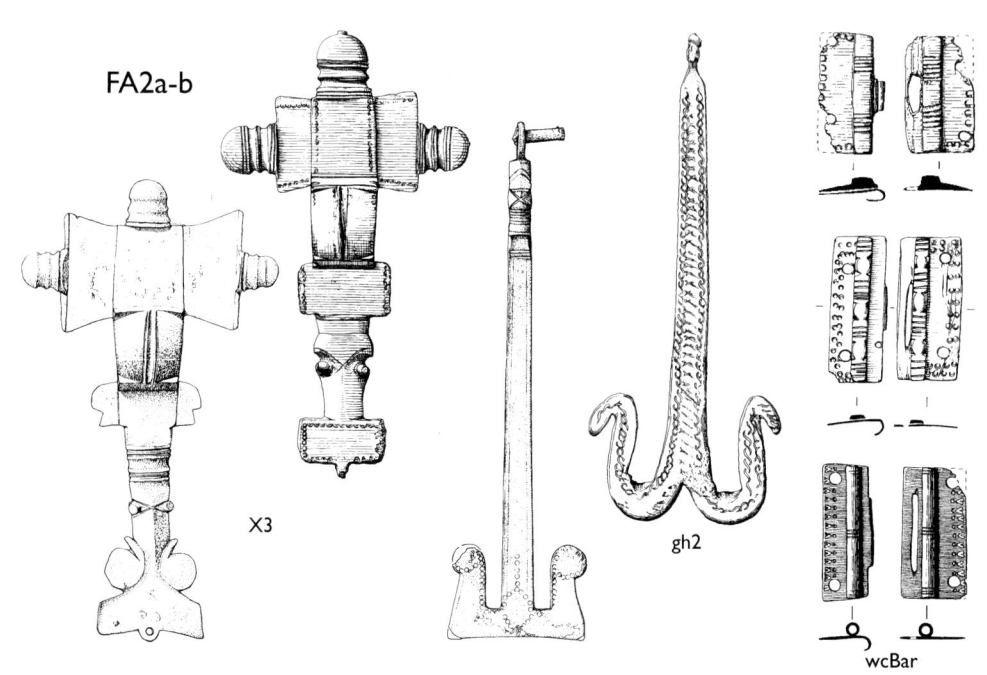

Figure 5.23 The four cemeteries. Types of object defining Phase FA2a–b. Not to scale

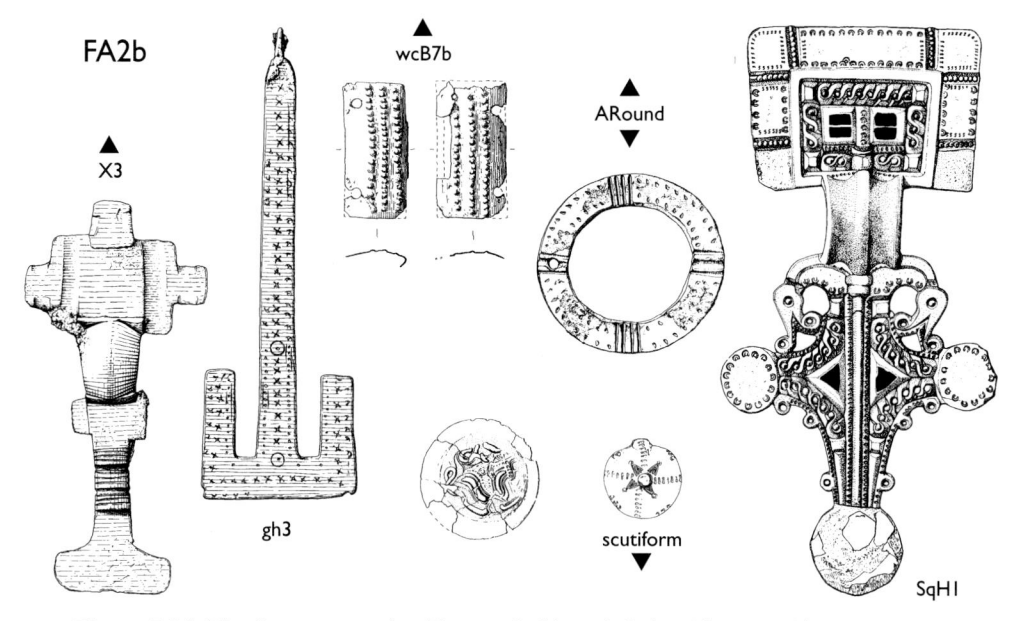

Figure 5.24 The four cemeteries. Types of object defining Phase FA2b. Not to scale

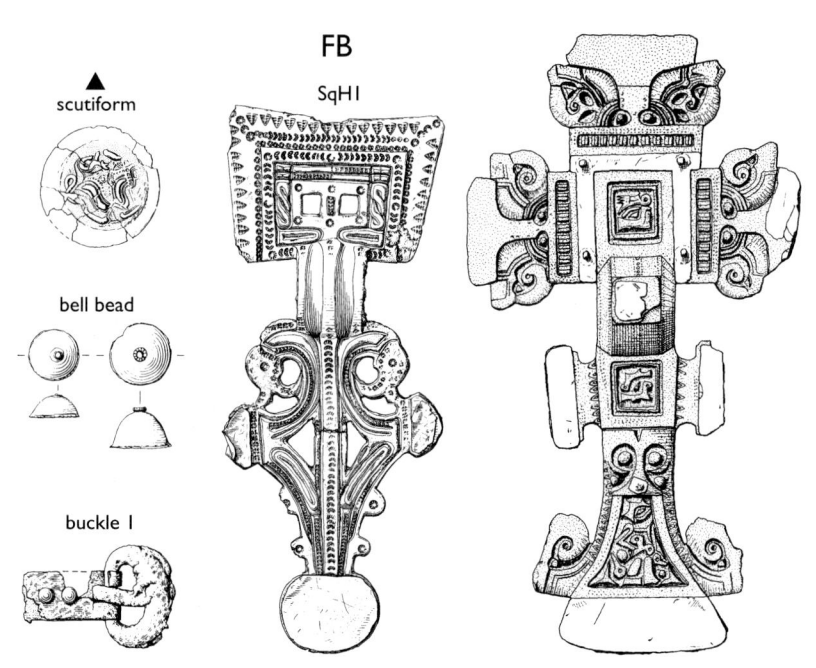

Figure 5.25 The four cemeteries. Types of object defining Phase FB.
Not to scale

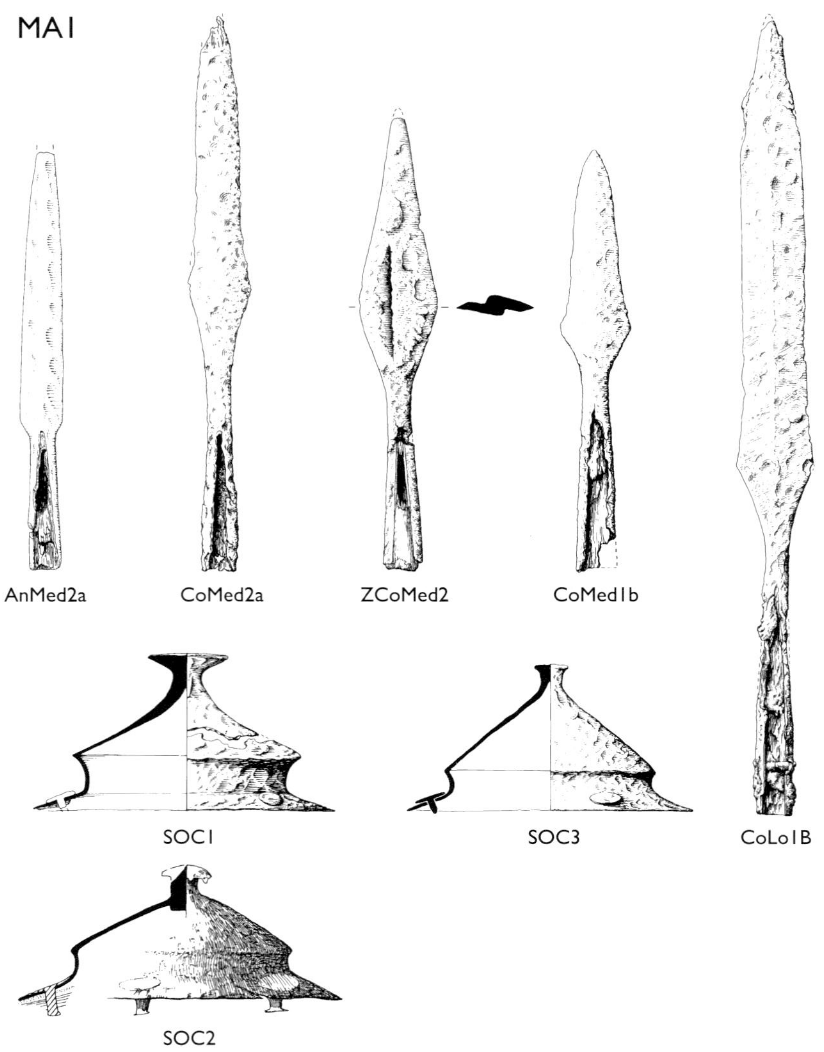

Figure 5.26 The four cemeteries. Types of weapon defining Phase MA1. Not to scale

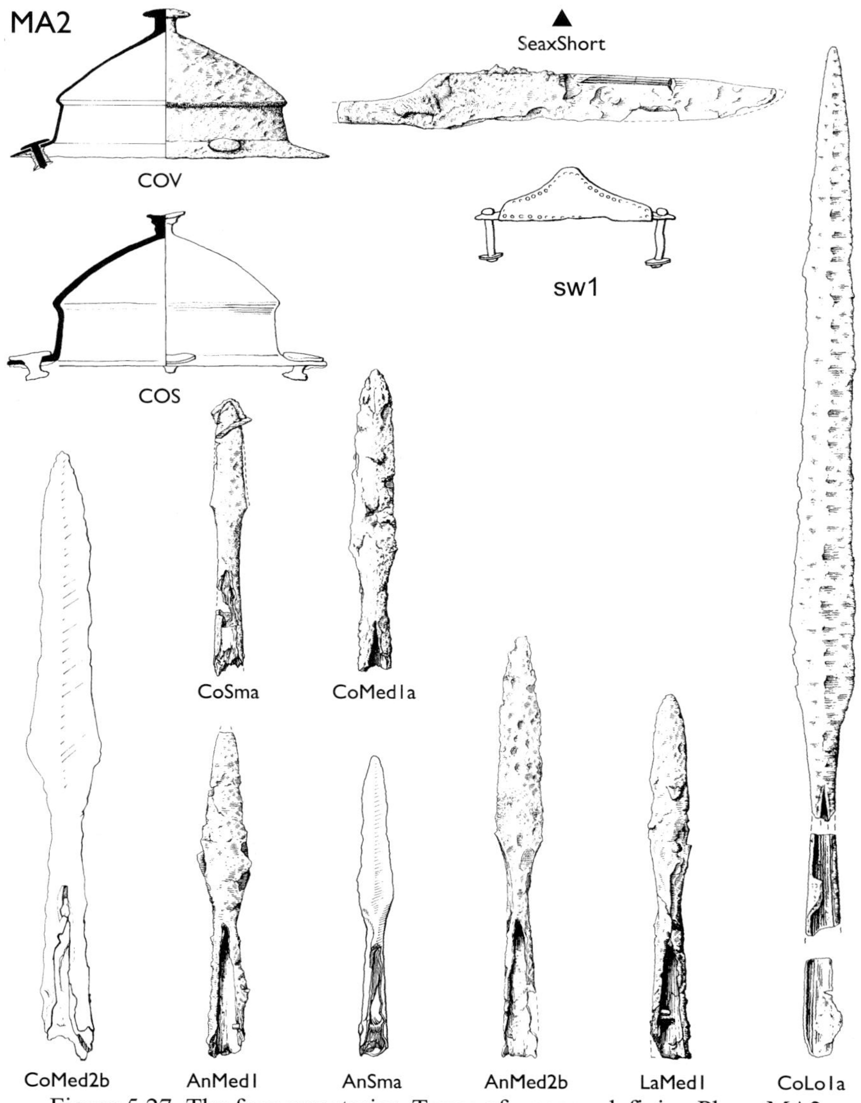

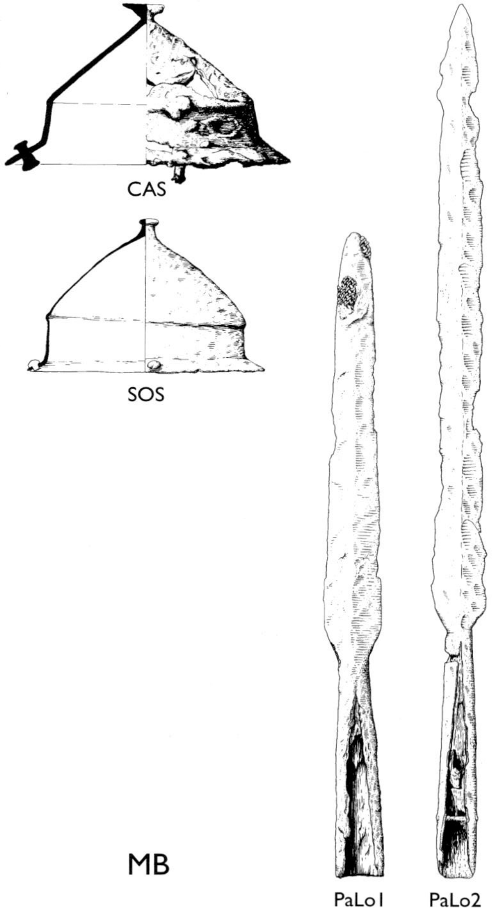

Figure 5.28 The four cemeteries. Types of weapon defining Phase MB. Not to scale

Figure 5.27 The four cemeteries. Types of weapon defining Phase MA2. Not to scale

6. Burial practice

6.1 Background

In Chapter 5, a chronological framework has been developed that is almost exclusively based on types of grave-goods and their distribution in the graves of the four cemeteries. This has shown aspects of continuity and change from the 5th to 7th centuries in East Anglian material culture. Some of these changes were the result of new designs for well-established types of objects, in particular dress accessories, others are likely to have been the result of changes in the choice of these functional types for burial and thus related to burial practice rather than everyday life. A closer look at the burial practice in the four cemeteries can support this chronological framework, a fact that explains the cross references to this chapter in Chapter 5. An analysis of the burial practice is also needed as a basis for an evaluation of the four cemeteries as a source of information on social structure because changes in burial practice can change the type and range of data available for study. Burial practice is likely to reflect some aspects of the social structure of the burial communities and to obscure others. Therefore, a survey of the graves and their layout is given below.

6.2 Grave lengths and depths

Due to the poor preservation of bones, in particular at Morning Thorpe, Spong Hill and Bergh Apton, many graves are identified as such on the basis of objects interpreted as grave-goods found in a mostly oval grave-shaped feature. 'Unfurnished' features cause a problem in this respect because the shape and to some extent orientation of the feature are the only basis for an identification. This problem is reflected in the classification of features as 'possible graves', in particular of small features at Morning Thorpe that may or may not have been the graves of children.

Grave lengths at the four cemeteries, measured along the axis of the graves, varied between c. 0.5m and c. 4m. All measurements were taken from the published grave-plans and are approximate because the plans from Spong Hill, Morning Thorpe and Bergh Apton were published at a scale of 1:20, the plans from Westgarth Gardens at a scale of 1:24 (West 1988, notinum). Preserved grave depths reached 120cm at Spong Hill (Fig. 6.2) and 95cm at Morning Thorpe (Fig. 6.4). Information on grave depths at Bergh Apton and Westgarth Gardens is not published.

The distribution of shallow and deep graves at Spong Hill and Morning Thorpe does not indicate that such variations were the result of different topsoil loss in different areas. Though there was an overall tendency for longer graves to be dug deeper, variations in the depths of graves of the same length indicate that grave depth was a means of differentiation in burial practice. At Westgarth Gardens, infants in graves of their own and most juveniles are buried in smaller graves than adults, a general tendency in Anglo-Saxon graves.

Comparison of grave-lengths shows that minimum and maximum lengths varied between sites. The smallest and the largest graves were dug at Morning Thorpe (Fig. 6.3). Spong Hill had a high proportion of graves 2.10m or more in length (Fig. 6.1) but few graves at Bergh Apton (Fig. 6.5) and Westgarth Gardens (Fig. 6.6) measured over 2.10m. On the latter sites, these graves were distributed surprisingly evenly across the excavated areas at a maximum distance of c. 3m.

Unfortunately, the depths of the graves at Bergh Apton and Westgarth Gardens were not recorded and it is therefore impossible to say whether the graves were not only shorter but on average also shallower than at Morning Thorpe and Spong Hill. As the sides of graves were rarely vertical, it would seem possible that variations in length and depth were not entirely the result of local differences in burial practice but on a small scale also due to topsoil loss.

Comparison between the lengths of undisturbed graves that can be identified as those of females or males shows a greater average length of the graves of males than of females. The most reliable evidence for this comes from Westgarth Gardens with the highest proportion of sexed individuals. It indicates that there was an overall difference in the length of graves for males and females, though not as pronounced as it appears in sets of data based entirely on grave-goods and therefore selectively on the graves of males designed to accommodate weapons.

Table 6.1 lists the known average length of the undisturbed graves of those individuals identified as male or female on the basis of grave-goods. These show an overall decrease over time in the lengths of graves for females but not in the lengths of graves of males. This suggests that differences in the average lengths of graves at the four cemeteries were not local variations but to some extent chronological phenomena. Spong Hill with the longest graves on average (2.26m among undisturbed graves over 1.50m) has a high proportion of early graves while Bergh Apton with the lowest average grave length (1.86m) has a high proportion of later graves (Table 5.1). At Morning Thorpe, with an average grave-length of 2.07m, fewer long graves were dug in the south-western part of the cemetery than in the north-western part (Fig. 6.3). The relatively high ratio of short graves in the south-east does not correlate with overall shallower graves in this area (Fig. 6.4). It seems likely that the distribution pattern is related to the distribution of graves dated to Phases MB and FB and reflects an overall decrease in grave lengths. It seems possible, however, that this tendency is exaggerated by the age ranges represented by the dated graves. Phase FB may include a higher ratio of sub-adults than the previous phases, which may have an effect on grave-lengths. It seems however, that the majority of individuals buried in Phase FB/MB were not only buried with fewer objects but also in shorter graves.

Stoodley (1999, 67) noted that on a national scale 'Except in the first adult group where two very long female graves have given this sex a greater average, male

	FA1	average length	FA2	average length	FB	average length
Spong Hill	4 graves	2.39m	15 graves	2.11m		
Morning Thorpe	6 graves	2.02m	41 graves	2.02m	14 graves	1.75m
Westgarth Gardens	4 graves	1.95m	5 graves	1.63m	1 grave	1.34m
Bergh Apton			16 graves	1.80m	5 graves	1.74m

	MA1	average length	MA2	average length	MB	average length
Spong Hill	5 graves	2.54m	5 graves	2.45m		
Morning Thorpe	11 graves	2.15m	22 graves	2.10m	6 graves	2.14m
Westgarth Gardens			9 graves	2.05m	1 grave	2.06m
Bergh Apton	1 grave	1.84m	6 graves	1.91m	1 grave	2.34m

Table 6.1 The four cemeteries. Grave lengths sorted after sites, gender and chronological phases

graves have longer averages throughout the period. Interestingly, over time their average length increases, and consequently in the 7th century the largest difference between the sexes is observed'. One of the long graves of a female noted by Stoodley is Grave 26 at Spong Hill dated in Phase FA1. Though the evidence from the four cemeteries suggests that female graves were dug shorter over time, instead of male graves dug longer, the observed trend is the same: an increase in differences between the graves for males and females.

6.3 Double graves

Anglo-Saxon inhumation burial practice favoured individual interment instead of a repeated use of communal structures. This does not exclude occasional double or multiple interments either contemporary or sequential. In his survey of 'multiple' Anglo-Saxon inhumation graves (with two or more interments), Stoodley (2002, table 1) listed one grave for Spong Hill, two graves for Bergh Apton and four graves for Westgarth Gardens. Establishing the exact nature of these double graves is problematic. Grave 31 at Spong Hill with the bones of a male individual and a child was probably disturbed (see below). The outline of the grave pit that contained the females numbered 29, 34 and 35 at Bergh Apton suggests two of them were buried in the same grave, but the stratigraphic relationship is far from clear. The grave-goods found in Grave 65 suggest the burial of two individuals, but again the stratigraphic relationship is not clear. At Westgarth, the skeletal remains of a male and a female suggest the burial of two individuals in a grave that was only 84cm wide. The infant in Grave 9, the grave of a young adult female, is not mentioned in the grave description in the catalogue but listed in a table on age and sex (West 1988, table 2). The outline of Grave 30 could not be discerned and the assumption that more than one male was buried is based on the relative position of two spears.

Morning Thorpe was presumably not included in Stoodley's sample because in many cases the lack of bones and the indistinct grave fill made it impossible for the excavators to establish the stratigraphical relationship of graves, which may have been contemporary or consecutive 'multiple' burials or intercutting individual burials. In some graves it was only the association of grave-goods that indicated more than one burial. Graves 80, 108, 129, 337, and 370 may have been the graves of two individuals buried side by side. This is particularly likely in the case of Graves 80 and 108 because the grave-good associations date both individuals to the same phase, FA2. In Graves 129, 337 and 370 females dated to Phases FA1–2 were associated with undated males.

In his survey on Anglo-Saxon 'multiple' graves, Stoodley (2002) interpreted contemporary multiple burials as a practice that dealt with the unusual and threatening situation of individuals of a small community dying at the same time. In a different context he noted that 'although weapon males in single graves had more grave-goods than their counterparts in multiple burials, feminine individuals sharing a grave had a greater quantity of grave-goods than those in single graves' (Stoodley 1999, 94). At Morning Thorpe, the unusual combination and position of grave-goods is the best indicator for more than one interment, and there may have been an unknown number of double graves not indicated by grave-goods. A problem, for example, is posed by a damaged half of a wrist-clasp in Grave 126 at Morning Thorpe. This object is the only indication that the grave may have been disturbed. As it is the non-functional half of a wrist-clasp and an object that would most likely have been associated with a brooch in the grave of a female, it is assumed that this is an intrusion in the fill.

Further evidence for double graves at Morning Thorpe may include the remains of 'stacked' graves, *i.e.* the burial of an individual placed on top of another in the same pit and in some cases disturbing the first one. If the individuals in these graves were not buried in the same but in consecutive pits, the second pit must have considerably disturbed the first one. Accidental disturbance after a lapse of time is unlikely in most of these cases: the grave-good associations in Grave 30 are dated to Phases FA1 and FA, in Grave 97 to Phases FA1 and MA1b, in Grave 140 both to Phases FA2, in Graves 238 to Phases MA2 and FB, in Grave 293 to Phases FA2 and FB, in Grave 351 to Phase FA2 and MB, in Grave 358 to Phases FA2 and FA2b, in Grave 362 to Phases FA2a and MA, and in Grave 369 to Phases FA2b and FA2. The only datable associations not of the same or immediately following phases were found in Grave 371, which involved interments dated to Phases FA2a and FB. In view of this evidence it seems possible that the 'chamber' Grave 31 at Spong Hill was not robbed soon after the grave had been dug (*cf.* Hills 1977a, 171) — there are no objects missing that one would expect to have seen — but that the child was interred soon after the adult, possibly before a mound was built over Graves 31 and 32 and encircled by the ring-ditch.

Figure 6.1 Spong Hill. Schematic site plan showing grave lengths and ring-ditches. Scale 1:300

Figure 6.2 Spong Hill. Schematic site plan showing grave depths and ring-ditches. Scale 1:300

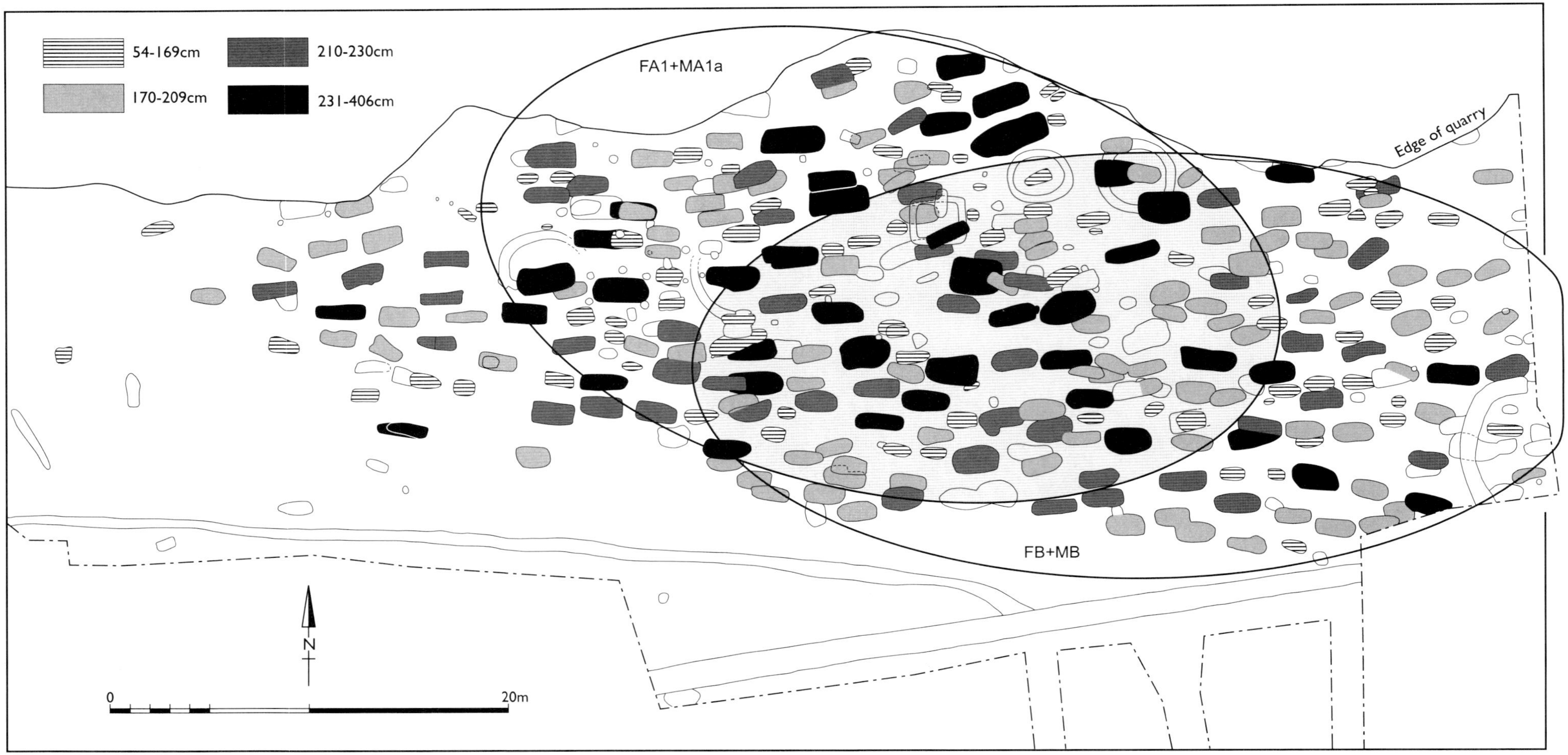

Figure 6.3 Morning Thorpe. Schematic site plan showing grave lengths and the distribution area of graves dated to Phases FA1/MA1a and to FB/MB. Scale 1:300

Figure 6.4 Morning Thorpe. Schematic site plan showing grave depths. Scale 1:300

Morning Thorpe seems to be in line with the 'multiple' burials in Stoodley's national sample, which includes the double burials of 143 males and females without clear bias for either sex (Stoodley 1999, 53 ff.). Such burials are interpreted as largely those of relatives or individuals of the same household. In a different context, Stoodley (2002, 114) pointed out that consecutive burials using the same grave pit include cases in which the later burial disturbed the earlier one, and he interpreted these disturbances as accidental. He concluded that 'the lack of any clear structure governing the deposition of consecutive burials' speaks against the interpretation of consecutive burials as principally family-related. On the Continent, however, early medieval consecutive burials are interpreted differently.

In a survey of double and multiple burials from continental row-grave cemeteries, Lüdemann (1994) showed a wide variety of types including burials side by side in the same grave pit, variations of 'stacked' burials and semi-detached grave pits with a partition made of wood or stone. Interments on the same level in the same pit were not necessarily contemporary as is shown by cases in which the remains of the primary interment were shifted to make space for a second interment. Among the 'stacked' graves were two types: interment in the same grave pit with the second body placed directly on the first, in some cases facing in the opposite direction, and stacked graves with a substantial layer between the upper and the lower interment. The difference between burials side by side and closely spaced 'stacked' burials was interpreted as a matter of available space in the original grave pit. According to Lüdemann (1994, 436 ff.) the 'stacked' version shows that no provision had been made for a secondary burial when the original grave pit was dug, and suggests that 'stacked' burials with reverse orientation were the result of very little space in a coffin. These conclusions were based on a detailed analysis of grave features.

The re-use of grave pits poses some practical problems also addressed by Lüdemann (1994, 516 f.). He argued that early medieval grave pits were not back-filled but given a cover that protected the body and grave-goods such as vessels from the fill of the grave. The concept of the 'living' dead housed with possessions and provisions would argue for such a burial custom. This idea is not only supported by direct evidence for coffins and wooden or stone grave structures but also indicated by evidence such as large stones at the base of the grave, which could have originally secured the cover, and smashed skulls or vessels, which could have been damaged when the grave cover collapsed. This interpretation might explain the large stones in Grave 47 at Spong Hill, for which the cemetery report discusses the possibility of a 'deliberate sacrifice' (Hills *et al*. 1984, 8). There was, however, no need for a covering to be elaborate because planks or branches covered with bushes, reed, or fur would have been enough (Lüdemann 1994, fig. 24).

Lüdemann (1994, 522 ff.) suggested that double burials were used to express a particularly close relationship between the members of a household. He pointed out that this relationship in most cases seems to have spanned no more than one generation. This interpretation is supported by the dating evidence for the Morning Thorpe graves listed above.

Most of the double and multiple graves on the Continent are dated to the 7th century. An increase in relation to the 6th century to some extent reflects the larger overall number of excavated burials of the later period (Lüdemann 1994, 512f.). Martin (1990, 101ff.), however, suggests that changes in burial practice led to an increase in double and multiple burials. At first, individuals were buried side-by-side, occasionally at the same time but more often in a sequence. At this stage, care was taken not to disturb the position of previously interred bodies. Later graves showed less respect for the remains of previous burials, a development related to the increased use of stone structures. Bodies were shifted aside or bones collected in a pile. This may have been the case with the remains of two individuals in the relatively narrow Grave 5 at Westgarth Gardens.

Stoodley's assessment suggests that the Anglo-Saxon evidence on multiple graves is similar to the continental: small but persistent numbers of contemporary and consecutive burials increasing in the 7th century (Stoodley 1999, 54, 97). Stoodley's and Lüdemann's interpretations of the Anglo-Saxon and continental evidence is, however, opposite. According to Stoodley, the disturbance of earlier burials indicates the lack of a relationship between the individuals buried, while Lüdemann and Martin interpreted the continental evidence as part of a burial practice that culminated in the re-use of stone sarcophagi. An interpretation of 'stacked' graves as an expression of a close relationship between the individuals involved is supported by evidence from Edix Hill, Barrington, Cambs (Malim and Hines 1998) and Buckland, Dover (Parfitt and Anderson forthcoming).

Lüdemann's interpretation of continental burial features explains how and why secondary burials were placed in an existing grave. Lüdemann took less notice of our modern attitude to corpses than Stoodley, implying in his interpretation that the disturbance of a body was not a sign of disrespect but could be made part of the burial practice. This implies a robust attitude towards corpses, which was in fact demonstrated by evidence for grave robbery on the Continent. This includes graves robbed at a time when the organic matter of the corpses had not yet disintegrated and the gender if not the identity of the individuals was known to the robbers. This has been interpreted as a 7th-century development connected to Christians laying claim to possessions of their pagan ancestors (Stork 1997). Written sources suggest that consecutive burial on the Continent was a burial practice that increased after the conversion and was opposed, but also inadvertently encouraged, by the church (Nehlsen 1978, 161ff.). The same may apply to Anglo-Saxon England.

6.4 Grave features

Relatively few graves produced structural evidence that suggests the inhumation graves at the four cemeteries were more than elongated pits in the ground. Ledges were found in Grave 14 at Spong Hill, Grave 35 at Morning Thorpe and Grave 82 at Bergh Apton. Further ledges at Morning Thorpe may have been disguised by the amorphous nature of the fill in most graves, which made it difficult to establish the relationship or even existence of intercutting graves. Spong Hill was the site that produced most of the evidence for structural features or coffins, biers *etc.*

Grave 31 at Spong Hill was published as a 'chamber grave' on the basis of evidence for a wooden 'box or chamber', probably disturbed soon after (Hills 1977a, 168–171). In the light of the discussion on double burials above (Ch. 6.3), a subsequent interment also seems possible.

Of the 'chamber' in Grave 31, only the base and *c.* 20cm of the upright planks were preserved together with what may have been a flint packing. There is no certain evidence for a lid. The term 'chamber grave' implies a structure made within the grave instead of being lowered into it as would be the case with a coffin (*cf.* Hinz 1969, 56ff.). On the Continent, the term 'chamber grave' is used for early medieval graves with a closed wooden structure that was large enough to enclose a coffin or bier and to provide space for objects such as weapons or containers alongside the body (Martin 1976, 13). These chambers were constructed as a box or grave-lining and more or less fitted the grave pit. It does not seem quite consistent with the concept of a 'chamber' grave that the shield boss and possibly also the spearhead from the Spong Hill grave seem to have been positioned outside the wooden structure (see Hills 1977a, 170), though this does not represent an isolated case (*cf.* Hinz 1969, 59). At *c.* 1.10m by 2.10m, the structure from Spong Hill is small by continental standards (see Martin 1976, 18) and though it seems to have been too large to be classified as a mobile coffin, it does not quite meet the definition of a chamber in continental terms.

Remains of planks on the floor of Grave 40 indicate a second, undisturbed 'chamber' grave at Spong Hill. The fill in this grave suggests that the wooden structure filled the entire grave pit and the function of the flints at the head and foot end of the grave is not clear. The excavators point out that there was no evidence for a separate coffin (Hills *et al.* 1984, 93).

The rectangular area of fine dark soil covering the floor of Grave 71 at Bergh Apton filled almost the entire rectangular grave pit and is described in the catalogue as the probable remains of a wooden structure. The grave plan and section show that this layer covered an area of 90cm by 180cm, was *c.* 20cm thick and included the remains of upstanding sides. The ?remaining depth of the grave is only 40cm, too little for a chamber grave, and the section does not indicate anything that could be interpreted as a collapsed structure.

Tim Pestell (Filmer-Sankey and Pestell 2001, 240) has pointed out that the interpretation of features in Anglo-Saxon graves as the remains of coffins often follows a stereotype: 'In only a few cases can it be proven conclusively that the stains observed are those of a coffin, and recent excavations in the churchyard of St Lawrence Jewry, Guildhall, London, have shown that even in the 11th century coffins as we might think of them were not being used, but (here surviving through waterlogging), could consist of loosely-pegged trays, boards under or over the body, or even two planks resting against one another like a pitched 'roof'…'. This holds true for most of the dark stains that were observed in graves at the four cemeteries but exceptions are formed by the evidence from Grave 46 at Spong Hill that included the base, sides and lid of a wooden structure, and in some cases by the level at which objects were found, suggesting they had been placed on a cover. As there is no evidence for these structures to have been constructed in a way that made them portable, it seems best to use the term 'coffin' in an Anglo-Saxon context for a box that may have been constructed in the grave and may not have been fit for transport.

Hills *et al.* (1984, 6) listed 'thirteen clear coffin stains, eight further graves with traces of wood which are likely to have been part of a coffin and several more graves with diffuse stains which might have been the remains of coffins at Spong Hill (Graves 4, 10, ?12, 13, 14, 22, ?24, 27, 32, ?34, ?35, 36, 41, 42, 46, 51, 55, 56, and 57). Rectangular areas of dark soil in graves at Morning Thorpe (Graves 35, 140, 155, 157, 178, 200, 208, and 362) indicate the existence of similar structures. Graves with a particularly regular and almost rectangular outline (Graves 19, 20, ?31, 36, 42, 54, 57, 80, 97–99, 124, 125, 140, 173, 231, 289, 335, and 364) may indicate original grave linings but only Grave 140 combined both features. The two dark linear stains on the base of Grave 353 are slightly 'boat-shaped'. They may have been created by two planks or some soft organic material. The rectangular stain along its side may suggest that the conditions for the preservation of organics were particularly good in this grave. Irregular areas of dark soil in some graves at Morning Thorpe may have been the remains of funeral structures or organic grave-goods.

Graves 6 and 27 at Bergh Apton showed dark stains on the floor that were interpreted as the remains of coffins or biers. The outlines of Graves 12, 16, 21 and 29 were almost rectangular, possibly because they were lined. It seems that Grave 26 was given a small recess to accommodate the spearhead in this grave. At Westgarth Gardens no remains of wooden structures were noticed but the almost rectangular pits of Graves 51, 55, 60, 62 and 66 may indicate linings.

The filling of some graves included large flints that formed deliberate features. At Spong Hill, these features were mostly combined with evidence for wooden structures. In Graves 12, 31 and 40 they may have formed packings along the upstanding sides of such structures. The large flints in Grave 47 were found in the upper fill and may have secured the cover of some structure. At Morning Thorpe, lines of flints were probably used to support wooden funerary structures at their base (Graves 17, 35, 78, 86, 126, 157, 178, 208, 396, and 403). The same may have been the case in Graves 6 and 62 at Bergh Apton.

In Graves 61 (undated) and 68 (Phase MA1b) at Morning Thorpe, impressions of ?grass were found on the shield studs and on the outside of the shield boss respectively. Stoodley's national sample suggests that 'a bed of grass or bracken on which the deceased was laid is a male-linked rite' but he also points out that 'The strong male correlation in this sample may be spurious — a result of the preservation of grass on iron weapons' (Stoodley 1999, 60). At Morning Thorpe, the evidence came from the top of the applications and therefore suggests a cover of vegetation such as discussed by Pestell from evidence at Snape and elsewhere, rather than a bed of vegetation (Filmer-Sankey and Pestell 2001, 242).

There is relatively little evidence for grave structures above ground at the four cemeteries, though the organisation of the cemeteries suggests the graves were visible throughout the period during which the sites were used. The most substantial grave-markers in the

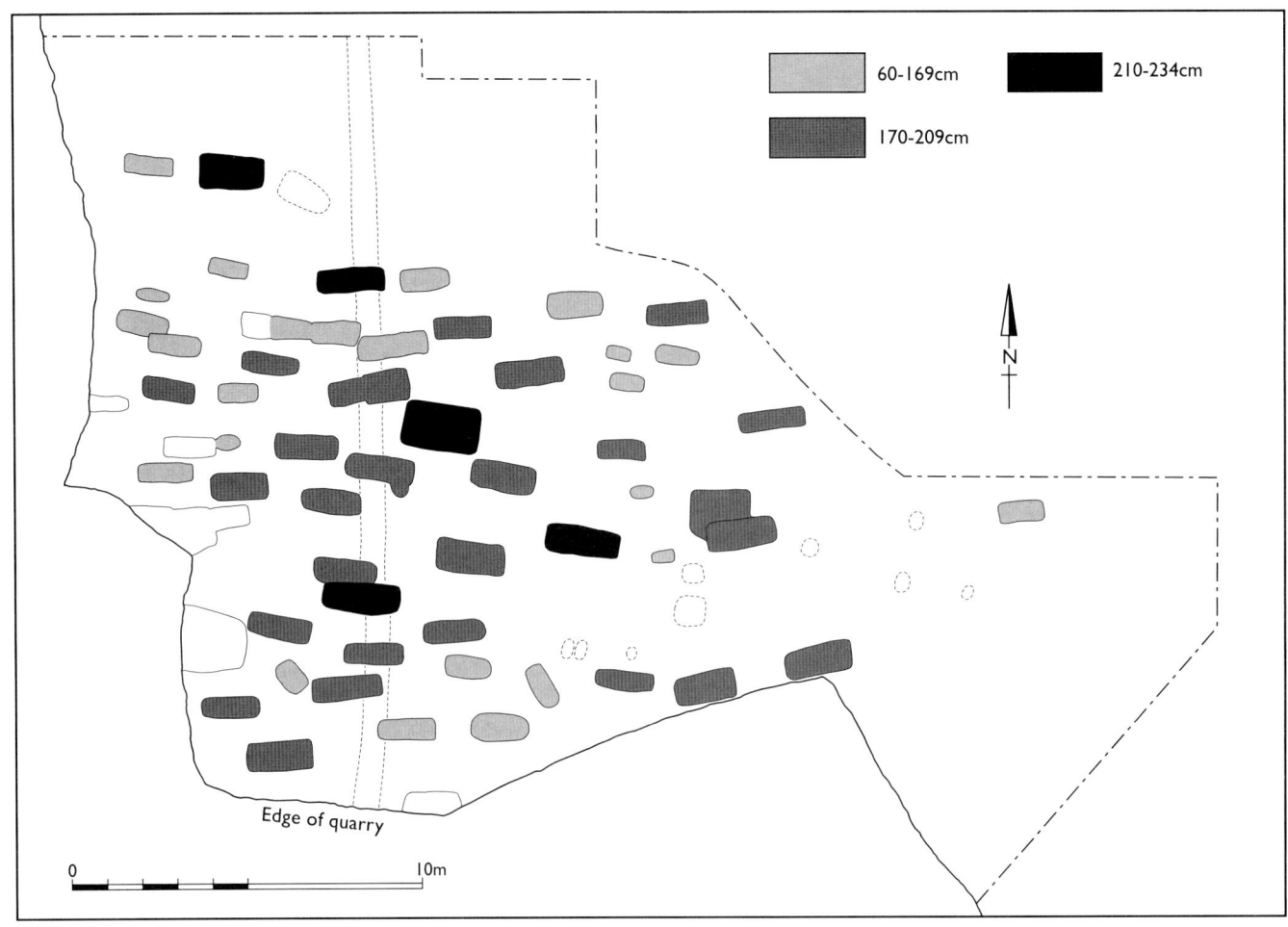

Figure 6.5 Bergh Apton. Schematic site plan showing grave lengths. Scale 1:200

archaeological record are the ring-ditches with diameters of 5–10m encircling the 'chamber' and other graves at Spong Hill (Graves 31, 32, 40, 41 and 46) and ring-ditches with diameters of 3–4m at Morning Thorpe (Graves 38, 227 and ?157). It seems likely that these ring-ditches encircled barrows created by the spoil from the grave pits and the ditches. Further graves may have had (shallow) ditches and barrows, not only graves with enough space around them for such features, but possibly others as well. This is suggested by the evidence from Spong Hill which shows the deliberate cutting of ditches by both ditches and graves.

Two or possibly more graves at Morning Thorpe were framed by post-holes which may indicate funerary structures above ground, possibly roofs or huts (Graves 62 and 148, neither of them particularly well furnished). Reconstructions of such features have been published for an Anglo-Saxon cemetery at Apple Down, Sussex (Down and Welch 1990, 15; pl. 52f.). The rectangular Ditch 28 cuts the graves in this area and is cut by an undated pit. It may post-date the use of the cemetery.

While graves with an almost rectangular outline and ditches were dug in all phases, graves with coffins/biers *etc.* seem to have been in use mostly during Phases FA/MA. 'Chamber grave' 31 at Spong Hill is dated to Phase MA1 and seems to have shared a ring-ditch and probably a barrow with Grave 32 of Phase MA2 with a likely coffin. The ditch cuts the ditch of Grave 40, a possible chamber grave dated to Phase MA2. The earliest

ditches at Spong Hill were probably the small ones around Grave 41 with a coffin/bier *etc.* dated to Phase MA1, and around Grave 46 with a coffin dated to Phase FA1. The only datable ditch at Morning Thorpe belongs to Grave 227 of Phase FB. None of the graves with certain or possible evidence for coffins and/or flint features was dated to Phases FB/MB. At Morning Thorpe, the graves with such features were dug in the north-west of the excavated area, which seems not to have been use in Phases FB and MB. It therefore seems likely that the undated graves with flint packings and dark soil indicating wooden structures also fall in Phases FA1–2 and MA1–2. It seems that the decline of 'furnished' burial in the four cemeteries went along with not only smaller graves for the majority of individuals, but also simpler grave designs.

6.5 Grave orientation and body position

Grave orientation at Spong Hill, Morning Thorpe and Westgarth Gardens is discussed in the cemetery reports (Hills *et al.* 1984, 2ff., fig 2; Green *et al.* 1987, 6, fig. 7, 8; West 1988, 7f., fig. 5). The published plan of the graves at Bergh Apton shows that as at Spong Hill, Morning Thorpe and Westgarth Gardens, most graves were dug with an approximate east-west orientation, following a general trend in Anglo-Saxon cemeteries (Stoodley 1999, 63f.). Hills *et al.* (1984, 6) pointed out that the individual orientation of a grave may have been related to the

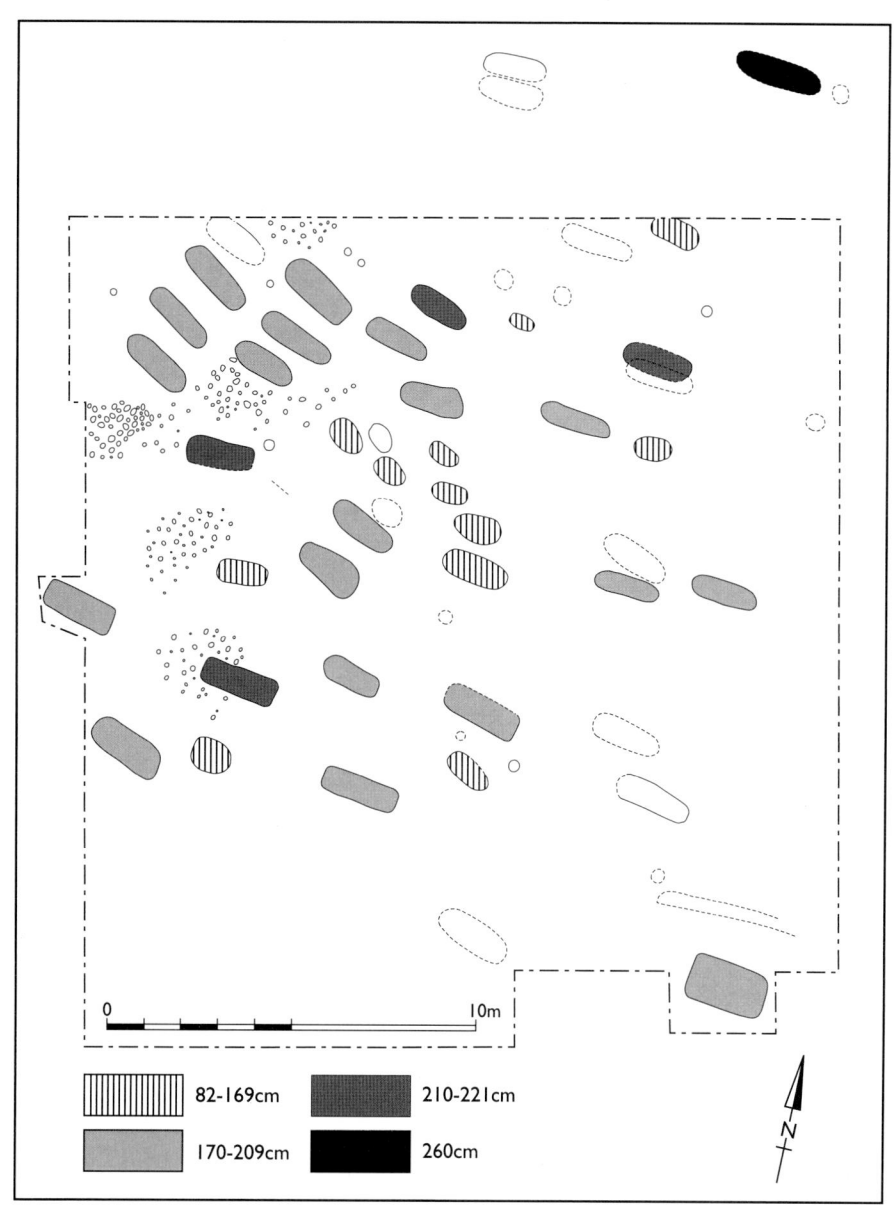

Figure 6.6 Westgarth Gardens. Schematic site plan showing grave lengths.
Scale 1:200

topography of a site rather than to a universal concept such as the position of the rising sun on the day of burial. This was part of an ongoing debate that has been summarised by Stoodley (1999, 63). Topographical reasons for local variations in the overall westerly range of grave orientations at the four cemeteries seems a likely concept. Stoodley (1999, 66) noted 'very little variation' in the orientation of graves in his East Anglian sample, a result supported by the Morning Thorpe evidence.

Some graves are noteworthy because the individuals were not buried with their heads towards the west but to the east. At Spong Hill, this applies to the females in Graves 19 and 44, both dated to Phase FA2. The position of brooches in Graves 153 (Phase FA1) and 207 (Phase FA2) at Morning Thorpe indicates that females were buried with their heads to the east. The grave plan of Bergh Apton suggests that four individuals were buried with their heads to the east (Green and Rogerson 1978, fig. 5), though the evidence seems not quite clear in the case of Grave 7 because the positions of the objects in the grave as shown in the grave plan are consistent with a position of the head of the individual to the west. The position of the dress accessories in Graves 5, 6 and 21, all dated to Phase FA2, however, suggests a position in the east. At Westgarth Gardens there was no evidence for 'reverse' burial.

As the evidence for unusual body positions is mostly based on the position of female dress accessories, it is not surprising that only the graves of females are listed here. The original number of 'reverse' burials may have been larger and may have included males. The dating of the graves suggests that reverse burial was not a practice either early or late in the period in which the cemeteries were used and therefore does not indicate some change over time. It may, however, be significant that the individuals in 'reverse' position were buried in adjacent graves at Morning Thorpe (Graves 153 and 207) and at Bergh Apton (Graves 5 and 6) and that all of these graves were well enough furnished to be dated. The plans of Graves 32 and 60 at Westgarth Gardens suggest that the males were placed on their left sides and partly turned to the grave floor, but not in a fully prone position. Children were buried flexed.

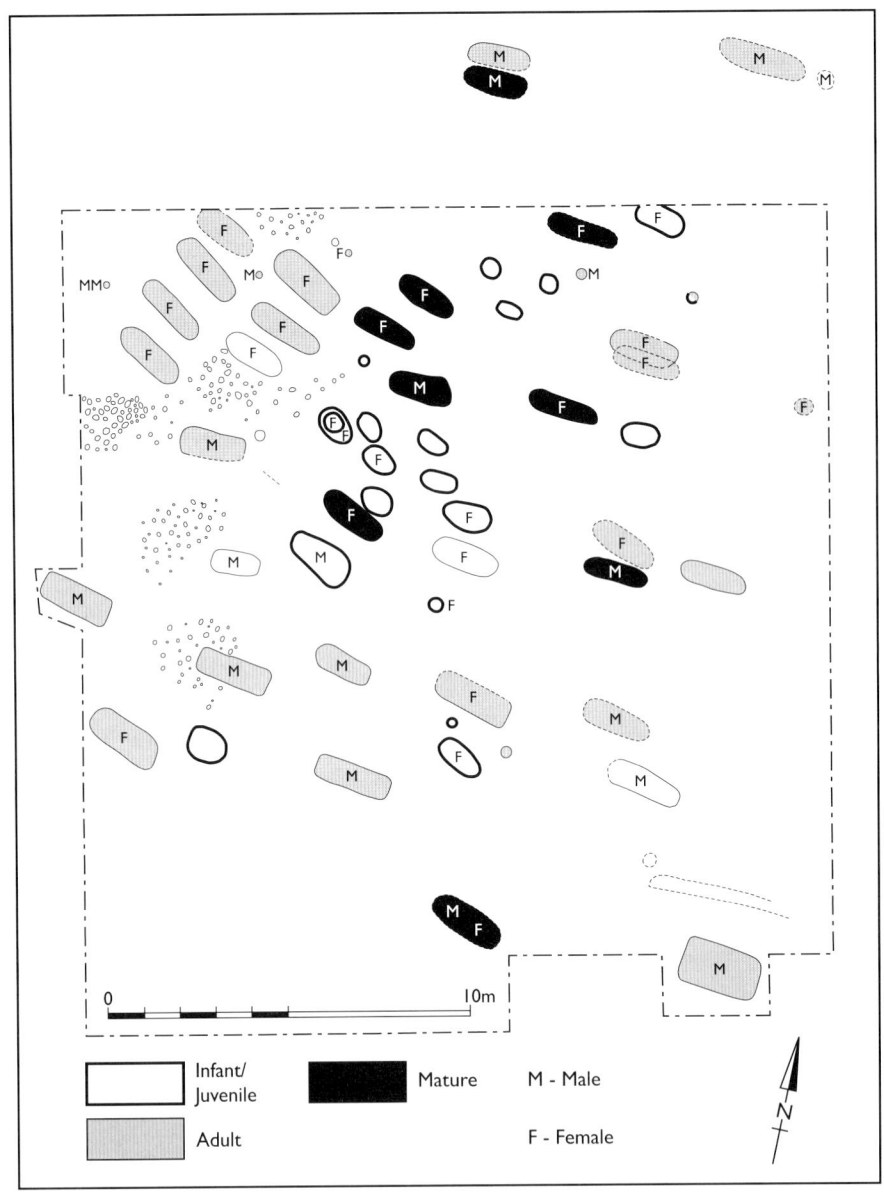

Figure 6.7 Westgarth Gardens. Distribution of age and sex.
Scale 1:200

Evidence on body positions is relatively sparse at the four cemeteries due to the poor preservation of bones. Hills *et al.* (1984, 2) pointed out that the 'normal' practice at Spong Hill was an extended body position. Crouched burials were found in Graves 19, 42 and 44 dated to Phase FA2 and the undated Grave 47. Two of these graves have been noted for their 'reverse' position and/or were apparently dug into the ring-ditch of Grave 40. The preservation of long bones at Bergh Apton indicated the burial of bodies with legs in an extended or flexed position (Graves 27, 32 and 71) and varying positions are also shown by the better preserved skeletons at Westgarth Gardens. The dating evidence suggests that extended and flexed positions were contemporary. Stoodley (1999, 58) concluded on the basis of his national sample: 'Deposition does not show any clear-cut sex patterns, the underlying cause of extended, half-turned, and extended on the side positions may be variation in sex but the associations are not really strong enough to base any firm conclusions on'. There is no evidence from Morning Thorpe to the contrary.

6.6 Cemetery layout

The layout of the graves in the excavated areas of the four cemeteries is basically the same: the sites are formed by graves of roughly the same orientation positioned in patterns that vary between rows and random scatters including touching and intercutting graves. At Spong Hill (Hills *et al.* 1984, fig. 4), Morning Thorpe (Green *et al.* 1987, fig. 6), Bergh Apton (Green and Rogerson 1978, fig. 5) and Westgarth Gardens (Fig. 6.7) there is some evidence for the clustering of the graves of males, females and the smaller graves of children, but not to not an extent that would justify describing these clusters as distinct sex/gender and age-related plots.

The distribution of dated graves at the four cemeteries suggest that the layouts are the results of spacious scatters of graves becoming filled with later graves over time, and that the sites therefore are polycentric, though there are few indications that the earliest graves formed centres rather than scatters. The area used for the earliest graves at Morning Thorpe expanded to the west and to the east in the late 5th century. This area seems too large to form just an extension of existing plots and therefore indicates a growth of the burial community using the site. It seems that in the second half of the 6th century, the north-westerly part of Morning Thorpe was given up, as was the east of the Bergh Apton site. There is no evidence for an expansion of the site elsewhere, but the evidence is inconclusive in this respect because neither site was fully excavated and their full extent is not known.

At Morning Thorpe, most of the graves of Phases FB and MB dug in the south-easterly part of the site added to the crowded layout of the site. These areas of densely packed and intercutting graves are different from the more spacious layout of the other sites. The spacing of the graves in the western part of Morning Thorpe is more generous and compares particularly well with the layout of graves at Bergh Apton. It seems that this part of Morning Thorpe was in use over a relatively short period of time. A spacious layout of graves can also be seen at Spong Hill, in use from the second half of the 5th to the first half of the 6th century, in the north-eastern part of Bergh Apton, mainly in use in the first part of the 6th century, and at Westgarth Gardens. Children's graves were given less surrounding space, but this seems to be a response to their smaller size. Their layout is different from the distribution of medium-sized graves that seem to be a feature of Morning Thorpe and Bergh Apton in the second half of the 6th and 7th centuries (Phases FB/MB).

The dating evidence from some of the closely spaced, intercutting and stacked graves from the site, however, suggests that these were not the result of space reclaimed after a lapse of time but that some of the dense pattern was created from early on (Ch. 6.3), a burial practice that may be echoed by the triple or quadruple Graves 29/34/35 at Bergh Apton. Research carried out on the Continent and on Dover Buckland (Parfitt and Anderson forthcoming) suggests that a lack of space was not the only or even the main factor that led to the disturbance of graves, but that proximity was an important aspect of Anglo-Saxon burial practice (see Ch. 6.3). The choice between expanding a plot and associating a grave with an existing grave in the form of a touching, cutting, stacked or re-opened grave, may have been just as important in Anglo-Saxon burial practice as the size and depth of a grave and the objects placed in it. Family or household relations may thus have been expressed or defined in a way that reminds one of shared pits for cremation urns.

Identifying the extent of individual family or household burial plots at Morning Thorpe, to give some idea about the size of such a social group, seems impossible. There are few cases of graves of the earliest Phases FA1/MA1 clearly serving as a focus for later burials. The best example is given by Grave 370 of Phase FA1 with just enough space around it to suggest that it might have had a very small barrow or ditch, and surrounding graves of later phases. Grave 90 dated to Phase FA1 is the earliest grave among the impressive group of large and well-equipped graves at the northern edge of the quarry. Graves 231, 328 and 319 form the only group of neighbouring graves dated to Phases FA1/MA1a but there is no clear evidence that the graves served as a focus for burials of the following phase. The little ring-ditch to the northwest of these graves was probably dug only in the latest phase.

What seems to be important for an interpretation of the social structure of the community using Morning Thorpe for burial is, however, that the site had no focus of any sort that could be interpreted as the burial space of a social group rising above the rest. The layout of Spong Hill has more potential in this respect. The 'chamber' graves, ditches and generously spaced weapon graves in the east of the area are more impressive than the more closely spaced graves in the west. The site chronology does not support Ravn's interpretation of the layout of the site (see Ch. 3.2.1) but suggests that both areas were used at the same time.

6.7 Conclusions

It seems that the layout of each of the four cemeteries started out as graves scattered over much of the area later covered by the fully developed cemeteries. Evidence for double and intercutting graves suggests that an intense use of an area over time does not indicate that space was 'reclaimed' after a lapse of time but that such spaces were used continuously by the same groups, probably families or households maintaining plots. Sometime around the mid 6th century a decline in 'furnished' burial set in that went along with smaller grave pits and fewer grave structures. In this period, parts of the burial grounds at Morning Thorpe and Bergh Apton were abandoned. This later development suggests that changes in burial practice went along with social changes affecting the burial communities.

7. Social structure

7.1 Background

The age, sex and gender of the individuals buried in the four cemeteries and the investment of labour and material culture in their burials form the fabric of the patterns that can indicate aspects of the social structure of the burial communities using these sites. A survey of the evidence on age, sex and gender from the four cemeteries will be followed by a detailed analysis of the material culture in its burial context.

7.2 Age

An age range based on the skeletal evidence was assigned to about a third of the individuals from the four cemeteries, some of them tentatively. This includes about half of the individuals from Spong Hill, about a quarter from Morning Thorpe, none from Bergh Apton and about 85% from Westgarth Gardens. Almost all the identifications for Spong Hill and Morning Thorpe concerned adults. The under-representation of children at Anglo-Saxon cemeteries is a well-known phenomenon (see Parfitt and Anderson forthcoming) but the absence of mature individuals at Spong Hill may be significant as a local feature. Glenys Putnam (1984, 16) in her report on the human bones pointed out that the average age at death at approximately 25 years for females and 30 years for males is low, and considered the small size of the sample to be the most likely reason for this deviation. It seems, however, that the age ranges given in the report may not be entirely reliable (Sayer forthcoming), and that it may therefore be wise not to rely too heavily on the Spong Hill data when analysing the four cemeteries. At Morning Thorpe, all age ranges are represented (McKinley 1987, table 10) but the numbers are too small in relation to the number of unidentified individuals from the site to allow far-reaching conclusions on age patterns.

The evidence from Westgarth Gardens is the most complete. Unfortunately the terminology in the report is confusing in respect to sub-adults (a term used in the following not only for individuals 13–18 years of age (McKinley 1994 table 1) but literally, *i.e.* for all individuals younger than adult) because the graves listed as those of 'infants' in table 2 in West (1988) are described as 'juveniles' in the catalogue descriptions. Twenty individuals were identified as 'adults', presumably including mature individuals, twelve of them females and eight males. A further six individuals were given age ranges between 20 and 40 years (mostly males) and ten individuals were given age ranges from 40 years, six of them females and four males (Crawford 1991). The clustering of the graves of male adults, female adults and of sub-adults respectively in the relatively small excavated area (Fig. 6.7) warns against using the data for far-reaching conclusions on the demography of the part of the population using the excavated area or site.

The quality of the data on age from the other three cemeteries makes comparison difficult and does not invite a detailed analysis. Age, however, is an important factor for a social analysis and therefore age ranges have been subsumed under 'sub-adult' and 'adult'. This allows for an analysis of a group of sixty infants/juveniles and ninety-seven adults. Twenty-five of these adults were buried at Spong Hill but only one sub-adult. At Westgarth Gardens, 35% (n=53) of the individuals have been recognised as sub-adults, a high proportion in comparison to other Anglo-Saxon sites (see Parfitt and Anderson forthcoming, table 7.3). Comparison with Bergh Apton has to be based on grave-length. About a quarter of the graves have lengths of less than 1.50m, and further sub-adults may have been buried in some of the larger graves. These varying proportions of sub-adults in the records of the four cemeteries need to be taken into account when the four cemeteries are compared in terms of 'wealth' and 'status'.

7.3 Sex and gender

Stoodley (1999, 1) has commented in detail on the difference between the biological concept of sex and the cultural concept of gender and has pointed out that the close relationship between the two does not make them interchangeable. At Spong Hill almost half of the individuals could be sexed on the basis of skeletal remains, and at Westgarth Gardens slightly more than half. 'Because of the fragmentary nature and condition of the skeletal remains, the sexing of the burials is based on the grave-goods' at Bergh Apton (Green and Rogerson 1978, 5), a common practice at the time. Only three individuals at Morning Thorpe could be sexed with any certainty on the basis of the skeletal data and only another ten individuals could be sexed tentatively. As Spong Hill, Westgarth Gardens and Bergh Apton are included in Stoodley's sample, his results on gender-specific grave-goods (Stoodley 1999, table 43) can be used as a template for the analysis of the four cemeteries: weapons indicate male gender, and more than one brooch, wrist-clasps, more than two beads, pendants, bracelets, girdle items and weaving tools indicate female gender (for finger-rings compare Stoodley 1999, 35 and table 43). The range of types at the four cemeteries is smaller than the sample analysed by Stoodley because the four sites did not produce any toilet implements or sets other than tweezers and a scoop (no combs, horse bits, or definite evidence for bracelets or boxes).

On the basis of grave-goods signalling gender and skeletal evidence (from Spong Hill and Westgarth Gardens only), it is possible to assign male or female sex or gender to about half of the individuals buried at the four cemeteries (Table 7.1). Grave 124 at Morning Thorpe is the only one that indicates a possible conflict between skeletal and artefactual data: according to the catalogue, the skull has male characteristics (Green *et al.* 1987, 69) but the remains of keys suggest a female. The uneven numbers between males, females and unidentified individuals at the four cemeteries are largely the result of different ratios of individuals buried either with weapons

	male gender/sex	*male sex*	female sex/gender	*female sex*	unidentified
Spong Hill	14	6	27	3	15
Morning Thorpe	69	1	111	0	150
Bergh Apton	14	0	24	0	27
Westgarth Gardens	23	4	29	7	16

Table 7.1 The four cemeteries. The number of individuals identified as male or female on the basis of human bone (sex) and/or grave-goods (gender)

or with the dress accessories of females. Most of the unidentified individuals at Spong Hill and Bergh Apton would need to be males to even out the ratio between females and males from these sites. If this is the case, relatively few males at these sites were buried with weapons. Westgarth Gardens shows the most balanced ratio between males and females in the record, both in terms of sex and gender. The highest ratios of unidentified individuals are found at Morning Thorpe and Bergh Apton. According to Stoodley (1999, 85), the other East Anglian sites in his national sample produced roughly the same result in relation to ratio of identified males and females.

The graves at the four cemeteries, as those of any other site, can be divided into four groups recognisable at first sight: graves with dress accessories indicating females (34%), with weapons indicating males (21%), with objects that do not indicate gender (30%), and graves without objects (15%). These groups formed the basis for much of the chronological analysis: separate frameworks were developed for the first two groups, while datings for the latter two remain hazy at best. To what extent do these groups reflect or express Anglo-Saxon social structure?

Stoodley (1999, 76) pointed out that 'It was almost as common for individuals not to have their gender expressed via grave-goods' and concluded that 'On the available evidence the burying community chose not to display the gender identity of these individuals in the burial ritual'. This implies that Anglo-Saxons happened exclusively to use objects for the display of gender in their burial practice that have survived in the ground, and that there was a threshold for the display of gender in Anglo-Saxon burial practice that was dependent on material wealth. Rather than assuming that roughly half of the population were 'not given a gender in death' (Stoodley 1999, 91), an interpretation with far-reaching implications on social identity in Anglo-Saxon society, it seems more likely that the 'gendered' individuals in the archaeological record formed just the upper half of the proverbial iceberg and that there were possibilities of signalling gender that are not usually preserved in the ground, such as hair styles or clothes.

7.4 Grave-goods

7.4.1 Background
The method of counting objects and types for social analysis has been widely debated, and though the method and its interpretation are not as straightforward as it may seem, it is at least an approach that deals with the archaeological evidence directly and in some detail (see Ch.3.2.1). In his analysis of a national sample of Anglo-Saxon cemeteries, Stoodley (1999) used the average number of grave-goods and the average number of different types of grave-goods in the graves. He confirmed 'the often stated claim that female burials are 'wealthier' on average than male burials' because overall 'females had greater quantities and types of grave artefacts'. The four cemeteries is no exception. It is generally agreed that this broad difference between the graves cannot mean that in life, females were wealthier than males. This seems to be a casual reaction rather than the result of a careful assessment of the position of females in Early Anglo-Saxon society, and forms a stark contrast to interpretations that in other contexts happily equate quantity and quality of grave-goods with social status. The issue of 'wealthier' females does in fact highlight an important point: the value of scoring schemes. The quantity and diversity of grave-good associations need to be assessed carefully if they are used as an indicator for 'wealth' and 'status'. How many amber beads of 2 grams each paid for a sword, and how many spearheads paid for a silver gilt square-headed brooch? How did being a key-holder compare to being a land-owner? These are questions that will not find an answer in this volume. Therefore the quantity, quality and diversity of grave-goods will be used only in relative terms of absence or presence within gender and age groups.

A count of the average number of objects (in contrast to types of objects) in the graves of the four cemeteries was not attempted. If every single object in the graves is counted, the number of objects in a single grave at the four cemeteries goes up to 217, the highest numbers created by bead strings. If such a count is modified on the basis of typological considerations, problems arise. The average number of beads, for example, varied over time because of variations in the sizes of beads and the way they were worn over time (Brugmann in Parfitt and Anderson forthcoming). At the four cemeteries, the average number of beads in grave-good associations dropped from thirty-six beads in Bead Group A1 to twenty-five beads in Bead Group A2 and twenty beads in Bead Group B (see Ch. 4.3.3 for bead groups). Taking bead numbers into account would therefore introduce a chronological aspect to the analysis. Other types of objects also pose problems, for example wrist-clasps and brooches. Should wrist-clasps be counted as two objects, though a pair is a functional unit, and if so, should pairs of brooches be treated the same? Does a shield count as a single item, or should 'extras' such as mounts on the board be taken into account? Should spears with ferrules count as a single item or should the ferrules count separately? These are questions also relevant to a count of types of grave-goods. In the following, shield studs and spear ferrules are counted separately because they fulfil a non-essential

	number of graves	association scores
male & female		
glass vessel	2	7.5
copper-alloy vessel	2	6.0
pin	15	5.7
bucket/tub	4	5.5
gold	19	5.4
rim clip (wooden vessel)	12	4.6
pursemount/firesteel	7	4.6
tweezers/scoop	14	4.5
all buckles	118	3.8
knife	215	3.8
pottery	131	2.9
female		
weaving tool	2	7.5
finger ring	4	7.3
girdle-hanger	11	6.6
key	15	6.6
strap-end	23	5.9
iron ring	35	5.8
pendant	7	5.7
buckle	37	5.7
wrist-clasp	55	5.5
copper-alloy ring	19	5.4
brooch	108	4.6
bead	113	4.3
coin	2	4.0
slip-knot ring	11	3.1
male		
sword	4	7.3
ferrule	19	5.2
shield mount	20	5.1
shieldboss	44	4.6
buckle	47	4.4
seax	3	4.3
spearhead	84	3.8

Table 7.2 The four cemeteries. Association scores for the main types of objects from the graves, sorted into three groups: types indicating male or female gender; and objects found with both groups. The association score for buckles is not only given in the third group but also separately for male and female contexts

function while brooches were not further differentiated because numbers worn changed over time: fashion changed from sets of two or three small brooches to single large brooches. The types chosen for analysis are given in Table 7.2.

Analyses of changes over time are largely dependent on well-equipped graves because they tend to be the datable ones. Figure 7.1 shows the ratio of graves dated to Phases FA1, FA2, FB, MA1, MA2 and MB against undated graves, among the graves with one to ten different types of grave-goods in them. Since mostly the better equipped graves are dated, conclusions drawn from this data need to take into account that they are based on only about half the graves from the four cemeteries and cover about two thirds of the graves of known males or females. Graves without gender-indicating grave-goods are excluded from such analyses.

Figures 7.2a–b, based on undisturbed graves, show the number of graves dated to one of the main phases sorted according to the number of types of grave-goods in them. Here, the highest scores (graves with eight or nine different types of objects) are represented exclusively by graves dated to Phase FA2. Graves with only one, two or three different types of objects in them include a relatively high proportion of graves dated to Phase FB.

On average, graves dated in Phases FA2 and MA2 produced a wider range of objects than the previous and the following phases, not only because some types were in use that are rare in the other phases, such as strap-ends or 'status' vessels (see Ch. 7.4.2), but also because combinations tended to be more random. This suggests that Stoodley's observation that 'By the late 6th century both standard gender categories record their maximum average totals' (Stoodley 1999) needs to be slightly corrected for the four cemeteries, with a peak by the mid 6th century rather than later.

This indicates that an analysis of the four cemeteries not taking chronological developments into account is likely to define a 'high status' group largely made up of graves of Phases FA2 and MA2, and a group of lower status in which most of the earlier and later graves would be presented. This would also have the effect that the particularly well-equipped graves of Phases FA2 and MA2 would stand out more against the rest of the graves than they actually did in their own time.

These changes over time need to be taken into account in regard to the overall 'wealth' of a cemetery. The considerable variations in the average number of different types of objects in the 'furnished' graves in the four cemeteries might indicate burial communities with different economic backgrounds or different burial practices: Spong Hill produced an average of 3.7 types, Bergh Apton 3.6 types, Westgarth Gardens 3.1 types, and Morning Thorpe only 2.8 types. This suggests that Morning Thorpe and Westgarth Gardens were 'poorer' sites than Spong Hill and Bergh Apton. Comparison of the dated graves, however, does not produce such a clear picture. If the graves of only Phases MA2 and FA2 at all four cemeteries are compared, Bergh Apton and Morning Thorpe show the best average for females and Spong Hill and Westgarth Gardens for males. This suggests that the low overall score of Morning Thorpe and Westgarth Gardens can be put down to a substantial number of 7th-century graves in the equation rather than differences in local economic situations or burial practices.

7.4.2 Materials

Stoodley (1999) grouped precious metals and some other materials as follows:
 1. Tinned, lead, amber, crystal and ivory
 2. Silver and/or silvered; precious stones
 3. Gold and/or gilt; silver and precious stone.

For an analysis of precious metals in the graves of the four cemeteries, criteria slightly different from Stoodley's have been used. Ivory presumably was not preserved and precious stones were not found. Precious metals were used mostly in small quantities for the decoration of

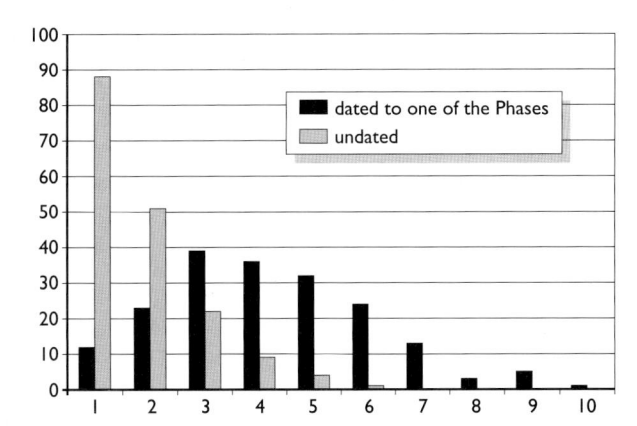

Figure 7.1 The four cemeteries. The ratio of undated and dated graves with one to ten types of objects as they are listed Table 7.2. Only undisturbed graves are included; only graves dated to one of the phases for males and females are counted as 'dated'

surfaces. As there is no common standard on which the occurrence of white metal from the four cemeteries was recorded, it does not seem wise to include this category in a detailed analysis. Gold appears as gilding on surfaces.

Most of the gold from the four cemeteries comes from the dated graves of females. This indicates quantity and quality go together, with the exception of Grave 55 at Westgarth Gardens with a low count of types because it contained three brooches, the equal-armed example among them gilt, but not associated with any other types of objects. Gold is particularly well represented in Phase FB, both in total and relative numbers. Six out of twenty undisturbed graves (30%) include gilt objects, a result that is largely based on the square-headed brooches in this phase. Only 6% of the many graves dated to Phase FA2 produced gold (six graves out of 104), compared to 23% in Phase FA1 (five graves out of twenty-two). This may indicate that the high total number of graves dated to Phase FA2 and the comparatively low number of graves dated to Phases FA1 and FB do not indicate a corresponding increase and drop in burial activity, but that the graves dated to Phases FA1 and FB form a more exclusive group than the graves dated to Phase FA2.

Precious metals are rare in Anglo-Saxon graves compared to copper-alloys and ironwork and can therefore draw only relatively few graves into a discussion on social status. The common use of copper-alloys and iron therefore merits a closer look. This shows that the use of copper-alloy and iron changed over time, a development that lies behind the rule of thumb where the grave of a female with mostly iron in it is usually dated to the 7th century, and grave-good associations dominated by copper-alloy in the 5th or 6th centuries.

The only type of object in Anglo-Saxon graves that shows a general replacement of one material for the other are bucket bindings (see Cook 2004). Other changes are subtler and correspond with changes in the quantity and quality of certain types of objects and in their range. There is too much of a hiatus between copper-alloy girdle-hangers and iron chatelaines to assume the one type replaced the other, but as objects suspended from the waist, they claimed the same space on the body. Copper-alloy wrist-clasps and strap-ends disappear from the burial record before the end of the 6th century, and at that time, copper-alloy brooches are less common but usually more substantial and elaborate (see below). Copper-alloy pins may not be rarer but certainly are smaller in the 7th century. The use of iron seems to become more lavish: knives are bigger on average; iron buckles are a fairly regular item in 7th-century graves (Geake 1997, 79), and boxes with iron handles appear in the burial record. In late burials, copper-alloy is mostly used for small items such as rivets, staples and hooks but not in the lavish quantities common in the 5th and first half of the 6th century. Instead, bits and pieces of iron, often of indeterminable use, indicate that there was more in the graves than is now apparent. Weighing the objects in a representative sample would probably make an overall change from copper-alloy to iron in the graves clearer than a count of types could do. It seems quite likely that such an overall change had to do with economic developments rather than a deliberate change in burial practice. It seems possible that these graves are not only the result of a concentration of resources in the hands of fewer individuals (see below) but also of a shortage of copper-alloy.

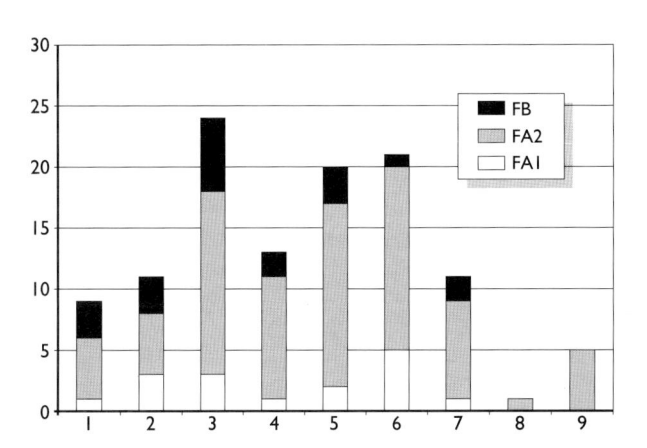

Figure 7.2a The four cemeteries. Graves dated to Phases FA1, FA2 or FB sorted according to the number of types of grave-goods in them (for type list see Table 7.2)

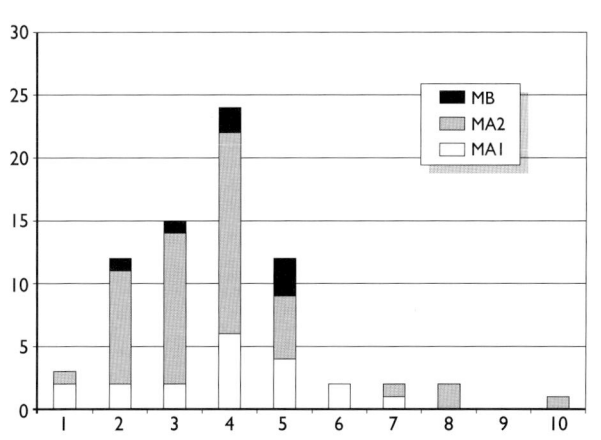

Figure 7.2b The four cemeteries. Graves dated to Phases MA1, MA2 or MB sorted according to the number of types of grave-goods in them (for type list see Table 7.2)

7.4.3 Association scores

An interesting aspect of the *Socistat* programme developed at the Institute for Archaeology, University College, London, and of a variation made available in the *Bonn Seriation and Archaeological Statistics Package* (see Ch. 3.2.1), is the calculation of a 'status index' for types of grave-goods as the mean number of different types in graves containing the type. This is a more sophisticated method of approaching the concept of 'wealth and status' than a simple count of the total number of associated grave-goods or of associated types in a grave. A bucket or glass vessel, for example, will score higher if always associated with at least five other types of objects and will score lower if also found on its own or combined with one or two objects. 'Status index' is an interpretative term for what is technically an 'association score', and therefore this more cautious term will be used in the following.

The association scores given in Table 7.2 sort types of grave-goods or their attributes such as materials into three groups: male and female contexts and objects found in both contexts. Strap-ends are listed with the female contexts because few were found in male contexts. Association scores for buckles are not only calculated for the entire dataset but also separately for male and female contexts based on the combination of sex and gender. Gilding is excluded from the calculation as such because it is not a type of object.

Most of the association scores in Table 7.2 meet established ideas about 'status goods' in Anglo-Saxon cemeteries. Beads scored less than brooches and wrist-clasps for example, and girdle-hangers and keys scored higher. In the graves of males, the established ranking of weapon types with spearheads at the bottom, swords at the top and shield bosses in the middle emerges. The low position of the seaxes is a surprise, though. The high scores of spear ferrules and shield mounts as separate categories were to be expected. In the group of objects not indicating gender, glass and copper-alloy vessels are at the top of the range and pottery and knives at the bottom. It seems that the association score used by *Socistat* can provide the statistical basis for evaluations that are often made intuitively. There are also, however, some surprises, in particular the high score buckles have in a female context (5.7). This suggests that buckles were not standard female equipment or randomly used but possibly the privilege of well-equipped females, though not necessarily in the context of girdle-hangers and keys because there is no particularly close correlation between them. The score for buckles is much lower for undisturbed graves in general (3.8), probably because buckles became more common when 'furnished' burial was otherwise in decline (see Ch. 5.4.3).

All the glass and copper-alloy vessels and the rims of wooden vessels from dated contexts at the four cemeteries fall in Phases FA2 and MA2. As far as their date ranges are concerned, all four sites could have produced these items. Both glass vessels, however, were found at Westgarth Gardens, the copper-alloy vessels at Spong Hill and Morning Thorpe, and the buckets and tubs everywhere but at Bergh Apton. None of the twenty-four Bergh Apton graves dated to Phases FA2 or MA2 produced a glass vessel, copper-alloy bowl or cauldron, or a bucket or tub, and only a single grave had rim-clips. There were also no swords.

The absence of these types of 'status goods' from Bergh Apton may be significant despite the small size of the excavated area, and indicate that in Phases FA2 and MA2, the site was used by a relatively 'poor' community. The absence of 'status' vessels and swords, however, may also be the result of a relatively high ratio of sub-adults in the excavated area, which leaves an even smaller number of graves in which such objects could be expected, considering that at the four cemeteries, an average of 2.0 types was found with sub-adults, compared to 3.5 types in the graves of adults. In terms of gilt objects, Bergh Apton seems on a par with the other three cemeteries. Five out of the eighteen graves from the four cemeteries with gilt objects were found on this site, two of them dated to Phase FA2 and three to Phase FB.

Thus, differences in 'wealth' between the four cemeteries need not indicate communities with different economic backgrounds or different local burial practices. Instead, overall changes in burial practice over time, small samples and different burial practices for different age groups may provide sufficient explanation. An analysis of the four cemeteries not taking chronological issues on board would be in danger of identifying a group of 'high-ranking' individuals on the basis of their 'wealth' that would be comprised of a high proportion of individuals buried at a 'wealthy' time and therefore not representative for the four cemeteries as such. This approach would in fact draw out the overall scale of 'wealth' observed in the material and could give the impression that in these terms, Anglo-Saxon society was more differentiated than was actually the case at any particular time.

7.4.4 Quantity and quality

The number of graves from the four cemeteries dated to individual phases varies considerably: twenty graves are dated to Phase FA1, 104 graves to FA2 and twenty-eight graves to FB; twenty-three graves to Phase MA1, fifty-six graves to MA2 and thirteen graves to MB. This is to some extent the result of differences in the date spans of the four cemeteries. All sites have substantial numbers of graves dated to the late 5th and first half of the sixth century, but the 5th century is not well represented at Bergh Apton, and Spong Hill has no graves of the second half of the 6th or later. The horizontal stratigraphy at Morning Thorpe suggests an expansion of the burial ground in Phase FA2 at a scale that indicates substantial growth of the burial community using Morning Thorpe, but none of these factors fully explains the almost six times as many graves in Phase FA2 than in FA1. Nor does the length of the individual phases provide an explanation. The question arises whether the high number of graves dated to Phases FA2 and MA2 are the result of an increase in burial activity or whether a higher proportion of graves of the late 5th and 6th centuries are datable on the basis of their grave-goods. The distributions of dated graves at the four sites show that the earliest tend to be widely scattered while the distribution of later graves is denser (Ch. 6.6). Some explanation for the relatively dense scatter of graves dated to this period may be found in changes in the material culture and its use in inhumation burial practice over the 5th to 7th centuries which may have led to a larger proportion of the population being buried with female dress accessories or weapons.

The backbone of the chronological framework for the females is formed by bead types that have a main distribution in Norfolk, so that in comparison to Spong Hill, Morning Thorpe and Bergh Apton, relatively few graves from Westgarth Gardens could be dated to Phase FA2. The beads were often associated with annular brooches and quite often also with wrist-clasps, a favourable combination for dating that explains much of the 'boost' in Phase FA2.

The age of the individuals buried with these dress accessories is likely to be a further factor that may speak against a steep rise in burial activity at the four cemeteries in Phase FA2. Of the twenty females dated to Phase FA1, eleven are adults and the others are unidentified. Of the 104 females dated to Phase FA2, twenty-five are adults, six sub-adults and the others are unidentified. Phase FB has four adults and sub-adults each among the twenty-eight dated females. Though the numbers are not conclusive because of the large proportion of unidentified individuals in all three groups, they may indicate a change in female dress or in burial practice that leads to an increase of datable sub-adult females in Phase FA2: none of the individuals dated to Phase FA1 was identified as sub-adults, though more than half could be identified as adult. In Phase FA2 the ratio of identified adults and sub-adults is 25:6, in Phase FB it is 4:4. This may indicate a steady increase in the number of sub-adults buried with (datable) dress accessories.

The average number of types in the graves of known adults and sub-adults indicates that sub-adults tended to be buried with fewer objects in Phase FA2: the average number of types in the graves of the identified adults is 5.3, of the sub-adults only 2.8. Wrist-clasps and girdle-hangers are absent in the latter group, which includes the only known grave of a sub-adult with a buckle, strap-end and key. Phase FA1 has no identified sub-adults whose grave-goods could be compared with the 4.1 types in the graves of the adults in this phase. In Phase FB, both identified adults and sub-adults were buried with an average of 3.7 types. This may indicate that some social differentiation between the age-groups in Phase FA2 was levelled out in Phase FB.

There are some indications that the wide but apparently differentiated use of female dress accessories in Phase FA2 went along with an overall decrease in the quality of the items from Phase FA1 to FA2: annular brooches as the most common type in Phase FA2 are remarkably unsophisticated in comparison to the cruciform and small-long brooches of Phase FA1, and weighing these brooches would probably show that the manufacture of annular brooches not only required less skill but also less copper-alloy. In Phase FA2, some cruciform brooches were made in larger sizes but on the whole, less effort was being put into the manufacture of cruciform brooches and girdle-hangers — the two types on which Style I decoration had been used in Phase FA1. Wrist-clasp production seems to have suffered from the same overall development: the latest type *wc7b* was no longer cast individually and was no more than cut-out copper-alloy sheets covered with repoussé dots. Strap-ends were made of two copper-alloy sheets riveted together at the base and therefore of lower quality than the contemporary cast bayleaf-shaped strap-ends with split ends from Kent. Some of the *Norfolk* types among the glass beads are noticeable for their careless manufacture, possibly another sign of quantity having been more important in dress accessories of Phase FA2 than quality.

This development may have been the cause or effect of wider access to copper-alloy dress accessories, which included a younger age group.

A similar development can be observed with regard to the weapon graves of Phases MA1 and MA2. Twenty-three graves are dated to Phase MA1, fifty-six to Phase MA2 and thirteen to Phase MB. The increase of weapon graves in Phase MA2 is not quite as dramatic as that of graves datable to Phase FA2 but is part of the general peak of Anglo-Saxon weapon graves in the first two-thirds of the 6th century (see Härke 1992, 217). According to Härke (1992, 182ff.; fig. 36) the minimum age at which boys were buried with weapons dropped around AD 500 and then rose steeply between the later 6th and mid 7th centuries. This had an effect on the weapon combinations of the first two-thirds of the 6th century. The average age of individuals buried with a combination of shield and spear was higher than that of individuals buried only with spears (Härke 1992, table 30). On average, older individuals were also buried with larger spearheads than younger individuals, a tendency that finds a convincing explanation in the length of spearheads as a status symbol, though the length of a spearhead is not a reliable indicator of the age of the individual buried with it (Härke 1992, 187, fig. 38). If these tendencies observed by Härke in his national sample are reflected in the evidence from the four cemeteries, Phase MA2 should have a higher proportion of spears not combined with other weapons, and shorter spearheads on average.

This is indeed the case. Of the individuals dated to Phase MA1 at the four cemeteries, 32% (n=22) were buried with a spear as the only weapon, in Phase MA2 this rose to 60% (n=51) and dropped again to 36% (n=11) in Phase MB. Average spearhead length dropped from 27cm in Phase MA1 to 23cm in Phase MA2 and rose to 41cm in Phase MB. The average length of spearheads associated with shields does not however vary significantly from the average length of all spearheads not associated with shields, which suggests that shorter spearheads were a general feature of Phase MA2. It seems that as with female dress accessories, quantity was given preference over quality, and members of a younger age group were buried with items that were previously the privilege of adults.

The skeletal evidence from the four cemeteries supports this interpretation to some extent: of the five individuals dated to Phase MA1 and identified as adults, four were buried with shields and one with a seax. Of the twelve known adults dated to Phase MA2, nine were buried with shields and one with a sword. The only known sub-adults with weapons are both dated in this phase; both have shields. Phase MB has three known adults, two of them buried with shields and swords.

The evidence from the four cemeteries in combination with Härke's research suggests that in Phase MA2, a larger proportion of males were buried with weapons and that this included a younger age group than before. In Phase MB weapon burial became more selective again, resulting in a range of particularly long spearheads. As is the case with Phase FA2, there is evidence for a burial practice in Phase MA2 that was less exclusive in respect to weapons than in Phases MA1 and MB.

After these changes between the late 5th and mid 6th centuries, Phase FB seems to have seen yet another change in the material culture and its use. The data on the age of the dated individuals are inconclusive but may indicate a drop in the average age of females buried with datable dress accessories. There seems to be a concentration of wealth: the beads of this phase are probably not of local production but imported, and square-headed brooches may be more evident as status objects. This is probably a development that started in Phase FA2, indicated by the two square-headed brooches from particularly well-equipped graves dated to this phase. Of the twenty undisturbed females in Phase FB, six were buried with gilt objects, mostly the square-headed brooches. This is more gilding than in any other context from the four cemeteries and suggests not only that weapon burial became more exclusive again towards the end of the 6th century, but that being buried with (datable) dress items also became the privilege of a relatively small group, including sub-adults. This may have been the start of a development observed by Geake (1997, 128f.) and Stoodley (1999, 113, 118) in their national samples. It seems that the trend from quality to quantity in Phases FA2 and MA2 was reversed in this period. This was part of a general development in Anglo-Saxon burial practice within the second half of the 6th century which led to the widening gap between a majority of 'unfurnished' and a minority of well-furnished graves characteristic of the 7th century.

7.4.5 Graves without gender-indicating grave-goods
How do individuals buried without gender-indicating objects relate to those males buried with weapons and females buried with dress accessories? Do they form a social group of their own, possibly the dependent and poor in Early Anglo-Saxon society? Such an interpretation would gain credibility if it could be shown that individuals buried without female dress accessories or weapons were never buried with 'status goods'. Stoodley (1999, 94), however, was able to demonstrate that on the basis of the average number of grave-goods and types, 'both standard gender categories record similar results, and significantly, so do all biologically sexed males and females, including individuals with no standard gender' in his date group 1 (c. AD 425–525). He concluded that 'The fact that feminine individuals do not have a greater number of goods from the inception of the period suggests that in the early years of settlement a conspicuous display of 'wealth' was not linked to the expression of this gender' and pointed out that 'In line with the evidence from wealth scores, only in the first date group are precious materials encountered with individuals without a visible gender in any quantity'. Later on, 'gendered burials consistently have greater averages than burials without a standard gender'.

The four cemeteries include few graves that have no gender-indicating grave-goods but more than knives, buckles or pots in them. Grave 200 at Morning Thorpe is the most impressive one, a large grave with evidence for a wooden structure, two copper-alloy vessels and a bucket but neither weapons nor dress accessories. Three further graves at Morning Thorpe without gender-indicating grave-goods show evidence for grave structures, a rare feature on this site: Graves 78 and 178 with belts as the only dress accessories, and Grave 17 with only a pot. At Spong Hill, where evidence for grave-structures was more common, rim-clips for a wooden vessel were found without any other objects in Grave 34. Four out of thirteen toilet implements and three out of seven pursemounts/firesteels from undisturbed contexts not associated with gender-indicating grave-goods are also noteworthy. A 5th-century date cannot be excluded for any of them, and the firesteels and decorated pots involved make a date later than the mid 6th century unlikely. Graves 17, 27, 36, 65, 87, 178, and 200 as the best-furnished gender-'neutral' graves at Morning Thorpe, were dug in the north-western part of the cemetery which was probably not in use in the latest phase. For Spong Hill, Graves 16 and 34 can be listed as 'neutral' graves with no more than knives, belts or pots, and Grave 12 joins the list for Westgarth Gardens. Stoodley's early date for such graves suggests that the absence of evidence from Bergh Apton is a result of the site not having produced much evidence of the earliest phase.

The changing role of dress accessories and weapons in Anglo-Saxon burial practice makes an assessment of the gender-'neutral' group in the archaeological evidence difficult. The *crux* is that graves of this group can rarely be closely dated, but a reasonably close date range is required to understand these graves in their specific context. Härke's and Stoodley's research has shown that age was an important factor in Anglo-Saxon burial practice (Härke 1992, 182ff.; Stoodley 1999, 105ff.). They were able to define thresholds for burial with female dress accessories or weapons based on biological and social criteria. According to Stoodley 'The age when an individual's gender was critical was for females from about 10–12 years to about 40 and for males from late teens to about 40. So although differences are noted early on in life, between the ages of 20–40, a stage in the lifecycle when gender was very important for both sexes is recognised'. The increase of 'gendered' burial from the late 5th century and its decline towards the end of the 6th century implies that in terms of social status, burying an individual around the age of thirty without either brooches or a spear was a particularly negative statement around AD 525. The gender-'neutral' group seems to have been the most heterogeneous one at all times, comprising children and mature individuals besides adults who were not buried with weapons or female dress items though they died at an age that would have qualified them for a 'gendered' burial. This group decreased in the late 5th century and increased again in the course of the 6th century.

7.5 5th- and 6th-century Anglo-Saxon social structure

In his survey of the Early East Anglian inhumation cemetery evidence, Scull (1993, 73) stated that 'Until the later 6th century, the cemetery evidence appears to reflect a greater degree of social differentiation within communities than between them', an important point picked up by Härke (1997, 147) in a survey of Anglo-Saxon social structure in which he noted a 'growing impression that the social differentiation seen in cemeteries may reflect status differences within rather than between families and/or households'. A household in this context is understood as a primary descent group in control of and economically supported by individuals of a different social status (*cf.* Stoodley 1999, 126). The 6th-century Anglo-Saxon settlement evidence suggests households of ten to fifteen individuals based on farmsteads, which could be clustered into hamlets of up to ten or possibly more contemporary units (Scull 1993, 72; Hamerow 1993; 2002, 93), which formed 'local community sizes of between a dozen and well over fifty people, but rarely touching one hundred' according to Härke (1997, 140).

Scull's estimate that even a site the size of Morning Thorpe 'need only represent a contributing population of around sixty individuals over 150 years' (Scull 1993, 72) is difficult to improve because reliable estimates for the four cemeteries would depend on a combination of data that is insufficient: indications that the site holds a cross-section of the population, age ranges for most of the individuals, the number of years in which the site was in use, and how steady the burial activity was over the period. None of the four cemeteries was fully excavated, the beginnings of Phases FA1/MA1, the end of Phases FB/MB are vague in absolute terms, and the skeletal data does not invite detailed interpretations. The analysis of the four cemeteries, however, supports Scull's model of 'broadly-equal, internally-ranked patrilineal, patrilocal descent groups' forming 'agrarian societies, with no market economy, money or large-scale specialised production' who operated on 'three levels of economic activity: subsistence, craft specialisation and exchange operating at a local level; and craft specialisation and exchange operating at a regional and inter-regional level' (Scull 1993, 73). It seems possible that the expansion of the burial ground at Morning Thorpe in Phases FA2 and MA1b–2 was the result of a settlement development that added new households to the burial community.

The emphasis on the interpretation of the archaeological evidence in respect to social structure has to be on 'broadly-equal, internally ranked' rather than on 'patrilineal' and 'patrilocal'. Härke (1997, 151) has pointed out that 'only a sophisticated analysis can achieve the distinction between household and family in the archaeological record, but the units we perceive in the organisation of cemeteries are better explained in terms of residential units with internal social differentiation (*i.e.* households) than kinship units (*i.e.* families)'. Making this distinction would seem to overtax the evidence from the four cemeteries, but there are some general aspects to the evidence that are worth pointing out.

The range of accumulated wealth displayed by the grave-good associations at the four cemeteries is created mostly by choices from a common pool of material culture. Variations in the quality of the metalwork such as brooches, wrist-clasps, girdle-hangers, decorative shield- and belt-mounts *etc.* would seem to be within the range of a workshop serving a corresponding range of demands. As in 6th-century Anglo-Saxon cemeteries in general, there is nothing in terms of quality or workmanship that would prepare for the stunning quality or quantity of finds made in Mound 1 at Sutton Hoo. Materials and objects that indicate far-distance exchange, such as gold, silver, rock crystal and amber, glass vessels, some glass bead types, copper-alloy vessels and possibly pattern-welded swords also seem to have been largely a matter of presence or absence rather than of quality ranges within the categories and we know that they were available in this form across all of Anglo-Saxon England. A detailed analysis of the material, however, may prove this to be wrong and reveal quality ranges of long-distance trade goods corresponding with other status indices.

The distribution of the various types of grave-goods across the four cemeteries is remarkably even and accordingly, the context of the individual graves is their main structuring element. At least half of the social group at the four cemeteries in the first half of the 6th century was buried with a small range of 'status goods' of comparable quality, which indicates a relatively low degree of social diversification at the time. Internal ranking is expressed by selective access to these common sources.

There is no evidence for hard and fast rules about the association of grave-goods apart from those concerning gender — with few known exceptions. There is a general consensus that on average, females were buried with more material wealth than males, but it is generally assumed that this cannot mean that females had more control over material wealth during their lifetimes. Stoodley's research on Early Anglo-Saxon lifestyles, however, suggests that in the early 6th century, being a woman with brooches (or a girl with the prospect of brooches) was an excellent position (that is before a relatively early death due to the risks of childbirth). This is suggested by a low rate of hypoplasia as an indicator for poor nutrition or prolonged illness, less caries and therefore better teeth than males, less hard physical labour indicated by arthritis and generally no exposure to physical violence. The evidence from the national sample analysed by Stoodley (1999, 125) suggests that living conditions for females deteriorated in the 6th century and 'that the position of women in early Anglo-Saxon England had declined by the 7th century'.

The lack of evidence for clear and simple rules about the use of 'status goods' for the definition and display of social rank among females may not be so much a matter of a blurred picture in the archaeological record but more a reflection of Anglo-Saxon social reality (*cf.* Stoodley 1999, 103f.). Considering that a household of ten individuals would have had to conduct the burial of a grown female member only about every ten years, and that the social status of this individual not only depended on her age but also on her position in the household at that particular time in relation to all the other household members and on the current economic situation of the household, a lot of room opens up for variations in burial practice. The same applies to the burial of males. A household fortunate enough not to have their head die while in office for two generations in a row may not have had the opportunity for a full-range burial in twenty or thirty years. In view of this, the clearer pattern presented by weapon burials in terms of internal ranking observed by Härke (1992) is almost surprising, but finds some explanation in the smaller range of objects involved and in the fewer thresholds in the life of males (Stoodley 1999, 117), because they give less room for variation.

Härke's research on a national sample suggests that clusters of weapon graves on sites such as Spong Hill, Bergh Apton and Westgarth Gardens are common in Anglo-Saxon cemeteries (see Härke 1992, 169). Such clusters mostly or entirely dated to Phase MA2 were also dug at Morning Thorpe, for example the neighbouring Graves 380, 381 and 409, and Graves 327, 337, 339, and 340. Härke's analysis of the distribution of weapon graves showed that despite such clusters, there was no evidence in the form of sword graves for a particular group to rise above the other(s) in a way that suggests a leading family in that community. This may be the result of the scenario described above: burial practice not as a fixed ritual which, for example, required a sword to be buried in every generation, but determined by variable factors.

The 'inflation' of gender-indicating status goods in the early 6th century coupled with what seems to be an overall decline in the quality used for what became a new standard ('cheap' dress accessories and overall shorter spears) came to an end in the mid 6th century at the latest, and was followed by a phase in which wrist-clasps and girdle-hangers were either not worn or not buried any more, and in which only annular brooches occasionally got into the graves. At the beginning of this phase, new types of square-headed brooches were worn by relatively few females who were buried with an item that required a lot of copper-alloy compared to annular brooches and for which gilding and silver-plating was used. Such a demonstrative concentration of wealth in the graves of relatively few individuals forms a stark contrast to the previously wide use of female dress accessories. It seems likely that square-headed brooches were used in this way only for a generation or so.

At Morning Thorpe, three graves with square-headed brooches were found close together on the southern fringe of the burial ground (Graves 214, 359 and 371) and in the vicinity of weapon graves dated to Phase MB, possibly an early indication of an accumulation of wealth as a result of peer competition that led to the development of a 7th-century elite (Scull 1993, 75). Another group of graves of Phases FB/MB is formed by Graves 218, 227 and 238 centred on a ring-ditch. Two of these graves produced buckets (one of them possibly associated with an earlier grave). The ring-ditch is particularly noteworthy because most graves dated to Phases FB/MB came to fill spaces between earlier graves, the main reason for the crowded layout of the site.

Evidence for burial activity after the mid 7th century at the four cemeteries is scant but Phases FB and MB appear to foreshadow the decline of 'furnished' burial. Though the evidence is by no means conclusive, it seems possible that the apparent abandonment of substantial proportions of the burial grounds at Morning Thorpe and Bergh Apton is related to the socio-economic changes leading to a reorganisation of settlement and a widespread abandonment of cemeteries founded in the 5th or 6th centuries (Hamerow 2002, 123). Whether the burial area in use contracted or just shifted, the fact remains that if the sites are interpreted as household plots, some must have been given up at Morning Thorpe in the 6th century. Whether this was a local phenomenon or part of a general development may become clearer in the course of future research on more cemeteries. The scant evidence for burial activity at Morning Thorpe and Westgarth Gardens after the mid 7th century suggests that if an elite emerged from the burial communities using the four cemeteries, this part of the community buried elsewhere.

7.6 Inhumation and cremation burial practice

The focus in this volume on the inhumation graves at the four cemeteries makes it easy to forget that at Spong Hill, Morning Thorpe and Westgarth Gardens cremation burial was also practised and that at Spong Hill, inhumation burials were in fact the exception. Do the inhumation graves nevertheless present a cross section of the Anglo-Saxon population in this part of East Anglia? Or do they represent a particular social group, such as the nuclear family of a household, for example?

Discussions on cultural differences indicated by the two burial practices tend to focus on the size of cremation sites such as Spong Hill with *c.* 2500 cremations, and the role of large cemeteries as central places. The difference between the just over 300 excavated inhumation graves at Morning Thorpe, which by Anglo-Saxon standards make a large inhumation cemetery, and the *c.* 2500 cremation graves and 55 inhumation graves at Spong Hill is indeed striking. Ravn (2003) interpreted the inhumation graves at Spong Hill as the burials of an emerging elite who used inhumation burial as a demonstrative act of separation (see Ch. 3.2.1). This raises the question whether the earliest graves at Morning Thorpe, Bergh Apton and Westgarth Gardens could also be seen in this light.

In some ways, the difference between cremation and inhumation burial practice may not have been as fundamental as the archaeological evidence seems to suggest at first sight. Though a pot filled with ashes presents evidence quite different from a grave pit with the skeletal remains of an individual and a number of grave-goods, much of the burial practice leading to these finds seems to have been the same. Both cremation and inhumation burial practice treated bodies individually and involved a particular range of material in their deposition. It seems that cremation burial to a large part involved the same range of objects that are found in inhumation burials, such as dress accessories and glass and copper-alloy vessels (McKinley 1987, 86). McKinley (1994, 92) concluded from her analysis of the cremated remains from Spong Hill that 'The grave-goods of various types illustrate the greater importance attached to the process of cremation than to burial of the remains. This was the stage at which the deceased was provided with her/his 'goods', be it personal ornaments, foodstuffs or other possessions'. Grave-goods deliberately not burnt are the exception rather than the norm: 'It seems somewhat out of keeping that particular items, *e.g.* bronze toilet sets, should be deliberately kept back from the pyre and only deposited in the urns which contained neither the complete remains of the deceased nor, very likely, the full remains of the grave-goods which accompanied them on the pyre' (McKinley 1994, 92).

The deposition of the cremated or inhumed individuals seems to have followed largely the same idea in terms of cemetery organisation: a communal space for burial plots presumably reflecting the household structure of the contributing farmsteads in the region. Cremation pits cut into inhumation burials as at Spong Hill and Morning Thorpe may also have been a form of 'shared space', like cremation pits with more than one urn. A transfer of this aspect of cremation burial practice onto inhumation burial practice might explain the intercutting of ring-ditches and inhumation graves at Spong Hill and the relatively large number of re-used and disturbed inhumations at Morning Thorpe, including cremations dug into inhumations (Ch. 6.6).

If the introduction of inhumation burial practice at Spong Hill and possibly also Morning Thorpe, Bergh Apton and Westgarth Gardens was indeed a demonstrative act of separation, what did the burial practice demonstrate? There was no funeral pyre, which must have robbed the occasion of an impressive element, and there was no investment of labour and resources in the building of this pyre. Labour and resources were diverted to the excavation of the burial pit, and in the case of Grave 31 into construction of what seems to have been a burial chamber. A major difference may have been that this activity was carried out at the central place formed by the cremation cemetery and not, as it seems from the lack of evidence for funeral pyres at Spong Hill, in a different and possibly less central place. The large ring-ditch around Graves 31 and 32 seems to have been dug only after Graves 18, 22 and 26, and Grave 46 with a coffin and the remains of a small shallow ditch. Here we may have founders after all, though not the ones suspected by Ravn (see Ch. 3.2.1). Graves 22, 26 and 46 were indeed in the top range of what was achievable in terms of grave-goods in the earliest phase (see Ch. 7.4).

Among the earliest graves of females further to the west are several graves of undated males with spearheads or no weapons, but a buckle (Grave 23) and an early pursemount (Grave 30). If inhumation burial was not largely restricted to females at this early stage, it is likely that some of these males were contemporary. Weapon burial was not so much of a status symbol at this time that it became later and therefore these graves do not necessarily speak against members of a rising elite (see Ch. 7.4). It seems possible that the general lack of evidence for weapons from cremation burial contexts reflects burial practice at the time, a practice continued in regard to early inhumation graves. Male inhumations may not have had to be that impressive to be of corresponding high status. As elsewhere, weapon burial at Spong Hill became more common only in the following phase, perhaps when inhumation burial practice as such had lost some of its force. It would take the definite graves of sub-adults dated to the earliest phase to convincingly argue that the inhumation graves at Spong Hill were for the members of an entire household and not for 'high status' members of one or possibly several households. The remains of a child in Grave 31 may have been contemporary with the male in this grave or a consecutive burial. Graves 3 and 16, both of sub-adults, most likely fall in Phase FA2.

The question remains whether inhumation burial actually had the demonstrative quality a rising elite would have wished to use. Detailed research on cremation sites might be able to suggest an alternative explanation: possibly cremation burial practice became economically and ecologically unviable towards the end of the 5th century because it put too great a strain on timber resources. The earliest inhumation graves at Spong Hill suggest that if this was the case, the answer was not found in a cheap solution which denied low-status household members a cremation burial. As at Spong Hill, the evidence from Morning Thorpe is not good enough to tell whether the earliest graves on the sites include individuals of all ages, indicating that all members of a household were inhumed in this phase. Evidence for children's graves at the four cemeteries suggests that sooner or later the whole range of household members was inhumed, in graves ranging from those that appear as 'unfurnished' in the archaeological record to those at the peak of what seems to have been economically viable in the 6th century in terms of grave-goods.

7.7 Summary

The layout of the four cemeteries, the material culture used in the burial practice, and the distribution and association of this material culture in the graves supports an interpretation of the cemeteries as the communal burial grounds of local farmsteads worked by families/ households with an internal social differentiation rather than a differentiation among these social units. The internal differentiation is indicated by gender- and age-specific grave-goods and their association in the graves. The range of grave-good associations from 'unfurnished' graves to assemblages which cover almost the full range of the types available to males or females is wide enough to represent a range of household members that covers anyone from a child or a possible servant to the heads of a household with access to 'status goods' obtained by distant exchange. Differences in grave 'furnishings' among individuals of the same sex/gender are a matter of degree rather than of groups of individuals clearly defined by their grave-goods. This is probably the result of a burial practice that was based on changing conventions and followed by groups too small to produce a clear pattern in their burials.

The archaeological and skeletal data from the four cemeteries are not sufficient for the identification of burial plots that would indicate the sizes of such households, or prove that the sites were indeed used for all members of such households. Until we find evidence for a burial practice different from both Anglo-Saxon cremation and inhumation burial practice, however, the model of communal burial grounds used by households based on farmsteads representing the local population is the best we have.

It seems that the analysis of the four cemeteries has answered certain questions and raised new ones. This demonstrates how important a chronological basis is for a detailed analysis of an Anglo-Saxon cemetery. Furthermore, the interpretation of the evidence has profited greatly from the context provided by research that has been carried out on various aspects of Anglo-Saxon material culture on the basis of national samples. In the future, regional surveys including metal-detector finds, settlement evidence and environmental data may fill the gap that presently exists between the study of individual cemeteries and national surveys on aspects of Anglo-Saxon burial practice and material culture.

8. Conclusions

Spong Hill, Morning Thorpe and Bergh Apton in Norfolk and Westgarth Gardens in Suffolk are the only substantial East Anglian inhumation cemeteries with date ranges between the mid 5th and 7th centuries which have been formally excavated and published so far (Green and Rogerson 1978; Hills *et al.* 1984; Green *et al.* 1987; West 1988). The *c.* 500 graves form 15–20% of the total number of inhumation graves recorded in East Anglia since the 19th century. The acidity of East Anglian soils on sands and gravels has often reduced the skeletal evidence to a few scraps of bone or stains at best. With the exception of Westgarth Gardens, the archaeological record is largely restricted to grave features and associated grave-goods. Only at Spong Hill could an area be fully excavated, and comparison of the four cemeteries in terms of size, duration, or their individual character as 'mixed' cemeteries with evidence for both inhumation and cremation burial is therefore limited.

The four cemeteries owe their joint discussion in this volume to the fact that the grave catalogues were published ahead of a detailed analysis expected to follow in due course. This publication policy makes East Anglia a particularly well represented region in national samples of mainly 6th-century sites. Spong Hill, Bergh Apton and Westgarth Gardens, together with Holywell Row and the earlier excavations at Little Eriswell in Suffolk and Swaffham in Norfolk (Gaz. nos. S62, S95 and N85), formed the regional samples for East Anglia in Härke's analysis of Anglo-Saxon weapon burials (Härke 1992) and Stoodley's study on aspects of gender in Anglo-Saxon burial practice (Stoodley 1999). A survey of glass beads included all four cemeteries in the national sample, but split them up as parts of regional samples for Norfolk and Suffolk (Brugmann 2004). While the weight of Härke's and Stoodley's East Anglian samples lie in Suffolk, the four cemeteries form a sample with a northern bias. An analysis of Eriswell, Lakenheath (Gaz. no. S95) may reveal regional variations in the material culture and burial practice of East Anglia that are not recognisable as such at the four cemeteries but might affect them as a regional sample.

The aim of the report was an analysis of material culture and inhumation burial practice at the four cemeteries as a source of information on Anglo-Saxon social structure. For this purpose, a chronological framework was created which allowed for distinctions between developments over time and contemporary diversity in the material culture and burial practice at the four cemeteries. This objective required a selective grave-good analysis focussed on a typology of objects suitable for correspondence analysis, on external dating evidence for types of grave-goods, and on the use of material culture in Anglo-Saxon burial practice. The relative chronological framework for the four cemeteries is based on correspondence analyses of grave-good associations and on the vertical and horizontal stratigraphy in particular at Morning Thorpe. This relative chronological framework is supported by results from research on a national sample of weapon graves carried out by Karen Høilund Nielsen and John Hines as part of the project *Anglo-Saxon England c. 570–720: the chronological basis* funded by English Heritage, and by a chronological framework for glass beads from Anglo-Saxon graves (Brugmann 2004). Absolute date ranges for the relative chronological phases defined on the basis of the results from correspondence analyses are based on types of objects which are dated by regional frameworks for Early Medieval cemeteries on the Continent, in particular for the Lower Rhine valley (Siegmund 1998) and southern Germany (Koch 2001).

The gender-specific types of objects — weapons and female dress accessories — in the graves of males and females required separate phasing schemes (Figs 5.20–28). It was possible to assign about half of the graves to either Phases FA1, FA2 or FB for female dress accessories or Phases MA1, MA2 or MB for weapons. Though further graves could not be dated individually, the analysis suggests some general changes in the burial practice at the four cemeteries over time. There seems to have been an overall decrease in grave length in Phase FB, which however did not affect males buried with weapons. An overall development from furnished to unfurnished burial seems to have had an impact on pots as accessory vessels but not on the presence of knives and buckles in graves.

The subdivision of the phases for males and females into Phases FA and FB and MA and MB denote major changes in the grave-good associations from the four cemeteries. Phase FA is characterised by associations of cruciform, small-long and annular brooches, wrist-clasps, girdle-hangers and certain glass bead types, Phase FB by different glass beads, silver bell beads and a type of square-headed brooch whose forerunners were introduced late in Phase FA. The main type of dress accessories linking Phases FA and FB are scutiform pendants. A major change in the weapon combinations is indicated by a very weak link in the correspondence analysis for the two groups of weapons defining Phases MA and MB. The absolute dates for the approximate time of change are different for male and female associations: *c.* AD 530/50 for the change from Phase FA to FB and *c.* AD 560/70 for the change from Phase MA to MB.

The subdivision of the Phases FA and MA into FA1/FA2 and MA1/MA2 mark changes in the grave-good associations which are more gradual than the changes from 'A' to 'B' and therefore even more artificial. The main change in female fashion defining Phase FA2 is the introduction of annular brooches as the most common type of dress accessory besides certain bead types. Subtler changes can be seen in typological details of cruciform and small long brooches, wrist-clasps and girdle-hangers. The change from Phase MA1 to MA2 is marked by the introduction of a new type of shield boss design. External dating evidence suggests a date around AD 480 for the subdivision of FA1 and FA2 and a date around AD 510 for the subdivision of Phases MA1 and MA2. The subdivision of Phase MA1 into sub-Phases MA1a and MA1b was useful for the correlation of Phase MA1 with Phases FA1 and FA2 but it is a construct based on a possibly unreliable tendency in the correspondence analysis of weapon combinations and by the horizontal stratigraphy at Morning Thorpe. It is so tentative that it will require further confirmation to be of value in any other context. The subdivision of Phase FA2 into sub-Phases FA2a and FA2b is also tentative but useful for a correlation of the phase with Phase MA1b.

External dating evidence for the beginning of Phases FA1 and MA1 is vague and provisionally put at c. AD 450. The end of Phases FB and MB is also difficult to assess. It may but need not have ended as late as c. AD 650. Only Morning Thorpe and Westgarth Gardens produced any evidence for material conventionally dated in the second half of the 7th century (lace-tags in Grave 2 at Morning Thorpe and an iron buckle with two tongues in Grave 350; a pin with a midrib in Grave 47 at Westgarth Gardens).

The four cemeteries were largely but not entirely contemporary. Spong Hill started in Phases FA1/MA1 and probably ended before the close of Phases FA2/MA2, which suggests a date span for the inhumation graves from c. AD 450 at the earliest to AD 550 at the latest. Morning Thorpe and Westgarth Gardens started in Phases FA1/MA1 (c. AD 450–480) and may have ended as late as the second half of the 7th century. Bergh Apton has a grave attributed to Phase MA1a but it seems that the excavated area was mainly in use in Phases FA2–FB and MA1b–MB, that is, from the late 5th century, and possibly not later than c. AD 600.

Inhumation burial at the four cemeteries seems to have started in the form of scattered graves covering an area filled in with graves in the following phases. Towards AD 500, the burial ground at Morning Thorpe was expanded on a scale that suggests more than the expansion of existing plots. In the second half of the 6th century, a substantial part of the site seems to have been given up both at Morning Thorpe and Bergh Apton. This development may be part of socio-economic changes that eventually led to the founding of 'Final Phase' cemeteries.

A detailed analysis of the grave-good associations from the four cemeteries confirms certain aspects of Härke's interpretation of Anglo-Saxon weapon burial practice and of Stoodley's research on gender. At the four cemeteries, as at other Anglo-Saxon sites, burial with female dress accessories or weapons became more common towards the end of the 5th century, and included individuals of younger age groups, who tended to be buried with more basic kits than adults, drawing out the scale of 'wealth' and 'status' indicated by grave-good associations. The evidence from the four cemeteries suggests that this development led to an 'inflation' of burials with female dress accessories or spears in the early 6th century and that this was related to a decline in the average manufacturing quality of copper-alloy dress accessories and in the length of spearheads. Around the mid 6th century wrist-clasps and girdle-hangers were either not worn or not buried any more, and annular brooches became rare grave-goods. By then, new types of great square-headed brooches had become the privilege of relatively few females who were buried with a dress accessory that required considerably more copper-alloy than annular brooches and wrist-clasps put together and on which gilding and silver-plating was used. It seems likely that these square-headed brooches fulfilled their display function for only a generation or so and marked the changes which led to the formation of a new elite in the 7th century, a development also indicated by the evidence from weapon graves. Weapon burial at this time was of spearheads and became mostly the privilege of adults. The concentration of wealth in the graves of males and females forms a stark contrast to the previously wide use of female dress accessories and spearheads.

This development over time demonstrates that 'wealth' is a relative term when applied to Anglo-Saxon cemetery evidence. East Anglia does not score highly among the regional samples analysed by Härke and Stoodley, in particular when compared to Kent as the Anglo-Saxon region with the richest record of status goods. Adding Morning Thorpe to the sample would not have changed that picture. Though objects indicating participation in exchange on an inter-regional level are relatively rare, they show the full range of what was available across Anglo-Saxon England in the 5th to 7th centuries: gold, silver, rock crystal, amber, glass vessels, and copper-alloy vessels. Though East Anglian burial practice seems to have used such status goods sparingly, it was not a backwater without access to them.

The evidence from the four cemeteries supports the interpretation of Anglo-Saxon inhumation cemeteries as the burial grounds of communities which 'may reflect status differences within rather than between families and/or households' (Härke 1997, 147). A household in this context is understood as a primary descent group in control of and economically supported by individuals of a different social status, about ten to fifteen individuals altogether. The distribution of 'status goods' across the four cemeteries is remarkably even and, accordingly, the context of the individual graves is their main structuring element. Internal ranking is suggested by a selective use of these 'status goods' and is a matter of degree rather than of clearly defined groups.

It would seem that at Spong Hill, the only fully excavated area, it would have taken one or two households to produce the number of graves found. An estimate of the number of households at Morning Thorpe, Bergh Apton and Westgarth Gardens is even more difficult because of incomplete data: these cemeteries were only partly excavated, half of the graves cannot be closely dated, the beginning of Phases FA1/MA1, the end of Phases FB/MB are vague in absolute terms, and the skeletal data does not invite detailed interpretation.

The chronological framework for the four cemeteries suggests that in East Anglia, cremation and inhumation burial practice was contemporary for at least fifty and possibly as many as 100 years. This raises the question whether the postulated households using the four cemeteries as their burial grounds represent a cross section through the population in that region at the time, or a particular social group. Ravn (2003) has suggested that inhumation burial practice at Spong Hill was used by an emerging elite as a demonstrative act of separation. This interpretation has far-reaching implications for the interpretation of the four cemeteries as a whole.

The earliest graves at Spong Hill and to a lesser extent the contemporary graves at Morning Thorpe and Westgarth Gardens include status goods that may support such an interpretation. The dating evidence is not sufficient to tell whether the earliest graves on the sites include individuals of all ages, indicating all members of a household were inhumed in this phase, or just 'high status' individuals. Evidence for children's graves at the four cemeteries suggests that sooner or later the whole range of household members were inhumed, ranging from what appears to be 'unfurnished' burial and graves with a pot as the only grave-good in the archaeological record to those buried with almost the full known range of grave-goods available to their gender.

Gazetteer of East Anglian cemeteries

Myres and Green (1973) listed the known Anglo-Saxon cemeteries of East Anglia, and subsequent discoveries have added greatly to their list, although the identification of some finds scatters as cemeteries may be more or less certain. The following Gazetteer is based upon the Sites and Monuments Records for Cambridgeshire, Essex, Norfolk and Suffolk, and other information, much of which will reflect the change in the discovery of possible cemetery evidence since the growth of metal-detecting as a hobby. For a definition of East Anglia as it applies to this gazetteer, see 2.3 above.

This gazetteer was compiled by Kenneth Penn from the County Sites and Monuments records of the four counties in 1994, with the assistance of Edwin Rose, Andrew Rogerson, Nesta Rooke, Alison Taylor, John Newman and Colin Pendleton. Subsequent finds from each county made before the summer of 2003 are listed under 'additions'. The form and final contents of the gazetteer were the responsibility of the author, and references are to the appropriate Sites and Monuments Record Numbers, to Meaney's Gazetteer, and to subsequent major references. A more detailed account of much of the Suffolk section is given by West's *Corpus of Anglo-Saxon finds from Suffolk* (West 1998). Grid references for the sites have been omitted. The accompanying map (Fig. 9.1) is on p.111.

Essex (north-western part, see 2.3 above)

E1 Great Chesterford 4939
Pre-1819, 1952. Mixed cemetery, 5th–6th century, excavated 1953–57. One hundred and sixty inhumations, thirty-three cremations.
Evison 1994; Meaney 1964, 85–6; Myres 1977, 90; Myres and Green 1973, no. 134.

E2 Wendens Ambo
1847. Weapons and pots, ?secondary in a barrow.
Meaney 1964, 89.

Cambridgeshire (southern part)

C1 Balsham or Fulbourn/Great Wilbraham 6386
1861. Inhumation(s) in Fleam Dyke.
Meaney 1964, 64; Myres and Green 1973, no. 123. (Not mapped).

C2 Babraham 6223
c. 1920. Worstead Street. ?Cemetery.
Meaney 1964, 71; Myres and Green 1973, no. 124.

C3 Barrington 3264, 2116, 9832
c. 1840, etc. Edix Hill Hole. Cemetery, 5th–6th century. Excavated 1861, etc. Two hundred inhumations (Barrington A).
Meaney 1964, 60; Myres 1977, 87; Myres and Green 1973, no. 129.

C4 Barrington 4853
1879–80. Hoopers Field. Cemetery, 5th–6th century. Excavated 1880. One hundred and fourteen inhumations (Barrington B).
Meaney 1964, 61; Myres and Green 1973, no. 130.

C5 Bartlow 6132
Single find.

C6 Bottisham 6726a
1860/1876. Barrow burial on Allington Hill, ?7th century.
Meaney 1964, 60; Myres and Green 1973, no. 109.

C7 Burwell 6764
c. 1884–6. Cemetery, 7th century, excavated 1925–9. *c.*One hundred and fifty inhumations.
Meaney 1964, 61; Myres 1977, 87; Myres and Green 1973, no. 107.

C8 Cambridge 5152b
Pre-1900. Madingley Road. ?Two burials. (Cambridge V).
Meaney 1964, 63; Myres 1977, 87.

C9 Cambridge 4997
c. 1887 Newnham (Barton Road). Finds. 1938, several burials found.
Meaney 1964, 68; Myres 1977, 89; Myres and Green 1973, no. 117.

C10 Cambridge 441 575 5109
1880, 1893, 1910, 1936. Crofts Lodge. Burials, ?inhumation/cremation
Proc. Cambridge Antiq. Soc. 38 (1938), 168

C11 Cambridge 5089a
Burial.
Medieval Archaeol. 15 (1971), 13–37

C12 Cambridge 4963c
1939. War Ditch. ?Single burial.

C13 Cambridge 5089a
Burial (?same as next) (Cambridge XX)
Proc. Cambridge Antiq. Soc. 16 (1912), 122–32

C14 Cambridge 4926
1888. St John's. Cemetery, mixed; 5th–7th century. 1888; 'many hundreds of burials', and *c.* one hundred cremations, excavated 1911, six burials (Cambridge I).
Meaney 1964, 62; Myres 1977, 89; Myres and Green 1973, no. 114.

C15 Cambridge 4889
1901. Rose Crescent. (Cambridge II).
Meaney 1964, 63; Myres and Green 1973, no. 115.

C16 Cambridge (Trumpington) 4955
Pre-1854. Finds, ?burials.
Meaney 1964, 70; Myres and Green 1973, no. 121

C17 Cambridge 4608a
1895. Jesus Lane. Finds, ?burial.

C18 Cambridge 4622
1847, 1870–. Barnwell. ?Several inhumations (Cambridge IV)
Meaney 1964, 63; Myres 1977, 87.

C19 Chatteris 3862
1757. Several burials, one with weapons and claw-beaker.
Meaney 1964, 63; Myres and Green 1973, no. 99.

C20 Cherry Hinton (Cambridge) 4965a
1949. Cemetery, 6th–7th century, with secondary burial in a Bronze Age barrow.
Meaney 1964, 63; Myres 1977, 87; Myres and Green 1973, no. 122.

C21 Cambridge 4628
Pre-1939. Burials in quarry.

C22 Chippenham 7512
1937. ?Secondary burials in Bronze Age barrow.
Meaney 1964, 63; Myres and Green 1973, no. 106.

C23 Downham 7150
1928. Chambers Pit, near parish boundary. Three 6th century inhumations.
Meaney 1964, 64; Myres and Green 1973, no. 98.

C24 Dry Drayton 1465
Post-1945. Bar Hill. Skeletons.
Medieval Archaeol. 14 (1970), 155

C25 Ely 2104
1947. Fields Farm. Cemetery, *c.*thirty inhumations, 5th–7th century.
Meaney 1964, 64; Myres and Green 1973, no. 102

C26 Ely 2074
1959. High Barns Estate. Burials, weapons and brooches.
Meaney 1964, 64; Myres and Green 1973, no. 97.

C27 Fen Ditton 6303
1957. Fleam Ditch, at High Ditch. Cemetery, *c.*nine inhumations, ?6th century.
Proc. Cambridge Antiq. Soc. 51 (1958), 1–5

C28 Foxton 3996
1935. Single burial.
Meaney 1964, 65.

C29 Foxton 4027, 4209
1922. Four burials.
Meaney 1964, 65.

C30 Foxton 3989
1921. Two burials.
Meaney 1964, 65; Myres and Green 1973, no. 131.
NB 28–30 may be parts of the same cemetery.

C31 Girton 5274
1871, *etc.* Cemetery, excavated 1871, 1881, 1886 etc. Over eighty inhumations, one hundred and thirty cremations, late 5th–6th century.
Meaney 1964, 65–6; Myres 1977, 87–8; Myres and Green 1973, no. 112.

C32 Grantchester 48543
1883. Inhumation and ?cremation.
Meaney 1964, 66; Myres and Green 1973, no. 120.

C33 Great Shelford/Stapleford 8193
Early 20th century. Golf Course. Single burial. (Not mapped).

C34 Haddenham 9831
1990. Three Kings PH. Two burials.
Excavation report.

C35 Haslingfield 4816
1865, 1872 *etc.* Cantelupe Farm. Mixed cemetery, over twenty burials.
Meaney 1964, 66; Myres 1977, 88–9; Myres and Green 1973, no. 128.

C36 Hauxton 4979b
1879. ?burials.
Meaney 1964, 67; Myres 1977, 87; Myres and Green 1973, no. 127.

C37 Hildersham 6070
?1916, 1944, 1946. Furze Hill. Three urns. 1944, single burial found in gravel pit.
Meaney 1964, 67; Myres and Green 1973, no. 137.

C38 Horningsea 6335
1932. Dredged from River Cam, sword, spear and shield. (Not mapped).

C39 Horseheath 7349
?1972. Single inhumation.
Proc. Cambridge Antiq. Soc. 64 (1973), 26–29

C40 Linton 6114
1934, 1935, 1936. Mixed burials. Linton A.
Meaney 1964, 67; Myres and Green 1973, no. 138.

C41 Linton 6179a
1853. Linton Heath. Bronze Age barrow with Anglo-Saxon cemetery. Excavated 1853. One hundred and four inhumations, late 5th–6th century; with several gilt square-headed brooches. Linton B.
Meaney 1964, 67–8; Myres 1977, 89; Myres and Green 1973, no. 139.

C42 Little Shelford 4803
Pre-1933. Burials.
Meaney 1964, 69; Myres and Green 1973, no. 126.

C43 Little Wilbraham 6330
Pre-1847. Streetway Hill. Cemetery, excavated 1851. Two hundred inhumations, one hundred and fifty cremations, 5th–6th century.
Meaney 1964, 70; Myres 1977, 89; Myres and Green 1973, no. 110.

C44 Lode 6866b
1887. Single urn
Meaney 1964, 60; Myres 1977, 87.

C45 Melbourn 3169
1951. Street Way. Cemetery, excavated 1952, twenty-eight inhumations, 7th century.
Meaney 1964, 68; Myres 1977, 89; Myres and Green 1973, no. 132.

C46 Mepal 5826a
1859. Mepal Fen. ?Secondary cremation in Bronze Age barrow.
Meaney 1964, 68; Myres and Green 1973, no. 100.

C47 Milton 5540
Pre-1923. Swan's Gravel Pit, Chesterton. ?Burial(s).
Fox 1923, 244; Meaney 1964, 63; Myres and Green 1973, no. 111.

C48 Oakington 5270
1928. Three burials. 1943. Single burial.
Meaney 1964, 69

C49 Sawston 4537
Pre-1816. Huckeridge Hill. Finds and a single burial (1816).
Meaney 1964, 69; Myres and Green 1973, no. 125.

C50 Shudy Camps 7368
1887. White Hills Field. Cemetery, 7th century. Excavated 1933. One hundred and fifty-eight inhumations.
Meaney 1964, 69; Myres 1977, 90; Myres and Green 1973, no. 140.

C51 Soham 7027
1856, 1865, 1867. Newmarket Road. Cemetery (Soham A and B).
Meaney 1964, 69; Myres and Green 1973, nos 103, 104.

C52 Soham 7506
1931. Waterworks. Cemetery, 6th–7th century. Excavated 1931, twenty-three inhumations, two cremations, (Soham C).
Meaney 1964, 69–70; Myres and Green 1973, no. 105.

C53 Stapleford 8211
18th century. Gog Magog Hills. Burials.

C54 Steeple Morden 2265
Pre-1923. Burials.
Meaney 1964, 104 (*sub* Ashwell).

C55 Swaffham Prior 6419,6427,11054b
1973. Eight burials. 1985. Two burials.

C56 Waterbeach 5351
Burial(s). Dredged from Car Dyke. (Not mapped).

C57 West Wickham 9142
1992. Metal-detector finds, excavation, at least three burials.

C58 Wicken 8152
Single burial. (Not mapped).

C59 Wimpole 3402
Pre-1742. Report of burials, ?Anglo-Saxon.
Meaney 1964, 71.

C60 Wimpole 8384
1990. Excavation, three burials.

C61 Wisbech 4012
1858. Corn Exchange. Finds, ?burial.
Meaney 1964, 71; Myres and Green 1973, no. 23.

Additions

C62 Duxford CB14768
Four burials

C63 Guilden Morden 14603
Burials

C64 Melbourn CB15238
Fifty-two burials, part of **3169**; C45?

This omits some of the scattered discoveries of Cambridge II, Town (Meaney 1964, 62); Myres 1977, 87; Myres and Green 1973, nos 118–9, and Cambridge III, St Giles, dredged from the River Cam (Meaney 1964, 62; Myres 1977, 87; Myres and Green 1973, no. 116).

Norfolk

N1 Aldborough 15189
c. 1974. Single decorated (?burial) urn.

N2 Beachamwell 4539
1985, 1988. (Metal-detector finds). Three bronze objects. ?Possible cemetery.

N3 Beachamwell 4562
1985. (Metal-detector finds). Four bronze objects. ?Possible cemetery.

N4 Beachamwell 12153
1987. Surface finds. Two bronze objects. ?Possible cemetery.

N5 Beachamwell 23536
1987. Surface finds; Eight bronze objects. ?Possible cemetery. From nearby came a single stamped sherd, found in 1915 near five unaccompanied burials, ?Anglo-Saxon (**4561**). Meaney 1964, 169.

N6 Bergh Apton 1011
1973. Inhumation cemetery, about seventy inhumations.
Green and Rogerson 1978.

N7 Bergh Apton 24171
1985–7. Metal-detector finds, nine bronze objects, possible cemetery, to the south west of **1011** (above).

N8 Blakeney 6153
1936. Langham. Secondary inhumation in Bronze Age barrow.
Meaney 1964, 177–8; Lawson *et al.* 1981, 40; Myres and Green 1973, no. 4.

N9 'Brettenham' 5653
1907, 1965, 1972, 1978. Bridgeham. Mixed cemetery. Burials, many surface finds.
Meaney 1964, 169; Myres and Green 1973, no. 67; Webster and Cherry 1973, 147; Wilson and Hurst 1966, 172.

N10 'Brettenham' 6076
c. 1753. Pre-1851. Shadwell/Rushford. One or possibly two cremation cemeteries.
Meaney 1964, 169; Myres 1977, 102; Myres and Green 1973, no. 68.

N11 Brooke 10132
1867–9. Inhumation cemetery (?one cremation).
Kennett 1977; Meaney 1964, 170; Myres 1977, 97.

N12 Broome 10628
Early 19th century. Broome Heath. Cremation urns. 1858, inhumation in a barrow, dubious.
Meaney 1964, 170; Myres and Green 1973, no. 49.

N13 Brundall 10234
1880–1900. Brundall Gardens. At least seven cremation urns.
Meaney 1964, 170; Myres 1977, 97; Myres and Green 1973, no. 41.

N14 Burgh Castle 10471
c. 1756. Cremation urns, ?cemetery. Three bronze objects may be from this site. (Also one hundred and fifty inhumations of ?7th to 10th-century date, excavated 1958–61).
Johnson 1983, 50–55, 119–20; Myres and Green 1973, no. 44.

N15 Burlingham 17429, 20248, 20249, 24348
1981–1989. metal-detector finds, six bronze objects, ?cemetery.

N16 Caistor St Edmund 9788
1814/15, 1818, 1822, 1831, 1948–9. White's Hill, Markshall. Cremation cemetery.
Meaney 1964, 178; Myres 1977, 101; Myres and Green 1973, no. 38.

N17 Caistor St Edmund 9794
1990. Harford Farm. Forty-six inhumations.
Penn 2000.

N18 Caistor St Edmund 9791
1754, 1814, 1932–8, 1976. Mixed cemetery. Over five hundred cremations and about sixty inhumations.
Meaney 1964, 171–2; Myres 1977, 97–100; Myres and Green 1973, no. 39.

N19 Caistor St Edmund 9787
1979, 1985–6. Metal-detector finds. Six bronze objects, ?cemetery.

N20 Caistor St Edmund 28200
1991–. Surface finds, by metal-detector; a few metal objects may indicate burials.

N21 Carleton Rode 21959
1983–9. Metal-detector finds. Six bronze objects, ?cemetery.

N22 Castle Acre/West Acre 3781
1857, 1877, 1891. Cremation cemetery. Excavated in 1891.
Meaney 1964, 172–3; Myres 1977, 99–100; Myres and Green 1973, no. 16.

N23 Colney 19139, 19191, 19825, 20859, 20861, 24833
1983–. Surface finds by metal-detector, probable cemetery.

N24 Congham 3569
1982. Surface finds by metal-detector. Probable cemetery. Other finds in this area may relate to a cemetery or to occupation here (County Sites 20505, 20975, 25765).

N25 Congham 23304
1986–7. Surface finds by metal-detector. Three objects, ?possible cemetery.

N26 Dersingham 1569
c. 1850. Single cremation urn.
Meaney 1964, 173; Myres 1977, 100.

N27 Downham Market 2444
19th century. Two cremation urns. (Not mapped).
Myres 1977, 100; Myres and Green 1973, no. 22a.

N28 Drayton 7853
1848–9. Cremation cemetery, about forty urns found.
Meaney 1964, 173; Myres 1977, 100; Myres and Green 1973, no. 35.

N29 Earsham 11110
1850, 1906. About ten cremation urns. Cremation cemetery, possibly associated with small mounds, ?barrows.
Meaney 1964, 173; Myres 1977, 100; Myres and Green 1973, no. 50.

N30 East Walton 1060
1964, 1975, 1986. Surface finds, some by metal-detector. Metal objects and urn fragments. Possibly mixed cremation and inhumation cemetery.

N31 Fakenham 2133
1869. Single inhumation.
Meaney 1964, 177; Myres and Green 1973, no. 9.

N32 Field Dalling 6164
1975, 1987. Saxlingham. Mixed cemetery. At least sixty cremation urns and two inhumations. Excavated 1975. Further surface finds by metal-detector in 1987.
Webster and Cherry 1976, 167.

N33 Fincham 14350
1984. Surface find by metal-detector. Single brooch, ?inhumation burial.

N34 Foulden 4801
1930, 1931, 1954, 1958, 1962. Everett's Farm. About seven burials, one with a dog, probably early Saxon.

N35 Gillingham 24254
1987–8. 1992. Surface finds by metal-detector. Possible ?mixed cemetery.

N36 Gissing 10961
1849. Single inhumation.
Meaney 1964, 175.

N37 Great Ellingham 9082
1960, 1987. Surface finds, some by metal-detector. Metal objects and sherds indicate a mixed cemetery.
Meaney 1964, 173.

N38 Great Walsingham 2030
c. 1658. Cremation cemetery, forty–fifty urns.
Meaney 1964, 184; Myres 1977, 100; Myres and Green 1973, no. 8.

N39 Great Walsingham 2024
1950. Surface finds. Three metal objects may indicate inhumations. Possibly the same as 2030 (above).

N40 Grimston 3573
1929, 1955, 1969. 'The Bell'. Inhumations. Excavated 1971. Six inhumations, one cremation urn.
Meaney 1964, 175; Myres 1977, 100; Myres and Green 1973, no. 19.

N41 Grimston 15404
1992. Surface finds by metal-detector indicate an inhumation cemetery, possibly associated with barrows.

N42 Gunthorpe 24620
1989. Surface finds by metal-detector indicate a probable cemetery.

N43 Hethersett 21862
1985–. Surface finds by metal-detector may indicate a cemetery.

N44 Hilgay 4453
1879. Churchyard. ?Cremation urn with other objects. Possible burial.
Meaney 1964, 175; Myres 1977, 100; Myres and Green 1973, no. 24.

N45 Hockwold-cum-Wilton 5587
1975–. Leyland's Farm. Surface finds may indicate a cemetery.
Scull 1985. (Other finds nearby (**19576**; N105) may indicate another separate cemetery to the north-west).

N46 Holkham 1780
1989. Howe Hill. Surface finds by metal-detector. (*NB* Early finds from here in *c*.1722).
Meaney 1964, 175–6; Myres and Green 1973, no. 3. (Other unlocated finds (**1781**) may be from the same site).

N47 Hunstanton 1142
c. 1860. Park Hill. single inhumation. 1900–02, excavations recovered at least twelve inhumations. 1969, single inhumation found.
Meaney 1964, 176; Myres 1977, 100; Myres and Green 1973, no. 1.

N48 Kempstone 4079
1988. Surface finds by metal-detector. Three metal objects, possible cemetery.

N49 Kenninghall 6228
1869. Inhumation cemetery.
Meaney 1964, 176–7; Myres 1977, 101; Myres and Green 1973, no. 62.

N50 Kettlestone 1050
1826, 1876, 1880–1. Pensthorpe. Cremation cemetery, associated with small barrows.

Lawson *et al* 1981, 41; Meaney 1964, 177; Myres 1977, 102; Myres and Green 1973, no. 11.

N51 Kirby Cane 10657
1853. Pewter Hill. Inhumations.
Meaney 1964, 177; Myres and Green 1973, no. 48.

N52 Kirby Cane 12380
1988. Surface finds by metal-detector indicate a cemetery, possibly the same as **10657** (above).

N53 Kirby Cane 9329
1988. Surface finds by metal-detector. Possibly the same site as **10657** (above).

N54 Little Snoring 2154
1943. Single inhumation.
Meaney 1964, 181; Myres and Green 1973, no. 10.

N55 Little Walsingham 2031
c. 1850. Single inhumation.
Meaney 1964, 184; Myres 1977,101; Myres and Green 1973; no. 7.

N56 Martham 15388
1979–. Surface finds by metal-detector. Several metal objects, may indicate a cemetery.

N57 Merton 5061
1980. Surface finds by metal-detector may indicate one or more inhumation burials.

N58 Morning Thorpe 1120
1974–5. Inhumation cemetery, with some cremations. Excavated, 365 inhumations and twelve cremations.
Green, Rogerson and White 1987.

N59 Mundesley 6872
1965. Nine cremation urns.
Myres 1977, 101; Myres and Green 1973, no. 13.

N60 Mundesley 16294
1980. Finds of metal objects may indicate an inhumation burial.

N61 Mundford 4985
1925. Mundford I. Single inhumation.
Meaney 1964, 179; Myres and Green 1973, no. 30.

N62 Mundford 4986
1967. Inhumation burial in pipe-trench. (1976. Finds in pipe trench at TL 789 939 **11799** may be from the same site).

N63 Mundford 5112
1951, 1954, 1956. Mundford II. Inhumations.
Meaney 1964, 179; Myres and Green 1973, no. 29.

N64 Mundford 11413
1976. Inhumation(s).

N65 Narford 3970
1939. Single inhumation.
Meaney 1964, 179; Myres and Green 1973, no. 17.

N66 North Elmham 1012
1711...1954, 1968, 1972–84. Spong Hill. Mixed cemetery of over 2000 cremations and 57 inhumations.
Hills 1977b; Hills and Penn 1981; 1984; 1987; 1994; Meaney 1964, 173–4; Myres 1977, 101–2; Myres and Green 1973, no. 15.

N67 North Elmham 25848
1990. Surface finds by metal-detector probably indicate a cemetery.

N68 North Pickenham 19449
1983. Surface finds by metal-detector may indicate a cemetery, possibly with some cremations.

N69 North Runcton 3348
1892, *c.*1907, 1925. Early finds include several ?cremation urns from the churchyard, and possibly, cremation and inhumation burials from just to the east.
Meaney 1964, 180–1; Myres 1977, 102; Myres and Green 1973, no. 20.

N70 Northwold 4811
1838–9. Inhumation cemetery, possibly associated with a ?barrow(s).
Clarke 1940, 226–7; Meaney 1964, 179–80; Myres and Green 1973, no. 28.

N71 Norwich 177N
1898. Eade Rd., Catton. Possible mixed cemetery. Urns and a square-headed brooch.
Clarke 1940, 227; Meaney 1964, 180; Myres 1977, 100; Myres and Green 1973, no. 36.

N72 Oxborough 25458
1989. Surface finds and subsequent excavation (1990) revealed ten inhumations (and traces of other burials) around a probable Bronze Age barrow.
Penn 1999

N73 Oxborough 1021
1984, 1987. Caldecote. Surface finds by metal-detector may represent a burial(s). (Another find from nearby TF 746 032 **2634** may be associated).

N74 Poringland 9898
Early 19th century. Poringland Heath. Early report of several spearheads, possibly indicating inhumation burials, perhaps in barrows.
Meaney 1964, 180; Myres and Green 1973, no. 40.

N75 Quidenham 1859
1859. Hargham. Some twenty–thirty urns found, of uncertain date, possibly Anglo-Saxon.
Meaney 1964, 175; Myres and Green 1973, no. 63.

N76 Rockland All Saints 1054 (and 11204)
1949, 1962, 1981–3. Mount Pleasant. At least twelve urned cremations.
Meaney 1964, 180; Myres 1977, 102; Myres and Green 1973, no. 64.

N77 Roudham 18464
1981–2. Surface finds by metal-detector probably indicate inhumation burials.

N78 Runcton Holme 2414
Pre-1869. Urn in gravel-pit.

N79 Sedgeford 1611, 1612.
Pre-1826. Cremation urns, at least two.
Meaney 1964, 181; Myres 1977, 102; Myres and Green 1973, no. 6.

N80 Shropham 9036
1829. Urned cremations, at least five.
Meaney 1964, 181; Myres 1977, 102; Myres and Green 1973; no. 65.

N81 Skeyton 22226–7
1986, 1988. Surface finds by metal-detector, possibly from inhumation burials.

N82 Smallburgh 8277
1856. A potsherd and beads may indicate an inhumation burial, possibly secondary in a barrow.
Lawson et al. 1981, 181; Meaney 1964, 181; Myres and Green 1973, no. 14.

N83 Snettisham 1529
1961. Single ?cremation in an urn.
Meaney 1964, 181; Myres 1977, 102; Myres and Green 1973, no. 5.

N84 Sporle-with-Palgrave 4598
1820. Inhumations in barrows, including a probable horse-burial.
Meaney 1964, 181–2; Myres 1977, 102; Myres and Green 1973, no. 33.

N85 Swaffham 1125
1968–70. The Paddocks. Nineteen inhumations and one cremation, part of a larger cemetery, possibly represented by earlier finds from Swaffham.
Hills and Wade-Martins 1976; Meaney 1964, 182; Myres and Green, no. 32.

N86 Thetford 1757
1911. Thetford Warren. Single inhumation burial.
Meaney 1964, 183; Myres and Green 1973, no. 70.

N87 Thetford 5758
1953. Thetford II, Bury Rd. Three inhumation burials.
Meaney 1964, 182; Myres and Green 1973, no. 69.

N88 Thetford 5860
c. 1868, 1929/1933. Thetford I, modern cemetery. Single inhumation with weapons. Finds made here in 1868 indicate a cemetery, associated with a barrow.
Meaney 1964, 182; Myres and Green 1973, no. 71.

N89 Thetford 25154
1989. Brunel Way. Salvage excavation, at least six inhumation burials.
Penn and Andrews 2000

N90 Thornham 1308
1955, 1956, 1960. Excavations within an Iron Age/early Roman enclosure revealed twenty-four inhumations.
Meaney 1964, 183; Myres and Green 1973, no. 2.

N91 Thorpe St Andrew 9628
1863. Probable inhumation, with weapons.
Meaney 1964, 183; Myres and Green 1973, no. 37.

N92 Tottenhill 2266
Pre-1890, 1890, 1942–3. Mixed cemetery, including at least forty urns.
Meaney 1964, 183; Myres 1977, 102; Myres and Green 1973, no. 21.

N93 Watton 8781
1952, 1957. Single inhumation.
Meaney 1964, 184; Myres and Green 1973, no. 34.

N94 Wereham (?) site unknown 4411, 4412
19th century finds of a spear and pots.
Meaney 1964, 184; Myres 1977, 102; Myres and Green 1973, no. 25.

N95 Wickmere 6659.
1915. Wolterton. Cremation urns.
Meaney 1964, 185; Myres 1977, 102; Myres and Green 1973, no. 12.

N96 Wicklewood 8897
1982, 1984. Surface finds by metal-detector may indicate burials.

N97 Wretham 1047
1949. Illington. mixed cemetery, over two hundred urns and three inhumations.
Davison and Green 1993; Meaney 1964, 176; Myres 1977, 100; Myres and Green 1973, no. 66.

N98 Wretton 4416
1913. Single inhumation burial, with shield, ?seax and knife, possibly Viking. (Not mapped).
Meaney 1964, 185; Myres and Green 1973, no. 26.

Additions

N99 Burston and Shimpling 23345
1986, 1987, 1990. Metal-detector finds, probable cemetery.

N100 Brundall 10232
1932. Single burial, ?Early Saxon.

N101 Burnham Market 18496
Metal-detector finds may indicate cemetery.

N102 East Walton 25856, 37195
1990, 1992. Metal-detector finds, probable cemetery

N103 Fincham 30049
1993–. Metal-detector finds include Early Saxon objects; probable inhumation cemetery. Possibly same as **14350** (see **N33** above)

N104 Hindringham 25474
1989, 1990–. Metal-detector finds indicate a probable cemetery.

N105 Hockwold-cum-Wilton 19576
1970s. Metal-detector finds. Possible cemetery.

N106 Hoe 37159
Cremations, single inhumation.

N107 Kilverstone 37349
Six graves, single cremation.

N108 Little Cressingham 35101
Surface finds.

N109 Morton on the Hill 29344
1994. Metal-detector finds. Probable inhumation cemetery.

N110 North Creake 30986
1994. Metal-detector finds. Possible cemetery.

N111 Shouldham 35988
Surface finds.

N112 Swannington 7438
1994. Metal-detector finds indicate a probable cemetery.

N113 West Acre 16841
1991. Metal-detector finds indicate a probable cemetery.

Suffolk

S1 Akenham Hall AKE Misc
Pre-1911. Two finds, ?burial. Imprecise location.
Meaney 1964, 224; Myres and Green 1973, no. 145.

S2 Badley (Needham Market) BAD 002
Pre-1865. Two bronze vessels, possibly associated, ?burials.
Meaney 1964, 224; Myres and Green; no. 142.

S3 Badley (Badwell Ash) BAA 008
1922–3. Mixed cemetery, thirty–forty inhumations and cremations.
Meaney 1964, 224; Myres 1977, 106; Myres and Green 1973, no. 58.

S4 Bardwell BAR 034
1988. Mill Farm. Finds scatter, may indicate a cemetery.

S5 Bardwell BAR Misc
Pre-1847. Finds of weapons, ?inhumation burials.
Meaney 1964, 224; Myres and Green 1973, no. 76.

S6 Omitted

S7 Barnham BNH 016
1914. Secondary burial(s) in Bronze Age barrow.
Meaney 1964, 224; Myres and Green 1973, no. 72.

S8 Barton Mills BTM 009
c. 1960. Single burial.

S9 Blaxhall BLX 007
1988. Finds scatter, may indicate a cemetery.

S10 Botesdale BOT 004
18th century. Back Hills. Cremation urns.

S11 Botesdale BOT Misc
18th century. Anglo-Saxon urns. (?Same as **BOT 004** above).
Meaney 1964, 225; Myres and Green 1973, no. 60.

S12 Bramford BRF Misc
Pre-1867. Single urn, ?cremation burial. (Uncertain location).
Meaney 1964, 225; Myres 1977, 106; Myres and Green 1973, no. 143.

S13 Brightwell BGL 017
1921. Excavation of three barrows (one of Anglo-Saxon date), with secondary cremation burials.
Lawson *et al.* 1981, 71; Meaney 1964, 225; Myres and Green 1973, no. 147; Vierck 1972.

S14 Bromeswell BML 009
1986. Surface finds, including 'Coptic' bucket, ?burials.
Mango *et al.* 1989.

S15 Bungay BUN 003
1951. Two burials.
Meaney 1964, 225; Myres and Green 1973, no. 51.

S16 Bungay BUN Misc
Pre-1855. Stow Park. Glass vessel.
Meaney 1964, 233; Myres and Green 1973, no. 52.

S17 Bury St Edmunds BSE 005
1955–59. Northumberland Avenue. Twelve burials. (Pre-1843. At least twenty burials found in Tollgate Lane).
Meaney 1964, 226; Myres and Green 1973, no. 81; West 1985, 155.

S18 Bury St Edmunds BSE 007
Pre-1958. Hardwick Lane. *c.* Three burials.
Meaney 1964, 226; Myres and Green 1973, no. 80; West 1985, 155.

S19 Bury St Edmunds BSE 028
1970. Baron's Road. Excavation of two–three burials, some 340m east of the Hardwick Lane site **BSE 007**.

S20 Bury St Edmunds BSE 030
1972. Westgarth Gardens. Cemetery, excavated. Sixty-five inhumations, four cremations.
West 1988.

S21 Cavenham CAM 011
1981. Surface finds. (An early record *c.*1900 of two probable Anglo-Saxon burials from nearby Park Farm **CAM 002** may be the same site as **CAM 011**).
Martin 1982, 156; West 1985, 156.

S22 Coddenham CDD 003
1958. Baylham Mill. Found during excavation of a Romano-British site, single urn.
Meaney 1964, 226; Myres 1977, 106.

S23 Coddenham CDD 017
Surface finds. Possible cemetery.

S24 Coddenham CDD 022,023,027
1985,1988. Surface finds. ?Cemetery
Gaimster *et al.* 1989, 208–9.

S25 Culford CUL Misc
Pre-1911. Single cremation urn.
Meaney 1964, 226; Myres 1977, 106; Myres and Green 1973, no. 83.

S26 Eriswell ERL 003
1915. Hardpiece Field, Foxhole Heath. Probably several burials.
Meaney 1964, 226; Myres 1977, 106; Myres and Green 1973, no. 93; West 1985, 159.

S27 Eriswell ERL 008
1957–59. Lakenheath Airfield. Burials. Excavations revealed a further thirty-three burials.
Meaney 1964, 230; Hutchinson 1966; Myres and Green 1973, no. 94.

S28 Eriswell ERL 046
1981. Lakenheath Airfield. Excavation of three burials (probably part of **ERL 008** above).
Martin 1982, 160. (Other finds from Lakenheath Airfield in the 1960s and recorded as **ERL 058** are probably part of **ERL 008** and **046**).

S29 Exning EXG 005,028
Pre-1892. Windmill Hill. Burials, probably ten or more.
1983. Excavation, six burials.
Meaney 1964, 227; Myres 1977, 106; Myres and Green 1973, no. 108. Martin 1984.

S30 Eye EYE 003
1818. Waterloo Plantation. Cemetery of one hundred and fifty cremation urns. Probable barrow.
Meaney 1964, 227; Myres 1977, 106; Myres and Green 1973, no. 55.

S31 Fakenham FKM 001
1946. Early Anglo-Saxon pottery and burial (?Anglo-Saxon) found on Iron Age and Romano-British site.
Meaney 1964, 227; Myres and Green 1973, no. 73.

S32 Finningham FNN 002
Pre-1849. Mixed cemetery.
Meaney 1964, 227; Myres and Green 1973, no. 57. (Also recorded as Cotton **COT 015**).

S33 Flixton FLN 008
1989. Flixton Park. Excavated Bronze Age barrow. Early Saxon secondary burial and metal-detector finds.

S34 Framlingham FML 002
1954. Framlingham Castle. Excavation, inhumation cemetery.

S35 Gisleham GSE 003/010
1758. Bloodmoor Hill, Pakefield. Burial (7th century?) in a barrow, with burials of 6th-century date.
Meaney 1964, 231; Myres and Green 1973, no. 46; Newman 1996a, b

S36 Gisleham GSE
Surface finds. Probably the same site as **GSE 003**.
Martin *et al.* 1983, 230. (The above sites are also recorded as Carlton Colville **CAC 007, 008**).

S37 Great Thurlow TUG 004
1891. Inhumation burial.
Meaney 1964, 235.

S38 Hacheston HCH 013
1986. Gallows Hill. Romano-British cemetery with Early Anglo-Saxon *grubenhaus* and barrow-burial.
Martin 1987.

S39 Hasketon HSK 006, 008
Surface finds suggest inhumation burials.

S40 Hinderclay HNY 017
1988–90. Surface finds by metal-detector, ?inhumation cemetery.

S41 Icklingham IKL 026
Pre-1888. Mitchell's Hill. Inhumation cemetery, over twenty-five burials, possibly associated with a Bronze Age barrow, and a horse-burial.
Meaney 1964, 231; Myres 1977, 106; Myres and Green 1973, no. 85; West 1985, 157.

S42 Ipswich IPS 016
1906–7. Hadleigh Road. Excavation of a mixed cemetery of about twelve cremations and one hundred and sixty-two inhumations.
Meaney 1964, 228; Myres 1977, 106; Myres and Green 1973, no. 144; Scull 1985.

S43 Ipswich IPS 053
1975. Elm Street. Excavation of a single burial.

S44 Ipswich IPS 228
1987–8. Buttermarket. Excavation of a 7th-century cemetery.
Newman 1991.

S45 Ipswich IPS 231
1990. Boss Hall. Cemetery, 6th century, with a single burial of *c.* AD700.
Newman 1991.

S46 Ixworth IXW 002
Single urn.
Myres 1977, 106.

S47 Ixworth IXW 005
1868, 1871. Cross House Meadow. Single burial, with further finds. 1950–1, excavation of seven cremation urns.
Meaney 1964, 228–9; Myres and Green 1973, no. 78. (Later finds, unlocated, may be from this site **IXW Misc i, ix, xi**).

S48 Ixworth Thorpe IXT 002
1940–5 Single inhumation.
Meaney 1964, 229; Myres and Green 1973, no. 77. (Further finds of urns and brooches may also be from this site **IXT Misc i**).

S49 Ixworth Thorpe IXT 007
Holmes Wood. Cremation burials.

S50 Kesgrave KSG Misc i
Pre-1852. Urn.
Meaney 1964, 229; Myres 1977, 106; Myres and Green 1973, no. 146.

S51 Lackford LKD 001
1914, 1945. Mill Heath. Cremation cemetery. Excavation in 1947 recovered about five hundred urns.
Meaney 1964, 229; Myres 1977, 106–8; Myres and Green 1973, no. 86.

S52 Lakenheath LKH 010
Saham Field and Pashford Wood. Surface finds.
West 1985, 159.

S53 Lakenheath LKH 017
1958. Surface finds. Pottery and cremations.

S54 Lakenheath LKH 041
1880s. Inhumations, possibly Anglo-Saxon.

S55 Lakenheath LKH 042
1952–3. Cremation cemetery, excavated. (This may be the same site as LKH 010).
Myres and Green 1973, no. 96.
[The four Lakenheath sites LKH 010, 017, 041 and 042 may represent a single cemetery].

S56 Lakenheath LKH Misc
19th century. Undley Fen. Surface finds may indicate a cemetery.
Meaney 1964, 235; West 1985. (There are other early reports relating to Lakenheath but not all can be located or identified).

S57 Langham LGH 005
Pre-1958. Inhumations, ?Anglo-Saxon.
Meaney 1964, 230.

S58 Little Bealings BEL 010
1966. ?Mixed cemetery, fragmentary urns and other finds, in gravel-pit.

S59 Little Cornard COL 001
1868. Scatter of finds and bone may indicate burials, possibly Anglo-Saxon.
Meaney 1964, 226.

S60 Martlesham MRM 028
1984. Finds scatter, possible burial(s).

S61 Mildenhall MNL 001
1820, 1866, 1875–77, 1881. Warren Hill (or Three Hills). Cemetery, perhaps associated with a Bronze Age barrow, and a ?horse-burial.
Meaney 1964, 236; Myres 1977, 108; Myres and Green 1973, no. 91.

S62 Mildenhall MNL 084
1851. Holywell Row. Excavated 1931. Inhumation cemetery, over 100 burials.
Meaney 1964, 228; Myres and Green 1973, no. 92; West 1985.

S63 Mildenhall MLN Misc
1906. Single burial.
Meaney 1964, 230; Myres and Green 1973, no. 90.

S64 Moulton MUN 011
c. 1965. Single urn.

S65 Oakley OKY 010
1979–80. Surface finds by metal-detector may indicate an inhumation cemetery.

S66 Pakenham PKM 006, 028
1944. Grimstone End. Excavations 1953,1957. Multi-period site with three burials, doubtfully Early Saxon.
Myres and Green 1973, no. 79.

S67 Parham PRH 002
1734. Single burial.

S68 Playford PLY 010
Surface finds may indicate an inhumation cemetery (and ?settlement).

S69 Redgrave RGV 004 (and ?005)
Late 18th century. Moneypot Hill. ?Cremation cemetery.
Meaney 1964, 231; Myres 1977, 108; Myres and Green 1973, no. 61.

S70 Rendlesham RLM 006
Pre-1837. Cremations in urns.
Meaney 1964, 231; Myres and Green 1973, no. 152.

S71 Rickinghall Inferior RKN 012
1936. Excavation of burial, possibly Anglo-Saxon. Two more ploughed out in 1945.
Meaney 1964, 232; Myres and Green 1973, no. 59.

S72 Risby (Barrow) RBY 001
1771, 1784, 1813. Barrow Bottom. Secondary burials in a Bronze Age barrow.
Martin 1976; Meaney 1964, 224; Myres and Green 1973, no. 88.

S73 Risby (Barrow) RBY 003
Pre-1869, ?1959. Bronze Age barrow with Anglo-Saxon secondary cremation burial.
Meaney 1964, 232; Myres 1977, 108.

S74 Rougham RGH 002
1843. Eastlow Hill. Barrows, one with ?Anglo-Saxon secondary burial (dubious).

S75 Snape SNP 007
1827, 1862–3, 1985–90. Mixed cemetery with ship-burials, barrows.
Bruce-Mitford 1955; Filmer-Sankey 1984; 1988; 1992; Filmer-Sankey and Pestell, 2001; Gaimster *et al.* 1989, 209; Meaney 1964, 232; Myres 1977, 108; Myres and Green 1973, no. 156.

S76 Snape SNP 020
c. 1828. Round Hill. Undated barrow with ?Anglo-Saxon finds, ?burial.

S77 Sutton SUT 004–6,038
c. 1860, 1938–9. Sutton Hoo. Mixed cemetery with *c.*fifteen barrows and with ship-burials under barrows. Excavated 1966–71, 1983–92.
Bruce-Mitford 1975; 1978; 1983; Carver 1992; 1998; Meaney 1964, 233–5; Myres and Green 1973, no. 150.

S78 Tuddenham St Mary TDD 001
c. 1894. Cemetery, with thirteen inhumations, and possibly cremations.
Meaney 1964, 235; Myres 1977, 108; Myres and Green 1973, no. 89; West 1985, 157–8.

S79 Tuddenham St Martin TDM 002
Surface finds by metal-detector may indicate burials.

S80 Tuddenham St Martin TDM 006
Surface finds by metal-detector may indicate burials.

S81 Ufford UFF Misc
1819. *c.*Three inhumation burials.
Meaney 1964, 235; Myres and Green 1973, no. 151. (Other early finds may be from this site **UFF 002, UFF Misc**).

S82 Waldringfield WLD 001
Pre-1864. Single cremation burial.
Meaney 1964, 235; Myres 1977, 109; Myres and Green 1973, no. 149.

S83 West Stow WSW 003
1849, 1852. Mixed cemetery, probably of over one hundred inhumations and one or more cremations.
Meaney 1964, 233; Myres 1977, 109; Myres and Green 1973, no. 84; West 1985.

S84 Wickham Market WKM Misc i
1907. Bronze 'Coptic' bowl, and comb; probably the remains of a burial.
Meaney 1964, 236; Myres and Green 1973, no. 153.

S85 Woodbridge WBG 022
1873. Barrow, with Early Saxon burial with spear.
Meaney 1964, 236.

Additions

S86 Barnham BNH 030
1950. possible burial

S87 Barton Mills BTM 011
1935. Station Yard. Burial.

S88 Bury St Edmunds BSE 183
Single burial.

S89 Coddenham, Smyes Corner CDD 050
Late 7th-century cemetery.

S90 Flixton FLN 053
43 burials.

S91 Hemingstone, Church Farm HMG 019
Surface Finds.

S92 Lackford LKD 045
Surface finds.

S93 Rushmere St Andrew RMA 013
Surface finds, possible cemetery.

S94 Wenhaston WNH 004, 005
Surface finds, possible cemetery

S95 Eriswell ERL 104
1998. RAF Lakenheath (just west of S27). 261 inhumation burials.

S96 Bromeswell BML 018
National Trust visitor centre. Excavated 2000. Eastern edge of mixed cemetery. 17 cremations, some with small ring-ditches, 19 inhumations. 6th/early 7th-century. (Very close to **BML 009** above). (Not mapped).
Newman 2005, 483.

This omits a number of early finds of uncertain identity or precisely known location. These are:

Ashby   ABY Misc (Ashby Dell 'boat burial').

Bury St Edmunds   BSE Misc i

Chilton   CHT Misc
(Myres and Green 1973, no. 141).

Fakenham   FKM Misc

Felixstowe   FEX Misc

Fornham St Genevieve	FSG Misc (Myres and Green 1973, no. 82).	Lakenheath	LKH 017,041.
Fornham St Martin	FSM Mis	Mildenhall	MNL misc
Freckenham	FRK Misc	Stanton	SNT Misc (Myres and Green 1973, no. 75).
Hoxne	various finds, including HXN Misc i,ii (Myres and Green 1973, no. 54).	Thorndon	TDH Misc i (Myres and Green 1973, no. 56).
Icklingham	Ick Misc	Wangford	WNG Misc (Myres and Green 1973, no. 95).
Ingham	urns, unknown location.	Wattisfield	WSF Misc
Ixworth	IXW Misc i,ix,xi (Meaney 1964, 228–9).		

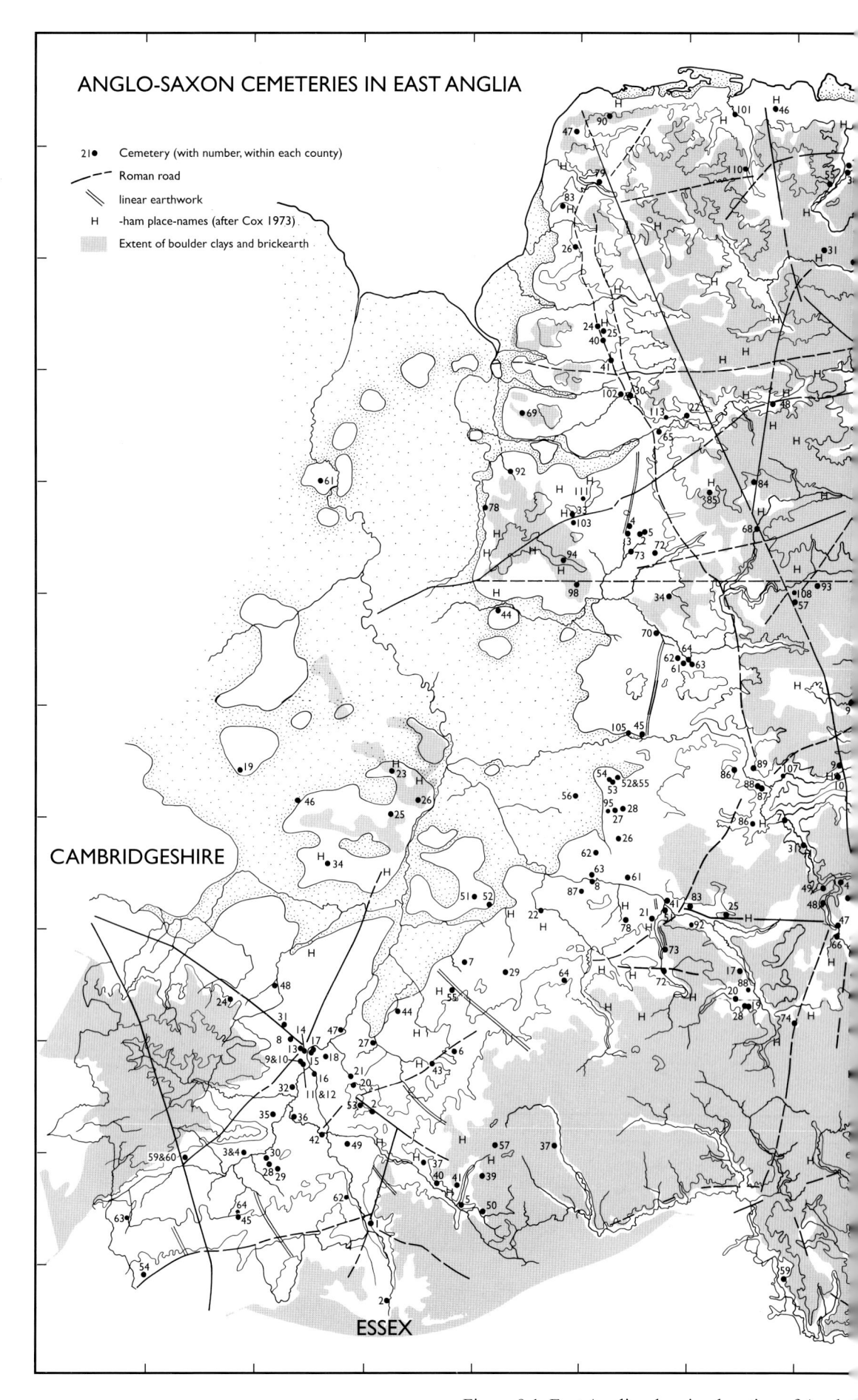

Figure 9.1 East Anglia, showing location of Anglo

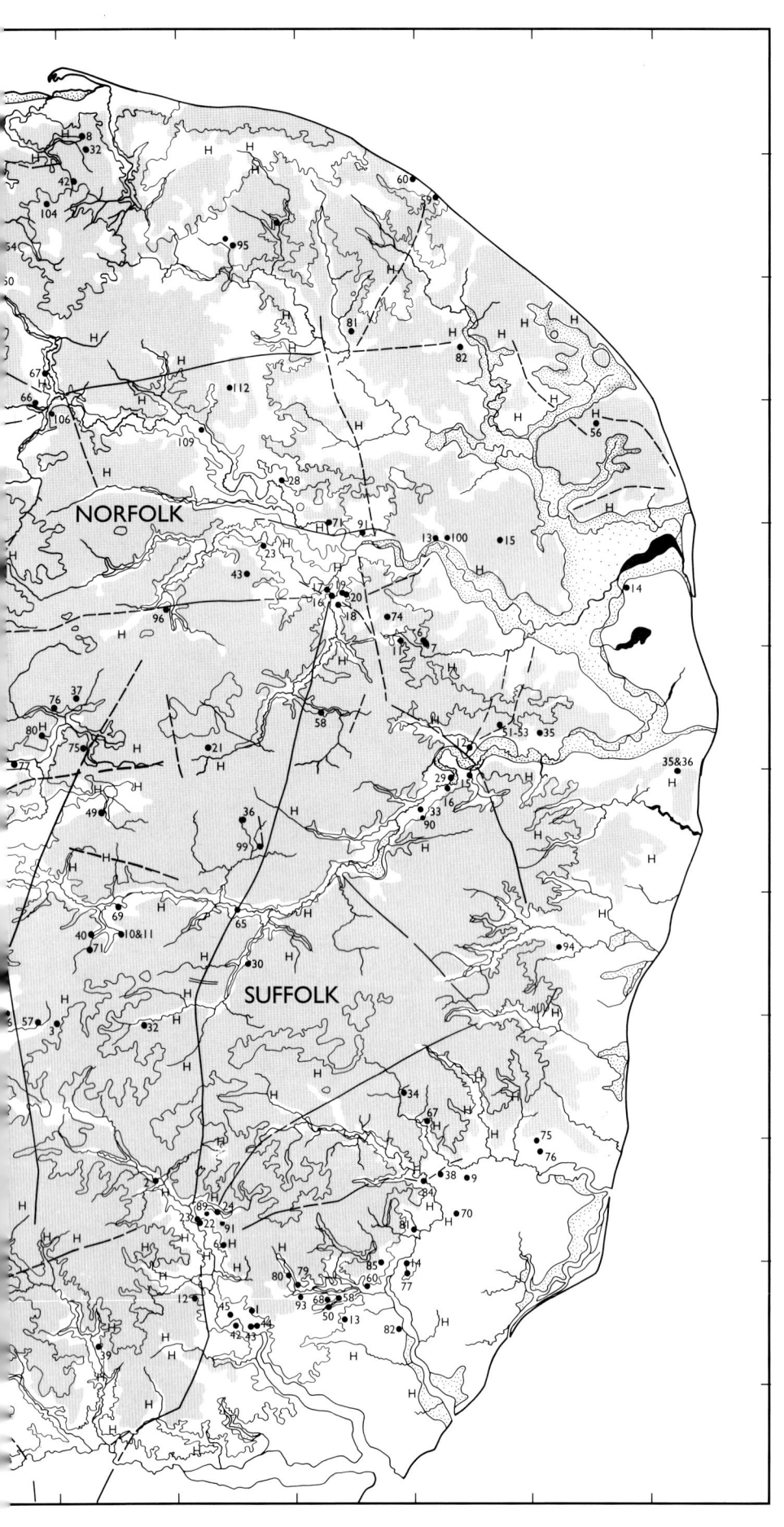

Saxon cemeteries listed in the gazetteer

Bibliography

Åberg, N., 1926 — *The Anglo-Saxons in England, during the Early Centuries after the Invasion* (Uppsala)

Adams, B. and Jackson, D., 1988–9 — 'The Anglo-Saxon Cemetery at Wakerley, Northamptonshire; Excavations by Mr D. Jackson', *Northants Archaeol.* 22, 69–183

Ager, B., 1985 — 'The Smaller Variants of the Anglo-Saxon Quoit Brooch', *Anglo-Saxon Studies in Archaeology and History* 4, 1–58

Arnold, C., 1980 — 'Wealth and Social Structure: a Matter of Life and Death', in Rahtz, P., Dickinson, T. and Watts, L., (eds) *Anglo-Saxon Cemeteries 1979*, Brit. Archaeol. Rep. 82 (Oxford), 81–142

Bede (The Venerable) — *H.E. Ecclesiastical History of the English People*, ed. and trans. Colgrave, B. and Mynors, R.A.B., 1969 (Oxford)

Bemmann, J. and Hahne, G., 1994 — 'Waffenführende Grabinventare der jüngeren römischen Kaiserzeit und Völkerwanderungszeit in Skandinavien. Studie zur zeitlichen Ordnung anhand der norwegischen Funde', *Bericht der Römisch-Germanischen Kommission* 75, 283–653

Bode, M.-J., 1998 — *Schmalstede. Ein Urnengräberfeld der Kaiser- und Völkerwanderungszeit*, Urnengräberfriedhöfe Schleswig-Holsteins 14 / Offa Bücher 78, (Neumünster)

Böhme, H.W., 1974 — *Germanische Grabfunde des 4. bis 5. Jahrhunderts zwischen unterer Elbe und Loire*, Münchner Beiträge zur vor- und Frühgeschichte 19, 2 vols (München)

Böhme, H.W., 1986 — 'Das Ende der Römerherrschaft in Britannien und die angelsächsische Besiedlung Englands im 5. Jahrhundert', *Jahrbuch des Römisch-Germanischen Zentralmuseums* 33, 466–574

Böhner, K., 1958 — *Die fränkischen Altertümer des Trierer Landes*, Germ. Denkmäler Völkerwanderungszeit B, 1 (Berlin)

Bonney, D.J., 1966 — 'Pagan Saxon burials and boundaries in Wiltshire', *Wilts. Archaeol. Natur. Hist. Mag.* 61, 25–30

Bonney, D.J., 1972 — 'Early boundaries in Wessex', in Fowler, P.J., (ed) *Archaeology and the Landscape* (London), 68–86

Bonney, D.J., 1979 — 'Early boundaries and estates in southern England', in Sawyer, P.H., (ed) *Medieval Settlements* (London), 72–82

Brenan, J., 1984–5 — 'Assessing social status in the Anglo-Saxon cemetery at Sleaford', *Bull. Institute Archaeol.* 21–22, 125–131

Brenan, J., 1991 — *Hanging Bowls and their Significance*, Brit. Archaeol. Rep. 220 (Oxford)

Brenan, J., 1997 — *Social Status Analysis*, (archive report)

Brooks, N.P., 1989 — 'The formation of the Mercian kingdom', in Bassett, S., (ed.) *The Origins of Anglo-Saxon Kingdoms* (Leicester), 159–170

Brown, P.D.C., 1977 — 'Firesteels and pursemounts again', *Bonner Jahrbücher* 177, 451–77

Bruce-Mitford, R.L.S., 1955 — 'The Snape Boat-Grave', *Proc. Suffolk Inst. Archaeol.* 26, 1–26

Bruce-Mitford, R.L., 1975 — *The Sutton Hoo Ship Burial*, 1 (Trustees of the British Museum)

Bruce-Mitford, R.L.S., 1978 — *The Sutton Hoo Ship Burial*, 2 (Trustees of the British Museum)

Bruce-Mitford, R.L.S., 1983 — *The Sutton Hoo Ship Burial*, 3 (Trustees of the British Museum)

Brugmann, B., 2004 — *Glass beads from Early Anglo-Saxon graves* (Oxford)

Brush, K., 1994 — *Adorning the Dead: the Social Significance of Early Anglo-Saxon Funerary Dress in England* (unpublished PhD thesis: Cambridge)

Carver, M.O.H., 1989 — 'Kingship and material culture in early Anglo-Saxon East Anglia', in Bassett, S., (ed) *The Origins of East Anglian Kingdoms* (Leicester), 141–158

Carver, M.O.H., 1992 — 'The Anglo-Saxon Cemetery at Sutton Hoo: an Interim Report', in Carver, M.O.H., (ed) *The Age of Sutton Hoo* (Woodbridge), 343–371

Carver, M.O.H., 1998 — *Sutton Hoo. Burial Ground of Kings?* (London)

Carver, M.O.H., 2005 — *Sutton Hoo: a 7th-century Princely Burial Ground and its Context*, (British Museum Press)

Clarke, R.R., 1940 — 'Norfolk in the Dark Ages, 400–800 AD', *Norfolk Archaeol.* 27(2), 215–49

Cook J.M., 2004 — *Early Anglo-Saxon Buckets. A Corpus of Copper-Alloy and Iron-bound Stave-built Vessels*, edited by Birte Brugmann, Oxford Univ. School of Archaeol. Monogr. 60 (Oxford)

Crawford, S., 1991 — 'When do Anglo-Saxon children count?' *J. Theoret. Archaeol.* 2, 17–24

Darby, H.C., 1971 — *The Domesday Geography of Eastern England* (Cambridge)

Davies, W. and Vierck, H. 1974 — 'The contents of the Tribal Hidage: social aggregates and settlement patterns', *Frühmittelalterliche Studien* 8, 223–93

Davison, A. and Green, B., 1993 — *Illington: a Study of a Breckland Parish and its Anglo-Saxon Cemetery*, E. Anglian Archaeol. 63

Dickinson, T.M. 1993 — 'An Anglo-Saxon 'cunning woman' from Bidford-on-Avon', in Carver, M.O.H., (ed) *In Search of Cult* (Woodbridge), 45–54

Dickinson, T M. and Härke, H. 1992 — 'Early Anglo-Saxon Shields', *Archaeologia* 110

Down, A. and Welch, M.G., 1990 — *Chichester Excavations VII: Appledown and the Mardens* (Chichester)

Evison, V.I., 1969 — 'Five Anglo-Saxon inhumation graves at Great Chesterford, Essex', *Berichten van de Rijksdienst voor het Oudheidkundig Bodemonderzoek* 19, 157–73

Evison, V.I., 1987 — *Dover: The Buckland Anglo-Saxon Cemetery*, English Heritage Archaeol. Rep. 3 (London)

Evison, V.I., 1994 — *An Anglo-Saxon Cemetery at Great Chesterford, Essex*, Counc. Brit. Archaeol. Res. Rep. 91

Evison, V.I., 2000 — 'Glass vessels in England AD 400–1100', in Price, J., (ed.), *Glass in Britain and Ireland AD*

	350–1100 British Museum Occasional Paper 127, 47–98 (London)	Härke, H., 2000	'Social analysis of mortuary evidence in German protohistoric archaeology', *J. Anthropological Archaeol.* 19, 369–384
Evison, V.I. and Hill, P., 1996	*Two Anglo-Saxon Cemeteries at Beckford, Hereford and Worcester*, Counc. Brit. Archaeol. Res. Rep. 103	Haughton, C. and Powlesland, D., 1999	*West Heslerton Anglian Cemetery*, Landscape Research Centre Archaeol. Monogr. Ser. 1 (Nottingham)
Fernie, E., 1993	*An Architectural History of Norwich Cathedral* (Oxford)	Hawkes, S. and Dunning, G.C., 1961	'Soldiers and Settlers in Britain, fourth to fifth century; with a catalogue of animal-ornamented buckles and related belt-fittings', *Medieval Archaeol.* 5, 1–70
Filmer-Sankey, W., 1984	'The Snape Anglo-Saxon Cemetery and Ship Burial: the current state of knowledge', *Bulletin of the Sutton Hoo Research Committee* 2, 13–15	Higham, N., 1992	*Rome, Britain and the Anglo-Saxons* (Seaby: London)
Filmer-Sankey, W., 1988	'Excavations at Snape, 1986' *Bulletin of the Sutton Hoo Research Committee* 5, 13–17	Hills, C.M., 1977a	'Chamber Grave from Spong Hill, North Elmham, Norfolk' *Medieval Archaeol.* 21, 167–176
Filmer-Sankey, W., 1992	'Snape Anglo-Saxon cemetery: the current state of knowledge', in Carver, M.O.H., (ed), *The Age of Sutton Hoo* (Woodbridge), 39–51	Hills, C.M., 1977b	*The Anglo-Saxon Cemetery at Spong Hill, North Elmham, Norfolk Part I*, E. Anglian Archaeol. 6
Filmer-Sankey, W. and Pestell, T., 2001	*Snape Anglo-Saxon Cemetery: Excavations and Surveys 1824–1992*, E. Anglian Archaeol. 95	Hills, C.M., 1978	Sächsische und Angelsächsische Keramik', in Ahrens, C., (ed.), *Sachsen und Angelsachsen* (Katalog Ausstellung Harburg 1978–9), Veröff Helms-Museums 32 (Hamburg), 135–152
Fox, C., 1923	*The Archaeology of the Cambridge region* (Cambridge)		
Gaimster, D.R.M., Margeson, S. and Barry, T., 1989	'Medieval Britain and Ireland in 1988' *Medieval Archaeol.* 33, 161–241	Hills, C.M., 1993	'Who were the East Anglians?' in Gardiner, J. (ed.), *Flatlands and Wetlands'*, E. Anglian Archaeol. 50, 14–23
Gaimster, M., 1992	'Scandinavian gold bracteates in Britain. Money and media in the Dark Ages', *Medieval Archaeol.* 36, 1–28	Hills, C.M., 1994	'The chronology of the Anglo-Saxon cemetery at Spong Hill, Norfolk', in Stjernquist, B., (ed), *Prehistoric graves as a source of information*, Symposium at Kastlösa 1992 (Stockholm) 41–49
Geake, H. 1994	'Anglo-Saxon double-tongued buckles' *Medieval Archaeol.* 38, 164–6		
Geake, H., 1997	*The Use of Grave-Goods in Conversion-Period England, c.600–c.850*, Brit. Archaeol. Rep. 261 (Oxford)	Hills, C.M. and Penn, K.J., 1981	*The Anglo-Saxon Cemetery at Spong Hill, North Elmham, Norfolk: Part II*, E. Anglian Archaeol. 11
Gilmour, B., 1984	'X-Radiography of two objects: the weaving batten (24/3) and the sword (40/5)', in Hills, C.M., *et al. The Anglo-Saxon Cemetery at Spong Hill, Norfolk: Part III*, E. Anglian Archaeol. 21, 160–161	Hills, C.M., Penn, K.J. and Rickett, R.J., 1984	*The Anglo-Saxon Cemetery at Spong Hill, North Elmham, Norfolk: Part III*, E. Anglian Archaeol. 21
		Hills, C.M., Penn, K.J. and Rickett, R.J., 1987	*The Anglo-Saxon Cemetery at Spong Hill, North Elmham, Norfolk: Part IV*, E. Anglian Archaeol. 34
Goodier, A., 1984	'The formation of boundaries in Anglo-Saxon England', *Medieval Archaeol.* 28, 1–21		
Green, B. and Rogerson, A., 1978	*The Anglo-Saxon Cemetery at Bergh Apton, Norfolk*, E. Anglian Archaeol. 7	Hills, C.M., Penn, K.J. and Rickett, R.J., 1994	*The Anglo-Saxon Cemetery at Spong Hill, North Elmham, Norfolk: Part V*, E. Anglian. Archaeol. 67
Green, B., Rogerson, A. and White, S., 1987	*The Anglo-Saxon Cemetery at Morning Thorpe, Norfolk*, E. Anglian Archaeol. 36 (2 vols)	Hills, C.M. and Wade-Martins, P., 1976	*The Anglo-Saxon cemetery at The Paddocks, Swaffham*, E. Anglian Archaeol. 2, 1–44
Halsall, G., 1995	*Settlement and social organization: the Merovingian region of Metz* (Cambridge)	Hines, J., 1984	*The Scandinavian Character of Anglian England in the Pre-Viking Period*, Brit. Archaeol. Rep. 124 (Oxford)
Hamerow, H., 1993	*Excavations at Mucking. Vol 2: The Anglo-Saxon Settlement*, English Heritage Archaeol. Rep. 21	Hines, J., 1992	'The seriation and chronology of Anglian English women's graves: a critical re-assessment' in Jørgensen, L., (ed) *Chronological Studies of Anglo-Saxon England, Lombard Italy, and Vendel Period Sweden* (Copenhagen), 81–93
Hamerow, H., 2002	*Early Medieval Settlements. The Archaeology of Rural Communities in Northwest Europe 400–900* (Oxford)		
Härke, H., 1989	'Knives in Early Saxon burials: blade length and age at death', *Medieval Archaeol.* 33, 144–148	Hines, J., 1993	*Clasps Hektespenner Agraffen: Anglo-Scandinavian Clasps of Classes A–C of the Third to Sixth Centuries AD*, (Kungl. Vitterhets Historie Och Antikvitets Akademien, Stockholm)
Härke, H., 1992	*Angelsächsische Waffengräber des 5.–7. Jahrhunderts*, Zeitschrift für Archäologie des Mittelalters Beiheft 6, (Köln)	Hines, J. 1997	*A Corpus of Anglo-Saxon Great Square-headed Brooches*, Rep. Res. Comm. Soc. Antiq. London 51 (London)
Härke, H., 1997	'Early Anglo-Saxon Social Structure', in Hines, J., (ed.), *The Anglo-Saxons. From the Migration Period to the Eighth Century, An Ethnographic Perspective*, Studies in Historical Archaeology 2, (Woodbridge), 125–159	Hines, J., 1999a	'Angelsächsische Chronologie: Probleme und Aussichten', in von Freeden, U., Koch, U. and Wieczorek, A., (eds), *Völker an Nord- und Ostsee und die Franken*, (Akten des 48.

	Sachsensymposiums in Mannheim vom 7. Bis 11. September 1997), Kolloquium Vor- und Frühgeschichte 3, (Bonn), 19–30	Lawson, A.J., Martin, E.A. and Priddy, D., 1981	*The Barrows of East Anglia*, E. Anglian Archaeol. 12
Hines, J. 1999b	'The sixth-century transition in Anglian England: an analysis of female graves from Cambridgeshire' in Hines, J., Høilund Nielsen, K. and Siegmund, F. (eds), *The Pace of Change. Studies in Early-Medieval Chronology*, Cardiff Studies in Archaeology (Oxford: Oxbow Books), 65–79	Lawson, G. 1978	'The Lyre from Grave 22' in Green, B. and Rogerson, A., *The Anglo-Saxon Cemetery at Bergh Apton, Norfolk*, E. Anglian Archaeol. 7, 87–97
		Lawson, G., 1987	'Report on the Lyre Remains from Grave 97', in Green, B., Rogerson, A.R. and White, S., *The Anglo-Saxon Cemetery at Morning Thorpe, Norfolk*, E. Anglian Archaeol. 36, 166–171
Hinz, H., 1969	*Das fränkische Gräberfeld von Eick, Gemeinde Rheinkamp, Kreis Moers*, Germ. Denkmäler Völkerwanderungszeit B, 4 (Berlin)	Lawson, G., 2001	'The Lyre Remains from Grave 32', in Filmer-Sankey, W. and Pestell, T., *Snape Anglo-Saxon Cemetery: Excavations and Surveys 1824–1992*, E. Anglian Archaeol. 95, 215–223
Hirst, S., 1985	*An Anglo-Saxon Cemetery at Sewerby, Yorkshire*, York University Archaeol. Publications 4		
Hodges, R., 1989	*The Anglo-Saxon Achievement: Archaeology and the Beginnings of English Society* (London)	Layard, N.F., 1907	'An Anglo-Saxon cemetery in Ipswich', *Archaeologia* 60, 2, 325–52
Hodson, F., 1977	'Quantifying Hallstatt', *American Antiquity* 42, 394–411	Leeds, E.T., 1945	'The distribution of the Angles and Saxons, archaeologically considered', *Archaeologia* 91, 1–106
Hoeper, M., 1999	Kochkessel – Opfergabe – Urne – Grabbeigabe – Altmetall. Zur Funktion und Typologie der Westlandkessel auf dem Kontinent', in Brather, S., Brückner, C. and Hoeper, M., (eds), *Archäologie als Sozialgeschichte. Studien zur Siedlung, Wirtschaft und Gesellschaft im frühgeschichtlichen Mitteleuropa* (Festschrift für Heiko Steuer zum 60 Geburtstag), Internat. Arch. Studia Honoraria 9, (Rahden/Westfalen), 235–249	Lethbridge, T.C., 1931	*Recent excavations in Anglo-Saxon cemeteries in Cambridgeshire and Suffolk*, Cambridge Antiq. Soc. Quarto Publ. new ser. 3
		Lethbridge, T.C., 1936	*A cemetery at Shudy Camps, Cambridgeshire*, Cambridge Antiq. Soc. Quarto Publ. new ser. 5
		Lethbridge, T.C., 1951	*A Cemetery at Lackford, Suffolk*, Cambridge Antiq. Soc. Quarto Publ. new ser. 6
Høilund Nielsen, K., 1995	'From artefact to analysis by way of correspondence analysis', *Anglo-Saxon Studies Archaeol. Hist.* 8, 111–43	Lucy, S., 1998	*The Early Anglo-Saxon Cemeteries of East Yorkshire*, Brit. Archaeol. Rep. 272 (Oxford)
Høilund Nielsen, K., 1997	'The schism of Anglo-Saxon chronology', in Jensen, C.K. and Høilund Nielsen, K. (eds), *Burial and Society* (Arhus), 71–99	Lucy, S., 2002	'Burial practice in early medieval eastern England: constructing local identities, deconstructing ethnicity', in Lucy, S. and Reynolds, A., (eds) *Burial in Early Medieval England and Wales*, Soc. Medieval Archaeol. Monogr. Ser. 17, 72–87
Høilund Nielsen, K., 2003	*The male graves of four cemeteries from Norfolk and Suffolk: Bergh Apton, Morning Thorpe, Spong Hill, Westgarth Gardens*, (archive report)		
Høilund Nielsen, K. and Hines, J., 1997	*The search for a chronological sequence: correspondence analysis of the grave assemblages*, (archive report)	Lucy, S. and Reynolds, A., (eds) 2002a	*Burial in Early Medieval England and Wales*, Soc. Medieval Archaeol. Monogr. Ser. 17 (Leeds)
Housman, H., 1895	'Exploration of an Anglo-Saxon cemetery', *Norfolk Archaeol.* 12, 100–04	Lucy, S. and Reynolds, A., 2002b	'Burial in early medieval England and Wales: past, present and future', in Lucy, S. and Reynolds, A., (eds) *Burial in Early Medieval England and Wales*, Soc. Medieval Archaeol. Monogr. Ser. 17, 1–23
Hutchinson, P., 1966	'The Anglo-Saxon Cemetery at Little Eriswell, Suffolk', *Proc. Cambridge Antiq. Soc.* 59, 1–32		
Jensen, C.K. and Høilund Nielsen, K., 1997	'Burial data and correspondence analysis', in Jensen, C.K. and Høilund Nielsen, K. (eds), *Burial and Society* (Arhus), 29–61	Lüdemann, H., 1994	'Mehrfachbelegte Gräber im frühen Mittelalter', *Fundberichte aus Baden-Württemberg* 19.1, 421–589
		MacGregor, A. and Bolick, E., 1993	*A Summary Catalogue of the Anglo-Saxon Collections (Non-Ferrous Metals)*, Brit. Archaeol. Rep. 230 (Oxford)
Johnson, S., 1983	*Burgh Castle: Excavations by Charles Green, 1958–1961*, E. Anglian Archaeol. 20		
Kennett, D.H., 1977	'Anglo-Saxon finds from Brooke, Norfolk', *Proc. Cambridge Antiq. Soc.* 66, 93–118	McHugh, F., 1999	*Theoretical and Quantitative Approaches to the Study of Mortuary Practice*, Brit. Archaeol. Rep. Int. Ser. 785 (Oxford
Koch, U., 1977	*Das Reihengraberfeld bei Schretzheim*, Germ. Denkmäler Völkerwanderungszeit A, 13, 1&2 (Berlin)	McKinley, J., 1987	'Report on the Skeletal Material' in Green, B., Rogerson, A. and White, S.,
Koch, U., 2001	*Das Alamannisch-Fränkische Gräberfeld bei Pleidelsheim*, Forschungen und Berichte zur Vor- und Frühgeschichte in Baden-Württemberg 60, (Stuttgart)		*The Anglo-Saxon Cemetery at Morning Thorpe, Norfolk*, E. Anglian Archaeol. 36, 188–9
		McKinley, J., 1994	*The Anglo-Saxon Cemetery at Spong Hill, North Elmham Part VIII: The Cremations*, E. Anglian Archaeol. 69
Kristoffersen, S., 2000	*Sverd og spenne. Dyreornamentikk og sosial ontekst*, Studia Humanitatis Bergensia 13	Mackreth, D., 1987	'A note on the Roman Brooches' in Green, B., Rogerson, A. and White, S., *The Anglo-Saxon*

	Cemetery at Morning Thorpe, Norfolk, E. Anglian Archaeol. 36, 165–6	Myres, J.N.L. and Green, B., 1973	*The Anglo-Saxon cemeteries of Caistor-by-Norwich and Markshall, Norfolk*, Rep. Res. Comm. Soc. Antiq. London 30 (London)
Malim, T., Penn, K., Robinson, B., Wait, G. and Walsh, K. 1997	'New evidence on the Cambridgeshire Dykes and Worsted Street Roman Road', *Proc. Cambridge Antiq. Soc.* 85, 27–122	Nehlsen, H., 1978	Der Grabfrevel in den germanischen Rechtsaufzeichnungen', in Jankuhn, H., Nelhsen, H. and Roth, H., (eds), *Zum Grabfrevel in vor- und frühgeschichtlicher Zeit. Untersuchungen zu Grabraub und „haugbrot" on Mittel- und Nordeuropa Bericht über ein Kolloquium der Kommission für die Altertumskunde Mittel- und Nordeuropas vom 14. bis 16. Februar 1977*, Abhandlungen der Akademie der Wissenschaften in Göttingen. Phil-Hist. Kl. 3. Folge 113, 107–187
Malim, T. and Hines, J., 1998	*The Anglo-Saxon Cemetery at Edix Hill (Barrington A), Cambridgeshire*, Counc. Brit. Archaeol. Res. Rep. 112		
Mango, M.M., Mango, C., Evans, A.C. and Hughes, M., 1989	'A 6th-century Mediterranean bucket from Bromeswell Parish, Suffolk', *Antiquity* 63, 295–311		
Martin, E.A., 1982	'Archaeology in Suffolk 1981', *Proc. Suffolk Inst. Archaeol.* 35(2), 155–60	Neville, R.C., 1852	*Saxon Obsequies*, (London)
		Neville, R.C., 1854	'Anglo-Saxon cemetery on Linton Heath, Cambridgeshire', *Archaeol. J.* 11, 95–115
Martin, E.A., 1983	'Archaeology in Suffolk 1982', *Proc. Suffolk Inst. Archaeol.* 35(3), 229–35	Newman, J., 1991	'The Boss Hall Anglo-Saxon Cemetery', *The Quarterly* (J. Norfolk Archaeol. Hist. Res. Group) 2, 16–23
Martin, E.A., 1984	'Archaeology in Suffolk 1983', *Proc. Suffolk Inst. Archaeol.* 35(4), 321–8		
Martin, E.A., 1987	'Archaeology in Suffolk, 1986', *Proc. Suffolk Inst. Archaeol.* 36(iii), 233–4	Newman, J., 1992	'The late Roman and Anglo-Saxon settlement pattern in the Sandlings of Suffolk', in Carver, M.O.H. (ed) *The Age of Sutton Hoo*, (Woodbridge), 25–38
Martin, M., 1976	*Das fränkische Gräberfeld von Basel-Bernerring* (Mainz)		
Martin, M., 1990	'Bemerkungen zur Ausstattung der Frauengräber und zur Interpretation der Doppelgräber und Nachbestattungen im frühen Mittelalter', in Affeldt, W., (ed.), *Frauen in Spätantike und Frühmittelalter. Lebensbedingungen — Lebensnormen — Lebensformen* (Sigmaringen), 89–103	Newman, J. 1996a	'Viking Battle Sites or Early Anglo-Saxon cemeteries', *The Quarterly* (J. Norfolk Archaeol. Hist. Res. Group) 6, 15–19
		Newman, J. 1996b	'New Light on Old Finds — Bloodmoor Hill, Gisleham, Suffolk' *Anglo-Saxon Studies Archaeol. Hist.* 9, 75–80
		Newman, J. 2005	'Survey in the Deben Valley', in Carver, M.O.H., *Sutton Hoo: a 7th-century Princely Burial Ground and its Context*, (The British Museum Press)
Marzinzik, S., 2003	*Early Anglo-Saxon Belt Buckles (late 5th to early 8th centuries AD): their classification and context*, Brit. Archaeol. Rep. 357 (Oxford)		
Meaney, A., 1964	*A Gazetteer of Early Anglo-Saxon Burial Sites* (London)	Nieveler, E. and Siegmund, F., 1999	'The Merovingian chronology of the Lower Rhine area: results and problems', in Hines, J., Høilund Nielsen, K. and Siegmund, F. (eds), *The Pace of Change. Studies in Early-Medieval Chronology*, (Oxbow Books: Oxford), 3–20
Meaney, A.L., 1981	*Anglo-Saxon Amulets and Curing Stones*, Brit. Archaeol. Rep. 96 (Oxford)		
Menghin, W., 1983	*Das Schwert im Frühen Mittelalter*, Wiss. Beibände zum Anzeiger d. Germ. Nationalmus. 1 (Stuttgart)	Nørgård Jørgensen, A., 1999	*Waffen und Gräber. Typologische und chronologische Studien zu skandinavischen Waffengräbern 520/30 bis 900 n. Chr.* Nordiske Fortidsminder B17 (Copenhagen)
Morris, C.A., 1994	'Find connected with wooden artefacts, woodworking and other tools', in Hills, C., Penn, K.J. and Rickett, R.J., *The Anglo-Saxon Cemetery at Spong Hill, North Elmham, Part V: Catalogue of Cremations*, E. Anglian Archaeol. 67, 30–34	Oosthuizen, S., 1998	'The Origins of Cambridgeshire', *Antiq. J.* 78, 85–109
		Pader, E-J., 1982	*Symbolism, Social Relations and the Interpretation of Mortuary Remains*, Brit. Archaeol. Rep. Int. Ser. 130 (Oxford)
Mortimer, C., 1990	*Some Aspects of Early Medieval Copper-Alloy Technology, as Illustrated by the Anglian Cruciform Brooch*, (unpublished D.Phil. thesis, University of Oxford)	Palm, M. and Pind, J., 1992	'Anglian English Women's Graves in the Fifth to Seventh centuries AD: a Chronological Analysis' in Jørgensen, L., (ed) *Chronological Studies of Anglo-Saxon England, Lombard Italy and Vendel Period Sweden* (Copenhagen), 50–80
Müller-Wille, M., 1995	'Boat-Graves, Old and New Views', in Crumlin-Pedersen, O. and Munch Thyre, B., (eds), *The Ship as Symbol in Prehistoric and Medieval Scandinavia* (Copenhagen), 100–109		
		Parfitt, K. and Anderson, T., forthcoming	*The Anglo-Saxon Cemetery at Dover Buckland. Excavations 1994*
Müssemeyer, U., Nieveler, E., Plum, R. and Pöppelmann, H., 2003	*Chronologie der merowingerzeitlichen Grabfunde vom linken Niederrhein bis zur nördlichen Eifel*, Materialien zur Bodendenkmalpflege im Rheinland 15, (Köln, Bonn)	Parfitt, K. and Brugmann, B., 1997	*The Anglo-Saxon Cemetery on Mill Hill, Deal, Kent*, Soc. Medieval Archaeol. Monogr. 14
		Parker Pearson, M., 1999	*The Archaeology of Death and Burial* (Stroud)
Myres, J.N.L., 1977	*A Corpus of Anglo-Saxon Pottery of the Pagan Period*, (Cambridge)	Paulsen, P., 1992	*Die Holzfunde aus dem Gräberfeld bei Oberflacht*, Forschungen und Berichte zur Vor-

Penn, K.J., 1999 *An Anglo-Saxon Cemetery at Oxborough, West Norfolk*, E. Anglian Archaeol. Occ. Papers 5

Penn, K.J., 2000 *Excavations on the Norwich Southern Bypass, 1989–91. Part 2: The Anglo-Saxon Cemetery at Harford Farm, Markshall, Norfolk*, E. Anglian Archaeol. 92

Penn, K.J., forthcoming *Excavations along the Bacton to King's Lynn Gas Pipeline, Volume II: Anglo-Saxon Cemetery at Tittleshall, Norfolk*, E. Anglian Archaeol.

Penn, K.J and Andrews, P., 2000 'An Anglo-Saxon Cemetery at Brunel Way, Thetford', *Norfolk Archaeol*. 43, 3, 414–440

Périn, P. 1998 'La question des 'tombes-références' pour la datation absolue du mobilier funéraire mérovingien' in Delestre, X. and Périn, P., (eds) *La datation des structures et des objets du haut moyen âge: méthodes et résultats* (Actes des Xve Journées intern. Arch. mérovingienne. Rouen, Musée des Antiquités de la Seine-Maritime 4–6 février 1994. Mémoires publiés par l'Assoc. française arch. Mérovingienne, Saint-Germain-en-Laye), 189–206

Pescheck, C., 1996 *Das fränkische Reihengräberfeld von Kleinlangheim, Lkr.Kitzingen/Nordbayern*, Germ. Denkmäler Völkerwanderungszeit A, 17 (Mainz)

Plunkett, S. J. 1994 *Guardians of the Gipping. Anglo-Saxon Treasures from Hadleigh Road, Ipswich* (Ipswich)

Putnam, G., 1984 'The human bones', in Hills, C.M., Penn, K.J. and Rickett, R.J., *The Anglo-Saxon Cemetery at Spong Hill, North Elmham, Norfolk: Part III*, E. Anglian Archaeol. 21, 15–17

Ravn, M., 2003 *Death Ritual and Germanic Social Structure (c. AD 200–600)*, Brit. Archaeol. Rep. Int. Ser. 1164 (Oxford)

Richards, J.D., 1987 *The Significance of Form and Decoration of Anglo-Saxon Cremation Urns*, Brit. Archaeol. Rep. 166 (Oxford)

Rickett, R.J., 1995 *The Anglo-Saxon Cemetery at Spong Hill, North Elmham, Norfolk: Part VII, The Iron Age, Roman and Early Saxon Settlement*, E. Anglian Archaeol. 73

Rigold, S.E., 1980 'The Sceattas' in Wade-Martins, P. *Excavations in North Elmham Park, 1967–72*, E. Anglian Archaeol. 9, 497–9

Ross, S., 1991 *Dress pins from Anglo-Saxon England: their Production and Typo-Chronological Development* (unpublished D.Phil. thesis, University of Oxford)

Sayer, D., forthcoming *Anglo-Saxon Cemetery Structure: a Question of Household or Kinship* (unpublished PhD thesis, University of Reading)

Schön, M., 1999 *Feddersen Wierde, Fallward, Flögeln* (Bremerhaven)

Schulze-Dörrlamm, M., 1990 *Die spätrömischen und frühmittelalterlichen Gräberfelder von Gondorf, Gem.Kobern-Gondorf, Kr.Mayen-Koblenz*, Germ. Denkmäler Völkerwanderungszeit B, 14 (Stuttgart)

Scull, C.J., 1985 'Further evidence from East Anglia for enamelling on early Anglo-Saxon metal work' *Anglo-Saxon Studies Archaeol. Hist*. 4, 117–24

Scull, C.J., 1992 'Before Sutton Hoo: Structures of Power and Society in Early East Anglia', in Carver M.O.H. (ed.), *The Age of Sutton Hoo*, (Woodbridge), 3–24

Scull, C.J., 1993 'Archaeology, Early Anglo-Saxon society and the origins of Anglo-Saxon kingdoms', *Anglo-Saxon Studies Archaeol. Hist*. 6, 65–82

Scull, C.J., 1995 'Approaches to material culture and social dynamics of the Migration period in eastern England' in Bintliffe, J. and Hamerow, H. (eds), *Europe Between Late Antiquity and the Middle Ages: Recent archaeological and historical research in Western and Southern Europe*, Brit. Archaeol. Rep. Int. Ser. 617 (Oxford), 71–83

Scull, C.J. and Bayliss, A., 1999 'Dating burials of the 7th and 8th centuries: a case study from Ipswich, Suffolk', in Hines, J., Høilund Nielsen, K. and Siegmund, F. (eds), *The Pace of Change. Studies in Early-Medieval Chronology*, Cardiff Studies in Archaeology (Oxford: Oxbow Books), 80–88

Seeberger, F., 1985 'Zur Identifizierung von Feuerstählen', *Archäologisches Korrespondenzblatt* 15, 257–259

Siegmund, F., 1998 *Merowingerzeit am Niederrhein. Die frühmittelalterlichen Funde aus dem Regierungsbezirk Düsseldorf und dem Kreis Heinsberg*, Rheinische Ausgrabungen 34 (Köln)

Smith, C.R., 1892 *Collecteana Antiqua* II

Stein, F., 1967 *Adelsgräber des Achten Jahrhunderts in Deutschland*, Germ. Denkmäler Völkerwanderungszeit A, 9, 2 vols (Berlin)

Steuer, H., 1982a *Frühgeschichtelicher Sozialstrukturen in Mitteleuropa: eine Analyse der Auswerkungs methoden des archaeologischen Quellen materials* (Göttingen)

Steuer, H., 1982b 'Schlüsselpaare in frühgeschichtlichen Gräbern', *Studien zur Sachsenforschung* 3, 185–247

Stoodley, N., 1999 *The Spindle and the Spear. A Critical Enquiry into the Construction and Meaning of Gender in the Early Anglo-Saxon Burial Rite*, Brit. Archaeol. Rep. 288 (Oxford)

Stoodley, N., 2002 'Multiple burials, multiple meanings? Interpreting the early Anglo-Saxon multiple interment', in Lucy, S. and Reynolds, A., (eds), *Burial in Early Medieval England and Wales*, Soc. Medieval Archaeol. Monogr. Ser. 17, 103–121

Stork, I., 1997 'Als Persönlichkeit ins Jenseits. Bestattungssitte und Grabraub als Kontrast', in *Die Alamannen* (Begleitband zu Ausstellung 'Die Alamannen' 14.6.–14.9.1997, Stuttgart), 418–432

Swanton, M.J., 1973 *A Corpus of Pagan Anglo-Saxon Spear-Types*, Brit. Archaeol. Rep. 7 (Oxford)

Thomas, G.W., 1887 'On excavations in an Anglo-Saxon cemetery at Sleaford in Lincs', *Archaeologia* 50, 383–406

Vierck, H., 1972 'Redwalds Asche', *Offa* 29, 20–49

Vierck, H., 1978a 'Sächsische und Angelsächsische Keramik', in Ahrens, C. (ed.), *Sachsen und Angelsachsen* (Katalog Ausstellung Harburg 1978-9), Veröff Helms-Museums 32 (Hamburg), 135–152

Vierck, H., 1978b 'Zur angelsächsischen Frauentracht' in Ahrens, C., (ed) *Sachsen und Angelsachsen* (Hamburg), 255–262

Wade, K., 2000	'Anglo-Saxon and Medieval (Rural)', in Brown, N. and Glazebrook, J., (eds), *Research and Archaeology: a Framework for the Eastern Counties*, E. Anglian Archaeol. Occ. Pap. 8, 23–26	West, S.E. 1988	*The Anglo-Saxon Cemetery at Westgarth Gardens, Bury St Edmunds, Suffolk*, E. Anglian Archaeol. 38
Wade-Martins, P. 1980	*Excavations in North Elmham Park 1967–1972*, E. Anglian Archaeol. 9 (2 vols)	West, S.E., 1998	*A Corpus of Anglo-Saxon Material from Suffolk*, E. Anglian Archaeol. 84
Walton Rogers, P., forthcoming	'Costumes and Textiles', in Parfitt, K. and Anderson, T., *The Anglo-Saxon Cemetery at Dover Buckland. Excavations 1994*	White, R.H. 1988	*Roman and Celtic objects from Anglo-Saxon graves: a catalogue and an interpretation of their use*, Brit. Archaeol. Rep. 191 (Oxford)
Webster, L. and Cherry, J., 1973	'Medieval Britain in 1972', *Medieval Archaeol.* 17, 149–50	Williamson, T., 1987	'Early coaxial field systems on the East Anglian Boulder Clays', *Proc. Prehist. Soc.* 53, 419–31
Webster, L. and Cherry, J., 1976	'Medieval Britain in 1975', *Medieval Archaeol.* 20, 167	Williamson, T., 1993	*The Origins of Norfolk* (Manchester)
West, S.E., 1985	*West Stow: The Anglo-Saxon Village*, E. Anglian Archaeol. 24	Wilson, D.M. and Hurst, D.G., 1966	'Medieval Britain in 1965', *Medieval Archaeol.* 10, 168–219

Index

Page numbers in *italics* denote illustrations

Åberg, N. 24
Adams, B. 31
Akenham Hall (Suffolk), cemetery 106
Aldborough (Norfolk), cemetery 103
Alde, River 5
Apple Down (Sussex), grave features 84
Arnold, C. 15
Ashby (Suffolk), boat burial 109
Aslacton (Norfolk), field system 10
axe 24, 42

Babraham (Cambs), cemetery 101
Badley (Suffolk), cemeteries 106–7
Balsham (Cambs), cemetery 101
Bardwell (Suffolk), cemeteries 107
Barnham (Suffolk), cemeteries 107, 109
Barrington (Cambs), cemeteries 2, 82, 101
barrows
    prehistoric 1, 6, 10, 11
    Anglo-Saxon 1, 84
Bartlow (Cambs), cemetery 101
Barton Mills (Suffolk), cemeteries 107, 109
Beachamwell (Norfolk), cemeteries 103
beads
    amber 26
    bell *73*, 98
    glass
        analysis 26, *27–8*
        chronology 16, 42, 48–58, 98
        correspondence analysis 48–50, *51*
        status 89, 92, 93, 94, 95
Beckford (Worcs), cemetery 4
Bede 7, 8
Bedericsworth 11
Bemmann, J. 22, 23
Bergh Apton (Norfolk)
    burial practice 87
        cemetery layout 86, *87*
        double graves 77
        grave features 82, 83
        grave length and depth 76–7, *84*
        grave orientation and body position 84, 85, 86
    chronological analysis
        correlation of male and female frameworks 58, *66–7*, 69, 71
        dress accessories 48–58
        weapons 42–7
    discussion 98–100
    grave-good analysis
        beads 26, *27–8, 29*
        brooches 24, 25
        buckles 31, *32*
        copper-alloy and wooden vessels 38
        firesteels/pursemounts 34
        girdle-hangers 30
        knives 34
        lyre 36
        necklet 31
        pendants 26
        pins 30–1
        pottery 38, 40
        shield bosses 22, 23
        spearheads 17, 18, 20, 21
        strap-ends 32
        swords 23–4
        wrist-clasps 28–9
    local context *8*, 9, 11
    location *xii*, 5
    previous research 12, 13, 15
    project background 1, 3, 4–5
    project methods 16
    social structure 97
        age 88

burial practice 96
    grave-goods 89–90, 92, 93, 94, 95, 96
    previous research 12, 13, 15
    sex and gender 88–9
biers 83, 84
Black Bourn, River 5
Blackwater, River 8
Blakeney (Norfolk), Langham, cemetery 1, 103
Blaxhall (Suffolk), cemetery 107
Bode, M.-J. 24
body positions 85–6
Böhme, H.W. 14, 22, 24, 25
Böhner, K. 34
Bonn Seriation and Archaeological Statistics Package 13, 92
Botesdale (Suffolk), cemeteries 107
Bottisham (Cambs), Allington Hill cemetery 1, 6, 101
boundaries 8
Bramford (Suffolk), cemetery 107
Breckland 5
Brenan, Jane 12–13
Brettenham (Norfolk), cemeteries 2, 103
Brightwell (Suffolk), cemetery 107
Bromeswell (Suffolk), cemeteries 107, 109
brooches
    analysis
        annular and penannular 25
        cruciform 24
        disc 26
        equal-armed 24
        great square-headed 25–6
        small-long 24–5
    chronology 48, 50, 58, *70, 72, 73*, 98
    distribution 6–7
    status 96, 99
        association score 90, 92
        materials 91
        previous research 13, 15
        quantity and quality 93, 94
Brooke (Norfolk), cemetery 103
Broome (Norfolk), cemetery 103
Brugmann, Birte 3, 48, 58, 59
Brundall (Norfolk), cemeteries 103, 106
Brush, K. 15
Buckland (Kent), cemetery
    burial practice 82, 87
    excavations 4
    knives 34
    pendants 26
    pins 30, 31
buckles
    chronology
        framework 42, 45, 48, 50, 58, 59
        horizontal stratigraphy *63*, 68–70
        Phase FB *73*, 98
    grave-good analysis 31–2, *33*
    status 13, 91, 92
Bungay (Suffolk), cemeteries 2, 107
Burgh Castle (Norfolk), cemetery 1, 2, 103
burial practice 76, 87
    cemetery layout 86–7
    double graves 77–82
    grave features 82–4
    grave lengths and depths 76–7, *78–81, 84*
    grave orientation and body position 84–6
Burlingham (Norfolk), cemetery 103
Burnham Market (Norfolk), cemetery 106
Burston and Shimpling (Norfolk), cemetery 106
Burwell (Cambs), cemetery 2, 101
Bury St Edmunds (Suffolk), cemeteries 11, 107, 109
Butley, River 5

Caistor St Edmund (Norfolk), cemeteries 2, 7, 9, 103–4
Cam, River 5, 8
Cambridge (Cambs), cemeteries 2, 5–6, 101–2

Cambridge Antiquarian Society 2
Carleton Rode (Norfolk), cemetery 10, 104
Carver, Martin 3, 6–7
Castle Acre/West Acre (Norfolk), cemetery 2, 6, 104
Cavenham (Suffolk), cemetery 107
cemeteries
    background 4–5
    discovery 1–3
    distribution
        geology 5–6
        parish boundaries 6
    evidence, nature of 12
    gazetteer 101–10
    location *111*
    previous research
        chronology 15–16
        social structure 12–15
    see also Bergh Apton; Morning Thorpe; Spong Hill; Westgarth Gardens
Chadwick Hawkes, S. 26, 32
chamber graves 83, 84
Chatteris (Cambs), cemetery 1, 101
Cherry Hinton (Cambridge), cemetery 101–2
Chet, River 5, 9
Chilton (Suffolk), ?cemetery 109
Chippenham (Cambs), cemetery 102
Christianity 82
chronological framework 42, 98–9
    correlation of male and female frameworks 71
        grave-goods 58
        horizontal stratigraphy 71; Bergh Apton *66–7*, 71; Morning Thorpe *60–3*, 68–70;
            Spong Hill *64–5*, 70–1; Westgarth Gardens *68–9*, 71
        vertical stratigraphy 59
    dress accessories 48–58
    objects defining *70*, 71, *72–5*
    weapons 42–5
    previous research 15–16
Coddenham (Suffolk), cemeteries 107, 109
coffins 83, 84
Colney (Norfolk), cemetery 104
comb 59
Congham (Norfolk), cemeteries 104
copper-alloy vessels 36–8, 58, 92, 95
copper-alloys 91
coprolite digging 2
correspondence analysis
    beads 48–50, 51
    dress accessories 50, 52–8
    weapons 42, 45, 46–7
cremations
    chronology 59, 99
    distribution 5
    excavations 4
    social structure 14–15, 96–7
    urns 14, 16, 38–40, 58
Culford (Suffolk), cemetery 107

Davidson, Septimus 1
Deben, River 5
Depwade Hundred 10
Dersingham (Norfolk), cemetery 104
Devil's Dyke 8
Dickinson, T.M. 22, 23, 26, 59
Diss and Earsham Hundred 10
Dove Lane 9
Downham (Cambs), cemetery 102
Downham Market (Norfolk), cemetery 104
Drayton (Norfolk), cemetery 104
dress accessories
    chronological framework
        absolute 58
        relative 48–58
    correspondence analysis 50, 52
    grave-good analysis 24–30
    see also beads; brooches; finger-rings; girdle-hangers; keys; pendants; slip-knot rings; wrist-clasps
Dry Drayton (Cambs), cemetery 102
Dunning, G.C. 32

Duxford (Cambs), cemetery 103

ear-scoop 36
Earsham (Norfolk), cemetery 1, 6, 104
East Anglia
    kingdom of 7–8
    see of 9
East Walton (Norfolk), cemetery 104, 106
East Yorkshire, cemeteries 12, 13–14
Eastry (Kent), cemetery 26
Eick (Germany), cemetery 22
Ely (Cambs)
    cemeteries 2, 102
    diocese 8
English Heritage 16, 17, 98
Eriswell (Suffolk), cemeteries 6, 107, 109; *see also* Lakenheath
Essex, kingdom of 8
estates, Saxon 6
Evison, V. 36
Exning (Suffolk), cemetery 107
Eye (Suffolk), cemetery 2, 107

Fakenham (Norfolk), cemetery 104
Fakenham (Suffolk), cemetery 107, 109
family plots 87
Felixstowe (Suffolk), ?cemetery 109
Fen Ditton (Cambs), cemetery 102
ferrules 18, 20, 21, 22, 45, 89–90
Field Dalling (Norfolk), cemetery 104
Fincham (Norfolk), cemetery 104, 106
finger-rings 29
Finningham (Suffolk), cemetery 2, 107
firesteels/pursemounts 34–6, 58
Fleam Dyke 8
Flixton (Suffolk), cemeteries 107, 109
'folk' cemeteries 3, 5
Fornham St Genevieve (Suffolk), ?cemetery 11, 110
Fornham St Martin (Suffolk), ?cemetery 11, 110
Foulden (Norfolk), cemetery 104
Foxton (Cambs), cemetery 102
Framlingham (Suffolk), cemetery 107
Freckenham (Suffolk), ?cemetery 110
Fulbourn/Great Wilbraham (Cambs), cemetery 101

gaming pieces 15
Geake, H. 32, 94
geology 5–6
gilding 90, 91, 94, 96, 99
Gillingham (Norfolk), cemetery 104
Gipping, River 5
girdle-hangers
    chronology 48, 50, 58, *70*, *72*, *73*, 98
    grave-good analysis 30
    status 13, 91, 92, 93, 96
Girton (Cambs), cemetery 102
Gisleham (Suffolk), cemeteries 1, 108
Gissing (Norfolk), cemetery 104
glass vessels 15, 36, 92, 95
gold 90, 91, 95
Goodier, A. 6
Granta, River 5, 8
Grantchester (Cambs), cemetery 102
grave depths 76, *79*, *81*
grave lengths 76–7, *78*, *80*, *84*, *85*
grave-goods
    analysis 17
        dress accessories and female objects 24–30
        male and female objects 30–41
        weapons 17–24
    social structure 89–90
        5th–6th-century 94–6
        association scores 91, 92
        cremations 96–7
        in gender-'neutral' graves 94
        materials 90–1
        quantity and quality 92–4
grave-markers 83–4
Great Chesterford (Essex), cemetery 5, 8, 101
Great Ellingham (Norfolk), cemetery 104
Great Shelford/Stapleford (Cambs), cemetery 102

120

Great Thurlow (Suffolk), cemetery 6, 108
Great Walsingham (Norfolk), cemeteries 1, 104
Great Wilbraham *see* Fulbourn/Great Wilbraham
Green, B. 2
Greenwell, Canon 1
Grimston (Norfolk), cemeteries 104
Guilden Morden (Cambs), cemetery 103
Gunthorpe (Norfolk), cemetery 104

Hacheston (Suffolk), cemetery 108
Haddenham (Cambs), cemetery 102
Hahne, G. 22, 23
Hallstatt (Austria), cemetery 13
Halsall, Guy 13
Härke, Heinrich, weapon graves, analysis of 12, 15, 16, 98, 99
   age 93, 94
   shield bosses 22, 23, 59
   social structure 94, 95–6
   spearheads 17
Hasketon (Suffolk), cemetery 108
Haslingfield (Cambs), cemetery 2, 102
Hauxton (Cambs), cemetery 2, 102
Hemingstone (Suffolk), cemetery 109
Hethersett (Norfolk), cemetery 104
Higham, N. 4
Hildersham (Cambs), cemetery 102
Hilgay (Norfolk), cemetery 104
Hills, C.M. 40, 83, 84–5, 86
Hinderclay (Suffolk), cemetery 108
Hindringham (Norfolk), cemetery 106
Hines, John, research by
   chronology 16
   grave-good analysis 17, 24, 25–6, 28, 29
   pottery 40
   weapon graves 42, 98
Hinz, H. 22–3
Hockwold-cum-Wilton (Norfolk), cemeteries 104, 106
Hodges, R. 4
Hoe (Norfolk), cemetery 106
Høilund Nielsen, Karen, research by
   chronology 16, 71
   grave-good analysis 15, 17
      brooches 6, 24, 50
      buckles 31, 32
      pottery 14, 40
   weapon graves 42, 98
Holkham (Norfolk), cemetery 104
Horningsea (Cambs), cemetery 102
horse-burials 1
Horseheath (Cambs), cemetery 102
Housman, H. 2
Hoxne (Suffolk), ?cemetery 110
human bones 16, 98
Hunstanton (Norfolk), cemetery 104

Icklingham (Suffolk), cemeteries 108, 110
Icknield Way 5, 6
infant burials 88, 99
Ingham (Suffolk), ?cemetery 110
Ipswich (Suffolk)
   cemeteries 2, 16, 25, 108
   museum 2
iron 91
Ixworth (Suffolk), cemeteries 108, 110
Ixworth Thorpe (Suffolk), cemeteries 108

Jackson, D. 31

Kempston cone beakers 36
Kempstone (Norfolk), cemetery 104
Kenninghall (Norfolk), cemetery 2, 104
Kesgrave (Suffolk), cemetery 108
Kettlestone (Norfolk), cemetery 9, 104–5
keys 13, 30, 92, 93
Kilverstone (Norfolk), cemetery 106
Kirby Cane (Norfolk), cemeteries 105
knives
   analysis 34, *35*
   chronology 59, 68–70
   status 91, 92

Koch, U. 22, 23, 30, 31, 34, 45
Krefeld Gellep (Germany), cauldron 36
KVARK 16

lace-tags 32–4, 58, 99
Lackford (Suffolk), cemetery 2, 108, 109
Lakenheath (Suffolk), cemeteries 108, 110
   Eriswell 1, 2–3, 4, 11, 15, 27, 98, 109
Langham (Suffolk), cemetery 108; *see also* Blakeney
Lark, River 5, 11
Larwood, G.P. 2
Lawson, G. 36
Layard, N.F. 2
ledges 82
Leeds, E.T. 24
Lethbridge, T.C. 1, 2
Linnet, River 5, 11
Linton (Cambs), cemetery 102
Linton Heath (Cambs), cemetery 1, 102
Little Bealings (Suffolk), cemetery 108
Little Cornard (Suffolk), cemetery 108
Little Cressingham (Norfolk), cemetery 106
Little Ouse, River 5
Little Shelford (Cambs), cemetery 102
Little Snoring (Norfolk), cemetery 105
Little Walsingham (Norfolk), cemetery 105
Little Wilbraham (Cambs), cemetery 1, 102
Lode (Cambs), cemetery 102
London, St Lawrence Jewry 83
Long Stratton (Norfolk), field systems 10
Long Wittenham (Oxon), bucket 38
Lucy, Sam 12, 13–14
Lüdemann, H. 82
lyres 36

Mackeprang, M. 26
McKinley, J. 96
Mackreth, D. 25
Madsen, Torsten 16
Mann, Commander-Surgeon F.R. 2
March (Cambs), island of 8
Martham (Norfolk), cemetery 105
Martlesham (Suffolk), cemetery 108
Marzinzik, S. 31, 32
materials 90–1, 95, 99
Meaney, A. 26
Melbourn (Cambs), cemetery 102, 103
Menghin, W. 22–3, 31
Mepal (Cambs), cemetery 102
Mercia, kingdom of 8
Merovingian cemeteries 13
Merton (Norfolk), cemetery 105
metal-detector searches 1, 4
Metz (France), Merovingian cemeteries 13
Mildenhall (Suffolk), cemeteries 1, 2, 108, 110
   Holywell Row cemetery 1, 2, *12*, 15, 26, 27, 98
Milton (Cambs), cemetery 102
Morning Thorpe (Norfolk)
   burial practice 87
      cemetery layout 86–7
      double graves 77–82
      grave features 82, 83, 84
      grave length and depth 76–7, *80–1*
      grave orientation and body position 84, 85, 86
   chronological analysis
      correlation of male and female frameworks 58, 69; horizontal stratigraphy *60–3*,
      68–9, 71; vertical stratigraphy 59, 71
      difficulties 42
      dress accessories 48–58
      weapons 42–7
   cremations 4, 9, 96–7
   discussion 98–100
   grave-good analysis
      axe 24
      beads 26, *27–8, 29*
      brooches 24, 25, 26
      buckles 31–2, *33*
      copper-alloy and wooden vessels 36, 38
      finger-rings 29

firesteels/pursemounts 34–6
girdle-hangers and keys 30
glass vessels 36
knives 34, *35*
lace-tags 32–3
lyre 36
pendants 26
pins 30–1
pottery *37*, 38, *39*, 40–1
seaxes and swords 23
shield bosses 22, 23
slip-knot rings 29–30
spearheads 17, 18, 20, 21, 22
strap-ends 32
tweezers 36
wrist-clasps 28–9
local context *9*, 10, 11
location *xii*, 5
previous research 13, 15
project background 1, 3, 4–5
project methods 16
ring-ditches 10, 84
social structure 97
    5th–6th-century 95, 96
    age 88
    grave-goods 89–90, 92, 93, 94, 95, 96
    previous research 13, 15
    sex and gender 88–9
Mortimer, C. 24
Morton on the Hill (Norfolk), cemetery 9, 106
Moulton (Suffolk)
  cemetery 108
  field system 10
Mundesley (Norfolk), cemeteries 105
Mundford (Norfolk), cemeteries 105
Müssemeyer, U. 23, 34
Myres, J.N.L. 2

Nar, River 5
Narford (Norfolk), cemetery 105
necklets 31
Neville, Hon. R.C. 1
Newman, J. 5
Nieveler, E. 23, 31, 34, 45
Norfolk Museums and Archaeology Service 2, 3
North Creake (Norfolk), cemetery 106
North Elmham (Norfolk)
  cemeteries 8, 105
  occupation site 8, 9
North Pickenham (Norfolk), cemetery 105
North Runcton (Norfolk), cemetery 105
Northwold (Norfolk), cemetery 105
Norwich (Norfolk)
  cemetery 105
  diocese 8

Oakington (Cambs), cemetery 102
Oakley (Suffolk), cemetery 108
Oberflacht (Germany), wooden objects 38
Oosthuizen, S. 6
orientation 84–5
Orwell, River 5
Oxborough (Norfolk), cemeteries 1, 105

Pader, E.-J. 12
Pakenham (Suffolk), cemetery 109
Palm, M. 16
Parham (Suffolk), cemetery 109
parish boundaries 6, 10
parochiae 6
pendants
  chronology 48, 50, *73*, 98
  grave-good analysis 26
    bracteates 26
    bucket 26
    scutiform 26
  status 13
Penn, Kenneth 13
Périn, P. 34
Pescheck, C. 34

Pestell, Tim 83
Pind, J. 16
pins
  chronology 42, 48, 58, 98
  grave-good analysis 30–1
  status 91
Playford (Suffolk), cemetery 109
Pleidelsheim (Germany), cemetery 22
Poringland (Norfolk), cemetery 9, 105
post-holes 84
pottery
  chronology 16, 58, 59, *63*, 68–70
  grave-good analysis *37*, 38, *39*, 40–1
  status 14, 15, 92
project
  aims 3
  archives 3
  background 1–3
pursemounts *see* firesteels/pursemounts
Putnam, Glenys 88

quarrying 2, 8, 9, 10
Queen's University (Belfast) 17
Quidenham (Norfolk), cemetery 105

railway construction 2
Ravn, M. 14–15, 87, 96, 97, 99
Redgrave (Suffolk), cemetery 1, 109
Rendlesham (Suffolk), cemetery 109
Rhee, River 5
Richards, J.D. 14
Rickinghall Inferior (Suffolk), cemetery 109
ring-ditches
  distribution 6
  Morning Thorpe 10, 84
  Spong Hill 59, *78*, *79*, 84, 97
Risby (Suffolk), cemeteries 1, 109
roads, Roman 6
  Bergh Apton *8*
  Morning Thorpe *9*, 10
  Spong Hill *7*, 8
  Westgarth Gardens *10*, 11
Rockland All Saints (Norfolk), cemetery 2, 105
Ross, S. 31
Roudham (Norfolk), cemetery 105
Rougham (Suffolk), cemetery 109
Runcton Holme (Norfolk), cemetery 105
Rushmere St Andrew (Suffolk), cemetery 109

Sandlings 5, 6
Sawston (Cambs), cemetery 36, 102
Schulze-Dörrlamm, M. 34
Scull, Christopher 4, 7, 15, 94, 95
seaxes 23, 42, 45, *75*, 92, 93
Sedgeford (Norfolk), cemetery 105
shield bosses
  analysis
    measurements 19
    types 22; low with convex cone 22–3; straight cones and concave walls 22;
      tall cones 23; tall convex cone and without apex 23; type S 23
  chronology 42, 45, *74*, *75*, 98
  status 13, 92, 93
Shimpling *see* Burston and Shimpling
ship burials 1, 5, 109
Shouldham (Norfolk), cemetery 106
Shropham (Norfolk), cemetery 105
Shudy Camps (Cambs), cemetery 2, 34, 102
Siegmund, F. 23, 31, 34, 45
Skeyton (Norfolk), cemetery 105
Sleaford (Lincs), cemetery 2
slip-knot rings 29–30
Smallburgh (Norfolk), cemetery 106
Smith, C. Roach 2
Snape (Suffolk), cemeteries 1, 5, 36, 83, 109
Snettisham (Norfolk), cemetery 106
social structure
  5th–6th-century 94–6
  age 88

grave-goods 89–90
   association scores 91, 92
   in gender-'neutral' graves 94
   materials 90–1
   quantity and quality 92–4
inhumation and cremation burial practice 96–7
previous research 12–15
sex and gender 88–9
summary 97
Socistat 13, 16, 92
Soham (Cambs), cemeteries 102–3
spangles 31
spearheads
   analysis *17*
      measurements 19
      size groups 17–18
      types *18*; angular *18*, 19, 20; concave *18*, 19, 20–1; corrugated *18*, 19, 21;
         lanceolate *18*, 19, 20; long socket/shank 19, 21; midribbed *18*, 19, 21;
         parallel *18*, 19, 21; rhomboid *18*, 19, 21
   chronology 42–5, *74, 75*
   status 13, 92, 93, 96, 99
Spong Hill (Norfolk)
   burial practice 87
      cemetery layout 86, 87
      double graves 77
      grave features 82–4
      grave length and depth 76–7, *78, 79*
      grave orientation and body position 84, 85, 86
   chronological analysis
      correlation of male and female frameworks 58, 69; horizontal stratigraphy *64–5*, 70–1; vertical stratigraphy 59
      dress accessories 48–58
      weapons 42–7
   cremations 4, 8, 14–15, 38–40, 59, 96–7, 99
   discussion 98–100
   grave-good analysis
      beads 26, *27*, 28
      brooches 24, 25–6
      buckles 31, 32
      copper-alloy and wooden vessels 36, 38
      finger-rings 29
      firesteels/pursemounts 34
      girdle-hangers and keys 30
      glass vessels 36
      knives 34
      pendants 26
      pins 31
      pottery 38–41
      shield bosses 22, 23
      slip-knot rings 30
      spearheads 17, 20, 21
      strap-ends 32
      swords 23
      tweezers 36
      weaving batten 30
      wrist-clasps 28–9
   local context *7*, 8–9, 11
   location *xii*, 5
   previous research 13, 14–15
   project background 1, 3, 4, 5
   project methods 16
   ring-ditches 59, *78, 79*, 84, 97
   social structure 97
      age 88
      burial practice 96–7
      grave-goods 89–90, 92, 93, 94, 95
      previous research 13, 14–15
      sex and gender 88–9
Sporle-with-Palgrave (Norfolk), cemetery 1, 6, 106
Stanton (Suffolk), ?cemetery 110
Stapleford (Cambs), cemetery 103; *see also* Great Shelford/Stapleford
Steeple Morden (Cambs), cemetery 103
Stein, F. 23
Steuer, H. 15
Stiffkey, River 5
stones 82, 83, 84

Stoodley, Nick, research by
   gender studies 12, 15, 16, 88, 89, 90, 94
      brooches 95
      buckles 31
      burial practice 76–7, 83, 85, 86, 98
      keys 30
      knives 34
      musical instruments 36
      multiple burials 77–82
Stour, River 5, 8
strap-ends 32, 90, 91, 92, 93
Strood (Kent), mount 38
suspension rings 13
Sutton Hoo (Suffolk), cemetery 1, 2–3, 5, 109
   buckets 38
   royal burial 7, 36, 95
Swaffham (Norfolk), cemetery 2, 15, 98, 106
Swaffham Prior (Cambs), cemetery 103
Swannington (Norfolk), cemetery 106
Swanton, M.J. 17, 20, 21
swords
   analysis 23
   chronology 42, 45
   status 13, 92, 93, 95, 96

Tas, River 5, 9, 10
territorial units 6–8, 15
Thet, River 5
Thetford (Norfolk), cemeteries 1, 106
Thomas, G.W. 2
Thor 15
Thorndon (Suffolk), ?cemetery 110
Thornham (Norfolk), cemetery 6, 106
Thorpe St Andrew (Norfolk), cemetery 106
Tittleshall (Norfolk), cemetery 27
Tottenhill (Norfolk), cemetery 106
trade 95, 99
tribal areas 7
Tribal Hidage 7
Tuddenham St Martin (Suffolk), cemeteries 109
Tuddenham St Mary (Suffolk), cemetery 109
tweezers 15, 36

Ufford (Suffolk), cemetery 109

vegetation 83
Vestland cauldrons 36–8
Vierck, H. 7

Waldringfield (Suffolk), cemetery 109
Wangford (Suffolk), ?cemetery 110
Waterbeach (Cambs), cemetery 103
Wattisfield (Suffolk), ?cemetery 110
Watton (Norfolk), cemetery 106
wealth 92, 94, 95, 96, 99
weapons
   chronology 16
      absolute chronology 45
      relative chronology 42–5
   correspondence analysis 42, 45, 46–7
   grave-good analysis 17–24
   status 13, 14, 15
   see also axe; seaxes; shield bosses; spearheads; swords
weaving batten 30, 58
Well Beck 9
Wendens Ambo (Essex), cemetery 5, 101
Wenhaston (Suffolk), cemetery 109
Wensum, River 5, 8, 9
Wereham (Norfolk), cemetery 106
West, S.E. 5, 6
West Acre (Norfolk), cemetery 106; *see also* Castle Acre/West Acre
West Heslerton (N Yorks), necklet 31
West Stow (Suffolk)
   cemetery 2, 109
   settlement site 15
West Wickham (Cambs), cemetery 103
Westgarth Gardens (Suffolk)
   burial practice 87
      cemetery layout *86*, 87
      double graves 77, 82

grave features 83
grave length and depth 76–7, *85*
grave orientation and body position 84, 85, 86
chronological analysis
correlation of male and female frameworks 58, *68*, *69*, 71
dress accessories 48–58
weapons 42–7
cremations 4, 96
discussion 98–100
grave-good analysis
beads 26–8
brooches 24, 25
buckles 31, 32
copper-alloy and wooden vessels 38
firesteels/pursemounts 34–6
girdle-hangers 30
glass vessels 36
knives 34
pendants 26
pins 31
pottery 38, 40, 41
seaxes and swords 23–4
shield bosses 22, 23
slip-knot rings 30
spearheads 17, 20, 21
strap-ends 32
tweezers 36
wrist-clasps 28–9
local context *10*, 11

location *xii*, 5, 6
previous research, social structure 12, 13, 15
project background 1, 3, 4, 5
project methods 16
social structure 97
age 88
grave-goods 89–90, *91*, *92*, 93, 94, 95, 96
previous research 12, 13, 15
sex and gender 88–9
Wicken (Cambs), cemetery 103
Wickham Market (Suffolk), cemetery 109
Wicklewood (Norfolk), cemetery 106
Wickmere (Norfolk), cemetery 106
Wimpole (Cambs), cemeteries 103
Wisbech (Cambs), cemetery 103
Wissey, River 5, 8
women, status 95
Woodbridge (Suffolk), cemetery 109
wooden vessels 36–8, 92, 96
Wremen (Germany), wooden objects 38
Wretham (Norfolk), cemetery 106
Wretton (Norfolk), cemetery 106
wrist-clasps
analysis 28–9
chronology 48, 50, 58, *70*, *72*, 98
distribution 7–8
status 13, 91, 92, 93, 96

Yare, River 9

East Anglian Archaeology

is a serial publication sponsored by ALGAO EE and English Heritage. It is the main vehicle for publishing final reports on archaeological excavations and surveys in the region. For information about titles in the series, visit **www.eaareports.org.uk**. Reports can be obtained from:

Phil McMichael, Essex County Council Archaeology Section
Fairfield Court, Fairfield Road, Braintree, Essex CM7 3YQ

or directly from the organisation publishing a particular volume.

Reports available so far:

No.1,	1975	Suffolk: various papers
No.2,	1976	Norfolk: various papers
No.3,	1977	Suffolk: various papers
No.4,	1976	Norfolk: Late Saxon town of Thetford
No.5,	1977	Norfolk: various papers on Roman sites
No.6,	1977	Norfolk: Spong Hill Anglo-Saxon cemetery, Part I
No.7,	1978	Norfolk: Bergh Apton Anglo-Saxon cemetery
No.8,	1978	Norfolk: various papers
No.9,	1980	Norfolk: North Elmham Park
No.10,	1980	Norfolk: village sites in Launditch Hundred
No.11,	1981	Norfolk: Spong Hill, Part II: Catalogue of Cremations
No.12,	1981	The barrows of East Anglia
No.13,	1981	Norwich: Eighteen centuries of pottery from Norwich
No.14,	1982	Norfolk: various papers
No.15,	1982	Norwich: Excavations in Norwich 1971–1978; Part I
No.16,	1982	Norfolk: Beaker domestic sites in the Fen-edge and East Anglia
No.17,	1983	Norfolk: Waterfront excavations and Thetford-type Ware production, Norwich
No.18,	1983	Norfolk: The archaeology of Witton
No.19,	1983	Norfolk: Two post-medieval earthenware pottery groups from Fulmodeston
No.20,	1983	Norfolk: Burgh Castle: excavation by Charles Green, 1958–61
No.21,	1984	Norfolk: Spong Hill, Part III: Catalogue of Inhumations
No.22,	1984	Norfolk: Excavations in Thetford, 1948–59 and 1973–80
No.23,	1985	Norfolk: Excavations at Brancaster 1974 and 1977
No.24,	1985	Suffolk: West Stow, the Anglo-Saxon village
No.25,	1985	Essex: Excavations by Mr H.P.Cooper on the Roman site at Hill Farm, Gestingthorpe, Essex
No.26,	1985	Norwich: Excavations in Norwich 1971–78; Part II
No.27,	1985	Cambridgeshire: The Fenland Project No.1: Archaeology and Environment in the Lower Welland Valley
No.28,	1985	Norfolk: Excavations within the north-east bailey of Norwich Castle, 1978
No.29,	1986	Norfolk: Barrow excavations in Norfolk, 1950–82
No.30,	1986	Norfolk: Excavations at Thornham, Warham, Wighton and Caistor St Edmund, Norfolk
No.31,	1986	Norfolk: Settlement, religion and industry on the Fen-edge; three Romano-British sites in Norfolk
No.32,	1987	Norfolk: Three Norman Churches in Norfolk
No.33,	1987	Essex: Excavation of a Cropmark Enclosure Complex at Woodham Walter, Essex, 1976 and An Assessment of Excavated Enclosures in Essex
No.34,	1987	Norfolk: Spong Hill, Part IV: Catalogue of Cremations
No.35,	1987	Cambridgeshire: The Fenland Project No.2: Fenland Landscapes and Settlement, Peterborough–March
No.36,	1987	Norfolk: The Anglo-Saxon Cemetery at Morningthorpe
No.37,	1987	Norfolk: Excavations at St Martin-at-Palace Plain, Norwich, 1981
No.38,	1987	Suffolk: The Anglo-Saxon Cemetery at Westgarth Gardens, Bury St Edmunds
No.39,	1988	Norfolk: Spong Hill, Part VI: Occupation during the 7th–2nd millennia BC
No.40,	1988	Suffolk: Burgh: The Iron Age and Roman Enclosure
No.41,	1988	Essex: Excavations at Great Dunmow, Essex: a Romano-British small town in the Trinovantian Civitas
No.42,	1988	Essex: Archaeology and Environment in South Essex, Rescue Archaeology along the Gray's By-pass 1979–80
No.43,	1988	Essex: Excavation at the North Ring, Mucking, Essex: A Late Bronze Age Enclosure
No.44,	1988	Norfolk: Six Deserted Villages in Norfolk
No.45,	1988	Norfolk: The Fenland Project No. 3: Marshland and the Nar Valley, Norfolk
No.46,	1989	Norfolk: The Deserted Medieval Village of Thuxton
No.47,	1989	Suffolk: West Stow: Early Anglo-Saxon Animal Husbandry
No.48,	1989	Suffolk: West Stow, Suffolk: The Prehistoric and Romano-British Occupations
No.49,	1990	Norfolk: The Evolution of Settlement in Three Parishes in South-East Norfolk
No.50,	1993	Proceedings of the Flatlands and Wetlands Conference
No.51,	1991	Norfolk: The Ruined and Disused Churches of Norfolk
No.52,	1991	Norfolk: The Fenland Project No. 4, The Wissey Embayment and Fen Causeway
No.53,	1992	Norfolk: Excavations in Thetford, 1980–82, Fison Way
No.54,	1992	Norfolk: The Iron Age Forts of Norfolk
No.55,	1992	Lincolnshire: The Fenland Project No.5: Lincolnshire Survey, The South-West Fens
No.56,	1992	Cambridgeshire: The Fenland Project No.6: The South-Western Cambridgeshire Fens
No.57,	1993	Norfolk and Lincolnshire: Excavations at Redgate Hill Hunstanton; and Tattershall Thorpe
No.58,	1993	Norwich: Households: The Medieval and Post-Medieval Finds from Norwich Survey Excavations 1971–1978
No.59,	1993	Fenland: The South-West Fen Dyke Survey Project 1982–86
No.60,	1993	Norfolk: Caister-on-Sea: Excavations by Charles Green, 1951–55
No.61,	1993	Fenland: The Fenland Project No.7: Excavations in Peterborough and the Lower Welland Valley 1960–1969
No.62,	1993	Norfolk: Excavations in Thetford by B.K. Davison, between 1964 and 1970
No.63,	1993	Norfolk: Illington: A Study of a Breckland Parish and its Anglo-Saxon Cemetery
No.64,	1994	Norfolk: The Late Saxon and Medieval Pottery Industry of Grimston: Excavations 1962–92
No.65,	1993	Suffolk: Settlements on Hill-tops: Seven Prehistoric Sites in Suffolk
No.66,	1993	Lincolnshire: The Fenland Project No.8: Lincolnshire Survey, the Northern Fen-Edge
No.67,	1994	Norfolk: Spong Hill, Part V: Catalogue of Cremations
No.68,	1994	Norfolk: Excavations at Fishergate, Norwich 1985
No.69,	1994	Norfolk: Spong Hill, Part VIII: The Cremations
No.70,	1994	Fenland: The Fenland Project No.9: Flandrian Environmental Change in Fenland
No.71,	1995	Essex: The Archaeology of the Essex Coast Vol.I: The Hullbridge Survey Project
No.72,	1995	Norfolk: Excavations at Redcastle Furze, Thetford, 1988–9
No.73,	1995	Norfolk: Spong Hill, Part VII: Iron Age, Roman and Early Saxon Settlement
No.74,	1995	Norfolk: A Late Neolithic, Saxon and Medieval Site at Middle Harling
No.75,	1995	Essex: North Shoebury: Settlement and Economy in South-east Essex 1500–AD1500
No.76,	1996	Nene Valley: Orton Hall Farm: A Roman and Early Anglo-Saxon Farmstead
No.77,	1996	Norfolk: Barrow Excavations in Norfolk, 1984–88
No.78,	1996	Norfolk:The Fenland Project No.11: The Wissey Embayment: Evidence for pre-Iron Age Occupation
No.79,	1996	Cambridgeshire: The Fenland Project No.10: Cambridgeshire Survey, the Isle of Ely and Wisbech
No.80,	1997	Norfolk: Barton Bendish and Caldecote: fieldwork in south-west Norfolk
No.81,	1997	Norfolk: Castle Rising Castle
No.82,	1998	Essex: Archaeology and the Landscape in the Lower Blackwater Valley
No.83,	1998	Essex: Excavations south of Chignall Roman Villa 1977–81
No.84,	1998	Suffolk: A Corpus of Anglo-Saxon Material
No.85,	1998	Suffolk: Towards a Landscape History of Walsham le Willows
No.86,	1998	Essex: Excavations at the Orsett 'Cock' Enclosure
No.87,	1999	Norfolk: Excavations in Thetford, North of the River, 1989–90
No.88,	1999	Essex: Excavations at Ivy Chimneys, Witham 1978–83
No.89,	1999	Lincolnshire: Salterns: Excavations at Helpringham, Holbeach St Johns and Bicker Haven
No.90,	1999	Essex:The Archaeology of Ardleigh, Excavations 1955–80
No.91,	2000	Norfolk: Excavations on the Norwich Southern Bypass, 1989–91 Part I Bixley, Caistor St Edmund, Trowse
No.92,	2000	Norfolk: Excavations on the Norwich Southern Bypass, 1989–91 Part II Harford Farm Anglo-Saxon Cemetery
No.93,	2001	Norfolk: Excavations on the Snettisham Bypass, 1989
No.94,	2001	Lincolnshire: Excavations at Billingborough, 1975–8

No.95,	2001	Suffolk: Snape Anglo-Saxon Cemetery: Excavations and Surveys
No.96,	2001	Norfolk: Two Medieval Churches in Norfolk
No.97,	2001	Cambridgeshire: Monument 97, Orton Longueville
No.98,	2002	Essex: Excavations at Little Oakley, 1951–78
No.99,	2002	Norfolk: Excavations at Melford Meadows, Brettenham, 1994
No.100,	2002	Norwich: Excavations in Norwich 1971–78, Part III
No.101,	2002	Norfolk: Medieval Armorial Horse Furniture in Norfolk
No.102,	2002	Norfolk: Baconsthorpe Castle, Excavations and Finds, 1951–1972
No.103,	2003	Cambridgeshire: Excavations at the Wardy Hill Ringwork, Coveney, Ely
No.104,	2003	Norfolk: Earthworks of Norfolk
No.105	2003	Essex: Excavations at Great Holts Farm, 1992–4
No.106	2004	Suffolk: Romano-British Settlement at Hacheston
No.107	2004	Essex: Excavations at Stansted Airport, 1986–91
No.108,	2004	Norfolk: Excavations at Mill Lane, Thetford, 1995
No.109,	2005	Fenland: Archaeology and Environment of the Etton Landscape
No.110,	2005	Cambridgeshire: Saxon and Medieval Settlement at West Fen Road, Ely
No.111,	2005	Essex: Early Anglo-Saxon Cemetery and Later Saxon Settlement at Springfield Lyons
No.112,	2005	Norfolk: Dragon Hall, King Street, Norwich
No.113,	2006	Norfolk: Excavations at Kilverstone
No.114,	2006	Cambridgeshire:Waterfront Archaeology in Ely
No.115,	2006	Essex:Medieval Moated Manor by the Thames Estuary: Excavations at Southchurch Hall, Southend
No.116,	2006	Norfolk: Norwich Cathedral Refectory
No.117,	2007	Essex: Excavations at Lodge Farm, St Osyth
No.118,	2007	Essex: Late Iron Age Warrior Burial from Kelvedon
No.119,	2007	Norfolk: Aspects of Anglo-Saxon Inhumation Burial